W9-CRA-065

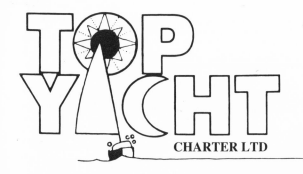

ANDREW HILL LANE
HEDGERLEY
BUCKS SL2 3UW
U.K.

Telephone: 44 (0) 1753 646636
Facsimile: 44 (0) 1753 645539

With Compliments

Turkish Waters &
Cyprus Pilot

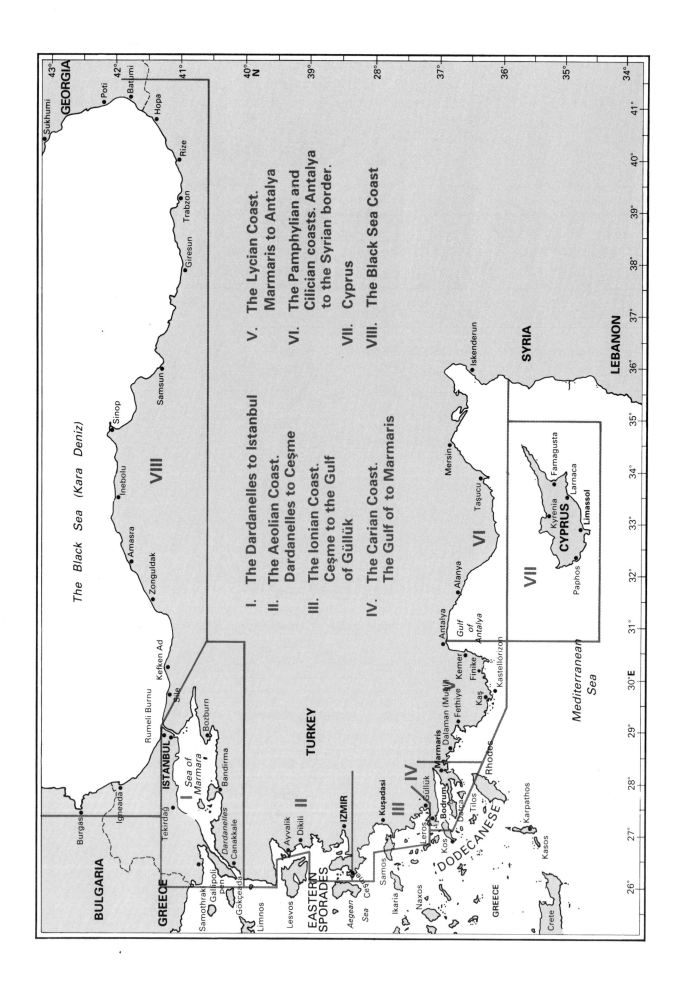

The Black Sea (Kara Deniz)

GEORGIA

Sukhumi
Poti
Batumi
Hopa

Rize

Trabzon

Giresun

Samsun

Sinop

Inebolu

Amasra

Zonguldak

Kefken Ad

Rumeli Burnu

Şile

VIII

I. The Dardanelles to Istanbul

II. The Aeolian Coast.
   Dardanelles to Çeşme

III. The Ionian Coast.
    Çeşme to the Gulf
    of Güllük

IV. The Carian Coast.
    The Gulf of to Marmaris

V. The Lycian Coast.
   Marmaris to Antalya

VI. The Pamphylian and
    Cilician coasts. Antalya
    to the Syrian border.

VII. Cyprus

VIII. The Black Sea Coast

BULGARIA

Burgas

İğneada

Tekirdağ

ISTANBUL

Sea of
Marmara

Bandirma

Bozburn

GREECE

Gallipoli
pen

Dardanelles

Çanakkale

Samothraki

Gökçeada

Limnos

Lesvos

Ayvalik

Dikili

EASTERN
SPORADES

II

TURKEY

İZMİR

Çeşme

Kuşadasi

Samos

Ikaria

Naxos

III

Güllük

Bodrum

Leros

Kos

Datça

Tilos

DODECANESE

Karpathos

Kasos

GREECE

Crete

Aegean
Sea

IV

Marmaris

Daçla

Dalaman (Muğla)

Fethiye

Kaş

Kemer

Finike

Kastellorizon

Rhodes

Mediterranean
Sea

V

Gulf
of
Antalya

Antalya

Alanya

Taşucu

Mersin

İskenderun

SYRIA

LEBANON

VI

VII

CYPRUS

Kyrenia

Famagusta

Larnaca

Limassol

Paphos

26° 27° 28° 29°E 30°E 31° 32° 33° 34° 35° 36° 37° 38° 39° 40° 41°

43° 42° 41° 40°N 39° 38° 37° 36° 35° 34°

Turkish Waters & Cyprus Pilot

A yachtsman's guide to the Mediterranean and Black Sea coasts of Turkey with the island of Cyprus

ROD HEIKELL

Imray Laurie Norie & Wilson Ltd
St Ives Cambridgeshire England

Published by
Imray, Laurie, Norie & Wilson Ltd
Wych House, St Ives, Huntingdon,
Cambridgeshire PE17 4BT, England
☎ +44(0)1480 462114 *Fax* +44(0)1480 496109
E-mail ilnw@imray.com
1997

All rights reserved. No part of this publication may be reproduced, transmitted or used in any form by any means – graphic, electronic or mechanical, including photocopying, recording, taping or information storage and retrieval systems or otherwise – without the prior permission of the publisher.

© Rod Heikell 1997
1st edition 1984
2nd edition 1987
3rd edition 1989
4th edition 1993
5th edition 1997

British Library Cataloguing in Publication Data.
A catalogue record for this book is available from the British Library.

ISBN 0 85288 363 3

CAUTION
Every effort has been taken to ensure the accuracy of this book. It contains selected information, and thus is not definitive and does not include all known information on the subject in hand; this is particularly relevant to the plans, which should not be used for navigation. The author and publisher believe that its selection is a useful aid to prudent navigation, but the safety of a vessel depends ultimately on the judgement of the navigator, who should assess all information, published or unpublished, available to him.

PLANS
The plans in this guide are not to be used for navigation. They are designed to support the text and should at all times be used with navigational charts.

Also by Rod Heikell
Greek Waters Pilot
Italian Waters Pilot
Mediterranean France & Corsica Pilot
Mediterranean Cruising Handbook
The Danube – A river guide
Mediterranean Sailing Adlard Coles Nautical
    Ltd
Ionian
Saronic
The Turquoise Coast of Turkey NET
Imray Mediterranean Almanac (editor)
Yacht Charter Handbook
Indian Ocean Cruising Guide

CORRECTIONAL SUPPLEMENTS
Imray pilot books are amended at intervals by the issue of correctional supplements. Supplements, if available, are supplied free of charge with the books when they are purchased. Further supplements are available from the publishers. A stamped-addressed envelope should be supplied and the following should be quoted:

1. Name of book.
2. Date of edition (see above).
3. Date of last supplement (if applicable).
4. Name and address to which supplement should be sent.

This work has been corrected to April 1997.

Printed in Great Britain at The Bath Press

Author's note
A large number of photocopies of my books circulate around the eastern Mediterranean. For those of you sitting and reading a photocopy of this book, I suggest you reflect on the fact that you forfeit your own moral basis for objecting to any theft from yourself or your boat. You have after all stolen something from me and my publishers, both in a moral and legal sense, so when you have something stolen, think about how it feels.

RJH

Contents

Preface

PREFACE TO THE FIRST EDITION

Turkey is a geographical and cultural bridge between Europe and Asia, a sort of no-man's land between East and West that presents the new arrival with a curious amalgam of the familiar and the unfamiliar. You will encounter all the trappings of a modern western country: blue jeans, modern apartment blocks, digital watches, traffic jams, television and over-amplified pop music. But side by side with all this is the unfamiliar: pencil-thin minarets and the wailing of the *muezzin* calling the faithful to prayer, the smells and sights of the bazaar, the lined Asiatic faces of Anatolian peasants, camels slow-stepping through village streets, Turkish carpets airing on balconies and a realisation that, behind the western façade, life is still very hard for most of the population. This blend of East and West assures the traveller of a gentle introduction to Asia and Islam, so that the unfamiliar is easily assimilated, and you wonder that you could ever have thought of Turkey as a strange and distant country.

You will find the modern Turk welcoming and friendly. Almost without exception, you will be greeted everywhere with *hoş geldiniz* – welcome. And later you will be asked a barrage of questions about yourself and the world, there being an intense curiosity about life outside Turkey. How much do you earn? How much did such and such cost? Do you have to go into the army? Are you married? What other countries have you been to? All these and endless other questions reflect a thirst for knowledge and opportunity outside Turkey. Although he knows full well that he stands in the back yard of the East, still he considers himself to be of the West.

Nowhere is this more evident than in the geographical entity of Istanbul. It straddles Europe and Asia across the Bosphorus and, while a thoroughly westernised city, still looks and feels like a gigantic eastern bazaar. In it the monuments of the great civilisations press against each other: Greek and Roman monumental architecture, Byzantine churches, Seljuk *caravanserais*, Ottoman mosques, the Istanbul Hilton. Geography and history mingle Europe and Asia, Christianity and Islam, to give a wonderful cultural jig-saw puzzle you can wander around in. Andrew Mango puts it thus: 'Geography and history, the two co-ordinates of the development of any human society, stand out in Turkey, establishing the place and the moment with a unique clarity, and the imaginative traveller can see not only a land and a people, part strange, part familiar, but also a living past and thus himself in history.'

I first sailed in Turkey in 1980, between Bodrum and Marmaris. Captivated by the country, I wanted to do a Turkish yachtsman's pilot after the Greek pilot was finished. As it turned out, I did not begin the Turkish pilot until 1983. After refitting *Tetranora* in Malta in early 1983, I sailed to Ceşme and pottered up the coast to Istanbul before returning south for the winter. I spent most of the winter in Bodrum, and in the early spring of 1984 left to finish the research along the rest of the Aegean and the southern coast. Now *Tetranora* is to be laid up in Bodrum until I can get back to her next summer. But I'm in no hurry to leave, I like the Turkishness of Turkey. It is a welcoming and friendly country, riddled with archaeological sites of great beauty, and possessed of spectacular cruising areas that will take you quite some time to exhaust. I'm taking my time.

Rod Heikell
Bodrum 1984

PREFACE TO THE SECOND EDITION

In three years, parts of the Turkish coast have changed considerably. Hotels have been built, and harbours dredged; simple restaurants have appeared as if by magic in previously deserted bays, and in the bigger resorts bright 'Hamburger' and 'Fast Food' signs are dotted around the streets. Yet, underneath, little has changed: the hospitality is still overwhelming, sometimes embarrassingly so, the paperwork for a yacht is just as tedious, and the coast is just as beautiful as it ever was.

Turkey is changing and must change as more people discover it, but the catch-cry 'get there before it is spoiled' is a misleading and selfish one that hardly looks underneath the surface of what is going on. For most Turks the way of life has changed minimally. Not far from the tourist centres and discos life is still very hard, a living must be gleaned from the soil or a small village shop, and a stranger is made welcome. It is to be hoped that we, as visitors to this country, treat the Turks as well as they treat us.

Rod Heikell
London 1986

PREFACE TO THE THIRD EDITION

My thanks to all who helped me with information for this new edition; though I cannot thank you all, I would like especially to mention W G Raper of SY *Ros Arcan* for his detailed sketches, Col. R E Nelson of SY *Cusar*, Sir Michael Clapham, and Bridgit Marsh, who crewed with me on *Rozinante* down the Danube.

Some of the information for this edition was collected at the tail-end of my trip down the Danube in the diminutive *Rozinante*. Arriving at the end of the Danube in Romania, I sailed *Rozinante* across the Black Sea to Istanbul and then down the Sea of Marmara and the Aegean coast to Bodrum. At just over 5 metres LOA and drawing less than a metre, it took me a while to get used to chugging into places I could not get into with *Tetra* and her 1·60-metre draught. *Rozinante* has now been sold and is to remain in Turkey, a far cry from her berth on the Thames at Twickenham. I'll be swapping grey skies for blue as well when I take *Tetra* back to Turkey this year.

Rod Heikell
Aix-en-Provence 1989

PREFACE TO THE FOURTH EDITION

Since the first edition of this book in 1984 the appearance of Turkey has changed radically. At least, so it seems.

Vast holiday villages now lie sprawled across coastal slopes, and five-star hotels have sprung up in once isolated coves. *Gulets* charge around parts of the coast where once few yachts could be seen. Yachting facilities ashore have improved dramatically, and marinas to rival any in the Mediterranean have been built in the popular cruising areas.

It is easy, as I have commented before, to remark that Turkey has changed for the worse, and to come up with the sort of patronising phrases that are commonly heard to the effect that 'you should have been here five years ago to really see Turkey'. Any country must change; whether we approve of those changes is another matter. Personally I find some of the vast barrack-like holiday villages an affront to the eye, with little to distinguish them from coastal developments in other parts of the Mediterranean. That said, the yachtsman is in the enviable position of being able to get away from those patches of coast where holiday villages have been built to the greater part of the coast still relatively untouched, and still one of the most wonderful cruising grounds in the Mediterranean. Here it is apparent that Turkey has changed little, and the magnificent coast is matched by the warmth of the people. It is a gentle caress from another age, with the bonus of being able to return to a first-class marina with all home comforts and good facilities for the care and repair of a yacht not far away.

In this edition the book has been completely taken apart and put back together with additional text and many new plans as well as substantial alterations to the old plans where necessary. A chapter on the Black Sea has been included, although the text has been kept to a minimum so that the whole book does not get too unwieldy. Most of the information is from trips I made around the coast in doughty *Tetra* in 1990, 1991, and 1992. As with the other pilots, I must thank all those who have contributed information and apologise if I have not personally thanked you all – things can get chaotic and confused with my peripatetic lifestyle.

Rod Heikell
Homps and London 1993

PREFACE TO THE FIFTH EDITION

For this fifth edition of the pilot the notes and harbour plans have been amended and corrected as you would expect and a number of additional plans have been added or inserted where old plans were not as useful as they might be. Most plans now have waypoints although I have not been able to get everywhere or obtain data on all places. If you do make a note of a waypoint from your GPS for future editions it is helpful to know where the waypoint is located and also to reference it to WGS84 datum.

The pilot has also been supplemented by a number of aerial photos of the coast between Kuşadasi and Antalya. The mountainous nature of much of the coast became even more evident to me when taking these photos as we often had to fly towards what seemed to be vertical and not-too-far-from-the-plane slopes in order to get the sun behind us (more or less) for satisfactory photos. The photos were taken in August which is not the best time for photography because of the summer haze, but does show where yachts anchor or berth in a bay or harbour. While aerial photos are useful they do not show the view from seawards and so many of the black and white approach shots have been left in the book.

A number of people helped with information for this edition and, while I cannot include everyone, I would like to thank the following. For arranging the flight along the coast my thanks to Ali Pulat and Yusuf Civelekoglu. My thanks to Yusuf and his staff at Yat Lift, especially Jody and Tansu for checking the accents and other odd bits of information. My thanks to the Cruising Association, especially Nigel Morley, for their updates although libel laws mean not all comments can be included! Thanks also to Nick Kerr, Dr B Logan, Dr H Van Marken Lichtenbelt, Claire James, Tony Marciniec, Yener Gokcirmak, Etienne Roussel, Claude Mauge, Charles Guest and Peter Robson.

Rod Heikell
London 1997

Introduction

Yacht and equipment

Engines

A reliable engine is necessary for motoring through the inevitable calms a yacht will encounter. On other occasions it will be required to motor against strong winds and the short steep seas of the Mediterranean in order to get into harbour. A petrol engine, whether inboard or outboard, can be dangerous as, in the high temperatures, petrol vaporises easily and there is a constant risk of fire or an explosion.

Ventilation

Most British-built yachts have inadequate ventilation for the hot Mediterranean. Extra skylights and vents and additional insulation can help solve the problem. An air-scoop to funnel air down the front hatch is a good investment, and will repay its modest cost tenfold. Make your own, or buy one of the commercially produced scoops on the market.

Refrigerator

A refrigerator is considered by many a necessity in the Mediterranean. If it is going to draw power from your batteries it may be necessary to install an additional battery and revise your charging methods – a refrigerator is estimated to use around 50–60 per cent of the power consumption on yachts. The heat absorption and thermoelectric types do not work well in the high ambient temperatures of the Mediterranean. The type having a compressor working off the batteries (high current drain) or off the engine (expensive to purchase and install) with a holding plate has proved to be the best. As a general rule most refrigerators do not have adequate insulation – 10cm/4in should be the minimum. Get the top-opening type so that the cold air does not 'fall out' every time the refrigerator is opened.

Shower

A shower is useful inside a yacht, but in the Mediterranean it is perhaps more useful if it can be used outside on deck or in the cockpit to wash off after swimming in the sea. Large water tanks or even an additional water tank may be required.

The sun-shower, basically a black plastic bag with a shower rose attached that you haul up on a halyard, works well – but beware of the water getting too hot in July and August.

Anchors

Preference for different anchors varies with the individual, but the following information may be useful for coping with the different types of bottom found in the Mediterranean. Often the bottom will be hard sand covered with thick weed and some anchors have difficulty penetrating the weed and digging in. If the water is clear enough, pick a sandy patch to let the anchor down onto. It is common practice to go astern once the anchor is down to ensure that it bites.

In many bays it is very deep until close to the shore, so it is standard practice to lay out an anchor and take a long line ashore to a convenient tree or rock. With the *meltemi*, gusts blow down into some bays from a constant direction and you will feel more secure tied to a tree with an anchor out than swinging to an anchor in deep water where the holding may be uncertain. The constant direction of the wind in the summer makes this practice commonplace.

Bruce A good main anchor. It holds well, even on a short scope, and is good over a range of different holding ground. Some people have reported difficulties in getting the Bruce to dig through thick weed. It will sometimes collect a clump of weed and must be raised to clear it.

CQR A good main anchor. Holds well in mud and sand, though it will sometimes pull through soft mud. In weed it will often pick up a clump on the point and must be raised to clear it.

Delta A new anchor similar to the CQR, but with no moving parts. Its one-piece construction makes it strong, and it has been designed to turn itself over to a holding position however it lands.

Danforth Good for getting through weed, but like the CQR picks up weed easily. My favourite for a kedge.

Fortress A new Danforth lookalike, but constructed of aluminium and therefore very light. This anchor defies the long-held notion that an anchor must be heavy to hold, and in my experience works well, with the advantage that it is very easy to lay from a dinghy.

Fisherman Excellent for getting through weed, but doesn't have the holding power of the plough types. However, it will hold on rocky bottoms, in thick weed, and on very soft bottoms where other anchors don't get through the soft top layer. A good alternative to the Danforth for a kedge.

Grapnel types The folding grapnel anchors which can be bought in England are useless except on a rocky bottom. A few yachtsmen swear by the large grapnels used by the Turks, but I have never found them to be very good.

Berthing lines

It is useful to have two stout lines made up for the stern lines when mooring stern-to. A short loop of chain on the end of the line which can be dropped over a bollard (or unfastened with a carbine clip or shackle to go through a mooring loop) will reduce chafe on the line. However, care is needed not to brain bystanders or anyone helping you to berth when you are throwing the lines ashore. The line should be fairly heavy, as the surges which can develop in some harbours with gale force winds can be greater than those encountered in many other cruising grounds.

Berthing lines should be inspected regularly, as ultraviolet degradation, especially of some polypropylene types of rope, happens quickly in the fierce sunlight of the Mediterranean. In addition, you will need a strong long line (50 metres is not too long) to use when anchoring with a line ashore.

Gang planks (passerelles)

A gang plank can be an elaborate affair or simply a plank. It is useful to have a pair of small wheels at the outer end of the board so that the end of the board scraping over the quay does not annoy you or your neighbours. A small aluminium ladder can be easily made into a smart passerelle.

Sails

Under the hot Mediterranean sun a yacht's sails suffer from ultraviolet degradation faster than is the case in more northerly climes. It is a good policy to cover the mainsail and bag any headsails whenever they are not in use. If you have a roller-reefing headsail then have a sacrificial strip on the luff and foot to protect the sail when it is furled. Roller-reefing headsails are now more common than hanked-on headsails and speak volumes for the practicality of the system.

Awnings

A good sun awning is a necessary piece of boat equipment. Much of your time will be spent in the cockpit, and the awning should be designed to be a comfortable height above the cockpit seats, and have side curtains for when the sun is low in the evening. Make the awning from dark-coloured canvas, as light-coloured materials cause an uncomfortable glare and nylon and *Terylene* materials flap and crack in the slightest breeze.

A permanent awning over the cockpit, along the lines of the Bimini hood common in the Caribbean, keeps you cool not only in harbour, but also when motoring or sailing.

Navigation

A yacht will require no more navigation equipment than would be used around other coasts, and will in all probability use less in practice. Apart from a steering compass, a hand-bearing compass, and a log, little else is required.

A depth-sounder is useful although, after a while, you will become adept at judging depths in the clear water – it is not uncommon to see the bottom at 7–10 metres. However, remember that it takes a little time to get the 'hang of' judging the depth visually.

In general the following colour schemes apply: brown to yellow-brown means 2 metres or less, green 2–5 metres, blue-green 5–25 metres and dark green-blue 25 metres plus. Caution is needed interpreting these colours as, under 10 metres, the nature of the bottom confuses the scheme with sandy bottoms giving the clearest indication while rock and weed make things look darker and shallower. In murky water around busy harbours, off river mouths or where strong currents or wave action have whipped up the bottom, a reliable echo-sounder is worth its weight in gold.

A VHF radio is useful for talking to other yachts, calling up a marina to reserve a berth, or to request a weather forecast. By law Turkish yachts must be equipped with a VHF radio and the law advises that private yachts visiting Turkey should have a VHF radio installed.

Electronic navigation aids

The new breed of electronic navigation equipment has revolutionised position finding, but some care is needed if you are using it in Turkey.

GPS (Global Positioning System) The cost of receivers is plummeting all the time with a sub-£200–250 price tag at the time of writing and prices continuing to fall. With an accuracy of around 100-200 metres in its degraded form, GPS provides the most accurate position-finding system going. Remember, satellites are turned off for maintenance, and coverage for an area may be removed by the military during a war such as the Gulf War. The very accuracy of GPS can at times be a positive danger (see below).

RDF Few yachts these days are still equipped with Radio Direction Finding equipment, but nonetheless marine and aero beacons still transmit along the Turkish coast. Details are given on page 22.

Loran C Although the technology is dated compared to satellite position-finding systems, nonetheless good accuracy can be obtained throughout most of the Mediterranean with a little care. In the SE Mediterranean you are on the limits of signal reception and around the SE Aegean there is a hole in the coverage for the sea area around

Bodrum and points south.

Accuracy varies, but is normally within 0·1 mile to 0·5 mile when the relevant offsets are included. The latitude is usually within 0·1 mile with the longitude giving the maximum error. As with RDF or any radio signals, care is needed at dawn and dusk, when the signals can be refracted and inaccurate fixes result.

Chart plotters A number of yachts are fitting chart plotters which when interfaced to an electronic position-finding system show a yacht's position on a chart. The problem with chart plotters is the difficulty of storing the charts; they require a large memory and so, in practice, small-scale charts are scanned and then blown up on the screen to get a larger scale. Much information normally shown on a large-scale chart will not be displayed on a blown-up small-scale chart. In addition, the problems outlined below are exacerbated on electronic charts where an electronically derived 'real' position is displayed on a cartographically inaccurate chart.

Laptop computers A number of yachts now have laptop computers on board. There are a number of software packages which reproduce charts and if GPS, Loran, and radar are interfaced this can be a useful navigation tool. One of the problems with most systems is that the laptop is not fitted into the navigation area and so is difficult to use when conditions are rough. Most people don't want to risk their laptop slithering all over the place when things get a bit bumpy. If you are contemplating a laptop-based navigation system incorporating charts and instrumentation then some thought needs to go into securing the laptop on the navigation table or perhaps as a modular unit with the screen on a bulkhead and the keyboard secured on the chart table. There are also a number of remote waterproof screens available which can be installed in the cockpit to reproduce the charts, GPS position and other data where it is easy to see when sailing. Laptops are also commonly used for weatherfax systems using a HF receiver and the appropriate software.

Radar Now that radar is more compact and more economical with your amps, it can be a useful navigation tool. Its great value is in reproducing a map of what is, rather than a lat and long that you then plot on an (inaccurate) chart.

A word of caution Most of the charts for Turkey were surveyed in the 19th century, using celestial sights to determine latitude and longitude. Subsequent observations have shown considerable errors, in some cases up to 1 minute of longitude. While you may know your lat and long to within 100–200 metres, the chart you are plotting it on may contain errors of up to 1 mile. The practice of including the datum point for a chart and an offset to be used with electronic position-finding equipment only confuses a very complicated picture when the old charts have varying inaccuracies over the area they cover. For instance, one cape may be out by ½ mile whereas another cape on the same chart may be out by 1 mile, with an average offset somewhere between the two. The solution to the problem lies in the hands of the relevant hydrographic authorities, who could use satellite-derived photographs to re-survey the areas and produce new charts. This seems unlikely to happen in the near future and so we are left with what amount to basically 19th-century charts patched up here and there as best the hydrographic departments are able. The problem is further complicated because the old 19th-century 'fathoms' charts are being metricated and so look like new surveys – even when the attribution is to a new survey, the basis for this will still have been the original Admiralty 19th-century survey.

It hardly needs to be stated that you should exercise great caution in the vicinity of land or hazards to navigation – eyeball navigation rules OK!

Yacht facilities

Agents and touts
On the whole anything that goes through an agent or a tout will have his 10 or 20 per cent added to the price, and this is normal practice. However, some agents and touts in cahoots with the suppliers will produce 'official' receipts that bear little resemblance to the actual quantity or price involved. Thus they manage to get 150 litres into 100-litre tanks and wine and beer at around double the price. I speak from experience. There are good agents around, but do ask and find out first.

Fuel
Where fuel is shown in the pilotage notes as being close to or on the quay, I am referring in most cases to diesel fuel. In many places it will have to be carried in canisters from the local petrol station in town. Because fuelling points can be quite a distance apart it pays to top up your tanks whenever possible.

Gas
Camping Gaz is fairly widely available in Turkey, although it may take a day or so to get it in some places. The local gas is widely available and appears to work well with European appliances.

Paraffin (Kerosene)
Widely available and sold from bowser pumps at petrol stations. Methylated spirit is also available, usually from a grocer's shop that has a licence to sell it.

Water
The water is nearly always safe to drink, although in some out-of-the-way places it pays to treat it with caution. In certain places where there is a heavy demand on supplies from land-based tourism – in

Bodrum and Marmaris for instance – water can be in short supply in the summer.

Water from wells should be treated with caution. Water-purifying tablets are cheap and can be bought almost anywhere. Alternatively, a little bleach solution or a few grains of potassium permanganate will get rid of most nasties when added to water of doubtful quality.

In most harbours a 'waterman' is appointed who controls the water and charges for it. The charges are fixed by the local council, but usually vary a bit according to what the 'waterman' thinks he can get. A length of hosepipe about 25 metres long is useful for filling water tanks. A selection of connectors should be carried.

The recent mild and dry winters in Europe have meant that summer water supplies in the Mediterranean have been steadily eroded. Already centres of tourism along the coast drain over-stretched supplies, and it is becoming more common to find water rationed at harbours and marinas. Though many optimistically believe that we are experiencing a mini-climatic aberration that will right itself in a few years, the evidence for global warming continues to accumulate and, if it is correct, then water poverty in the Mediterranean is going to become a fact of life. I can see the day when reverse-osmosis water-makers become a common piece of equipment on board cruising yachts.

Ice

Ice will be found in most harbours as large blocks, or ice cubes can be bought in many places. Many fishing boats use ice, either to supplement their own refrigeration systems or, on smaller boats, as the sole means of keeping the catch cold. In most harbours it is usually a simple matter to locate the 'ice-man' or the local supplier. Some of the ice contains chemicals to keep it solid longer and is unsuitable for consumption in drinks. In some of the larger harbours used regularly by yachts, ice cubes, suitable for those all-important cold drinks, can be found.

Using ice, whether in blocks or in cubes, is the cheapest way of keeping food cool and, at the height of summer helps out refrigeration systems struggling to keep things cool.

Yacht spares

Imported equipment and spares are getting easier to find all the time, but there is still not a lot of imported equipment for sale in the chandlers. The chandlers in some of the bigger yachting centres (Kuşadası, Bodrum and Marmaris) carry the best collection of imported spares and some locally manufactured gear, mostly deck hardware. To offset the lack, the local engineer or blacksmith will attempt to construct almost anything if you can describe what you want. Stainless steel hardware of good quality can be fabricated in some places, and mild steel fabrication is good and can be galvanised cheaply. The big engineering workshops can adapt a wide range of good-quality spares for motors, including

bearings, fuel pump and injector spares, and gaskets.

Duty-free spares

Duty-free spares can be imported into Turkey, but not without considerable bother and some delay. For large items, engage an agent but still prepare yourself for long delays.

Turkey has recently been granted membership of the customs union with the European Union and in theory this should make importing duty-free goods for a yacht easier. In theory no customs formalities and no VAT is applicable. In practice the procedure varies from place to place with somewhere like Istanbul being relatively easy and somewhere like Bodrum being more difficult. It is necessary to have an agent or a company like a boatyard to import goods, as the onus for bonding requirements now rests with them. In the future it is to be expected that the practice will be ironed out nationally so that importing duty-free goods becomes a quick and easy process.

When flying into Turkey small items like electronic goods and small engine and equipment spares can easily be brought in packed with your personal belongings. Technically this is illegal as such goods should be declared but, in practice, most people do this without any bother. The other option is to have goods sent to Greece and then sail across to pick them up. On re-entering Turkey the goods can be listed on the Transit Log as part of the boat's inventory.

Antifouling

A yacht bottom fouls more quickly in the warm waters of the Mediterranean than it would in more northerly waters. Consequently, more potent antifouling must be used.

Eroding antifoulings such as *International Micron*, *Blake's*, and *Hempel's Blue* work well as long as your boat is moving and not sitting still at anchor or berthed for long periods, when the build-up of weed and coral worm overcomes the antifouling's ability to erode itself and rubbing down just takes the antifouling off.

Hard, scrubbable antifoulings like *Blake's tin-free Tiger*, *Hempel's Hard Racing* and *Veneziani* hard antifouling work well and, although they tend to foul more quickly than eroding antifoulings, they can be satisfactorily rubbed down without removing all the antifouling.

Locally manufactured antifoulings of the eroding and hard types are made in Turkey under several brand names (*Duratek* is one) and seem to work as well as the more expensive imported varieties.

Local antifouling of the soft type (*Dyo Tropicano* and *TransOcean* work well) is widely available, cheap, and effective – you cannot, of course, rub it down through the season. Generally, for an eight-month sailing season and four months on the hard, I find it copes well, with fouling just beginning in the eighth month. If you haul every winter then, in terms of cost-effectiveness, the local soft antifouling is difficult to beat – working out at around one-third the cost or less of more sophisticated antifoulings.

Hauling out

There are comparatively few places to haul out in Turkey, although it is likely that additional yards will open as the numbers of yachts in Turkish waters increase. Unless you are hauled out in a customs enclosure (such as Kuşadasi Marina) you must have an inventory of everything on board notarised and responsibility for the boat and equipment made over to the boatyard owner. The boat will be sealed by customs and the seal will be removed when you return.

There are four popular places for hauling: Kuşadasi, Bodrum, Marmaris and Kemer/Antalya. There are travel hoists at Atabay and Ataköy near Istanbul, Kuşadasi, Bodrum, Keçi Bükü, Marmaris, Kemer and the Setur Marina in Antalya commercial harbour. Yachts can be hauled on a sledge and cradle at various other places, notably Istanbul, Golden Dolphin Marina, Izmir, Yalikavak, Bodrum, Bozburun and Marmaris.

Berthing

In all harbours go stern or bows-to the quay with an anchor laid out from the quay or mole. It takes some skill to go stern-to, especially if there is a strong cross wind and perhaps nearby anchor chains. Always have plenty of fenders out and, when close to the quay, warp the yacht into place rather than using the engine. For yachts up to 10–12 metres long it is easier to go bows-to, as they can more easily be manoeuvred into a berth when going forward, and if ballasting extends for a short distance underwater (as it often does), then damage to the rudder is avoided. Moreover, there is a gain in privacy, as people on the quay cannot see into the cockpit or cabin. Going stern or bows-to rather than alongside prevents vermin, particularly cockroaches, from coming on board, and avoids damage to a yacht from wash or surge in the harbour. Even if there is room to go alongside it is nearly always better to go stern or bows-to.

Gulet skippers

Care is needed in the vicinity of many *gulet* skippers, who charge around everywhere at great speed, but particularly in and out of harbours. An element of machismo is at work here and there have been instances where yachts berthed on the quay or at anchor have been damaged by *gulets* hitting them. Most of the skippers do not understand the nautical 'rules of the road' and many do not have boat skills equal to their machismo.

Insurance

A comprehensive insurance policy for the Mediterranean is not excessively expensive, but shop around the various companies to get the best deal. Many insurance companies do not cover anything E of 34°, which includes part of Cyprus and the Turkish coast, in their standard policy for the eastern Mediterranean. It is possible to get special extensions for this area as the main thrust of this policy requirement is to exclude some of the risky war zones in the Middle East in the standard policy for the eastern Mediterranean.

All insurance policies require that due care and seamanship be exercised. If you use photocopied charts or pilots, this may be construed as contrary to good seamanship and may influence claims.

Ship's papers

The Small Ships Register papers issued by the Department of Transport in Swansea, or full (Part I) registration papers, are accepted. At the time of writing the Turkish authorities are lenient over registration papers, but things may get tougher in the future. A certificate of competency is rarely asked for and, if it is, the RYA Helmsman's Certificate of Competence or Yachtmasters is acceptable. A ship's stamp is useful and can be made cheaply. Below is a suggested crew list and port form with the details in English and Turkish.

Name of yacht	*Yatin Ismi*
Country of registration	*Sicil Memleketi*
Registration number	*Sicil numarasi*
Registered tonnage	*Net tonilato*
Length	*Uzunluk*
Beam	*Genişlik*
Draught	*Cektiğisu*
Type of vessel	*Geminin Cinsi*
Captain	*Yatin kaptani ve*
Passport number	*Pasaport numarasi ve*
Address	*Adresi*
Owner address	*Yatin sahibi ve adresi*
Crew names and	*Murettebatin Isimleri ve*
passport numbers	*pasaport numaralari*
Time and date of arrival	*Limana varis tarihi ve*
in port	*saati*
Last port of call	*Geldiği son ziyaret limani*
Next port of call	*Gideceği ilk ziyaret limani*

Mooring bows-to is easier and more private

Garbage

The steady increase in man-made disposables found in the oceans and seas of the world is saddening. Around the shores of Turkey there has recently been an increase in plastic refuse of all types. When I was in Turkey in 1980 it was rare to be given a plastic bag when shopping and there was very little in the way of prepacked food. In fact, plastic bags were at such a premium that they were never thrown away but jealously hoarded. As a result the sea and shore were comparatively free of litter. Today plastic bags and prepacked food are common, and the increase in plastic refuse in the sea and on the beaches is frightening. Much of it is thrown into the sea by the Turks themselves, especially from the local charter boats, but shore-based tourists and, sadly, some yachtsmen are also to blame.

In nearly every harbour there are containers for garbage and it is here and not in the sea that it belongs.

Rescue services

A coastguard service, in distinctive cream patrol boats with a diagonal orange stripe (the Sahil Güvenlik), was established in 1982. The coastguard patrols prohibited areas, may ask for your papers, will assist if you are in distress and can supply a weather forecast for you. The new patrol boats listen on VHF Ch 16 and have radio operators who speak English.

The relevant coastguard telephone numbers are as follows:

Coastguard Marmara and Straits Area Command at
  Istanbul ☎ (212) 242 9710/11/12
Coastguard Canakkale Group Command at Canakkale
  ☎ (286) 854 8262
Coastguard Aegean Sea Command at Izmir
  ☎ (232) 365 5820/366 6666/366 6667
Coastguard Marmaris Group Command at
  Marmaris/Muğla ☎ (252) 412 7722/412 6386
Coastguard Antalya Group Command at Antalya
  ☎ (242) 248 1450/248 1451
Coastguard Mediterranean Sea Command at Mersin
  ☎ (324) 237 1919/237 2222
Coastguard Samsun Group Command
  ☎ (362) 445 0333/445 0334
Coastguard Trabzon Group Command
  ☎ (462) 230 0882
Coastguard Enez ☎ (284) 821 4442
Coastguard Igneada ☎ (288) 692 2129
Coastguard Ayvalik ☎ (266) 312 1730
Coastguard Fethiye ☎ (252) 614 8460
Coastguard Iskenderun ☎ (326) 614 2311
Coastguard Karatas ☎ (322) 681 2579
Coastguard Kaş ☎ (242) 836 2455
Coastguard Golçuk ☎ (262) 414 6601
Coastguard Ceşme ☎ (232) 724 8355
Coastguard Botas ☎ (322) 613 5859
Coastguard Cevlik ☎ (326) 594 9018

Charges

Charges are made in the marinas around the coast and in some municipal harbours. Marina fees are often calculated in Deutschmarks or dollars because high inflation quickly deflates the lira against hard currencies.

In this pilot, there is a rough guide to prices, based on a banding system from 1 to 5. Prices for the different charge bands are given below, but it must be emphasised that charges change often and arbitrarily. The charge bands are intended to give an indication only. For weekly, monthly and annual contracts, prices come down on a sliding scale, often as much as 50 per cent for an annual contract. Winter rates are usually much less than summer rates.

Charges are for the daily high season rate for a 12-metre yacht, at the exchange rates current when this volume went to press. Prices are in GBP sterling. For smaller or larger yachts make an approximate guesstimate.

1. No charge
2. Low cost (under £15)
3. Medium cost (£16–£25)
4. High cost (£26–£35)
5. Very high cost (over £36)

General information

Tourist offices

In the cities and larger towns there are tourist offices. These can often provide free brochures and maps detailing local itineraries and places of interest, as well as helping you with any small problems you may encounter.

Banks

Eurocheques, Postcheques, major credit cards (Visa, Access/Mastercard, American Express and Diners) and travellers' cheques are accepted in the cities, larger towns and popular tourist spots. In most larger towns and tourist resorts, and a surprising number of small resorts, there are ATM ('hole-in-the-wall') machines that will take credit cards (Visa or Access). Machines operated by *Pamukbank*, *Isbank*, *Yapi Kredi* and several others work with Visa and Access and even have instructions in English to help you along. Credit cards and charge cards are also commonly accepted in many shops and some restaurants.

In general there are few places of any size where you cannot change money, either in a bank, in a post office, or at a travel agent who will usually have a sideline in changing money. Banks are open from 0830–1200 and 1330–1800 Monday to Friday. Hours may vary in the summer. Getting money sent to Turkey from outside the country is a tedious and prolonged affair – expect it to take literally weeks longer than you anticipate.

Public holidays

January 1	New Year's Day
April 23	Children's Day
May 1	May Day
May 19	Youth Day

May 27   Freedom and Constitution Day
August 30   Victory Day
October 29, 30   Republic Days
Where the holiday falls on a weekend the following Monday will be a holiday.
Movable
Seker bayrami (sugar holy days)
Kurban bayrami (holy days of sacrifice)

Laundry

In most places laundry will be taken in and returned crisp and neatly folded. Ascertain the cost first as prices vary considerably.

Security

On the whole the Turks are an honest nation and you will be little troubled by theft. In the cities and tourist resorts it pays to take normal precautions.

Drugs

Contrary to popular opinion, *narghiles*, the hubble-bubble water pipes smoked by elder Turks in some cafés, are not stuffed with hashish but with ordinary tobacco! There are strict penalties for using drugs such as hashish in Turkey and your boat may be confiscated if you are found to have drugs on board. The possession of hard drugs incurs extremely severe penalties.

Health

Medical facilities vary from good in the cities to poor in the villages. Dental treatment can be horrifying, especially when the common treatment seems to be to pull out the offending tooth. Dental treatment is best in the largest cities.

Medicines

Specially prescribed drugs should be bought in sufficient quantities before departure. Most drugs, including antibiotics and antihistamines, can be bought over the counter, although they may be under different brand names from those you are used to.

Mail

The Turkish postal system is reliable but muddled. Letters arrive quite quickly, but parcels can take up to two months to arrive, as they are all opened by customs and, at busy periods, a backlog builds up. Items sent *poste restante* cost a small sum each to extract from the post office.

Telecommunications

All towns and most villages have a post office where local and international calls can be made. In some towns and tourist resorts telephone cards can be purchased and these can be used for international calls. In most post offices calls are metered and you pay at the counter.

Many travel agents and hotels have metered telephones and fax machines that you can use, although charges can be steep – the record so far is £15 for a single-page fax to England!

Making telephone calls and sending faxes can be a tedious business, and it may take some time to get through. Try to avoid business hours if at all possible.

Mobile phones Digital cellular phones with GSM (Global System for Mobile Communications) capacity can now be used in Turkey. Along the coastal region the signal will be picked up by either a Turkish or a Greek provider, whichever is the stronger. There are licensing agreements between both Turkish and Greek providers and, in practice, the system works well. Hand-held sets are limited to around 2 watts so you will not be able to transmit when too far away from any particular station. Portables (around 5 watts) or proper marine installations have a greater range. Portable phones, like VHF sets, are limited by the distance from the receiving and transmitting station and are also shut out by high land. Enclosed bays or high islands and mountains will cast a transmitting shadow over the phone.

Fax connections from digital phones are available with dedicated PC cards for your specific cellular phone. You will need a PC, a fax PC card or modem, some sort of software to run it, and an interface between the portable phone and fax PC card or stand-alone modem. Transmission rates are currently 9,600 baud.

Internet There are internet providers in Turkey although, at the time of writing, the transmission rate is slow, at least in practice. Compuserve has nodes in Istanbul and Ankara and although the reported baud rates are highish, in practice they can be slow. For text-based e-mail the rates are adequate.
Compuserve Ankara ☎ (312) 468 8042
    SCI 1,200–9,600 baud
Compuserve Istanbul ☎ (212) 293 2191
    INF 300–28,800 baud
Compuserve Istanbul ☎ (212) 234 5168
    SCI 1,200–9,600 baud

Provisioning

In all but the smallest villages basic provisions can be found and fresh produce is excellent. Imported goods can be found in large towns and tourist centres. Luxury goods made in Turkey (and this includes paper towels, toilet paper, long-life milk, hard cheeses, salad dressing, etc) can also be difficult to find away from the tourist centres.

In the large villages and towns there is a market day once a week, usually on Fridays, where all manner of fresh produce, fruit and vegetables, dried fruit and nuts, poultry, cheese, herbs and spices are brought from the surrounding countryside for sale. The quality of the produce, especially the fruit and vegetables, would be hard to better in the eastern Mediterranean. Not without reason is Turkey known as the market garden of Europe but, of course, the choice is limited by the seasons.

Shopping hours vary somewhat, but are generally 0830–1400/1530 and 1600–1930 Monday to Saturday. Some shops will open on Sundays. The following brief comments give you some idea of what is available in Turkey and its quality.

Meat Reasonably priced and always fresh. It is not hung and is butchered in a haphazard fashion so that it is difficult to know which part of the carcass you are getting. Since Turkey is a Moslem country, pork is not commonly for sale, although wild boar is occasionally available. Remember that the latter may be host to a whole range of worms and other nasties.

Fish No longer cheap, and prized fish like grouper is expensive. Crayfish and prawns are also expensive. Other types of fish, especially mackerel and tunny in season, are good value.

Fruit and vegetables Excellent throughout the year and comparatively cheap. The choice is seasonal.

Staples Most basics can be found, although some items, such as rice and pasta, tend to be of poor quality.

Cheese Local soft cheeses (feta types) are cheap and good. Locally made and prepacked hard and processed cheeses are adequate and reasonably priced. Imported cheeses (usually Camembert and blue cheeses) are expensive.

Canned goods Reasonable choice of canned goods although there are not a lot of meat-based stews and the like. Canned vegetables, beans and fruit are good and relatively cheap.

Coffee and tea Imported instant coffee is available although comparatively expensive. Filter coffee is also available. Local coffee can be ground coarsely to make an acceptable cup. The packaged ground coffee is very fine for Turkish coffee and tends to clog filters if you are making filter coffee. Imported tea is available for the traditional 'cuppa'. Local tea doesn't make a British cuppa but is drinkable. Drink it Turkish-style: strong, black, and sweet.

Wines, beer and spirits Local wines are quite palatable and some of the more expensive ones are good. However, on the whole, they are neither cheap nor consistent. Try *Dikmen*, *Villa Doluca*, *Dardanelles*, and *Kavaklidere* for reds, and *Kavaklidere*, *Villa Doluca*, *Sungurlu*, and *Çankaya* for whites. Wine cannot be bought in bulk from a barrel. Local beer (commonly *Efes* or *Tuborg*) is of the lager type, cheap, and eminently drinkable although a bit gassy. The local spirit, the aniseed-flavoured *raki*, is moderately priced and lethal. It is normally drunk 'half and half' with water. Local brandy is hardly palatable. Imported spirits, if you can find them, are expensive, but local gin and vodka are reasonably priced and drinkable.

Formalities and laws relevant to the yachtsman

Entry and exit formalities

A yacht entering Turkey must go to a port of entry where the necessary officials for clearing a yacht in are stationed. The order in which the various officials are seen varies, but is generally as follows: harbourmaster, health, passport police, customs, customs patrol.

When leaving you see these officials in more or less the same order, although, as I have mentioned, there are local variations. The passport police will stamp you into the country for a three-month period. Customs may want to come aboard your yacht to search it, but this is usually a cursory procedure and seldom occurs in popular yachting ports of entry. The health authority will get you to fill in a form; no documents are required. The harbourmaster will make a moderate charge for harbour dues and light dues for boats over 30 tons.

In 1984 a Transit Log for yachts was introduced to replace the cumbersome collection of papers previously required. The Transit Log cost 30 dollars US in 1997, but the charge may be reviewed each year. In recent years there have been 'requests' for 'overtime' or 'extra time' payments to customs in some harbours during normal working hours, and for these you will often get receipts which mean nothing. The 'request' cost around £9–£10 in 1996, but appears to have been less frequently asked for in a number of harbours of late. There is a legal overtime charge of around £15 for outside office hours and weekends.

The Transit Log is valid for three months only except in the circumstances outlined below. At your first port you are required to list your itinerary in the Transit Log. If you alter your route there is a section in the log that you must fill out. Similarly any changes of crew must be recorded in the log. At any subsequent ports of call the customs will want to inspect your log. Between ports of call where customs officers are stationed the coastguard (Sahil Güvenlik) may ask for your papers while doing the rounds.

When leaving Turkey you must surrender your Transit Log. Since a new Transit Log must now be obtained after three months and, because visitors cannot remain longer than three months at any one time, the normal practice is simply to nip across to Greece on your yacht; when you return you will automatically be given a further three months.

Documents

A valid passport or identity card is required. Most visas can be obtained at the port of entry (such as the visa required for British passport holders) but check with your consulate if you are unsure. Most EU countries and many other countries do not require a visa. Ship's papers are required and these may be either the RYA Small Ships Register papers or full Part 1 registration papers. Photocopies will be regarded with suspicion and are not normally allowed. If your registration papers do not show ownership of the yacht then it is wise to have a notarised document showing that you are the owner.

Yachts with more than one owner are admissible with a ceiling of four owners for the yacht to be regarded as a private yacht in Turkey. Each owner may own as much or as little as wished, but the names and shares of the owners must be listed on the registration documents or the bill of sale. Yachts owned by clubs are regarded as for shared ownership. Again, there must not be more than four owners and they must be listed on the registration document or bill of sale. Company yachts must be accompanied by notarised documents showing that whoever is on board is a shareholder of the company. Headed notepaper and the like is not acceptable proof of someone being a shareholder.

Owners

The owner of a yacht must be aboard it in order for the yacht to cruise in Turkish waters. This applies to friends and family who cannot use a yacht even if they are related to the owner or have permission from him/her. The yacht can only cruise in Turkish waters with the owner on board. As there can be up to four owners of a yacht then it is possible for each one to use the boat without penalty. Friends and family can be registered as part owners (they need only own 1 per cent or so) although the complications and possible ramifications will rule this out as an option for most people. The easiest thing to do is to cross to Greece to pick up friends and family and then return to Turkey with them on board when they will be cleared into the country in the normal way.

Only one crew change is allowed per Transit Log. If you change crew on a subsequent occasion then you will have to purchase another Transit Log. This applies equally to family and friends.

Leaving a yacht in Turkey

A yacht may remain in Turkey for up to five years and on the hard for up to two years. Whether the yacht is ashore in a yard or afloat, it must be bonded with customs if the owner is leaving the country. As your passport is stamped with the boat's name when you enter, you cannot leave without getting the stamp annulled by customs. When the yacht is bonded, the yacht itself and the inventory is transferred to the responsibility of a recognised agent, usually a boatyard or a marina.

Agents

The procedure for leaving a yacht in Turkey can be carried out by the owner, but is often easier left to an agent. Enquire on prices between agents as they can vary substantially. An agent can also be used to clear a yacht in and out of Turkey although this is perfectly feasible (although time consuming) to do on your own.

Fines

Large fines are levied on yachts discharging waste into the sea, particularly in harbours. The maximum official fine is in the region of £150–£200. However fines have been known to be as much as £400 and, in one case, £1000. Ports strictly enforcing heavy penalties are Bozburun, Gocek, Kalkan and Kaş. There is some hypocrisy over this matter as I have personally witnessed *gulets* pumping out their holding tanks in several harbours for which action no fines have been levied. It is thought that *gulet* skippers and shoreside locals will report foreign-flag yachts. That said, yacht skippers should never pump out holding tanks in harbour or at anchor whether threatened by a fine or not.

Transit Log explanation

Overleaf is the translation on the back of the Transit Log.

Yacht charter

There are extensive regulations governing yacht charter in Turkey, some of which are included in the regulations reproduced opposite. Chartering regulations for foreign flag yachts are entirely different and require the services of an authorised Turkish charter operator or the payment of a charter fee if a foreign flag yacht arrives from another country (inevitably Greece). For practical advice the best thing to do is to contact a yacht charter company operating in Turkey. The Turkish regulations can be obtained abroad from a Turkish tourist office or in Turkey from the Ministry of Culture and Tourism.

Ports of entry

Istanbul, Bandirma, Canakkale, Ayvalik, Dikili, Izmir, Ceşme, Kuşadasi, Güllük, Bodrum, Datça, Marmaris, Fethiye, Kaş, Finike, Kemer, Antalya, Alanya, Anamur, Taşucu, Mersin, Iskenderun. (See frontispiece map.) In the Black Sea Trabzon, Samsun, and Tekirdağ are also listed, but see the notes on the Black Sea (Chapter VIII).

Other regulations

1. It is strictly prohibited to take any archaeological souvenirs from the coast or the sea bed, with the possible penalty of confiscation of the yacht. A certain percentage of yachts all taking 'just one little souvenir' adds up to an awful lot of ancient history disappearing, and I have every sympathy for the archaeological authorities who must enforce this law and none for the yachtsman who breaks it. You should also be wary of touts at archaeological sites selling ancient coins and ceramics since most are fakes. Either way you may lose: if you purchase a real antique you stand to lose your yacht; alternatively you may buy a worthless (although often quite good) fake.
2. Underwater diving with bottles is prohibited (as is underwater fishing) in Turkish waters, except under the supervision of an authorised guide.

-Please read the following before filling in the Certificate.

- The Certificate will duely be filled in by the captain of yacht in block letters

- Yachts entering and departing Turkey will practice the same through border points (Trabzon, Samsun, Tekirdağ, İstanbul, Çanakkale, Bandırma, Akçay, Ayvalık, Dikili, İzmir, Çeşme, Kuşadası,Güllük, Bodrum, Datca, Marmarıs, Fethiye, Kaş, Kemer, Antalya, Anamur, Alanya, Taşucu, Mersin and İskenderun)

- The yacht, while entering the Turkish territorial waters, will be registered in the passport of yacht captain, or in a document to be found acceptable by the Customs authorities.

- During departure, the registration wiil be cancelled again by the customs authorities at the seaport where the yacht have formerly anchored.

-Captain of the yacht will always keep this Certificate in the yacht, and demonstrate it to the authorities concerned whenever required.

-This Certificfate is issued to those bearing Yacht Registration Certificatet to ensure their depature abroad after entering of the yacht into the country and performing journey among the Turkish seaports. The yachts entering into the Turkish territorial waters from abroad will mark on the Certificate sheei the Entry into Turkish Seaports Box, and those journeying among the domestic seaports will mark the Domestic Journey Box

-The yachts mentioned are allowed to leave the country through the use of Y2 copy of this Certificate. In case of departure from the country, yachts bearing no certificate will mark the Departure from Turkish Seaports Box after having obtained the Certificate in question.

Y1 COPY

This copy will duely be filled in after seizure of the Certifificate. The movable stocks of yacht will be registered in the movable stock list attached to this copy. Other stocks which are not in the list, but actually exist in the yacht will be included in a separate sheet of movable stock list and wil be approved by the Customs authorities. Further, each of the relevant public authorities concerned appearing on Y1 copy will be approached, submitted declarations and ensured that their singatures and seals be secured without missing. Y1 copy, originals of the movable stock list and Y2 Copy will be withheld in the yacht, and other copies will remain with te public authorities concerned.

Y2 COPY

Part Y1 of this copy is arranged in following cases;

1. Winter lay-up,

2. Departure of yacht from the Turkish seaports,

3. Change in owner(new transit log number will be written on Y2 copy)

4. Expiry of validity of the Certificate;

    (a) the validity period of the Certificate is for one year for the Turkish flag private yachts.

    (b)The validity period of the Certificate is for three months for foreign flag yachts (except the cases stated in Part Y1)

5. Change in declaring person (new transit log number will be written on Y2 Copy)

6. Termination of tours for commercial journeys.

    Yacht Registaration Cerficates of those sailing among the domestic seaports are delivered to the relevant public authorities will be approached, submitted declarations and ensured that their singatures and seals have been secured without missing. Similary, copies of these Certificates will be kept with the public authorities concerned.

PART VII and VIII OF THİS COPY

The route during sailling is fixed in case of any change in yacthsmen and crew, and parts covering these changes are approved by the Harbour Master's Office

-To ensure the yacois to sail, approval of the Harbour Master's Ofice at the first seaport landed will suffice, and the approval of other authorities will not be required provided that they remain in the Turkish territorial waters, or sail among the Turkish seaports.

-During arrivals and departures, declarations will be made to the Turkish authorities at the first place visited due to

extra- ordinary situations of force majeure, or the liabilities foreseen in the law no: 4922 regarding the Protection of Life and Properties on the Sea.

---

1. PURPOSE OF USE:

This Certificate covers the declarations and transactions, at the first seaport or at the final destination point for winter lay-up, of the Turkish flag private yachts arriving from foreino seaports and the Turkish and foreing flag commercial yachts.

This Certificate can not be used for passanger transporting vessels (even if they have the status of a yacht) sailling between a Turkish seaport and a foreing seaport or between the Turkish seaports. However, this can be used in the yachting activites of the operations licenced by the Turkish Ministry of Tourism.

II. REASONS OF CANCELLATION OF THE CERTIFICATION

1. Winter lay-up

2. Departure of the yacht from the Turkish seaports

3. change in owner.

4. Expiry of validity of the Certificate

5. Change in declaring person

6. Termination of tours for commercial journeys

III. ROUTE

Foreing flag yachts and foreign driven Turkish flag yachts can sail on route as manifested on the saling document. They may approach to places and lay anchor on route where exists no custom office provided that they are free from restrictions. Any change in route will be declared in part VI of Y2 copy, and submitted to the approval of the Habour Master's office.

IV. HEALTH DECLARATION

Health service rendered for the yacths are valid within the given period of the Yacht Registration Certificate so long as that they do not stop by any foreing seaport. Any case of contagious disease or death which may occur on board will be reported to the Coastal Health Center at the nearest seaport.

V. CUSTOMS TRANSACTIONS

1. Transactions regarding the yacht.

Should there be the movable stocks and items to be used for handling the yacht, they will be registered in the Movable Stock List From attached to Y1 copy of this Certificate. The list is checked during the procedures of departure or the entry to the seaport for winter lay-up.

2. Transactions regarding the yachtsmen and the crew:

(a) Part of personal belongings, having enjoyed the exemption applied on personal belongings and gift ilems, are returned to owers without Customs Tax Charges. Personal use of an item owned is considered a personal belonging For example; a photographic camere, coffee and alchoholic drinks etc. in certain quantities.

(b) Items, temporarily brought in and designed to be taken out of country again and subject to Customs duties and qualified non-commercial, are permitted to bring into the country free of customs charges through the registering of the case in the passport of the declaring person or in a document acceptable by the Customs Authorities. For example; sports and camping material and equipments.

(c) Necessary permits are to be obtained from the Authorities concerned for items subject to special permit for their entry into the country . For example; diving tubes, fire arrms etc.

VI. GENERAL INFORMATION

1. Foreigners entering into Turkey in their own yachts are allowed to leave the country by a different means of transportation after having deposited their yachts in a licenced yacht harbour for a maximum period of two years for lay-up, mintenance and repair purposes.In such cases, necessary transactions are performed in their passports at the time when they apply the Customs Office, together with a document to be obtained from the Yacht Harbour Master's Office where their yachts have been deposited earlier.

2. "Lighthouse Dues" are charged from yachts over 30 NRT.

3. Persons or groups wishing to skin-dive at the Turkish areas of certain coordinates are expected to bear a Certificate obtained from the national organisations or the authorised bodies of their countries.

4. Skin-divers are obliged to perform their activities under the supervision of the Turkish Diving Guides.

5. Permissions should be obtained from the Regional Tourist Offices or the person authorised by the same Office regarding the areas intended for skin-diving.

Customs will want to know if you have diving bottles on board and, if so, will seal them.

3. Only wild boar can be hunted in the hunting season.

4. Commercial fishing by foreigners is prohibited and carries heavy penalties.

Marine life

Marine life in the Mediterranean is, at first, disappointing to the yachtsman used to life around the Atlantic coast or in the Red Sea. It is not as prolific or as diverse as you might imagine; there are fewer seabirds, good eating fish are more scarce and difficult to catch and, in places, the sea bottom can be quite bereft of interest compared, say, with the Red Sea or the west coast of France.

There are a number of reasons for the relative paucity of marine life. The first is the non-tidal nature of the sea, which means that there is no inter-tidal zone in which a varied and rich amount of life can live and contribute to the whole marine ecosystem. The second is the fact that the Mediterranean has been fished far longer and more intensively than any other sea area.

Although the marine life is initially disappointing, the yachtsman is in a unique position to discover and explore what life there is in the Mediterranean. Dolphins, whales, turtles, flying fish, tuna, swordfish and sunfish will be seen in many places and, with a mask and snorkel, the warm water invites exploration.

Whales and dolphins (cetaceans)

Dolphins, sadly, are becoming less common in Turkish waters than they were even a few years ago. You will still see dolphins and, occasionally, a school of dolphins will come up to a yacht and play around it. At night the phosphorescence created by dolphins around a yacht is something marvellous to behold.

The numbers of dolphins have decreased for several reasons. Food stocks, especially mackerel and tuna, have decreased. Drift-netting, common in Italy and, unfortunately, recently resumed there, catches dolphins as well as swordfish and tuna. Estimates of the numbers killed in this manner vary, but are thought to be in the thousands rather than hundreds. Lastly, pollution, in the form of heavy metals, PCBs and other carcinogenic compounds, and spills of toxic chemicals, have caused a form of flu similar to that which killed many seals around British coasts. I can only suggest that you support any of those groups fighting for the continued survival of this magnificent mammal which has never harmed humans and, anecdotal trivia aside, is known to have actively aided humans in distress in the water. Renew your subscription to Greenpeace, Friends of the Earth or the Environmental Investigation Agency.

In antiquity the dolphin was mentioned and often depicted in mosaics. Aristotle and Pliny mention it as a friend of man, Plutarch provides us with much information about the classical legends in his treatise *On the Intelligence of Animals*, Aesop wrote the fable *The Monkey and the Dolphin* concerning dolphin behaviour, and good old Herodotus also tells a number of tales concerning dolphins. Most of these tales relate how the dolphin has befriended man and exhibited great intelligence, particularly to those in distress in the sea. Athenaios tells us of a youth from Iassos (in the present, Güllük Körfezi) who befriended a dolphin which eventually would take him on its back and play with him in the water. Such was the friendship that one day the dolphin tried to follow the boy ashore, was stranded on the beach, and died. The citizens of Iassos were so impressed that they engraved their coins with the image of the dolphin after the event. Pausanias relates the story of the dolphin from Poroselene (in the present-day archipelago around Ayvalik) that was rescued by a young boy from fishermen and which later stayed in the vicinity and took him for rides on its back.

In the eastern Mediterranean most of the cetaceans seen are toothed whales, which are fish-eaters and so possess teeth to grip their prey. To this class belong the porpoise, dolphin, pilot whale and killer whale. The common dolphin (*Delphinus delphis*) will often be seen. Less common are the larger bottle-nosed dolphin (*Tursiops truncatus*) and the common porpoise (*Phocoena phocoena*). The pilot whale (*Globicephala melaena*) is fairly common and grows up to 8·5 metres long. The bottle-nosed whale (*Hyperoodon ampullatus*), Risso's dolphin (*Grampus griseus*) and the killer whale (*Orcinus orca*) have been sighted in the eastern Mediterranean.

Good eating fish

Numerous good eating fish are caught off the Turkish Aegean and eastern Mediterranean coasts, and equally numerous restaurants specialise in fish. Fish is good simply grilled or fried, but one wishes that some of the traditional Turkish fish recipes were to be found in these restaurants. Alan Davidson in his excellent *Mediterranean Seafood* details mouth-watering recipes such as fish baked with apple and onion, gurnard with almond sauce, turbot cooked with vegetables, and mussels with beer and tartar sauce, all Turkish recipes but, alas, not found in the fish restaurants, where frying or grilling is the standard method of cooking. However, in Istanbul, where fish and, in particular, swordfish and bonito are easily caught migrating through the Bosphorus, restaurants serving fish in a variety of interesting ways can be found. On Galata Bridge there are numerous, often humble, restaurants offering tempting fish dishes in colourful surroundings; alternatively you can explore further afield and discover other excellent restaurants in the city which is the culinary capital of Turkey.

In out-of-the-way spots in the Aegean and eastern Mediterranean you will sometimes be offered fish by local fishermen and so can perform your own culinary experiments. One of my favourites, first demonstrated to me by a friend, Richard Wilson, is to stuff a largish fish, such as a sea bream or grouper, with chopped onions, carrots, parsley, a little rosemary and fresh ginger, and steam it over whatever vegetables you are having. The following list of good eating fish is a brief one, and the reader should consult Alan Davidson's *Mediterranean Seafood* for more detailed information.

Tuna *(Orkinos)* Tuna (and swordfish) pass through the Bosphorus in large numbers when migrating to the Black Sea for summer spawning and back again to the Mediterranean in the autumn and winter. Also found off the Aegean coast. Firm flesh, delicious grilled or fried.

Swordfish *(Kiliç)* Delicious as a steak grilled or fried with a squeeze of lemon. Sometimes smoked in Istanbul.

Grouper *(Sari hani, Orfox)* Flaky white flesh without too many bones. Excellent eating.

Red mullet *(Barbunya)* Tasty fish but bony.

Sea bream *(Sinarit)* Tasty and not too bony.

Flounder and sole *(Dere pisisi and Dil)* Delicious fried in butter with a sauce. Flatfish are most common in the Sea of Marmara and the Black Sea.

Prawns *(Karides)* Good if fresh (they are often frozen) but expensive.

Lobster/crawfish *(Böcek); **flat lobster** (Ayi istakozu)* Crawfish and particularly the flat lobster (*cigale*) are often offered in restaurants. Those unfamiliar with the flat lobster should not be put off by its appearance as it is every bit as good as lobster proper.

Squid *(Kalamar)* Delicious deep fried.

Octopus *(Ahtapot)* Often offered cold in a vinaigrette as a starter. Excellent if fresh.

Fishing methods

Fewer fishing boats will be encountered in Turkey than in Greece, Italy and points west. Most fishing is with long lines or nets, either small set nets or trawled nets. The only practice of potential danger is when one or two fishing boats place a net, just below the surface, across the entrance to a bay or creek. If you see a fishing boat lurking near the entrance to the bay, keep an eye out for a net just under the water.

Fish farms

In a number of bays, coves and bights there are floating rafts of fish farms. In some the space for anchoring is severely diminished and in others care is needed to avoid the raft anchors on the bottom. Fish farms are frequently moved so the pilotage notes may not always be accurate.

Dangerous marine animals

In the Mediterranean there are no more dangerous marine animals than you would encounter off the English coast, but the warm sea temperatures mean that you are in the water more often and therefore more likely to encounter these animals.

Sharks Probably the greatest fear of a swimmer, yet in all probability the least to be feared. Films such as *Jaws* and *Blue Water, White Death* have produced a phobia amongst swimmers that is out of all proportion to the menace. After a dozen and more years of sailing around the eastern Mediterranean I have positively identified a shark in the water on only three occasions. Fishermen occasionally bring in sharks from the deep water – usually the mackerel shark or sand shark. I have not been able to establish one fatality from a shark attack in Turkey and, as far as I know, the total recorded number of fatalities for the Mediterranean is six.

Moray eels Of the family *Muraenidae*, these eels are quite common in the eastern Mediterranean and are often caught by fishermen. They inhabit holes and crevices in rocks and can bite and tear if molested. Usually they will retire and are not aggressive unless wounded or sorely provoked.

Octopus Are very shy and do not attack. They have much more to fear from man than man from them.

Stingrays The European stingray (*Dasyatis pastinaca*) is common in the Mediterranean. It inhabits shallow waters, partially burying itself in the sand. If it is trodden on accidentally it will lash out with its tail and bury a spine in the offending foot. Venom is injected which produces severe local pain, sweating, vomiting and rapid heart beat, but rarely death. Soak the foot in very hot water and seek medical help.

Weeverfish Members of the family *Trachinidae*. The two most common are the great weever (*Trachinus draco*) and lesser weever (*Trachinus vipera*). The dorsal and opercular fins contain venom spines. When disturbed or annoyed, the

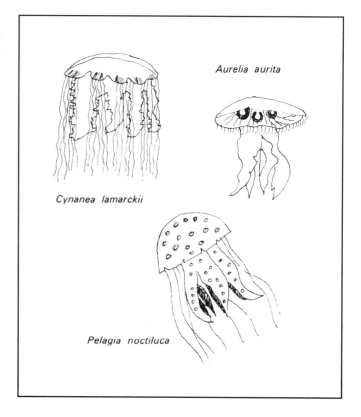

weever will erect its dorsal fin and attack. The venom injected produces instant pain which spreads to other parts of the body and is very severe. The victim may lose consciousness and death sometimes occurs. There are no known antidotes. Bathe the wound in hot water and seek medical help as soon as possible.

Note When walking in water where stingrays or weevers are thought to be, wear sand-shoes and shuffle the feet along the bottom. Do not handle dead weevers or stingrays.

Jellyfish Of all the animals described, those you are most likely to encounter are jellyfish. At certain times of the year and in certain places there will be considerable numbers of jellyfish in the water. All jellyfish sting, for this is the way they immobilise their prey, but some species have more powerful stings than others and consequently deserve greater respect.

Aurelia aurita The common jellyfish. It has a transparent dome-shaped body with four purple-violet crescents grouped around the centre. Transparent or light violet mouth arms hang below. Up to 25cm in diameter. A light contact with the stings is something like a nettle, but prolonged contact can hurt.

Pelagia noctiluca A mushroom-shaped jellyfish up to 10cm in diameter. It is easily identified, being light brown-yellow in colour and covered in 'warts'. It has long trailing tentacles and can inflict severe and painful stings.

Cyanea lamarckii A blue-violet saucer-shaped jellyfish up to 30cm across. It can be identified by the frilly mass of mouth arms underneath. It has long tentacles which can inflict severe and painful stings. There is a brown variety (*Cyanea capillata*) which can grow up to 50cm in diameter.

Charybdea marsupialis Mediterranean sea-wasp. A transparent, yellow-red box-shaped 'umbrella' up to 6cm high. Rarely seen but can inflict severe and painful stings.

Physalia physalis Portuguese man-of-war. Has a large conspicuous float (pneumatophore) above water growing to 30cm long and 10cm wide. Below it stream very long tentacles. Rarely seen but can inflict dangerous stings.

Rhizostoma pulmo Dome-shaped blue-white jellyfish up to 90cm in diameter. Its mouth arms are fused in a grey-green 'cauliflower' mass below the body. It has no long tentacles and is not known as a vicious stinger.

There are no known antidotes to jellyfish stings, but there are a number of ways of obtaining relief. Antihistamine creams have proved useful in some, but not all, cases. Diluted ammonium hydroxide, sodium bicarbonate, olive oil, sugar, and ethyl alcohol have been used. In general use a weak alkali. A tip which I have not tried but which sounds promising is to use a meat tenderiser, which apparently breaks down the protein base of the venom. Gloves should be worn when hauling up an anchor in jellyfish-infested water as the tentacles, especially those of *Pelagia*, can stick to the anchor chain.

Bristleworms In some locations numbers of bristleworms, probably of the family *Nereidae*, will be found. They are black and may grow up to 25cm long. The setae can produce a mild irritation, similar to that caused by a stinging nettle, if touched.

Sea urchins In some places on rocky coasts large colonies of sea urchins (*Paracentrotus lividus* and *Arbacia lixula*) will be found. While they do not have a venom apparatus, the spines penetrate and break off when the urchin is trodden on and are very painful. Care must be taken not to get a secondary infection.

Pollution

The Mediterranean is a closed sea supporting a large population around its shores. About 120 million people live in the coastal region and this number may double in summer. It has a small tidal difference, with about half of the water that is lost through evaporation coming from the rivers flowing into the Mediterranean and the other half coming from the Atlantic Ocean over the ledge at the Strait of Gibraltar (about one million cubic metres every second).

With most of the sewage from the coastal population being pumped into the sea untreated, with tankers and oil installations causing hydrocarbon pollution, and with industrial waste being discharged directly into rivers and so, ultimately, the sea, the waters around Turkey suffer from some pollution, although not as much as the western Mediterranean. The worst affected areas are around Istanbul and the Bosphorus, particularly in the Golden Horn and the neighbourhood of Izmit, where hydrocarbon and industrial waste pollutants are particularly bad; in the Bay of Izmir, where the water can no longer support marine life and swimming is banned; and at Mersin, where hydrocarbon pollution from the oil installations scars the sea and coast.

Up until recently nothing was being done about the increasing pollution in the Mediterranean but, in 1975, a United Nations environment committee decided to get together the culturally and politically diverse countries around the Mediterranean and work out a programme to clean up the sea. In 1980 all the countries (except Albania) agreed to a 10-billion dollar programme to go ahead with UN recommendations. Part of the anti-pollution plan may affect yachtsmen in the future. No thinking yachtsman should ever throw garbage into the sea – especially plastic. Yachtsmen can be fined for dumping waste oil into a harbour or close to the coast. In the future it is possible that holding tanks will have to be fitted, although few pumping-out points exist in marinas or harbours. The yachtsman may curse the extra cost involved, but must acknowledge the necessity of such regulations when so much of the Mediterranean, and for that matter the other seas and oceans of the world, is threatened by pollution of all types.

Food

The Turks eat better than anyone else in the eastern Mediterranean. This is partly to do with the plentiful and varied ingredients available in Turkey and partly to do with the care taken in the serving of food.

The cuisine is characterised by grilled or fried meats and stews of meat and vegetables. Starters are usually cold and often include cold cooked vegetables in a vinaigrette – cauliflower, beetroot and spinach are common.

Prices vary from cheap to reasonable. Even those on a tight budget will be able to find a small restaurant to suit their pocket. In the more expensive restaurants I have had meals that would not disgrace a moderately priced restaurant in London, but at less than half the price. The Turks are beer and *raki* drinkers, so you may find the choice of wines limited; otherwise you will eat and drink well for little.

For starters try the cold vegetables, *börek* (flaky pastry rolls stuffed with cheese, spinach, or meat, and deep fried), yoghurt dishes (with garlic, chopped spinach, aubergine, etc), stuffed vine leaves, bean salads (with chopped vegetables and a vinaigrette sauce), Russian (potato) salad, sometimes called American salad, and peppery tomato and garlic purée dips.

For the main course you will most likely be offered charcoal-grilled kebabs, steak, chops, chicken liver or kidney. Fish is usually offered grilled and occasionally as kebabs (tuna and swordfish in season). *Döner* kebab consists of slices of lamb roasted on a vertical spit, usually in a restaurant specialising in kebab dishes of one type or another. Various stews of lamb or beef with vegetables are usually made for the midday meal, but may be served in the evening. Variations on these basic meals are many, and in the more sophisticated restaurants you may be lucky enough to encounter delicious dishes such as bread-crumbed steaks stuffed with tomato and cheese, Circassian chicken (croquettes with herbs and pounded walnuts), fish salads and fish stew. Salads, usually tomatoes, onion, cucumbers and parsley, are good. Inevitably you will get chips, chips with everything in the humblest to the most expensive restaurant.

Desserts are simple but delicious affairs of fresh fruit, sometimes with chopped nuts and steeped in honey, and often with a hollowed-out orange or lemon atop the whole affair with a candle inside, so that at the end of a meal this becomes the centrepiece. For pastries you must go to a pastry shop. Coffee is of the Turkish type, strong, thick and sweet, with the grounds in the cup.

In most towns and resorts you will find sandwich shops. The sandwich is usually half a large loaf of bread stuffed with a variety of fillings (you choose) and flattened on a hot plate so that you can fit it in your mouth – a cheap and filling snack. There are cafés in the smallest village serving tea (*çay*), Turkish coffee, beer and *raki*.

History and culture

The following brief history helps place the events and epochs mentioned in the text. For detailed accounts the reader must turn elsewhere.

Prehistory (550 BC)

Numerous sites, from Palaeolithic through Neolithic to Chalcolithic, have been found. The earliest finds have come from around Antalya at Hacilar. We know little of the people, but some of their art survives, including the earliest landscape painting – an erupting volcano. Agriculture and the domestication of animals probably occurred in Upper Mesopotamia around 6500 BC.

Bronze Age (3000–1200 BC)

The first settlement at Troy has been dated to about 3000 BC. In the Anatolian plateau the Akkadian dynasty established itself at numerous sites. Assyrian traders arrived on the scene around 1900 BC. In northern central Anatolia (near Ankara) the Hatti peoples flourished, and from them the developing Hittite dynasty borrowed much, particularly their art forms. The Hittites, an Indo-European race, assumed control of western and southern Turkey in 1900 BC, and their rule lasted for nearly a thousand years. The Hittites developed a civilised society with written law, used silver for currency, developed agricultural methods and had an artisan class. They evolved a strong army and fortifications to protect the kingdom.

The Dark Age (1200–700 BC)

In the south, the Assyrians conquered the Hittite cities, and in the north the Thracian tribes from the Balkans moved in on the Hittites. For several centuries there was a so-called Dark Age, although along the coastal regions numerous city-states were evolving. Aeolia and Ionia were founded by Greek colonists, while Lydia, Caria and Lycia evolved from Anatolian sources. Along the coast Greek culture was pre-eminent, with the Pan-ionic League formed around 800 BC.

The Persians (700–479 BC)

The Greek colonies along the coast prospered, and we find the beginnings of Greek science and philosophy in Ionia from 600–500 BC. The Persians, attracted by the new wealth along the coast, brought most of the area under their dominion. Cyrus the Great, Darius and Xerxes figure in this period. It ended with the Persian defeats by the Greeks at Marathon, Salamis, Plataea and Mycale between 490–479 BC.

Classical and Hellenistic periods (479–130 BC)

After the Persian defeats the Greek coastal cities flourished. The Persians arrived again in 401 BC under Xenophon, only to be defeated by Alexander the Great's lightning campaign through Asia Minor.

He crossed the Hellespont in 334 BC, and by 330 Asia Minor was his. After his death in 323 numerous successors and would-be successors wrangled over the territory. Pergamon became prominent between 260–240 BC, and in 113 BC the Pergamene kingdom was handed over to Rome.

Rome (130 BC–AD 330)

Under Rome, Asia Minor was unified, although it took until 60 BC and the defeat of the Pontic King Mithridates. Many of the ruins along the coast date from the Roman occupation, which on the whole was a period of considerable prosperity. Many fine buildings and works of art have survived. The period also ushered in Christianity, and in AD 330 Constantinople was declared the capital of the Eastern Holy Empire.

Byzantium (AD 330–AD 1453)

For nearly eight centuries Turkey was a predominantly Christian country ruled from Constantinople. Around the coast there are numerous castles and ruined churches built during the Byzantine era. Three phases of the period can be distinguished.

The late Roman period lasted from AD 330 to the 7th century, when the Slavs and Avars besieged Constantinople and the Arabs invaded in the east, with the empire caught in the middle of the unintended pincer movement. But the Iconoclast Emperors, beginning with Leo III, managed to hold off the Arabs, and after centuries of fighting the Byzantine Empire was re-established in the 10th century. In the 11th century the Selçuk Turks arrived and gradually nibbled away at Byzantium. The Crusaders from the west slowed the process to some extent, but in the end it was inevitable that the old empire would be replaced by the new.

The Selçuks were ousted by the Ottomans and the Karamans, both Turcoman tribes from different regions, and Ottoman power grew rapidly. Under Mehmet II, Constantinople was conquered in 1453 and its name changed to Istanbul.

Ottoman period (AD 1453–1923)

After the conquest of Constantinople, Ottoman power spread quickly so that by the 16th century the empire included all of Turkey, Syria, Palestine, Egypt, Algeria and southern Europe. In 1571 the

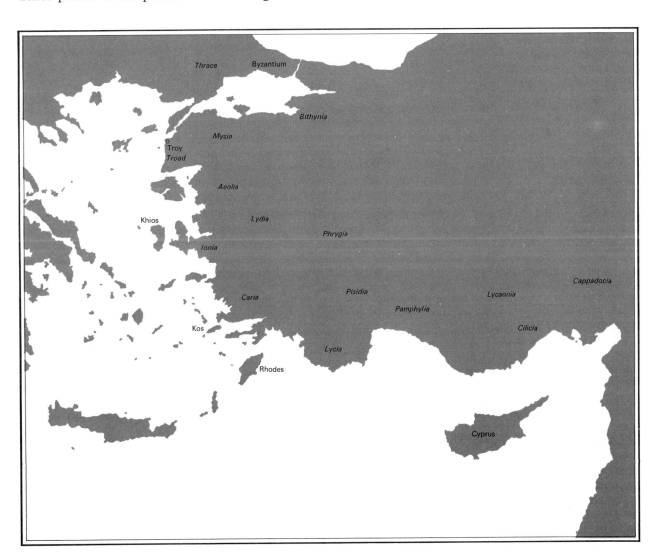

The ancient regions of Asia Minor

defeat of the Turkish fleet at Lepanto stopped further Ottoman expansion. By the 19th century Ottoman territory was much diminished, and in 1832 after the Greek War of Independence the islands in the Aegean were lost. In 1912–13 Turkey lost Macedonia and part of Thrace in the Balkan Wars. Turkey entered the First World War as a German ally and at the end of the war the country was fragmented between the victorious powers. In 1922 Ataturk started to turn the tide with the defeat of the Greeks at Smyrna (Izmir), and in 1923 Turkey was declared an independent state under the Treaty of Lausanne.

Modern period (AD 1923 to the present)

Ataturk was elected the first President of the Turkish Republic and until his death in 1938 he forcibly propelled Turkey into the 20th century. He made Turkey a secular state, abolished the fez, made sweeping changes to the education system, improved internal communications and, probably most of all, gave the nation a feeling of security and pride in its country.

He is revered to this day, and his portrait is an obligatory part of the furniture in every house, shop and office. Turkey was a neutral power for most of the Second World War, only entering the war in 1945, on the side of the Allies. In 1980 the army intervened after a period of unrest, but in 1984 elections, albeit tightly controlled ones, were held. In the recent elections in 1996 the RIFA party, dedicated to returning Turkey to Islamic practices, won an overwhelming majority. It remains to be seen how it copes with double and triple digit inflation and whether it can right the country's economic problems while holding onto the Islamic values it espoused in the elections.

A note on the chapter titles

The chapter titles for the Aegean and Mediterranean coasts are taken from the early inhabitants of the various regions who were prominent and often left numerous memorials behind. Thus there are the Aeolian coast, the Ionian coast, the Carian coast, the Lycian coast and the Pamphylian and Cilician coast. I do not pretend that the area covered in each chapter exactly corresponds with the ancient boundaries, which in any case changed constantly, but by and large each section roughly covers the area described in the title of the chapter. I much prefer these titles to the modern ones coined by the Tourist Office, which, in the modern idiom, are the Blue Coast, the Turquoise Coast, the Emerald Coast, the Turkish Riviera, etc.

Archaeological sites

Along the coast of Turkey there are literally acres of ancient ruins, dating from the proto-Greek period to the Byzantine period. Most sites have an accumulation of buildings, so that Byzantine structures are built atop earlier Roman structures that are in turn built over Greek structures and so on. However, there are also sufficiently intact buildings from the different periods, so that you do not always have to sort through this archaeological palimpsest to see what a Greek or Roman structure looked like.

Some of the sites have been extensively excavated and partially reconstructed (Pergamon and Ephesus come to mind) but most of the sites are only open excavated and many are totally overgrown. Some of the sites along or close to the coast occupy spectacular positions, and in my opinion the ancient ruins of Asia Minor are the most picturesque in the Mediterranean. At many of the sites or in the provincial capitals there are excellent museums that imaginatively display finds from the surrounding area.

I will reiterate my plea here that you should not remove artefacts from these sites. Although you may consider that taking a couple of mosaic tiles, a pottery sherd or two, an amphora or an old coin will make little difference when there is so much just lying about, it must be remembered that every little bit taken is a step down the road to the destruction of the site. Furthermore, when the archaeologists come along the often innocent vandalism caused by visitors presents problems that might have been avoided. It is also illegal, with the confiscation of your yacht the possible penalty for collecting souvenirs.

Architecture

To a large extent the Turks have built for God and for public glory. Private houses, until the introduction of the ubiquitous reinforced concrete, were largely of wooden construction, and the Turkish word for a mansion, *kanak*, means literally a resting place on a journey. Many of these houses have been destroyed, and they are not common today, although you can see them in the old quarters of villages or towns.

The most obvious architectural monuments are of course the mosques (*cami*) and the pencil-thin minarets from which the call to prayer is made. Few Selçuk mosques remain (with the notable exception of the Fluted Minaret in Antalya); most of the mosques seen today date from the Ottoman period or after. Outside a mosque there is a fountain for the ritual ablutions which must precede prayer. Although most Turks do not pray five times a day as prescribed in the Koran, many do so on Fridays, traditionally the market day when everyone is in town. Mosques may be visited by non-believers when prayers are not in progress, but you must remove your footwear and women should cover their hair. Both men and women should be modestly attired.

Apart from mosques there is the public architecture of Koranic colleges (*medrese*), inns and caravanserai (*han, Kervansaray*), palaces (*saray*), and Turkish baths (*hamam*).

Most inns and caravanserai have disappeared from the countryside, but in the towns they can still be found, although they are rarely used for the original purpose for which they were built. They are often in the market or bazaar area. Palace architecture is best represented in Istanbul, by Topkapi Palace. This is a marvellous example of the Turkish-style palace, where a number of small buildings inside a fortified wall replace the European monumental style of palace.

Turkish baths will be found in even quite small villages, as ablution was mandatory after sexual intercourse. For men, the baths were also private meeting places away from the home. Most of them consist of two rooms, a changing room and a steam room, the domed roof of the latter often studded with thick glass windows. Men and women use the same *hamam*, but at different times. Foreigners can use a *hamam* and the adventurous can try a massage. Towels are normally provided and a small charge is made.

Carpets and *kilims*

There are no bargains to be had buying a carpet in Turkey and a good carpet or *kilim* is expensive. *Hali* are the tufted carpets and *kilims* are the cheaper woven rugs. Most carpets and *kilims* are still hand-made, although industrial dyes have largely replaced the vegetable dyes formerly used. A good-quality older carpet will usually cost more than a newer carpet, and various towns and villages are renowned for the quality of the carpets produced there.

There are carpet shops throughout Turkey, but unless you know something about carpets and *kilims* I suggest you take your time over buying one. Prices vary tremendously, as much as six times over and above what the price should be in my experience. Moreover, carpet touts are quite sophisticated (they are called *avci*, the hunter) and it may be several hours before you cotton on to the fact that the nice young man showing you the sights does not just happen to have a 'cousin' with a carpet shop nearby. Nonetheless you may, like me, become enamoured of Turkish carpets and *kilims* and discover that looking in carpet shops is an addictive habit.

Technical information

Weather forecasts

A weather forecast in English is broadcast on TRT National Radio on or around 96 MHz FM after the 0900 (local time) news.

On VHF Ch 67 (advice on Ch 16) there is a weather forecast in English at 1500 local time.

You can use the relevant part of the Greek national programme forecasts for the Aegean; these are as follows:

Athens 738kHz (412m)
Thessaloniki 1043kHz (288m)
Corfu 1007kHz (298m)
Rhodes 1493kHz (201m)
Khania 1511kHz (198m)
Patras 1485kHz (202m)
Volos 1484kHz (202m)

Broadcasts at 0630/0700 in Greek and English and at 1310/1325, 1330, 2145/2200 in Greek only. All local times.

There is also a forecast in English on a Greek station which can be picked up in many places on or around 89 MHz FM at 0630 and 0750 local time.

On the national television channel a weather forecast in Turkish (but with a synoptic chart with wind direction and forces shown) is given after the news at 2130–2200 local time.

In most of the marinas (Ataköy, Kuşadasi, Bodrum, Marmaris, Kemer, Setur Antalya and Antalya) a weather forecast in English is posted daily or is available on request.

Weatherfax (WX) broadcasts

Madrid (Facsimile)

3650	10
6918·5	10
10250	10

Map areas

CE	1:24 000 000 (c)	EP	1:15 000 000 (c)
51°N 78°W	51°N 59°E	45°N 15°W	45°N 9°E
32°N 9°W	9°N 12°E	33°N 32°W	34°N 7°E
AP-1	1:10 000 000 (b)	AP-2	1:15 000 000 (b)
59°N 41°W	63°N 21°E	50°N 45°W	58°N 16°E
27°N 18°W	27°N 9°E	28°N 27°W	27°N 10°E
AP-3	1:24 000 000 (c)	504	1:10 000 000 (b)
35°N 42°W	54°N 31°E	48°N 54°W	65°N 16°E
25°N 26°W	28°N 20°E	15°N 23°W	18°N 26°E
M	1:15 000 000 (c)		
52°N 46°W	56°N 60°E		
25°N 17°W	27°N 33°E		

Schedule

AP-1 Surface Anal.	0350(00) 1545(12) 120/576		
AP-2 300 hPa Anal.	0402(00) 1558(12) 120/576		
AP-2 500 hPa Anal.	0415(00) 1750(12) 120/576		
EP 12h 300, 500, 700	0430(00) 0900(00)		
and 850 hPa Prog.	1650(12) 2230(12) 120/576		
EP Significant Wx	0440(00) 0910(00)		
	1700(00) 2240(12) 120/576		
AP-2 700 hPa Surface Anal.	0600(00) 120/576		

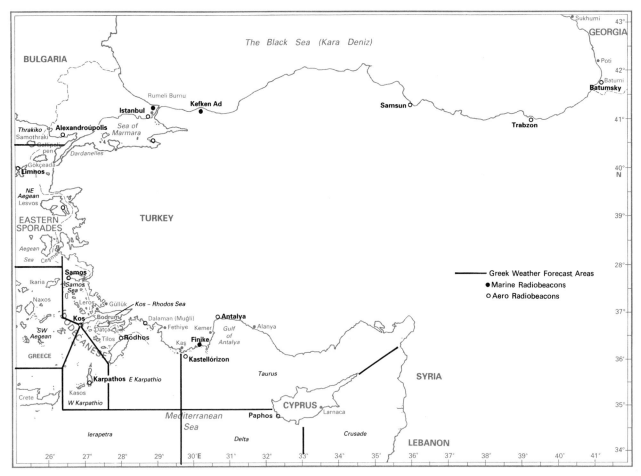

Radiobeacons and Greek weather areas

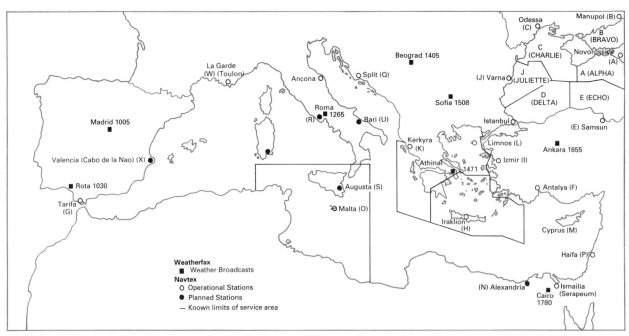

Navtex and weatherfax services

AP-2	850 hPa Surface Anal.	0615(00)	120/576
AP-3	Surface Prog.	0630(00)	120/576
504	Wave Anal.	1105(06)	120/576
AP-1	12h Surface Prog.	1120(12)	120/576
504	Wave Prog.	1215(06)	120/576
504	Sea surface temp.	1714(12)	120/576
504	Wave Anal.	1730(12)	120/576
AP-2	12h 700hPa Anal.	1810(12)	120/576
AP-2	12h 850 hPa Anal.	1830(12)	120/576
504	24h Wave Prog.	1215(06)	120/576
504	Sea surface temperature	1710(12)	120/576
M	300 hPa Prog.	1904(12)	120/576
M	500 hPa Prog.	1938(12)	120/576

Rota (AOK) (US Navy)

7595kHz	4·0	1800–0600
9050kHz	4·0	H24
10542kHz	4·0	0600–1800

Map areas

1 (a)
65°N 25°W.65°N 55°E
25°N 25°W.25°N 55°E

2.(a)
55°N 7°W.55°N 37°E
30°N 7°W.30°N 37°E

3 (a)
65°N 80°W.65°N 20°E
10°N 80°W.10°N 20°E

Schedule

2	FSME 1 LERT		
	Prog. blend	0015 0400	
		1215 1600	120/576
2	OSME 1 LERT Significant		
	wave height	0030 0415	
		1230 1615	120/576
1	Surface P/W/K Anal.	0048 1248	120/576
1	1000 hPa H/T/W Anal.	0100 1300	120/576
1	850 hPa H/T/W Anal.	0112 1312	120/576
1	500 hPA H/T/W Anal.	0124 1324	120/576
1	300 hPa H/T/W Anal.	0136 1336	
1	24h Surface P/W/K Prog.	0148 1348	120/576
1	24h 1000 hPa H/T/W Prog.	0200 1400	120/576
1	24h 850 hPa H/T/W Prog.	0212 1412	120/576
1	24h 500 hPa H/T/W Prog.	0224 1424	120/576
1	24h 300 hPa H/T/W Prog.	0236 1436	120/576
3	36h Surface P/W Prog.	0248 1448	120/576
3	60h Surface P/W Prog.	0300 1500	120/576
3	96h Surface P/W Prog.	0312 1512	120/576
3	72h 500 hPa H/W Prog.	0324 1524	120/576
3	96h 500 hPa H/W Prog.	0336 1536	120/576
2	Sea surface temp. Anal.		
	(Mediterranean)	0348 1548	120/576
	Schedule	0430 1630	120/576
	(including weather warnings for the N Atlantic)		
	Schedule	0442 1642	120/576
	(including weather warnings for the Mediterranean)		
1	72h ECMWF Surface P		
	Prog.	0500 1700	120/576
1	72h ECMWF 500 hPa		
	H Prog.	0512 1712	120/576
1	96h ECMWF Surface P		
	Prog.	0524 1724	120/576
1	96h ECMWF 500 hPa		
	H Prog.	0536 1736	
1	Surface P/W/K Anal.	0548 1748	120/576
1	1000 hPa H/T/W Anal.	0600 1800	120/576
1	850 hPa H/T/W Anal.	0612 1812	120/576
1	500 hPa H/T/W Anal.	0624 1824	120/576
1	300 hPa H/T/W Anal.	0636 1836	120/576
1	24h Surface P/W/K Prog.	0648 1848	120/576
1	24h 1000 hPA H/T/W Anal.	0700 1900	120/576
1	24h 850 hPa H/T/W Anal.	0712 1912	120/576

1	24h 500 hPa H/T/W Anal.	0724 1924	120/576
1	24h 300 hPa H/T/W Anal.	0736 1936	120/576
1	500 hPa H/V Anal.	0748 1948	120/576
1	24h 500 hPa H/V Anal.	0800 2000	120/576
1	36h Surface P/W/K Prog.	0824 2024	120/576
1	36h 1000 hPa H/T/W Prog.	0836 2036	120/576
1	36h 850 hPa H/T/W Prog.	0848 2048	120/576
1	36h 500 hPa H/T/W Prog.	0900 2100	120/576
1	36h 300 hPa H/T/W Prog.	0912 2112	120/576
1	48h Surface P/W/K Prog.	0924 2124	120/576
1	48h 1000 hPa H/T/W Prog.	0936 2136	120/576
1	48h 850 hPa H/T/W Prog.	0948 2148	120/576
1	48h 500 hPa H/T/W Prog.	1000 2200	120/576
1	48h 300 hPa H/T/W Prog.	1012 2212	120/576
2	NORAPS Surface P/W Anal.	1024 2224	120/576
2	NORAPS 500 hPa H/T/W Anal.	1036 2236	120/576
2	24h NORAPS Surface P/W Prog.	1048 2248	120/576
2	24h NORAPS 500 hPa H/T/W Prog.	1100 2300	120/576
2	36h NORAPS Surface P/W Prog.	1112 2312	120/576

Roma (IMB) (Facsimile)

(IMB 51)	4777·5kHz	5·0
(IMB 55)	8146·6kHz	5·0
(IMB 56)	13597·5kHz	5·0

Map Areas

B 1:20 000 000(c)
52°N 31°W 45°N 61°E
24°N 10°W 21°N 37°E

B1 1:15 000 000(c)
52°N 31°W 45°N 61°E
24°N 10°W 21°N 37°E

D 1:15 000 000
49°N 25°W 49°N 45°E
28°N 10°W 28°N 30°E

S 1:10 000 000
45°N 6°W 41°N 39°E
29°N 1°W 26°N 31°E

Schedule

D	3h Pressure changes	0400(00) 1030(06)	120/576
	chart	1700(12) 2322(18)	
B¹	Surface Anal.	0415(00)[1] 0457(00)[2]	120/576
		1045(06) 1645(12)	
B	Freezing level chart	0425(00) 1810(12)	120/576
	Test chart	0813	120/576
B	24h surface Prog.	1030(06) 2322(18)	120/576
S	Med. Sea state Prog.	1153(06) 2230(18)	120/576
B	Surface Anal.	2312(18)	120/576

[1]. Summer only
[2]. Winter only

Beograd (Belgrade) (YZZ) (Facsimile)

(YZZ1)	5800	10

Map Areas

A 1:2 500 000 (b)
47°30'N 12°30'E
47°30'N 24°30'E
48°00'N 5°00E
48°N 25°00'E

B 1:2 500 000 (b)
40°30'N 13°00'E
40°30'N 24°30'E
37°30'·N 7°30'E
38°N 23°30'E

D 1:7 500 000 (b)
64°N 28°W
56°N 56°E
53°30'N 22°W
54°00'N 40°E

D 1:15 000 000 (c)
33°N 15°W
28°N 34°E
40°00'N 8°W
30°30'N 27°E

Schedule

A Plotted surface data
0045(00) 0345(03)
0645(06) 0945(09)
1245(12) 1545(15)
1845(18) 2145(21) 120/576

B Surface Anal. with plotted data
0140(00) 0440(03)
0740(06) 1040(09)

		1340(12) 1640(15)	
		1940(18) 2240(21)	120/576
C	Surface Anal. with plotted data	0245(00) 0840(06)	
		1445(12) 2045(18)	120/576
D	24h surface Prog.	0600(00) 1805(12)	120/576
D	36h surface Prog.	0720(00) 1915(12)	120/576

Athinái (SVJ4) (Facsimile)

(SVJ4)	8530kHz	5·0	0845–0945

Map Areas

A	1:15 000 000	B	1:5 000 000
	50°N 20°W 50°N 40°E		Central–Eastern
	30°N 10°W 30°N 40°E		Mediterranean Sea

Schedule

B	30h wave Prog.	0845(12)	120/576
B	36h wave Prog.	0855(12)	120/576
B	42h wave Prog.	0905(12)	120/576
B	48h wave Prog.	0915(12)	120/576
A	Surface Anal.	0925(06)	120/576
A	24h Surface Prog.	0935(06)	120/576

Ankara (YMA20) (Facsimile)

	3377	5·0	1610–0500
	6970	5·0	0500–1610

Map Area

A	1:10 000 000(b)	
	54°N 13°W	53°N 76°E
	18°N 7°E	17°N 55°E

Schedule

A	24h and 36h 500hPa Anal.	0330(12)	90/576
A	Surface Anal.	0430(00) 0610(03)	
		0940(06) 1240(09)	
		1610(12) 1840(15)	
		2152(18)	90/576
	Test chart	0500	90/576
A	500hPa Anal.	0640(00) 1910(12)	90/576
A	300hPa Anal.	0710(00) 2015(12)	90/576
A	24h significant Wx	0740(00) 1710(12)	90/576
A	24h 700hPa Anal.	0810(00)	90/576
A	24h 300hPa Anal.	0840(00)	
A	48h and 72h 500hPa Anal.	0910(12)	90/576
A	Significant Wx	1010(00)	90/576
A	Maximum wind Anal.	1040(00)	90/576
A	200hPa Anal.	1940(12)	90/576

Cairo Meteo (SUU) (Facsimile)

4526·5kHz	10·0	1900–0700
10123kHz	10·0	0700–1900

Note Tune facsimile recorders +400Hz for White and −400Hz for Black. Bcsts are intended to be received throughout Africa, Europe and West Asia.

Map Area

A	1:20 000 000 (a)	
	60°N 20°W 60°N 80°E	
	10°S 20°W 10°S 80°E	

Schedule

Note All products use the same map area. The transmission time for each product extends approx. 20 mins from the time given.

Surface Prog.	0000(06) 0600(12)	120/576
	0640(00) 1200(18)	
	1800(00) 1840(12)	
Surface Anal.	0020(18) 1220(06)	120/576
Upper air 300mb Anal.	0040(12) 1300(00)	120/576
Upper air 500mb Prog.	0340(12) 0940(18)	
	1540(00) 2140(06)	120/576

Upper air 300mb Prog.	0400(12) 1000(18)	
	1600(00) 2200(06)	120/576
Upper air 200mb Prog.	0420(12) 1020(18)	
	1620(00) 2220(06)	120/576
Significant Wx Prog.	0440(12) 1040(18)	
	1640(00) 2240(06)	120/576
Tropopause Max wind Prog.	0500(12) 1100(18)	
	1700(00) 2300(06)	120/576
Upper air 700mb Prog.	0520(12 1120(18)	
	1720(00) 2320(06)	120/576
Upper air 250mb Prog.	0540(12) 1140(18)	
	1740(00) 2340(06)	120/576
Upper air 850mb Anal.	0700(00) 1900(12)	120/576
Upper air 700mb Anal.	0720(00) 1920(12)	120/576
Upper air 500mb Anal.	0740(00) 1940(12)	120/576
Upper air 300mb Anal.	0800(00) 2000(12)	120/576
Upper air 250mb Anal.	0820(00) 2020(12)	120/576
Upper air 200mb Anal.	0840(00) 2040(12)	120/576
Tropopause Max wind Anal.	0900(00) 2100(12)	120/576
Upper air 100mb Anal.	0920(00) 2120(12)	120/576
Satellite Imagery – Wind Anal.	1240(00)	120/576

Navtex (N4) transmitters

Navtex

The Mediterranean is covered by Navtex (N4) transmitters as follows. Reliability is generally good.
For full operational details of NAVTEX, together with the times of each scheduled MSI bcst, see the relevant ALRS
Volume 3 station number, shown in column (2). All MSI bcsts are in English unless otherwise stated in column (5).
NI = No information   TBD = To be decided

Country	COAST STATION Name (NAVTEX character) (ALRS volume-station number, if applicable)	Position	Range NM	Status of implementation (Date of Operation) Remarks
(1)	(2)	(3)	(4)	(5)
Spain				
South Coast	Tarifa (G) (3-1040)	36°01'N 5°34'W	400	Operational. English & Spanish
Mediterranean Coast	Valencia (MRCC) (3-1069) Remote-controlled station			On trial
	Cabo de la Nao (X)	38°43'N 0°09'E	NI	English
France				
Mediterranean Coast	La Garde (CROSS) (W) (3-3113)	43°06'N 5°59'E	250	Operational
Italy				
Sardegna	Cagliari (T) (3-1180)	39°13'N 9°14'E	320	Planned (1996). English & Italian
	Roma R (3-1250)	41°37'N 12°29'E	320	Planned (1996). English & Italian
Sicily	Augusta (S) (3-1295)	37°14'N 15°14'E	320	Planned (1996). English & Italian
Sardegna	Bari (U) (3-1315)	40°26'N 17°25'E	320	Planned (1996). English & Italian
Croatia	Split (Q) (3-1390)	43°30'N 16°29'E	85	Operational
Malta	Malta (O) (3-1440)	35°49'N 14°32'E	NI	Operational
Greece	Kerkyra (K) (3-1450)	39°37'N 19°55'E	280	Operational. English & Greek
	Iraklio (H) (3-1460)	35°02'N 25°07'E	280	Operational. English & Greek
	Limnos (L) (3-1492)	39°52'N 25°04'E	280	Operational. English & Greek
Bulgaria	Varna (J) (3-1505)	43°04'N 27°46'E	NI	Operational
Ukraine	Odesa (C) (3-1550)	46°29'N 30°44'E	280	Operational
	Mariupolí (B) (3-1595)	47°06'N 37°33'E	280	Operational
Russia				
Black Sea Coast	Novorossiysk (A) (3-1600)	44°42'N 37°44'E	300	Operational
Turkey				
Black Sea Coast	Samsun (E) (3-1640)	41°17'N 36°20'E	NI	Operational
Sea of Marmara	Istanbul (D) (3-1660)	41°04'N 28°57'E	NI	Operational
Aegean Coast	Izmir (I) (3-1672)	38°21'N 26°35'E	NI	Operational
Mediterranean Coast	Antalya (F) (3-1681)	36°53'N 30°42'E	NI	Operational
Cyprus	Cyprus (Troodos) (M) (3-1700)	35°03'N 33°17'E	220	Operational
Israel				
Mediterranean Coast	Hefa (Haifa) (P) (3-1760)	32°49'N 35°00'E	200	Operational
Egypt				
Mediterranean Coast	Alexandria[1] (N) (3-1775)	31°11'N 29°52'E	200	Planned
	Serapeum (Ismailia)[2] (N) (3-2800)	30°28'N 32°22'E	200	Operational

1. Currently operational through Serapeum. 2. 4MHz service planned (before 1.2.1999)

Coast radio stations

Istanbul (TAH) (41°04'N 28°57'E)
RT (MF) Transmits on 2182, 2670kHz (24hrs). Receives on 2182kHz. Traffic lists on 2670kHz every H+05 and H+35.
VHF Transmits and receives on Ch 16 (24hrs), 01, 26, 87,

Canakkale (TAT) (40°08'N 26°24'E)
RT (MF) Transmits on 2182, 1850kHz (24hrs). Receives on 2182kHz
VHF Transmits and receives on Ch 16 (24hrs), 01, 25, 85
VHF Transmits and receives on Ch 16 (24hrs), 25, 27

Izmir (TAN) (38°22'N 26°36'E)
RT (MF) Transmits on 2182, 1850, 2760 (24hrs). Receives on 2182kHz
VHF Transmits and receives on Ch 16 (24hrs), 04, 24

Kuşadasi (TAE3) (37°52'N 27°16'E)
VHF Transmits and receives on Ch 16 (24hrs), 03, 26

Oren (TAE9) (37°02'N 27°57'E)
VHF Transmits and receives on Ch 16 (24hrs), 26, 87

Bodrum (TAE5) (37°02'N 27°26'E)
VHF Transmits and receives on Ch 16 (24hrs), 04, 05, 25, 85, 87

Datça (TAE7) (36°45'N 27°39'E)
VHF Transmits and receives on Ch 16 (24hrs), 05, 24, 84

Marmaris (TAE4) (36°51'N 28°16'E)
VHF Transmits and receives on Ch 16 (24hrs), 04, 24, 85

Fethiye (TAE6) (36°37'N 29°07'E)
VHF Transmits and receives on Ch 16 (24hrs), 25, 28

Kaş (TAC2) (36°12'N 29°38'E)
VHF Transmits and receives on Ch 16 (24hrs), 02, 25, 28, 84

Finike (TAC3) (36°18'N 30°09'E)
VHF Transmits and receives on Ch 16 (24hrs), 23, 27 (24hrs)

Antalya (TAL) (36°53'N 30°42'E)
RT (MF) Transmits on 2182, 2693kHz. Receives on 2182kHz
VHF Transmits and receives on Ch 16 (24hrs), 25, 27

Alanya (TAC4) (36°33'N 32°00'E)
VHF Transmits and receives on Ch 16 (24hrs), 25, 27, 84

Anamur (TAC6) (36°05'N 32°50'E)
VHF Transmits and receives on Ch 16 (24hrs), 23, 26, Continuous.

Taşucu (TAC5) (36°19'N 33°53'E)
VHF Transmits and receives on Ch 16, 02, 03 (0800–2400),

Mersin (TAM) (36°49'N 34°36'E)
RT (MF) Transmits on 2182, 2820kHz (24hrs). Receives on 2182kHz
VHF Transmits and receives on Ch 16 (24hrs), 24, 28

Iskenderun (TAI) (36°37'N 36°07'E)
RT (MF) Transmits on 2182, 2629, 3648 kHz (24hrs). Receives on 2182kHz
VHF Transmits and receives on Ch 16 (24hrs), 26, 27

Cyprus (5BA) (35°10'N 33°26'E)
RT (MF) Transmits on 2182, 2670, 2700, 3690kHz (24hrs). Receives on 2182kHz. Traffic lists on 2700kHz every H+33.
VHF Transmits and receives on Ch 16 (24hrs), 26, 24, 25, 27

Radiobeacons

Marine radiobeacons

Rumeli Burnu (41°14'·3N 29°06'·65E) *RB* 301·1kHz 150M Seq 1, 2. Grouped with Kefken Adasi *KF* 150M Seq 3, 4.
Finike (36°16'·83N 30°09'·5E) *FR* 297kHz 150M In fog: Continuous. In clear weather: At H+00, 30.

Aero radiobeacons

Trabzon (41°00'·01N 39°46'·43E) *TRN* 371kHz 75M.
Samsun (41°16'·47N 36°17'·92E) *SMN* 350kHz 50M.
Istanbul (41°00'·72N 28°54'·45E) *TOP* 370kHz 50M.
Alexandroúpolis (40°51'·45N 25°56'·65E) *ALP* 351kHz 100M.
Lesvos (39°03'·1N 26°36'·4E) *LVO* 397kHz 25M.
Sámos (37°41'·18N 26°55'·02E) *SMO* 375kHz 80M.
Kos (36°47'·70N 27°05'·5E) *KOS* 311kHz 25M.
Ródhos, Paradisi (36°25'·17N 28°07'·12E) *ROS* 339kHz 150M.
Finike (36°16'·75N 30°09'·1E) *FR* 297kHz 150M. Fog: Cont Clear: H+00, 30
Dalaman (Muğla) (36°41'·43N 28°46'·95E) *DAL* 346 kHz.
Antalya (36°52'·53N 30°47'·43E) *YT* 302kHz 50M.
Paphos (34°43'·10N 32°28'·77E) *PHA* 328kHz 100M.
Larnaca (34°49'·27N 33°33'·28E) *LCA* 432kHz 150M.

The radiobeacons on the nearby Greek islands are also useful.

Climate and weather

At the beginning of each chapter there is a description of the weather patterns for that area. Here I will confine myself to general remarks for Turkish waters.

Wind strength

Wind strength is described as a force on the Beaufort scale. To get the approximate wind speed in knots from its force, multiply the force by 5 and then subtract 5 (up to Force 8).

Winds

In the summer months the winds in the Sea of Marmara and the Aegean are predominantly from the north, curving around the coast to blow from the west. In the Aegean the constancy of the northerly winds in the summer has been noted from ancient times, when they were called the etesians, from *etos* (annual); today the wind is commonly called the *meltemi* or *meltem*, although some areas have a local name, as at Izmir, where it is called the *imbat*. This wind begins blowing in May and June, reaches full strength in July and August, and dies off in September and October. In the Sea of Marmara the *meltemi* blows from NE down through the Dardanelles, where it curves to follow the coast and blows from the N, except where a gulf interrupts the coastline, when the wind usually curves in from the W. It blows from the NW between Kos and Bodrum, and from the W in Rhodes Channel. It

BEAUFORT SCALE OF WIND STRENGTH

Sea State	Beaufort No.	Description	Velocity in knots	Velocity in km/h	Term	Code	Wave height in metres
Like a mirror	0	Calm glassy	<1	<1	Calm	0	0
Ripples	1	Light airs Rippled	1–3	1–5	Calm	1	0–01
Small wavelets	2	Light breeze wavelets	4–6	6–11	Smooth	2	0·1–0·5
Large wavelets	3	Gentle breeze	7–10	12–19	Slight	3	0·5–1·25
Small waves, breaking	4	Moderate breeze	11–16	20–28	Moderate	4	1·25–2·5
Moderate waves, foam	5	Fresh breeze	17–21	29–38	Rough	5	2·5–4
Large waves, foam and spray	6	Strong breeze	22–27	39–49			
Sea heads up, foam in streaks	7	Near gale	28–33	50–61	Very rough	6	4–6
Higher long waves, foam in streaks	8	Gale	34–40	62–74			
High waves, dense foam, spray impairs visibility	9	Strong gale	41–47	75–88	High	7	6–9
Very high tumbling waves, surface white with foam, visibility affected	10	Storm	48–55	89–102	Very high	8	9–14
Exceptionally high waves, sea covered in foam, visibility affected	11	Violent storm	56–62	103–117	Phenomenal	9	Over 14
Air filled with spray and foam, visibility severely impaired	12	Hurricane	>63	>118			

also blows from a westerly direction along the Mediterranean coast as far as Finike Körfezi. In effect, the *meltemi* describes an arc from the NE in the Sea of Marmara through north to the west along Turkey's Mediterranean coast. It does not blow along Turkey's southern coast eastward of Finike Körfezi. In strength it varies from Force 3/4 to Force 6/7 in July and August.

The *meltemi* is a consequence of a pressure gradient between a low pressure area over Pakistan (the Asian monsoon low), which extends its influence as far as the eastern Mediterranean, and the high pressure over the Azores, which affects the western Mediterranean. The pressure gradient between these two stable areas produces the constant northerlies in the summer.

Along Turkey's southern coast between the Gulf of Antalya and the Syrian border, winds are predominantly land and sea breezes, with the latter coming in from between south and southwest. In the morning there will often be a land breeze blowing from the north.

In the winter the pressure gradients over the eastern Mediterranean are not pronounced at all and winds are not from any constant direction. An almost equal proportion of northerly and southerly winds can be expected.

Depressions

Gales in the winter result from small depressions moving in an easterly direction, either south-eastward towards Cyprus or north-eastward to the Black Sea. Although these depressions are usually of small dimensions, they can give rise to violent winds. The depressions can develop rapidly and are often difficult to track, as they move fast and then stop before moving off again. Depressions often linger in the southern Aegean.

Coptic calendar

Below is reproduced an extract from the Coptic almanac which shows when strong winds can be expected. The Copts are a Christian sect living in Egypt and Ethiopia, the Christian descendants of the ancient Egyptians who became Monophysites and split from the general church at the Council of Chalcedon in AD 451. About 12 per cent of Egypt's population are Copts. I reproduce the extract from the almanac for the reader to use with discretion, but I have found the accuracy to be about 60 per cent. Why or how such a chart works I haven't a clue, but any aid to forecasting gales, however odd it may appear, is a welcome bonus to the other more commonly accepted methods.

The meltem

The list of gales shows the date on which the gale can be expected, the Arabic name (phonetically rendered as nearly as possible), the direction, the translation of the Arabic name and the duration of the gale. Deviation is rarely more than 48 hours either way.

ADDITIONAL NOTES ON THE COPTIC CALENDAR

This Coptic calendar of the gales has been expanded and commented on by Cmdr John S Guard RN, who combines it with an annual Turkish storm table (below) and adds valuable comments on the whole

Date	Name	Direction	Type	Duration
27 Sept	El Saleeb	W	Cross	3 days
21 Oct	El Saleebish	W	Crusade	3 days
26 Nov[1]	El Micness	W	Broom	3 days
06 Dec[1]	Kassim	SW	Gale	7 days
20 Dec	El Fadrel Saggra	SW	Small gale	
11 Jan[1]	El Fadrel Saggra	S	Strong gale	3 days
19 Jan	El Fedra El Kibirain	W	Feeder	5 days
27 Jan	El Fedra El Kibirain	W	Feeder	2 days
18 Feb[1]	El Shams El Saggira	NW	Feeder	5 days
10 Mar	El Hossom	SW	Brings the equinox	8 days
20 Mar[1]	El Shams El Kabira	E	Big sun gale	2 days
25 Mar	Hawa	E	A wind	
29 Apr	Khaseen	E	Sand wind	2 days
16 Jul	El Nogia	E	Black wind	2 days

1. Indicates a severe gale!!

The Coptic calendar

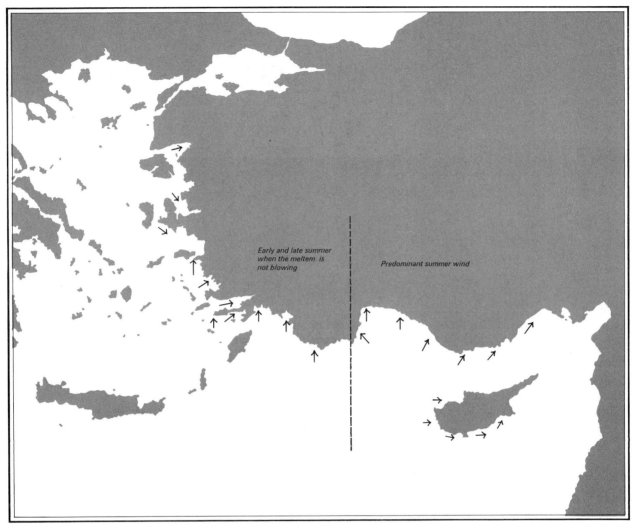

The afternoon summer breeze

ensemble. I am indebted to Cmdr J Guard and *Latitude 37* magazine for permission to reproduce this storm table and the valuable commentary on it. If I have any comment to make it is that the Turkish storm table predicts a higher percentage of gales than are actually encountered, and therefore must get some of them right on a hit or miss basis.

Annual storm table

A Turkish annual storm table appears in various publications. This lists many 'storms', seldom gives their direction (though this can be inferred) and does not specify the sea area to which they apply, but it is safe to assume that this is mainly the Aegean. That strong winds occur off the Turkish Aegean coast on approximately the same dates each year is a well established and widely believed tradition shared by the Greeks.

The predictions for each month in the Turkish table and the Coptic almanac are compared below, and the winds which tradition holds we should expect during these months are deduced. Sources differ, and readers who possess a published Turkish table may find that it differs from the list below.

What is a *firtina*?

The Turkish word *firtina* means 'storm, gale' (it derives from the Italian *foruna di mare* – 'storm at sea') but in this context it should not be interpreted literally in relation to the Beaufort Scale. This tradition was evolved by, and for, seafarers in small craft propelled by oars and sail. For them a wind of, say, Beaufort Force 6 or more was, quite reasonably, a 'storm'. To avoid confusion with Beaufort, *firtina* is used throughout.

Origins of the tradition

The similarities between the Coptic almanac and the Turkish table leave us in no doubt that they came from a common source. There are strong indications that this source was of Egyptian, and probably ancient, origin and was based on scholarly research. In other words, it was lore, or accumulated wisdom. As it filtered down to the simpler folk it became folklore and, like most folklore, became less precise. With time more *firtina* were added (without scientific justification), names changed and became confused, variable dates became fixed, and so on.

How reliable are the predictions?

Tradition has it that a predicted *firtina* may occur one or two days before or after the given date. For obvious reasons, *firtina* with names are more likely to occur than anonymous ones. Comparison of the predictions with the climatic tables in the British Admiralty pilot shows no correlation at all, but this proves nothing. Winds in the Aegean are notoriously local in effect, and the pilot's two observation stations (Izmir and Rhodes) are not typical of the Aegean as a whole.

In assessing the reliability of the predictions one must take into account days when there is a *firtina* somewhere in the area, if not where one happens to be, and days when the synoptic situation is such that even a slight change of pressure distribution or gradient could have caused a *firtina*.

Predictions

March

Turkish table
1   Firtinasi
11   Kocakari Soğuğu (old women's cold spell). The old name for this was berdelecuz, with a gale (Ahiri berdelecuz) at the end of it on 17 March.
12   Husum (enemy) Firtinasi
15   Firtina (Ahiri berdelecuz)
21   Firtina (unnamed, but at the equinox)
24   Koz Kavuran (which blights the walnuts) Firtinasi
26   Caylak (kite-the bird) Firtinasi

Coptic almanac
10   eight days. Southwest. 'El Hossom'
20   two days. Strong easterly. 'El Shams El Kabira' (big sun gale)

Comment The Coptic and the Turkish predictions accord well. Strong southwesterlies in the Nile Delta forecast area mean strong northerlies in the Aegean; easterlies in the Delta imply southerlies in the Aegean.

The Turkish *Husum* and the Coptic *El Hossom* are obviously related, if not the same word, and an indication of a common source.

Throughout the year a number of *firtina* are named after birds and refer to their migration, to the north in spring and to the south in autumn. From this one can infer the direction of the *firtina*.

Inference In the second and third weeks of March there will be a cold spell with strong northerlies lasting about a week. This will be followed by strong southerlies around the equinox.

April

Turkish table
8   Kirlangiç (swallow) Firtinasi
11   Firtina
16   Kuğu (mute swan) Firtinasi
29   Firtina, three days (Ahiri sittei sevir)

Coptic almanac
29   two days. Easterly, 'Khoseen' (sand wind)

Comment Sittei sevir is the six-day period between 20 April and 20 May when the sun is in Taurus (astrology), which by tradition ends with a severe gale (*Ahiri sittei sevir*). Obviously this varies from year to year, but some sources fix it on 20 or 26 April – an example of where a variable, but predictable, date is becoming fixed, and part of the whole tradition lost.

The Coptic prediction suggests southerlies in the Aegean, and a 'sand wind' that may be a sirocco.

Inference In April winds will be predominantly southerly, strong at times but not for long periods, probably caused by vigorous depressions passing far to the north over Europe. Northerlies, if any, will not be strong or prolonged. At the end of the month there may be a period of *sirocco*.

May

Turkish table
4   Ciçek (flower) Firtinasi
7   Firtina
13   Firtina (Ahiri eyyami matar)
17   Filiz Kiran (that destroys young buds) Firtinasi
20   Kakulya (Cardamom) Firtinasi
21   Firtina

Some Turkish sources also predict a *Mevsimsiz Soğuklar* (unseasonable cold spell) 10–13 May.

Coptic almanac No predictions.

Comment Ahiri eyyami matar – 'the end of the blessed season of rain'. The meaning of *Filiz Kiran* suggests a cold northerly. *Kakulya* suggests a wind off the land, therefore easterly.

Inference There will be a series of short, sharp *firtina*, southerly going northerly, caused by local depressions. In the middle of the month there may be a spell of cold north/northeast winds (*Poyraz*).

At this time of year, looking forward to summer, we tend to expect fine, settled weather, but, as the table shows, May weather is usually unsettled.

June

Turkish table
22   Gün Dönümü (solstice) Firtinasi
28   Kizil Erik (red plum) Firtinasi
29   Yaprak (leaf, probably vine) Firtinasi

Coptic almanac No predictions.

July

Turkish table
11   Cark Dönümü Firtinasi (old name: Ahiri siyahi bevarih)
16   Firtina (two days)
25   Firtina (three days)
30   Kara Erik (black plum) Firtinasi

Coptic almanac
16   Easterly 'El Noggia' (black wind) (two days)

Comment There are some puzzles about the July *firtina*, which invite comment.

Ahiri siyahi bevarih means 'the end of the period of the black summer wind', and by tradition that wind is southerly. All Turkish sources place it on about 9 July. The Coptic 'black wind' must be the same, but the date is different!

Cark Dönāmā means something like 'the turning of the firmament wheel of destiny' – perhaps simply the change of season, because one thing is certain – this is the start of the *meltemi* summer season.

Turkish sources are also contradictory about the two 'plum' *firtina* in June and July.

Inference The winds will settle to the summer *meltemi* regime about the middle of the month. Before this there is likely to be a period of sirocco, which must be the 'black wind'.

August

Turkish table
14   Firtina
17   Firtina
20   Firtina (two days)
31   Mercan Firtinasi ('mercan' is a fish, Red Sea bream)

Coptic almanac No predictions.

Comment With the possible exception of the *Balik Firtinasi* in October, *Mercan Firtinasi* is the only one named after a fish, which may be significant.

Inference Not a lot! Apparently, by tradition, the *meltemi* will be unusually strong on or about the dates shown, but in my experience nobody really knows how strong the *meltemi* will be even a few hours in advance. It does seem to have some connection with the relative humidity on the preceding night, but I have never been able to establish a simple rule about this.

September (to 20th)

7   Bildircin (quail) Firtinasi
13   Caylak (kite – the bird) Firtinasi

Comment Firtinasi named after birds refer to their migrations. In autumn they move south on northerly winds. In the Aegean the *meltemi* fades fairly quickly early in September and thereafter the weather usually sets fair with little wind.

Inference In September the winds, if any, will be northerly, and may be strong on the dates shown.

September (from 21st)

Turkish table
25   Firtina
28   Kestane Karasi Firtinasi (see below)
30   Turna (crane) Firtinasi

Coptic almanac
27   three days westerly El Salieb (cross).

There is no obvious connection with the Turkish table.

Comment Gales named after birds refer to their migration. In autumn they move south on northerly winds. *Kestane* means chestnut; *kara* means ground, land, or black, dark or gloomy. The meaning of

Kestane Karasi is not clear, but it is a strong northerly blowing over the Black Sea – the only traditional *firtina* that I know definitely to be connected with that area.

In the Aegean the *meltemi* fades fairly quickly early in September and thereafter the weather usually sets fair with little wind. This monthly list is, therefore, one of the least reliable, except that it does show that winds are still northerly and that the autumnal equinox (unlike the vernal) is not marked by strong winds. At this time Black Sea weather is more unsettled, and perhaps other September predictions are for that area.

Inference In September the winds, if any, will be northerly, and may be strong on the dates shown.

October

Turkish table
4   Koç Katimi (mating of rams and ewes) Firtinasi
15   Meryem Ana (Virgin Mary) Firtinasi
18   Kirlangiç (swallow) Firtinasi
22   Bağ Bozumu (spoiling of the vineyard) Firtinasi
27   Balik (fish) Firtinasi

Coptic almanac
21   three days westerly El Shabeesh (crusade), which corresponds to the Turkish table.

Comment Why the 15 October *firtina* should be so named is not clear. In the western church the feast of the Virgin is 15 August, but perhaps the Orthodox or Coptic church has a different day. Lost in the mists of time there may be some connection with the Coptic 'crusade' winds a week later. *Meryem Ana Firtinasi* usually occurs as a strong southerly that shifts north.

Balik Firtinasi is also something of a puzzle. Aegean fishermen might name a *firtina* after a seasonal arrival of a certain species, but not just 'fish'. On the other hand, at about this time occurs a high season for fishing in the Black Sea/Bosphorus area, with a run of various species. *Balik* also means the zodiac sign of Pisces, but the associated period is February/March.

Inference The settled northerly regime of summer winds will finally be broken by a southerly gale, possibly severe, around the middle of the month.

November

Turkish table
2   Kus Geçimi (migration of birds) Firtinasi
76   Kaşim Firtinasi (see below)
28   Firtina

Coptic almanac
26   three days strong westerly 'El Micness' (broom), which accords fairly well with the Turkish prediction.

Comment Kaşim in modern Turkish means November, but its original meaning was '28 November', traditionally the start of the winter period ending 5 May. The Coptic almanac dates *Kaşim* as a month later, which might be explained by the difference in latitude. However, a traditional Turkish saying is

'Kaşim yüz elli, yaz belli', meaning 'Summer is certain (to have arrived) 150 days from *Kaşim*'. From Turkish *Kaşim* to 5 May is 180 days – from Coptic Kaşim to 5 May is 150 days! Strong westerlies in the Delta suggest northerlies in the Aegean.

Inference In general November is not a windy month, but there may be strong northerlies on the dates shown.

December (to 21st)

Turkish table

2 Ulker Dönümü Firtinasi (helical setting of Pleiades)
9 Firtina (Ahiri sukutu evrak)
12 Karakiş (depths of winter) Firtinasi
19 Firtina
21 Gün Dönümü (solstice) Firtinasi

Coptic almanac

6 seven days strong southwest; Kaşim (see remarks in previous instalment)
20 Southwesterly 'El Fadrel Saggara' (a small gale). Both accord with the Turkish table.

The old name *Ahiri sukutu evrak* means 'the end of the period of falling leaves' – not an apt name in the Aegean where most leaves fall later. This is also not the most severe part of winter in the Aegean, so Karakiş seems more applicable further north.

Inference December is a windy month! The timing of these predictions suggests the passing of three major weather systems, but no prolonged period of high wind.

December (from 21st)

Turkish table

21 Gün Dönümü (solstice) Firtinasi
28 Firtina
31 Firtina

Coptic almanac

20 Southwesterly 'El Fadrel Saggara' (small gale). Accords with the Turkish table.

Inferences December is a windy month! The timing of these predictions suggests the passing of major weather systems but no prolonged period of high winds.

January

Turkish table

2 Firtina (three days)
8 Zemheri Firtinasi (see below)
17 Firtina
18 Firtina
23 Firtina - Kişin şiddeti (the hardship of winter)
28 Ayandon Firtinasi (see below)

Coptic almanac

11 Three days, 'El Fadrei Saggara' (small gale)
19 Five days, westerly 'El Fedra El Kibrain' (feeder)
27 Two days, westerly, same name as 19 January gale

The dates of the Coptic predictions accord well with

the Turkish ones but, unfortunately for these theories, the names do not!

Comment The three days around 2 January are probably *poyraz* (strong, cold NE winds). *Zemherir* is another word which translates as 'the dead of winter', but, more precisely, it is the forty days 22 December–30 January. As it is an Arabic name, it might have been expected to appear in the Coptic almanac.

Kişin şiddeti suggests a northerly.

Ayandon (from Greek) is St Anthony (the Abbot) (c. AD 251–356). He is, or was, particularly revered by Greek seamen. In the western church his feast day is 17 January, but Orthodox feast days are commonly some days later. St Anthony was Egyptian, which would suggest a 'Coptic Connection', but the Coptic almanac does not show it.

Inferences About 2–8 January there will be a prolonged period of cold northeast winds. Thereafter, around 17/18 and 23/25 January and 28 January/1 February three depressions will pass, probably local depressions in the eastern Mediterranean/Aegean. As the last one bears a Greek name and requires the special attention of St Anthony, the 28 January/1 February weather system will be a bad one!

February

Turkish table

1 Firtina
4 Firtina (three days)
7 Firtina (three days)
10 Firtina
13 Firtina
23 Firtina (three days)

Coptic almanac

18 Five days, strong southwesterly

Comment The above is one published Turkish list for February; there are other, shorter ones. With one possible exception (see below) February gales have no names, which suggests recent additions or corruption of the lore. This list has so many gales that it is almost impossible to distinguish one from another to make useful references.

According to a related tradition, three distinct 'radiations of heat' from the sun fall successively into the air, water and earth in February and March, known as Cemre 1, 2 and 3. Opinions vary as to whether these are marked by strong winds – a most interesting tradition, suggesting an origin in some ancient pre-Christian, pre-Islamic religion.

Conclusion

The table and almanac may now be regarded as folklore, at least in part, but folklore usually has some basis in fact. In this case I am convinced that their basis was ancient scholarly research and systematic observation. It may not be too fanciful to suggest that this lore was lost when the great library of Alexandria was burned in AD 641.

The Turkish table certainly appears to be in need of 'cleaning up' to resolve, if possible, the confusion of names and dates of gales which has undoubtedly arisen over the years, and to eliminate those *firtina* which seem to be duplicates or more recent additions. It may also be possible to establish that some of the predictions originally referred to particular areas of Turkey's long coastline.

Cmdr John S Guard RN

Local names for the winds

Meltemi/meltem Describes the prevailing summer northerlies in the Aegean.

Imbat Local name for the *meltemi* in the Gulf of Izmir.

Other names for the winds are taken from points of the compass in Turkish (see diagram).

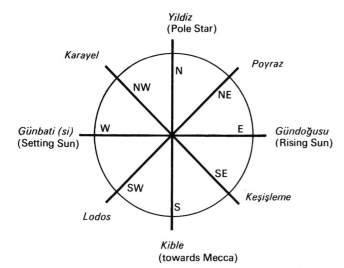

Climate (at Izmir)

	Av max °C	Av min °C	Highest recorded	Relative humidity	Days 1mm rain	Sea temp °C
Jan	13	4	23	62%	10	13
Feb	14	4	23	51%	8	12
Mar	17	6	29	52%	7	13
Apr	21	9	33	48%	5	14
May	26	13	41	45%	4	15
Jun	31	17	41	40%	2	18
Jul	33	21	42	31%	0	22
Aug	33	21	42	37%	1	24-25
Sep	29	17	39	42%	1	24
Oct	24	13	37	49%	4	23
Nov	19	9	32	58%	6	20
Dec	18	11	24	69%	11	19

Thunderstorms

These are most frequent in the spring and autumn. They are usually accompanied by a squall, but seldom last for more than an hour or two.

Fog and visibility

Fog is not frequent in this area in the summer, being reported at less than one per cent for observations. In the winter, fog is most frequent at the entrance to the Dardanelles, being reported at 3·9 per cent in January and 3·5 per cent in October. Along Turkey's southern shores, in the summer, there is frequently a radiation fog in the morning, which can reduce visibility to less than a mile at times. In the Gulf of Antalya visibility was less than two miles, and less than half a mile for a seven-day period, in June 1984. It had always cleared by midday, although visibility was still not good.

Visibility can also be reduced to as little as two miles, but rarely less, by dust particles suspended in the air in the summer months. When the first rain comes in the autumn and clears the air, visibility is improved and the clarity can be startling.

Humidity

Humidity is low for most of the region, except from Anamur Burnu to the Syrian border, where it is high in summer.

Sea temperature

In winter there are considerable differences in the mean sea temperature from north to south. In February the temperature is 10°C in the Sea of Marmara, 15°C around Bodrum, and 16°C in Iskenderun Körfezi. In August it is 24°C in the Sea of Marmara, 24°C at Bodrum, and 28°C in Iskenderun Körfezi.

Swell

Although there is not the large swell encountered in the Atlantic, a heavy swell can set onto the southern coast of Turkey where there is a long fetch across the eastern Mediterranean from Tunisia and Libya. This is apparent once you leave the shelter of the Aegean islands when going east along Turkey's southern coast. The afternoon land breeze will often augment any ground swell in this area, causing a heavy surf on the coast. In general the seas in the Mediterranean are shorter and steeper than seas around the British coast, and they are not to be underestimated. Going to windward in a stiff *meltemi* is always difficult – sometimes murderously so.

Currents

In general there is an anticlockwise circulation in the eastern Mediterranean, with the current following the coast in a general northerly and westerly direction. However, many of these currents are weak, and winds from a contrary direction can halve them and even reverse the current. In the NE Aegean, the N-going current meets the strong cur-

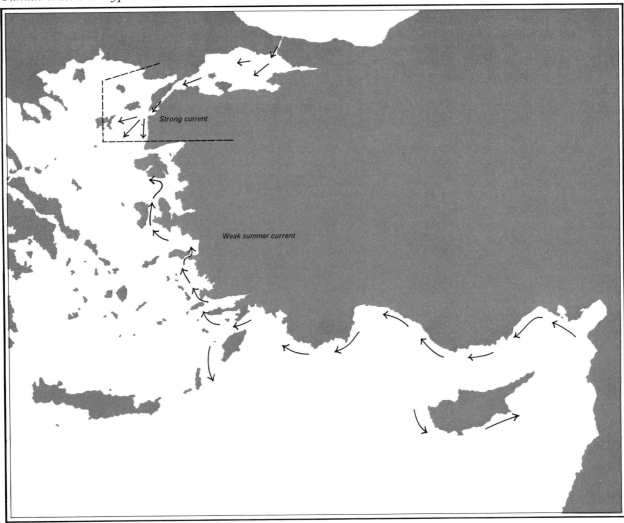

Currents. Predominant direction in the summer

rent flowing down from the Black Sea through the Sea of Marmara and the Dardanelles. This current is consistent and strong in the summer and winter.

Tides

In this area the tidal heights are everywhere less than 0·5 metres at springs. This tidal difference can be cancelled by strong contrary winds. For all intents and purposes tidal differences can be ignored.

Sea level

The wind is the prime cause of differences in sea level. The barometric pressure also influences the sea level. With a high barometric pressure and offshore winds the sea level is lowered, and with a low barometric pressure and onshore winds the sea level is raised. In the winter the mean sea level in Turkish waters may rise as much as 0·4m above normal.

Routes

The constancy of the summer wind from the north and west makes the planning of routes quite straightforward. In the spring a yacht should head north and west and plan to go south and east with the summer N-NW-W prevailing winds.

Buoyage

Buoyage is neither developed nor consistent. The Turkish government has accepted in principle the IALA System 'A' scheme, but no date has been given for implementation. The old system uses a black conical buoy on the starboard side of the channel and a red can buoy on the port side. Isolated buoys are variable in shape and colour. In recent years a number of cardinal buoys have been laid in busy yachting areas.

Lights

The coast is well lit around commercial harbours, but elsewhere lights are few and far between. Turkish lights, even major ones, are not always to be relied upon.

About the plans and pilotage notes

Nomenclature

In this edition, I have adopted the convention, in common with all hydrographic departments, of calling a place by the common Turkish name and by the Turkish name for the feature described. Thus cape = *burnu* or *burun*; bay = *bükü*; island = *adasi* or *ada*, and so on. A list of the Turkish names used on charts and their English equivalents is given in Appendix III.

In this century many of the villages, bays, capes, points, channels and islands along the Turkish coast have been renamed or so extensively modified as to be unrecognisable from the original. I have used where possible the modern Turkish names, with the old names and any variations in brackets afterwards. For some places whose Turkish names would be confusing to English speakers, for example the Dardanelles, which is known to the Turks as Canakkale Boğazi, I have used the better-known English name.

In the renaming of the coast, many of the places have been given the same name as a cape, island, bay, etc, a short distance away. There seems to be a lack of imagination in naming geographical features, with the result that there are numerous 'Black' (*Kara*) capes, islands and mountains; numerous 'Big' or 'Small' (*Büyük or Küçük*) capes and islands; and so on. This can be confusing where, for example, there are two capes of the same name a short distance apart. R P Lister makes the same observation:

'Turkish place-names show strikingly the limited nature of the Turkish imagination. Many of them are very pretty; but they are derived from a smallish stock of adjectives and nouns. Aksaray, the White Palace; Karaköy, the Black Village; Kizilirmak, the Red River; the same basic materials are combined and recombined over and over again until a certain monotony sets in. You could make a list of twenty Turkish adjectives and twenty Turkish nouns; and by the time you have deleted from the map all the place-names of Turkish origin that were made up from these elements in varying combinations, what you would have left would be a map with hardly any Turkish names left on it at all.'

R P Lister *Turkey Observed*

Abbreviations

In the pilotage notes compass directions are abbreviated to the first letter in capitals, as is common practice. So N is north, SE is southeast, etc.

Harbour plans

The harbour plans are designed to illustrate the accompanying notes, in the belief that the old adage 'a picture is worth a thousand words' is still true. It is stressed that many of these plans are based on the author's sketches and therefore should only be used in conjunction with official charts. They are not to be used for navigation.

Soundings

All soundings are in metres and are based on low water springs. For most of my soundings there will sometimes be up to half a metre more water than the depth shown when the sea bottom is uneven, but, in most cases, there is for all practical purposes the depth shown. It should be remembered that many of the harbours are prone to silting, and while many are kept dredged to a minimum depth, there may be others that are not dredged regularly.

For those used to working in fathoms and feet the use of metres may prove difficult at first, and there is the danger of reading the depth in metres as the depth in fathoms. For all practical purposes one metre can be read as approximately three feet and therefore two metres are approximately equal to one fathom. As a quick check on the depth in fathoms without reference to the conversion tables in the appendix, it is possible simply to divide the depths in metres by two. The result will be approximately equal to the depth in fathoms (e.g. 3 metres = 1½ fathoms, whereas accurately 3 metres = 1 fathom 3·8 feet).

Photographs

For this edition I braved the perils of leaning out of a small aircraft, for part of the time buffeted by the *meltemi* gusting over the high land in the gulfs, to take the aerial photographs of the harbours and anchorages featured. For someone who doesn't like flying in heavier-than-air machines all that much, it surprises me that there was not more camera-shake from the adrenaline pumping through my body. My thanks to the pilot and co-pilot of the Turkish Aviation Society and to Ali Pulat and Yusuf Civelekoglu for arranging things.

Most of the other photographs were taken by the author. Many were taken under difficult conditions – when navigating short-handed, in rough weather, under poor light conditions – and consequently the quality is not all that might be desired.

Bearings

All bearings are in 360° notation and are true.

Quick reference guide

At the beginning of each chapter there is a summary of important information: ports of entry; prohibited areas; radiobeacons; major lights. Following this there is a list of all the harbours and anchorages described in the chapter, with a classification of the shelter offered, mooring, and whether fuel, water, provisions and restaurants exist. Compressing information about a harbour or anchorage into such a framework is difficult, but the list can be useful for route planning, and as an instant memory aid for a harbour. Note that in the case of restaurants the classification reflects the number of restaurants and not the quality of the food served.

KEY

Shelter

A Excellent
B Good with prevailing winds
C Reasonable shelter but uncomfortable and sometimes dangerous
O In calm weather only

Mooring

A Stern-to or bows-to
B Alongside
C Anchored off

Fuel

A On the quay
B In the town
O None or limited

Water

A On the quay
B In the town
O None or limited

Provisioning

A Excellent
B Most supplies can be obtained
C Meagre supplies
O None

Eating out

A Excellent
B Average
C Poor
O None

Plan

• Harbour plan illustrates text

Charges

Charges are for the daily high season rate for a 12-metre yacht, at the exchange rates current when this volume went to press. Prices are in GBP sterling. For smaller or larger yachts make an approximate guesstimate.

1. No charge
2. Low cost (under £15)
3. Medium cost (£16–£25)
4. High cost (£26–£35)
5. Very high cost (over £36)

Key to symbols

⊕ : waypoint
3⌇₂ : depths in METRES
: shallow water with a depth of one metre or less
: rocks with less than 2 metres' depth over them
: rock just below or on the surface
: a shoal or reef with the least depth shown
: wreck partially above water
: eddies
: wreck
4 Wk : dangerous wreck
: rock ballasting on a mole or breakwater
: above-water rocks
: cliffs
⚓ : recommended anchorage
: prohibited anchorage
: mosque
✠ : church
: chimney
: ruins
: windmill
: castle
: houses
✈ : airport
: port police
: customs
: fish farm
: pine
: trees other than pine
: water
: fuel
: travel-hoist
YC : yacht club
i : tourist information
✉ : post office
℄ O.T.E. : overseas telecommunications exchange
⌇ : electricity
▲ : Port of entry
○ : Radiobeacon
: oil platform
: yachts
: yacht harbour
: yacht berth
: *caïques* or local boats (usually shallow or reserved)
✳ : light and characteristic
: lighthouse
○ : bn
: port hand buoy
▲ : starboard hand buoy
: mooring buoy
F : fixed
Fl : flash
Fl(2) : group flash
Oc : occulting
R : red
G : green
W : white
M : miles
s : sand
m : mud
w : weed
r : rock

I. The Dardanelles to Istanbul

This chapter covers the Dardanelles and the coasts and islands of the Sea of Marmara to the Bosphorus and Istanbul. The yachtsman in a low-powered yacht needs some perseverance to get up the Dardanelles against the prevailing winds and contrary current, but once into the Sea of Marmara he will be rewarded by a cruising ground amongst the islands and around the coast of Erdek Körfezi that is quite simply idyllic, and little frequented by yachts. Some of the local yachts based in Istanbul cruise around here, but most travel south to the Aegean for the summer.

You must remember that you are cruising along a giant crack between two continents. Occasionally you will have to pinch yourself and remember that Europe is on one side, Asia Minor on the other, and somewhere underneath giant tectonic plates are at work grinding over each other along the Anatolian fault line. Earthquakes have devastated the surrounding countryside since the dawn of written history. Looking over the records for 1938 to 1977, I found that there were 30 earthquakes along the Anatolian fault classified as major disasters with massive loss of life and property. Such massive earthquakes have perceptibly altered the seabed in places, and the yachtsman should treat even the most up-to-date charts with caution. Most of the alterations to the seabed have occurred, I believe, in the SW of the Sea of Marmara, around the archipelago including Paşalimani and Avşar Adalari in Erdek Körfezi.

Weather patterns

In the summer and the winter, winds are predominantly from the NE. In spring and early summer the winds are lightest; they often die at night and do not get up until midday. There may be southerlies in the spring and autumn (more frequently in the former), and these greatly aid passage up the Dardanelles. The prevailing NE winds gradually increase in strength through the summer, and often blow at Force 5–6 and occasionally more. In the autumn winds from the NE predominate, and at times may blow with some strength day and night. In the winter, winds from the NE again dominate, but there are occasional southerlies as well.

Gales are rare in the summer and occur in the winter for about 5 per cent of observations. They are usually (inevitably, it seems in this region) from the NE.

In the summer the climate in the Sea of Marmara is of the Mediterranean type, with little rainfall and high temperatures. The winter is dramatically different, and it can be chilly here in October. Snow falls around some of the coast, and in the Black Sea pack ice has been reported to extend to the northern entrance of the Bosphorus in a severe winter. Fifty miles S of the Dardanelles on the Aegean coast the winter temperatures are radically different and can be anything up to 5–10°C higher.

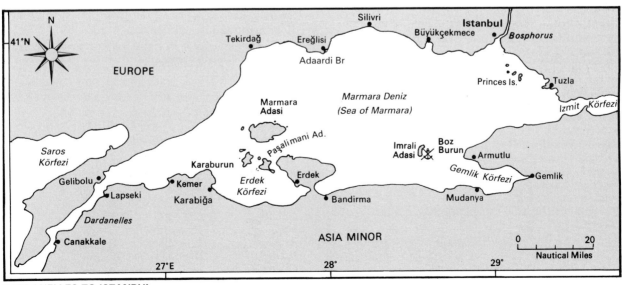

DARDANELLES TO ISTANBUL

Data

PORTS OF ENTRY
Canakkale
Bandirma
Istanbul

PROHIBITED AREAS
1. Landing on Bozcaada, Tavşan Adasi, and Gökçeada is prohibited without special authorisation, although in practice yachts use the harbours and anchorages on Bozcaada and Gökçeada with few problems.
2. Landing is prohibited on Saros Adasi (40°37'N 26°44'E) and on the coast between positions 40°36'·1N 26°49'·5E and 40°30'N 26°41'·3 E and between positions 40°28'·3N 26°44'·1E and 40°33'·3N 26°58'·8E.
3. It is prohibited to enter and anchor SE of the port in Erdek Limani.
4. It is prohibited to approach close to, anchor off, or land on Imrali Adasi.
5. Yachts are forbidden to enter much of Izmit Körfezi.

MAJOR LIGHTS
Gökçeada/Aydincik Br Fl(3)20s9M
Tavşan Adasi Fl.WR.5s14/10M

THE DARDANELLES
Kumkale Burnu Fl(2)10s8M
Mehmetçik Burnu Fl.WR.5s19/12M 350°-R-010°
Kanlidere Burnu Fl.5s10M
Canakkale Fl.RG.3s10M 341°-R-027°
Nara Burnu Fl(2)G.10s6M
Goçuk Burnu Fl.3s8M
Cardak Burnu Fl.G.3s7M
Gelibolu Fl.5s15M Siren(2)30s
Zincirbozan Fl.10s7M

SEA OF MARMARA
Ince Burun Fl(3)10s12M
Karaburun Fl(2)10s12M
Kale Burnu Fl.5s8M
Tavşan Adasi (Erdek) Fl.10s8M
Avşar Adasi Fl.5s8M
Kapidağ peninsula Fl(2)10s8M
Fener Adasi Fl.5s10M
Asmaliada Fl(3)15s12M
Domuz Burnu Fl.10s9M
Hayirsizada Fl.3s12M Siren(3)10s
Hoşköy Fl(2)10s19M
Ereğli Fl.15s15M
Karga Burun Aero 2 Oc.R.2·5s20/16M
Değirmen Burnu Fl.5s10M
Mersin Burnu Fl.10s9M
Marti Burnu Fl.10s10M
Boz Burun Fl.5s10M Siren(2)30s
Arnavutköy Burnu Fl(2)10s9M
Tuzla Burnu Fl.5s8M
Yesilköy Aero Al.Fl.WG.7·5s10M
Yesilköy Burnu Fl.10s15M Siren 30s
Kadiköy Iso.4s10M
Fenerbahçe Burnu Fl(2)12s15M Siren 60s
Sivriada Fl.3s13M
Yelkenkaya Burnu Fl.15s18M

Quick reference guide

	Shelter	Mooring	Fuel	Water	Provisions	Eating out	Plan	Charge band
Gökçeada								
S coast								
anchorages	O	C	O	O	O	O		
Aydincik	O	C	O	O	O	O		
Kuzu Limani	A	B	O	B	O	O	•	1
Kaleköy	C	BC	O	B	C	C		
Mainland coast								
Kabatepe Limani	B	AB	O	A	O	C	•	1
Küçükkemikli	O	C	O	O	O	O		
Anfartalar Köyu	O	C	O	O	O	O		
Erikli	C	C	O	B	C	C		
Ibrice Limani	B	AB	O	B	O	O	•	1
Kocaçeşme	C	C	B	B	C	C		
The Dardanelles								
Anit Limani	C	C	O	B	O	O	•	
Karantina Köy	C	C	O	O	O	O		
Canakkale	A	A	B	A	B	B	•	2
Eceabat	C	A	B	B	C	C		
Lapseki	C	AC	B	B	C	C		
Gelibolu	B	AC	B	B	C	B	•	1
Sevketiye	C	AC	O	B	O	C		
Kemer	C	AC	B	A	C	O	•	1
Sea of Marmara								
South shore								
Karabiga	B	ABC	B	B	C	C	•	1
Erdek	A	A	B	A	B	A	•	2
Ocaklar	C	C	O	O	O	O		
Narliköy	C	C	O	B	C	C		
Paşalimani Adasi								
Paşalimani	B	C	O	B	C	C	•	1
Balikli	C	C	O	B	C	C		
Avşar Adasi								
Turkeli	C	AC	O	B	C	B		
Marmara Adasi								
Cinarli	O	C	O	O	C	C		
Port Marmara	A	AB	A	B	C	B	•	1
Gundoğdu	O	C	O	O	C	C		
Topağaç	C	C	O	O	O	O	•	1
Asmaliköy	B	AB	O	B	C	O	•	1/2
Saraylar	A	AC	B	B	C	C	•	1
Kapidağ to the Princes Islands								
Ilhanköy	B	AB	O	A	C	C	•	2
Kapidağ N side anchorages								
Doğanlar	C	C	O	B	C	O		
Turan Köy	C	C	O	O	O	O		
Cayağzi	B	B	A	A	C	C		
Cakilköy	B	A	O	B	C	C		
Karsikaya	C	A	O	A	O	C		
Kum Limani	C	C	O	O	O	O		
Tatlisu	C	C	O	O	O	O		
Bandirma	A	AB	B	A	A	B	•	1/2
Kurşunlu	B	C	O	B	C	C		
Zeytinbaği	C	BC	B	A	B	B	•	1
Mudanya	C	BC	B	A	B	C		
Gemlik	C	BC	B	A	B	B		
Narli	B	BC	O	B	C	C	•	1
Armutlu	C	BC	O	B	C	C		
Esenköy	B	C	O	B	C	C	•	1
Cinarcik	B	A	B	A	B	B	•	2
Yalova	A	A	O	B	O	O		

Tuzla	B	C	B	B	B	B	•
Aydinli	C	AC	O	O	O	C	
Pendik	C	C	B	B	C	B	•
Princes Islands							
Büyükada	O	C	O	O	C	B	• 1
Heybeliada	B	C	O	O	C	B	• 1
Kinaliada	O	C	O	O	C	B	• 1
Sivriada	B	B	O	O	O	O	• 1
Istanbul and approaches							
Ataköy Marina	A	A	A	A	C	B	• 2/3
Kumkapi	C	B	B	A	C	C	•
Kalamis Marina	A	A	B	A	B	B	• 2/3
Haydarpaşa	A	C	B	B	A	A	•
The Bosphorus							
Bebek	B	AC	B	B	A	A	• 2
Istinye	B	A	B	A	C	B	2
Tarabya	B	AC	B	B	C	B	
Büyükdere	C	C	B	B	C	B	
Rumeli	A	B	B	B	C	C	• 1
Poyraz	B	AC	O	B	C	C	• 1
North shore							
Yesilköy	B	AC	B	B	C	C	
Büyükçekmece	C	AC	B	A	C	C	• 1
Selimpasa	C	B	B	A	C	C	
Silivri	B	AC	B	B	C	B	• 1
Ereğli	C	C	B	B	C	C	•
Tekirdağ	B	ABC	B	B	B	C	•
Kumbağ	C	AB	A	B	C	C	
Hoşköy	A	A	B	B	C	C	•
Sarköy	B	AB	A	A	C	C	• 2

The Dardanelles

Approaches

Most yachts approach the Dardanelles from due W between Gökçeada (Imroz) and Tavşan Adasi. A yacht coming from Limnos will have no trouble identifying these two islands. Less commonly, a yacht may approach the Dardanelles between Gökçeada and the Gelibolu peninsula from Alexandroupolis or Samothrace. A yacht may also approach from the S between Bozcaada and Tavşan Adasi and the Asiatic coast.

From any of these directions, but particularly the due W approach from Limnos, a careful eye should be kept on the large volume of traffic leaving and converging on the Dardanelles. This is one of the busiest waterways in the world, with hundreds of ships of all nationalities passing through it every week. Ships entering the strait must keep to the starboard side, but remember that VLCCs must start turning well before a corner and that they cannot easily change course or stop – a yacht should keep well clear of all ships and allow them absolute right of way.

Conspicuous

The islands of Gökçeada, Bozcaada, and Tavşan are easily identified. The white lighthouse and dwelling on Tavşan stand out well. At the entrance to the Dardanelles, the white lighthouse on the N side (on Mehmetçik Burnu, formerly Cape Helles) and the Turkish war memorial on Hisarlik Burnu (four square pillars topped by a flat square roof built of grey stone, 24m, 80ft, high) are conspicuous from some distance off. Closer in, the British war memorial, a tall obelisk close to the lighthouse on Mehmetçik Burnu, and a military observation platform on the southern side of the entrance (Kumkale) are conspicuous.

By night Use the lights on Tavşan Adasi (Fl.WR.5s 14/10M); on Mehmetçik Burnu (Fl.WR.5s19/12M, the red sector covers the shoal water off Kumkale); and on Kumkale (Fl(2)10s8M).

Currents

A yacht approaching the Dardanelles should be prepared for a significant current up to 15 miles off. From the entrance the current spreads out in a fan pattern so that it runs W along the southern coast of Gökçeada, SW between Tavşan Adasi and Bozcaada, and to the S between Bozcaada and the Asiatic coast. Off the southern tip of Bozcaada there can be a 1½ knot S-going current, and five miles W of the entrance there can be a 2-knot W-going current. In the entrance itself there can be up to a 3–4 knot current.

Passage in the Dardanelles

Low-powered yachts need to plan carefully for a passage up the Dardanelles. The prevailing wind blows straight down the channel, and combined with the strong current can cause considerable problems. Once through the entrance a yacht should follow the coast on the SE side where the current is weaker. There may occasionally be a weak countercurrent. The edge of the main current is readily identified by eddies welling up where the seabottom shelves from the deep channel to the 20 and 10 metre lines. In practice a yacht can keep just inside the eddy line and encounter the full force of the current only where the channel narrows. (*Tetranora* is nearly 7 tons and is powered by a 17hp diesel. At the entrance to the Dardanelles I covered slightly less than two nautical miles over the ground in one hour, but once inside the entrance and following the eddy line I covered two nautical miles in half an hour. Normal speed in flat water would have been slightly over 5 knots.)

Care must be taken of the amount of shipping using the Dardanelles

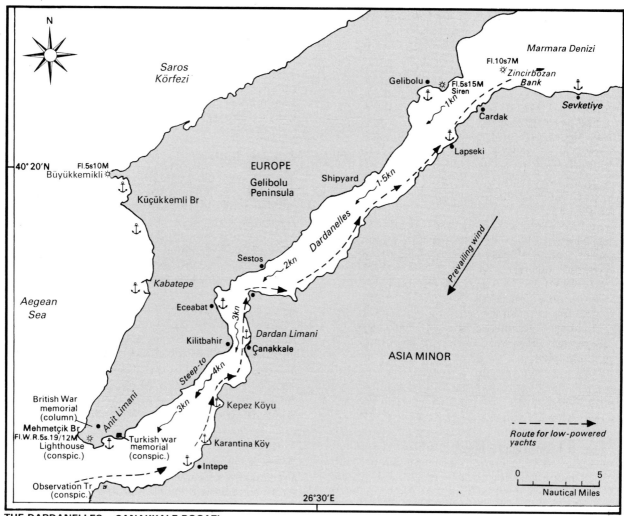

THE DARDANELLES – CANAKKALE BOGAZI

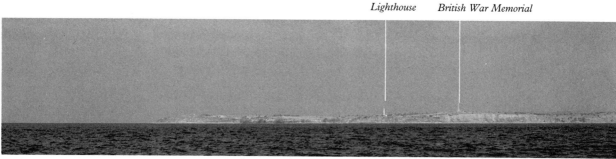

Lighthouse   British War Memorial

Northern side of the entrance to the Dardanelles looking N

Turkish war memorial conspicuous at the entrance to the Dardanelles looking NW

A yacht must clear in at Canakkale, and in any case this is a convenient place to break the passage up the Dardanelles. A yacht can then proceed to Gelibolu, again following the Asiatic coast to avoid the strong current in mid-channel and on the European side. The prevailing northerlies may drop at night, and a yacht should leave very early in the morning in order to get as far as possible before the wind gets up again.

Even if you have a powerful engine it is worth following the low-power route, which, although longer, is quicker overall. It also has the benefit of being out of the main shipping channel for the most part. On the return journey a yacht can follow the European coast to take full advantage of the current.

Note Admiralty chart 2429 of the Dardanelles, on a large scale showing currents and counter-currents, is essential for low-powered yachts proceeding up the Dardanelles. See also Imray-Tetra chart G2 (Northern Aegean).

Prohibited areas

1. Landing on Bozcaada (39°50'N 26°00'E), Tavşan Adasi (39°56'N 26°04'E), and Gökçeada (40°09'N 25°55'E) is prohibited without special authorisation. However, in practice no objection is made to yachts visiting Gökçeada and Bozcaada. See the notes on navigation for the islands concerned.
2. Landing is prohibited on Saros Adasi (40°37'N 26°44'E), and on the coast between positions 40°36'·1N 26°49'·5E and 40°30'N 26°41'·3E and between positions 40°28'·3N 26°44'·1E and 40°33'·33N 26°58'·8E. However, again in practice no objection is made to yachts visiting the harbours and anchorages in Saros Körfezi. Nonetheless it should be kept in mind that these are military areas with restrictions on landing and photography.

Gökçeada

(Imroz Adasi, Imbros)

This high bold island on the northern side of the approaches to the Dardanelles is easily recognised. A high mountain ridge runs along the N coast, dominated by the peak of Ilyas Dağ (672m/2184ft) in the middle of the island. From seaward, the island has a barren aspect. Off the W and S coasts there are extensive shoals extending seaward for up to half a mile.

There are several anchorages and harbours around the island, and although the island is a military area, no objection seems to be raised to yachts anchoring off the coast or berthing in the main harbour at Kuzu Limani.

ANCHORAGES ON THE S COAST

Pirgoz (Pirgos) In calm weather a yacht can anchor on the W or E side of Pirgoz Burnu near the SW tip of the island. Pirgoz Burnu is a white cliffy projection which stands out well. With even moderate winds from the NE a swell is pushed in and it is not comfortable. With strong NE winds it is untenable.

Kapikaya A large bay about 2½ miles E of Pirgoz. Slightly better shelter than Pirgoz, but still uncomfortable in NE winds and untenable with strong NE winds.

Aliki An anchorage in the roadstead under Tuzla Burnu. The coast is fringed by above and below-water rocks, and care is needed when navigating in the vicinity of the coast. Shelter as for Kapikaya.

AYDINCIK LIMANI

The large bay on the N side of Aydincik Burnu. Although completely open to the prevailing NE winds, it could be useful in the event of a blow from the S.

KUZU LIMANI

Approach

The harbour is situated under the NE tip of the island. The long breakwater protecting the harbour and several oil storage tanks on the coast are easily identified.

By night The entrance to the harbour is lit: Fl.G.3s5M and Fl.R.3s6M.

Mooring

Proceed into the large harbour and go alongside in the small inner basin. Good all-round shelter.

Authorities Customs. Harbourmaster.

Facilities

There is little at the harbour itself, and you will have to go into Gökçeada, some 7km away, for provisions

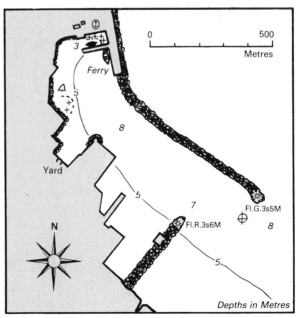

KUZU LIMANI
40°13'·8N 25°57'·3E (Fl.G. light)

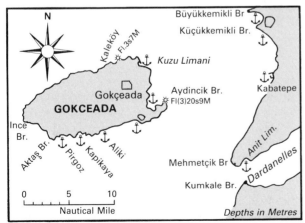

GOKCEADA TO THE DARDANELLES
Aydincik Burun light 40°09'·8N 26°00'·6E

and services. Ferry to Kabatepe on the mainland opposite.

General

Kuzu Limani is the ferry port for the island, and apart from that there is very little more to say. Since it offers good shelter, it is the obvious place to leave a yacht should you want to explore inland.

KALEKOY (40°14'·2N 25°54'E)

A bay and miniature harbour some 3 miles W of Kuzu on the N coast (Fl light). A yacht can anchor in the bay, where there is indifferent shelter from the prevailing winds. The harbour is very small and shallow, with just 1·5-metre depths in the entrance and mostly less than 1-metre depths inside.

The mainland coast opposite Gökçeada

On the coast opposite Gökçeada and N of the entrance to the Dardanelles between Mehmetçik Burnu and Büyükkemikli Burnu there are several anchorages, and the ferry harbour at Kabatepe.

KABATEPE LIMANI

A large harbour just over 10 miles NNE of Mehmetçik Burnu. The entrance is lit: Fl.R.5s6M/Fl.G.5s6M. There are 4–5 metre depths in the entrance and mostly 3–5 metre depths inside. Go stern or bows-to or alongside the quay at the S end of the harbour. Reasonable shelter from the prevailing winds. Water on the quay and a café ashore.

The harbour is ideally situated for a visit to the Gelibolu peninsula, and a taxi can be arranged for a tour.

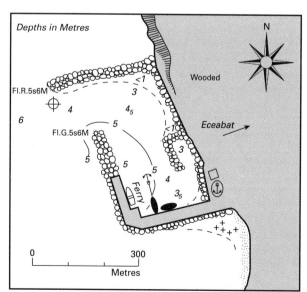

KABATEPE LIMANI
40°12'·3N 26°15'·9E

KUCUKKEMIKLI BURNU

A yacht can anchor off the long sandy beach here in calm weather.

ANFARTALAR KOYU

A large bay between Küçükkemikli Burnu and Büyükkemikli Burnu. Suitable in calm weather and light NE winds.

SAROS KORFEZI

The large gulf on the N side of the Gelibolu peninsula. On the N side of the gulf there are several anchorages and a small harbour at Ibrice that can be used.

Erikli A long sandy beach off which there are suitable depths for anchoring. Mediocre shelter only.

Ibrice Limani A small harbour on the E side of Toplar Burnu. There are 6–7 metre depths in the entrance and 1·5–2·5 metre depths off the quay in the SW corner. Go alongside. Reasonable shelter from the prevailing NE winds.

Kocaçeşme An open anchorage in the NE corner of the gulf.

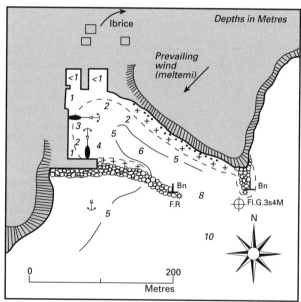

IBRICE LIMANI
40°36'·2N 26°32'·8E

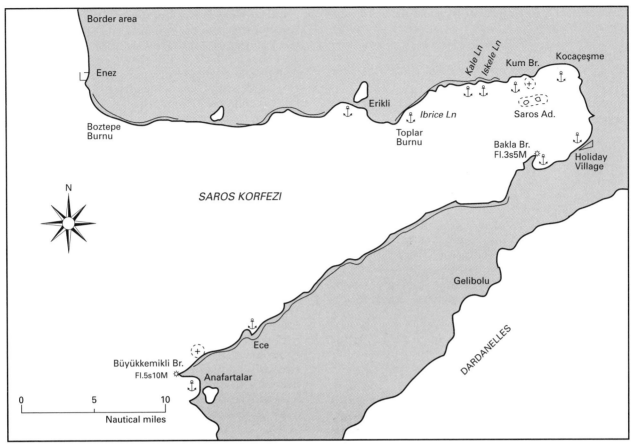

Border area

Enez

Boztepe
Burnu

Erikli

Ibrice Ln

Toplar
Burnu

Kale Ln

Iskele Ln

Kum Br.

Kocaçeşme

Saros Ad.

Bakla Br.
Fl.3s5M

Holiday
Village

SAROS KORFEZI

N

Gelibolu

DARDANELLES

Ece

Büyükkemikli Br.
Fl.5s10M

Anafartalar

0	5	10

Nautical miles

SAROS KORFEZI

The Dardanelles – general

At some time in prehistory, a fault in the mountains around what is now the Sea of Marmara opened up and the sea rushed in to separate Europe from Asia Minor along this narrow winding channel. By some quirk of nature the geography of the region appears to have been reversed: the European side of the Dardanelles is steep-to and appears barren, while the Asiatic coast is composed of gently rolling countryside richly cultivated with the vine and grain crops, the latter reminiscent of English or French farming land. In fact the European side is also cultivated, mostly with corn and wheat, and only appears barren from seaward. The Dardanelles was known in ancient times as the Hellespont, and is known to the Turks as Canakkale Boğazi.

This channel is a strategic stepping stone not only between Europe and Asia, but also between the Aegean Sea and the Sea of Marmara and so to the Black Sea. It has figured prominently in the affairs of men, and especially in the aspirations of warlike men, from ancient times to the present. The roll call begins with Troy and continues with Xerxes, Alexander, the Romans, the Byzantines and the Ottomans, to the Gallipoli campaign in the First World War.

The ruins of Troy lie a short distance inland on the Asiatic side. A pilgrimage to Troy is more of an intellectual journey than a journey to see the material remains of this most famous of Homeric cities. There is little for the uninformed layman to see: the trenches and debris created by archaeologists; the site on the mound at Hisarlik overlooking the Trojan Plain, ancient Tenedos and the approaches to the Dardanelles; the remains of the various Troys, covering three millennia of human existence, including the all-important Troy VIIa, the Troy identified as the Troy of Homer.

All in all 46 strata have been identified, with the phlegmatic Schliemann identifying Troy II as the real Troy. Now it is estimated to have existed about a thousand years before Priam's Troy. The exact identification of periods is still in dispute. Turkish archaeologists identify Troy VI as Priam's Troy. Professor Blegen asserts that Troy VII is the one mentioned by Homer. Take your pick. The remains are not much to look at, and are little helped by the replica of the Trojan horse (could the Trojans really have simply trundled this ancient time bomb into their city?) and the paucity of exhibits in the nearby museum. A pilgrimage to Troy is really a journey to see the wellhead of western European culture. Andrew Mango captures its importance neatly:

'The victory won by the Greeks at about 1250 BC provided them with a national epic and the beginnings of a sense of common identity, which survived the destruction of Mycenean civilization by the Dorian newcomers. From then on the history of Troy continued outside the city. Having given Greece a shared historical experience, it furnished Rome with a mythical noble origin in rivalry with that of Greece, the legend of Aeneas, noble Trojan emigrant to Rome, symbolising both the

39

incorporation of Rome into Greek culture and its attempt to define itself within it. Troy lived on abroad – from the Iliad through the Aeneid to the Lusiads, from the tragic and memorable Aeneas to the comic and forgotten Brut (founder of Britannia and presumably ancestor of Lud, who is at least remembered in pub names), from Hellenistic novelettes to the twelfth-century 'Roman de Troie' and then through Boccaccio, Chaucer and Lydgate to Shakespeare's 'Troilus and Cressida'.'

Andrew Mango Discovering Turkey

From Troy you can see two tumuli near to the Aegean coast, traditionally called the graves of Patroclus and Achilles. Homer mentions these in the *Odyssey*: 'In this your white bones lie, my lord Achilles, and mingled with them the bones of Menoetius's son Patroclus, dead before you, and separately those of Antilochus, who was your closest friend after the death of Patroclus. Over them all, we the soldiers of the Argive force built up a great and glorious mound, on a promontory jutting out over the broad waters of the Hellespont, so that it might be seen far out to sea by the sailors of today and future ages.' The wonder of it is that today the two tumuli are easily identified from seaward about one mile south of Kumkale.

In The Narrows the strait is barely 1300 metres across between Kilitbahir and Canakkale, and it is not much wider at the northern end between Sestos and Abidos. Kilitbahir means 'The Key to the Sea', and the castle so prominent from seaward was built in 1452 by Mehmet the Conqueror to control the straits prior to his siege of Constantinople. At the northern end of The Narrows, Xerxes sat on his marble throne on Abidos (Abydos) and watched his ships form a bridge from Sestos (Akbas) to Abidos. Herodotus tells us that the King of Persia shed tears over the grand spectacle below him, and also over the mortality of man: '...and it came into my mind how pitifully short is human life, for of all these many thousands of men not one will be alive in a hundred years' time.'

Sestos is named after the ancient Sestos, which is identified with the tragedy of Leander and Hero. Hero was a priestess in the temple of Aphrodite who fell in love with Leander. To meet her he had to swim across the Hellespont, and every night she put a lantern out to guide him to Sestos. One wintry night the lantern blew out and poor Leander, no doubt confused by the strong currents, drowned. Heartbroken, Hero drowned herself too. Byron swam the straits here on 3 May 1810, and according to H M Denham was swept some four miles below the point he set out from, although the strait is only one mile across at this point.

It is recent history that has given the Dardanelles a prominence above other sites in Turkey. The Gallipoli (Gelibolu) peninsula is dotted with the war graves and memorials of that ill-begotten campaign. The dead of England, France, Australia, New Zealand and Turkey lie here; more than a hundred thousand dead, of both sides, are buried amongst the debris of the war.

It was in the Gallipoli campaign that Mustafa Kemal (later Kemal Ataturk) made his mark as a commander in the Dardanelles. He played a decisive part in the defeat of the Allies, and went on to rally the Turks against the Greek expeditionary force and later to lead Turkey into the 20th century. Like a benign Big Brother, his portrait is to be found everywhere in Turkey, watching over customs officers and normal mortals alike.

At the northern end of the Dardanelles the straits widen into the Sea of Marmara. It is something of a relief to reach the sea after the narrow waters behind; partly to leave behind the opposing current and winds that make it difficult for a yacht to get up the channel, and partly to leave behind the oppressive memories of the Gallipoli campaign and the many graves of the dead. Rarely have I felt such anger at the pointlessness of so many young men losing their lives in a campaign managed wholly, it seems, with incompetence and disregard for life.

ANIT LIMANI (Morto Bay)

The large bay on the N side of the entrance to Canakkale Bogazi. The pilot station at Seddülbahir is situated on the W side of the bay and should not be approached. On the western side of the bay a reef extends 700 metres from the shore. Its eastern extremity is marked by a concrete beacon 5 metres high and exhibiting a light (Fl(4)R.15s5M). At the head of the bay there are several large mooring buoys.

A yacht should make for the NE corner of the bay and anchor in 2–5 metres on mud. Care should be taken of several detached underwater rocks off Hisarlik Burnu on the eastern side. Reasonable shelter from the *meltemi*. It is reported that there is a water tap at the root of the rough rock mole on the E side of the bay.

You are normally allowed ashore without special authorisation. You can wander around the war cemeteries and get a good idea of what it must have been like during the Gallipoli campaign from here.

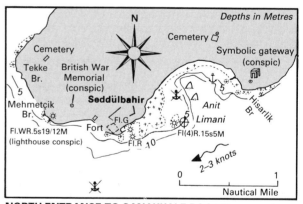

NORTH ENTRANCE TO CANAKKALE BOGAZI AND ANIT LIMANI 40°02'·6N 26°12'·1E

KARANTINA KOY and INTEPE

In settled weather a yacht can anchor off Karantina Köy in a shallow bight. Shelter is better than it looks on the chart, and the setting with wooded slopes behind is most attractive.

A yacht can also anchor further S in Intepe Limani. Neither anchorage is safe in strong northerlies, but the winds are often light here, while being stronger on the opposite side of the channel.

CANAKKALE (Canak, Chanak)

BA 2429

Approach

Conspicuous The most conspicuous object day and night is the fort on the western side of The Narrows at Kilitbahir. By day the fort is easily identified and at night it is floodlit. The light structure at

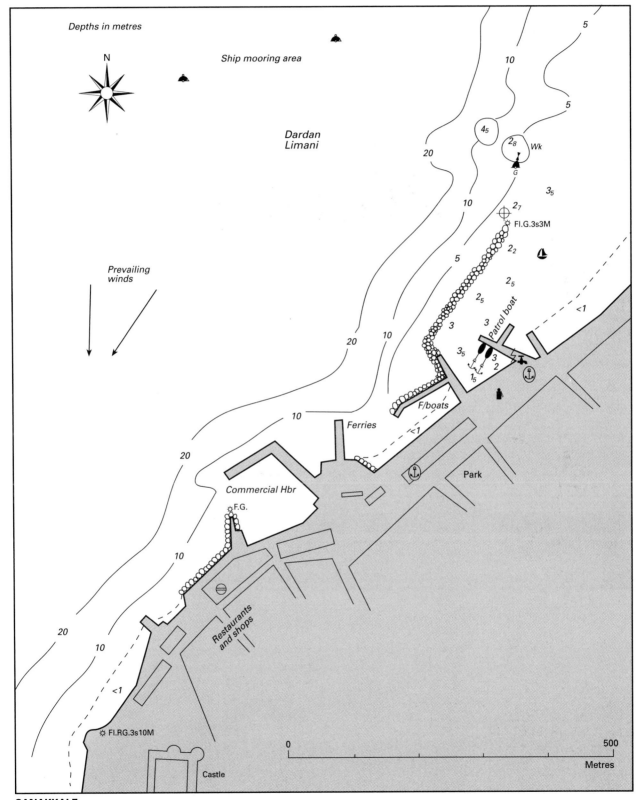

CANAKKALE
40°09'.3N 26°24'.4E

Namazgah (Kilitbahir) is also conspicuous. Closer in, Canakkale fort and the light structure can be identified. Once into Dardan Limani the harbour is easily spotted. There are always ships at anchor in Dardan Limani.

By night Straightforward. The Dardanelles are well lit. Use the light at Kilitbahir Fl.R.3s7M and the floodlit castle. Canakkale is lit by its castle Fl.RG.3s10M (027°-G-341°-R-027°). The commercial harbour is lit on the spur mole F.G.3M. The end of the yacht harbour breakwater is lit Fl.G.3s3M. The buoy is not lit. The yacht pier is floodlit.

VHF Ch 16 for port authorities.

Dangers

1. In Dardan Limani there are numerous unlit mooring buoys.
2. Ferries regularly cross from Canakkale to Kilitbahir and Eceabat on the opposite shores. They should be given a wide berth.
3. The green conical buoy at the entrance (W cardinal ⚲ topmark) marks a wreck. There are 2·7 metre least depths between the buoy and the end of the breakwater. Once around the breakwater depths are variable between 2–3m approximately 15–20m out from the breakwater. The bottom is mud if you go aground.

Note The prevailing wind gusts into The Narrows from the ENE. There is usually less wind outside The Narrows.

Canakkale: the approach to the yacht harbour, looking E

Canakkale: the harbour. Entrance to the yacht harbour is at the top of the picture

Mooring

Go stern or bows-to the yacht pier where shown. The bottom is mud and good holding. It is best to go bows-to, as a slight slop is set up by the prevailing wind and you will be more comfortable with your bows facing into it.

Canakkale: the yacht harbour, looking N

Canakkale, on the SE side of the Narrows, looking N

The Narrows, looking N

Kilitbahir castle (the Narrows), looking WNW

Shelter Good all-round shelter.

Authorities A port of entry, hence the full complement of authorities. Charge band 2.

Note There have been reports of the authorities being somewhat irksome here, and of overcharging for visas and Transit Logs by the authorities. There are also a number of agents to whom you may be referred for the paperwork, but there is no need to engage an agent or pay his fee. It may be better to clear into Turkey at Dikili or Ayvalik if you are proceeding up the coast, and to arrive at Canakkale with a Transit Log.

Facilities

Water On the quay. A modest charge is made.
Fuel On the quay.
Electricity 220V can be connected on request.
Repairs Mechanical and light engineering repairs can be carried out. A small chandler's, catering mostly for local fishermen, on the waterfront.
Provisions Good shopping for all provisions. Market on Fridays.
Eating out Good restaurants along the waterfront.
Other PO. Banks. Turkish gas. Hardware shops. Bus to Istanbul. Ferry to Eceabat.

General

Canakkale is a lively thriving town, the administrative centre for the area, the gateway to Troy and a base for visits to Gallipoli. You cannot call it an attractive spot, but it is a friendly and interesting town. Its origins are Turkish, Mehmet the Conqueror having built the fort here, which was originally called Sultan's Castle (Kale-i Sultaniyye) and later Pottery Castle after the well known local pottery.

For the Turks Canakkale is synonymous with the Gallipoli Campaign. On the slopes NE of the town a large sign gives the date '18 March 1915', while on the hillside opposite a picture of a soldier and a message picked out in white stones ask us to regard with reverence the place where so many young soldiers died. It is all too easy to forget that Turkish soldiers died here as well as ANZACs and British troops in this grand folly of a campaign.

ECEABAT

The ferry terminal on the European shore for Canakkale. A yacht can go bows-to near the extremity of the breakwater. Further in, the harbour is shallow and encumbered with underwater debris. The harbour is very uncomfortable and possibly dangerous with the prevailing winds, which set up a surge inside. The ferry uses the central pile pier.

LAPSEKI

The ferry terminal on the Asiatic side for the ferries from Gelibolu. In calm weather a yacht can anchor N of the ferry pier, leaving sufficient room for the ferries to manoeuvre. With strong northerlies a yacht should go to Gelibolu. Provisions and restaurants ashore.

GELIBOLU (Gallipoli)
Approach

The harbour lies on the S side of the headland with Gelibolu lighthouse on it.

Conspicuous The buildings of Gelibolu town are easily recognised. Behind the town a concrete water tower and the white lighthouse and dwelling on the cliff edge are conspicuous.

By night Use Gelibolu light (Fl.5s15M). The end of the pier of the commercial harbour is lit by a weak F.R (a street lamp painted red).

Dangers The bottom of the commercial harbour comes up quickly from 3–4 metres to less than one metre on the N side. The limit of the shallows is not marked.

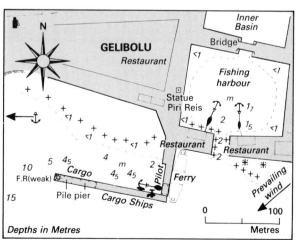

GELIBOLU
40°26'N 26°41'E

Shallow

Gelibolu: the small commercial harbour, looking ESE

Mooring

It may be possible to go stern or bow-to or alongside the pier in the commercial harbour. Much of the E corner is taken up by pilot boats, but have a look here first. The quay is very high making getting on and off difficult. Alternatively go bow-to just inside the entrance of the fishing harbour. The W side is usually favoured because you do not get as much wash from the ferries. Depths are irregular in the basin and there is a bit more water than shown on the plan. However care is needed and you must allow something under the keel to avoid being dumped on the bottom by the wash from the ferries coming and going.

Shelter Good shelter from the prevailing winds in the commercial harbour and in the fishing harbour.

Dangers The entrance to the fishing harbour is narrow and bordered by underwater rocks. A yacht must keep to the middle of the channel when entering. A good lookout must also be kept for the ferry which docks near the entrance.

Authorities Customs. Harbourmaster. A small charge is made.

Anchorage A yacht can also anchor out in the northern corner of the bay to the E of the harbour. Anchor in 3–5 metres on sand. There is a good lee from the prevailing winds here.

Gelibolu fishing harbour

Facilities

Water On the pier.

Fuel Near to the harbour, but you will have to carry it in jerry cans.

Repairs Mechanical and light engineering work can be carried out.

Provisions Good shopping for provisions in the town which straggles up the hillside. Large market on Tuesdays with huge range of fresh fruit and vegetables and local produce. A small fish market near the fishing harbour. Ice from the factory 3km away. Excellent *loukoum* in the shops.

Eating out Good restaurants around the waterfront.

Other PO. Banks. Turkish gas. Hardware shops. Bus to Istanbul. Ferry to Lapseki on the opposite shore.

General

Gelibolu, formerly Gallipoli, is the principal port on the European side of the Dardanelles. The fortress at Gallipoli was built by an Armenian Byzantine emperor, Philippicus Bardanes, in AD 713. The Turks captured it in 1357 and rebuilt it.

Gelibolu is celebrated as the birthplace and home of Piri Reis, the 16th-century map-maker and pilot. His charts of the Mediterranean, Africa and America are geographically detailed and include additional details such as wind roses, currents, recommended anchorages and notes on supplies and the inhabitants. His map of America is dated from around the time of Columbus' first voyage. A monument to this early navigator has been erected near the harbour, and a small museum at the tourist office has a few exhibits on Piri Reis. Some of his original pilots are on display in the naval museum in Istanbul.

The Sea of Marmara
(Marmara Denizi)

The sea takes its name from Marmara Island, which is composed almost entirely of marble, and hence means literally the 'Marble Sea'. The ancient Greeks called it Propontis or 'Fore-sea', the sea before the Aegean Sea proper.

A yacht proceeding from the Dardanelles to Istanbul will usually follow the southern shores of the Sea of Marmara. Here the prevailing NE wind is absent, or at best weak when a fresh breeze is blowing in the northern half of the sea. Hence a yacht can find an easy passage along the southern shore until the approaches to Istanbul. On the return journey it can follow the northern shore, where the prevailing winds make for a fast passage to the Dardanelles.

The cruising ground in Erdek Körfezi should not be neglected. There are many sheltered anchorages and harbours which are comparatively unfrequented, and the surroundings are delightful. Several weeks should be allotted to the gulf and the outlying islands, for this is the best part of the Sea of Marmara.

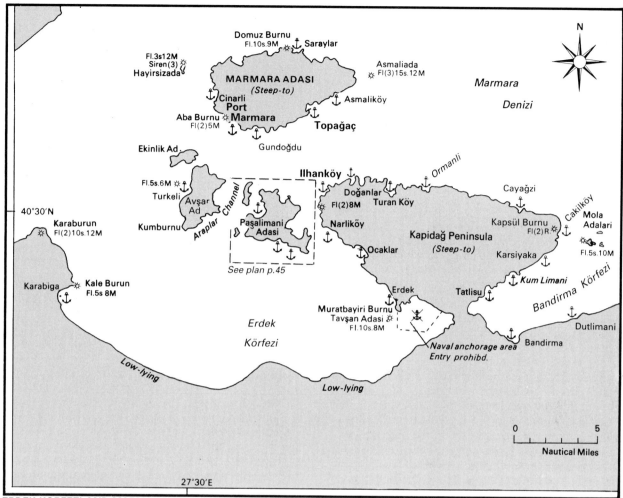

ERDEK KORFEZI AND MARMARA ADASI

ZINCIRBOZAN BANK

A shallow bank extending from the Asiatic coast at the northern end of the Dardanelles. The northern edge of the bank is marked by a light tower which is easily identified (Light: Fl.10s7M). A high girder tower near Cardak is conspicuous and the mast of a wreck just over a mile SE of Zincirbozan light tower is easily identified.

SEVKETIYE

A fishing harbour approximately 5½ miles E of Zincirbozan beacon. An old windmill will be seen on the W side of the harbour and a factory on the left side. Depths are reported to be variable and mostly fairly shallow inside, with just 2-metre depths in the entrance and 1–1·5 metre depths on the quay on the E side. It is usually very crowded with fishing boats.

KEMER

A large bay on the Asiatic coast lying close under Bodrum Burnu about 17½ miles E of Gelibolu. A yacht can anchor off, or use the small harbour if there is room.
1. Anchor in the NE corner of the bay where there is good shelter from the prevailing wind. Anchor close inshore opposite a house with four arches and take a line ashore.

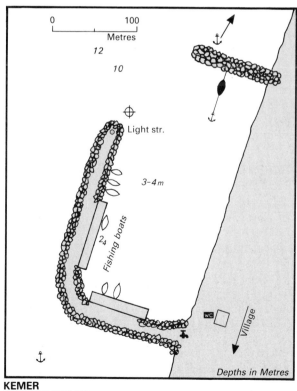

KEMER
40°25'·4N 27°04'E

2. Because the harbour is usually crowded with fishing boats, the only usable place is hanging off the stone breakwater on the N side. Alternatively, anchor off the S side of the harbour.

Fuel and water near the root of the breakwater. Some provisions and several *çay* houses. *Dolmuş* to Karabiga. The village is not a sophisticated place, but is convivial enough for a stop to be worthwhile. The anchorage is useful when plugging against the prevailing wind on the passage to Erdek Körfezi.

BUYUKADA

40°27'N 27°04'E

A new fishing harbour is reported here. It may be possible to anchor off the beach outside.

ERDEK KORFEZI (Gulf of Erdek)

This large gulf in the SW of the Sea of Marmara lies between Karaburun on the W and Kapidağ peninsula on the E. The Marmara Islands close it off to the N, and the low marshy Asiatic coast forms the southern side.

The winds in the gulf vary considerably. Around the western and southern shores, including Paşalimani Adasi, the winds are light and variable, although most often from the NE and NNE. Under the mountainous Kapidağ peninsula and Marmara Islands, there are strong gusts off the high land and down the ravines when there is only a moderate breeze on the northern and eastern sides. In general the winds are moderate when a fresh breeze is blowing on the northern side of the Sea of Marmara. Any sea the wind raises quickly moderates when the wind dies in the evening.

Prohibited area

Erdek Limani, the large bay under Kapidağ peninsula SE of Tavşan Adasi, is a naval anchorage. Turkish naval craft will frequently be seen entering or leaving the bay and exercises are often carried out in Erdek Körfezi. A yacht should keep out of the bay, and you should refrain from taking photographs.

KARABIGA (Karabuga)

Approach

The harbour lies WSW of Kale Burun.

Conspicuous Colossal sections of the medieval wall on Kale Burun can be seen from a considerable distance off. The light structure on Kale Burun is also conspicuous. Once into the bay, the village, the outer breakwater, and two white light towers on the breakwaters are easily identified.

By night Use the light on Kale Burun (Fl.5s8M). The outer breakwater is lit on its extremity F.G.7m5M. The end of the pier is lit F.R.7m5M.

Mooring

Go stern or bows-to or alongside the west quay or the pier. With strong NE winds go stern or bows-to

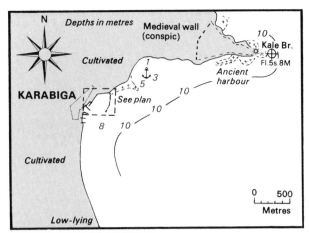

KARABIGA APPROACHES
KALE BURNU 40°24'·6N 27°20'·4E

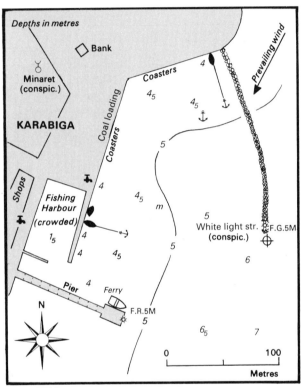

KARABIGA
40°24'·1N 27°18'·6E

in the NE corner of the harbour. The quay is sometimes used for loading coal, in which case it is best to anchor off in the NE of the harbour to avoid getting coal dust all over the boat.

Shelter Good shelter from the prevailing winds. The normal northeasterlies do not blow as frequently or as strongly in this corner of Erdek Körfezi.

Anchorage A yacht can also anchor off in the bay where shown. Anchor in 3–5 metres on sand and mud – good holding.

Facilities

Water A public fountain near the inner basin.
Fuel On the outskirts of the village, but near the harbour.
Repairs Minor mechanical repairs only. A yard hauls small *caïques* in the SE corner of the harbour.
Provisions Most provisions can be found in the

Karabiga: a section of the medieval wall so prominent from seaward

Entrance   *Light tower*   *Breakwater*

Karabiga: approach, looking W

Pier

Karabiga harbour, from the end of the central pier

village. Fish from the local boats is sold at the harbour.
Eating out A simple restaurant and several *köfte* shops.
Other PO. Bank. Bus to Istanbul.

General

Karabiga is a sleepy little village sustained by the surrounding farmland, and by marble. Marble mined inland at Can is loaded onto small coasters and caiques in the harbour. Coal mined at Can is also loaded here which can make it a bit grimy at times around the harbour area although this should not put you off visiting here. The village is little touched by tourism and exudes a delightful rustic atmosphere reminiscent of a small French farming village. I have not been able to track down any references to the massive medieval walls and town on Kale Burun – after all these years I am surprised that no-one has yet written to me with details.

ERDEK

Approach

The harbour lies on the eastern side of Erdek Körfezi, N of Tavşan Adasi and Muratbayiri Burun.

Conspicuous Tavşan Adasi and Muratbayiri Burun (from the distance the latter looks like an island as well) are easily identified. The town on the slopes behind the harbour can be seen from some distance off, and closer in the outer mole of the harbour is easily spotted.

By night Use the light on Tavşan Adasi (Fl.10s8M). The end of the breakwater is reported lit Fl.R.3s3M.

Mooring

Go stern or bows-to the quay or pier where convenient. The bottom is sand – excellent holding.

Shelter Good all-round shelter. The harbour is open to the S, but these winds are reported not to blow home. With strong southerlies a yacht could moor on the quayed section of the mole, which is partially protected from the S by the small islet.

Authorities Harbourmaster. A charge may be made.

Facilities

Water On the quay. A charge is made for it.
Fuel Near the harbour.
Repairs Limited mechanical repairs only.
Provisions Good shopping for all provisions in the town. A small fruit and vegetable market near the bus station. Small fish market at the harbour.
Eating out Excellent restaurants on the waterfront.
Other PO. Banks. Turkish gas. Hardware shops.
Dolmuş to Bandirma, where there are buses to Istanbul and Izmir. Ferry to the Marmara Islands.

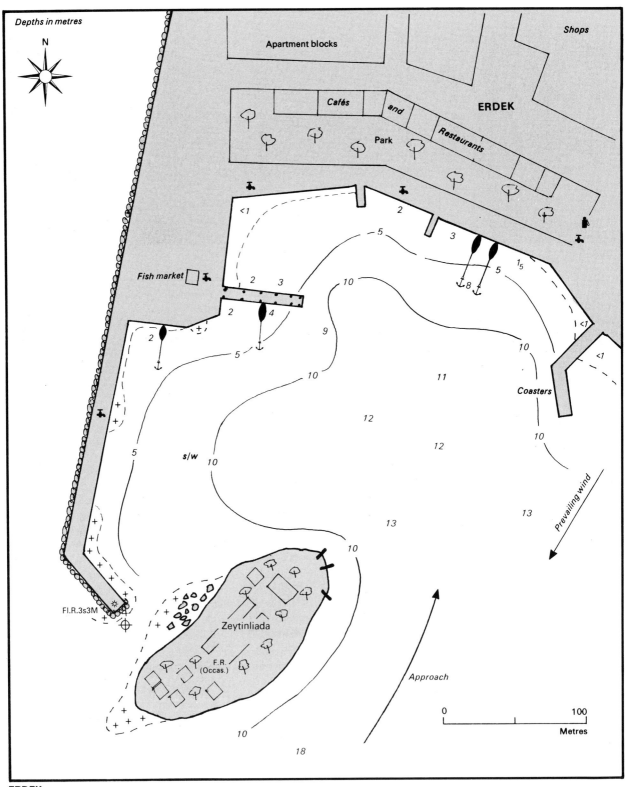

Depths in metres

N

Apartment blocks

Shops

Cafés and Restaurants

ERDEK

Park

<1

2

5

3

Fish market

2   3

1₅

5

2   4

<1

2

<1

5

9

10

Coasters

8

5

11

10

10

12

12

s/w   10

13

13

Prevailing wind

10

Zeytinliada

F.R.
(Occas.)

Fl.R.3s3M

1

Approach

0   100

Metres

10

18

ERDEK
40°23'·2N 27°48'·3E

Zeytinlada

Approach to Erdek looking E

Zeytinlada *Entrance* *Coaster pier*

Erdek harbour looking NNE

Entrance *Zeytinlada* *W mole*

Erdek

General

The setting, under wooded slopes in a sandy corner of the gulf, is exquisite. The town too is pleasing, with cobbled streets, shaded by trees, and a small park around the town quay. Few foreign tourists have discovered Erdek yet, it being largely a resort for those 'in the know' from Istanbul.

Nearby are the ruins of ancient Cyzicas, described by Strabo as one of the most splendid cities in Asia. Little of the ancient city remains to be seen.

Kapidağ peninsula

(Kapidağ Yaramadasi)

The mountainous peninsula forming the eastern side of Erdek Körfezi. The massif rises to a height of 791 metres (2595ft) at the sharp peak of Adamkaya Tepe, and everywhere drops precipitously into the sea. The slopes are extensively wooded and the narrow coastal flats well cultivated. The massif is separated from the comparatively low-lying Paşalimani Adasi by the Narliköy or Rhoda Channel. There are good depths in the fairway. A current of up to 2½ knots is reported to set southwards through the channel, though it is usually substantially less.

Apart from Erdek, which offers the best all-round shelter here, there are several other anchorages on the W side of Kapidağ.

Ocaklar A large bay in the southern approaches to Narliköy Channel. The best anchorage is in the NE corner in 3–5 metres on a sandy bottom. Local boats are kept on moorings in the SE corner of the bay off the small village of Ocaklar. The village and hinterland are most attractive.

Anchorage *Pier*

Narliköy, looking NW

Narliköy A village on the eastern side of the channel between Paşalimani and Kapidağ. Good shelter from the prevailing NE winds. With strong winds from the NE, anchor off the village, where the shelter is better than it looks on the chart. A short pier is used by the ferry and local fishing boats.

Paşalimani Adasi

The amoeba-like island lying close to Kapidağ peninsula, from which it is separated by Narliköy Channel. The island is comparatively low-lying, with gently rolling slopes much cultivated with the vine. There are several attractive anchorages around the island.

1. ***Paşalimani*** The large bay on the NW side of the island, partially protected by Koyun Adasi and Mamaliada. A yacht can enter the bay through the N passage or the W passage. There are good depths in the fairway of the N passage, which is free of dangers. The W passage is obstructed by underwater rocks on either side. The reefs off Koyun Adasi are clearly shown on the Admiralty charts (1004 and 1005), but a reef in the bay shown on these charts as having a minimum depth of 2·7m is in fact a good deal shallower than shown (1·5m and less – I know, I perched *Tetranora* on top of it in calm weather). A yacht should only attempt the W passage in calm weather, with someone up front keeping an eye on things.

   In the bay there are two hamlets: Harmanli on the S side and Paşalimani on the E side. Anchor off Paşalimani in 5–7 metres. The bottom is hard

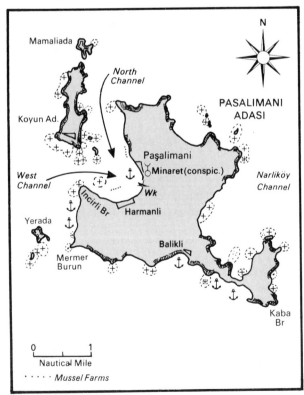

PASALIMANI ADASI
40°29′N 27°37′E

Paşalimani (minaret conspicuous), from the anchorage

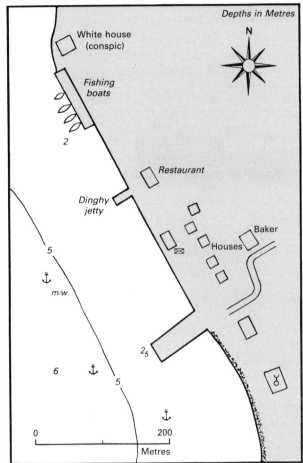

PASALIMANI

sand and weed – good holding once your anchor is in, but you may need to try several times before it digs in. Good shelter from the prevailing winds, which blow ENE off the land. If the wind blows into the bay it is reported there is better shelter about 50m off the mosque in 2·5m depths. There is a pier at Paşalimani, but it is in constant use by local ferries, trading *caïques* loading grapes, and fishing boats. Meagre provisions and a simple restaurant ashore.

Caution There are small mussel farms in the bay. The drums are painted white and easily seen. Their approximate positions are marked on the plan.

2. On the W side of the island between Incirli Burun and Mermer Burun there are several attractive bays useful as 'lunch stops'. They are sufficiently protected from the prevailing winds in settled weather for a yacht to stay overnight.

Harmanli, on Paşalimani, from the anchorage

Paşalimani – the hamlet

3. ***Balikli*** A small hamlet in a picturesque wooded
valley on the S side of the island. There is a short
pier used by the fishing boats and the ferry, but it
is better to anchor off. Anchor in 3–5 metres on a
hard sand bottom. Good protection from the prevailing winds. Meagre provisions and a *çay* shop
in the hamlet.

Balikli, from seaward

4. Three quarters of a mile E of Balikli there is a
small deserted cove close to the sandy isthmus
joining the southeastern part of the island to the
main part. Anchor in 3 metres. Good shelter
from the prevailing winds.

Asmaliada off the E end of Marmara Adasi, looking E

AVSAR ADASI (Turkeli, Araplar Ad)

The rocky and barren island lying close W of
Paşalimani Adasi, from which it is separated by the
Araplar Channel. Above- and below-water rocks
fringe the coast for some distance off, and care
should be taken in case the seabed has altered here
as it has in Paşalimani anchorage.

A yacht can anchor off the village of Turkeli on
the W coast. There may be room alongside a fishing
boat on the pier off the village, but it is more
comfortable to anchor off, as the prevailing wind
sets down onto here. Anchor in 3–6 metres off the
beach to the S of the pier. Ashore there are hotels
and restaurants, and provisions can be found.

A yacht might also find some shelter in
Kumburnu Limani, on the SE coast.

EKLINLIK ADASI

A small flat island lying close off the NW corner of
Avşar Adasi, from which it is separated by a shallow
channel less than a mile wide at the NE end. There
is a reported least depth of 7 metres in the fairway of
the channel. A current sets to the W at up to 1½
knots, causing eddies and counter-currents at the
edges.

Marmara Adasi

The largest island of the group. It is mountainous
and steep-to, with two mountain ridges running
approximately west to east along its length. There
are no clearly defined peaks. The geology of the
island varies remarkably from the north to the south.
The northern half of the island is composed of white
marble, and little but *maquis* grows on this side
except in some of the valleys. The southern half
consists of granite and slate, and the lower slopes are
well cultivated or covered in pine.

Approaching Marmara from the W, the island of
Hayirsizada shows up well; there is a light on the
island (Fl.3s12M). From the E, the small island of
Asmaliada, off the eastern tip of Marmara Island,
will not be seen until close in. A reef extends about
100 metres out from the W side of the islet, but
otherwise the passage between Asmaliada and
Marmara Adasi is clear of dangers. A light is
exhibited on it (Fl(3)15s12M). On the S coast a
detached reef, Laz Kayasi, lying off Topağaç village,
should be given a good offing. There is a reported
least depth of 2·7 metres over it.

When sailing along the northern coast the
numerous scars of the marble quarries show up well.
Marmara Adasi has long been celebrated for its
white marble, which has been quarried from ancient
times, by the Greeks and Romans, by Byzantines
and Ottomans, to the present day. The prize is
flawless white marble unblemished by grey or
haematite brown impurities – ideal marble for a
temple column or a statue, a sarcophagus or an
altar.

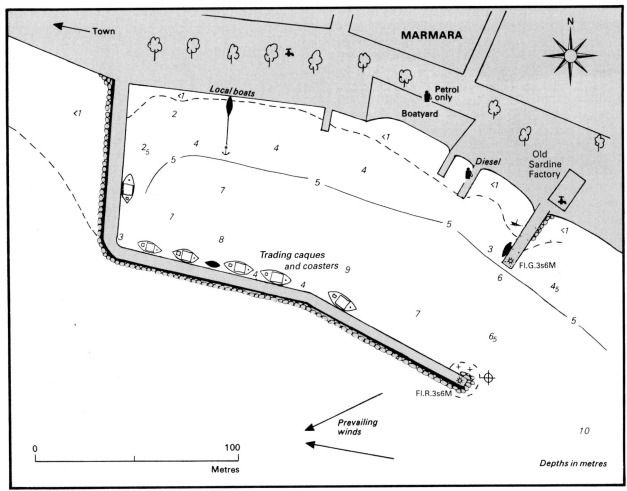

PORT MARMARA
40°35'·1N 27°33'·7E

Approach to Port Marmara, looking NW

Port Marmara, looking E from W quay

Nature has provided Marmara Island not only with an abundance of white marble but also with a natural harbour close by. Saraylar, or Palatia, as it was known not so long ago, has been used since antiquity for shipping the marble from the quarries. Close to the harbour an open air 'museum' exhibits a number of items left behind by Greek, Roman and Byzantine workmen for one reason or another. Most of the sarcophagi, columns, statues, and ornamental slabs have been rejected because a defect showed up in the marble after the craftsmen had begun work. Thus there are roughed-out statues and capitals, and many sarcophagi. A fascinating look in on a craftsman's skill of long ago, interrupted by the intractable nature of the material he worked in.

If you wish to visit the quarries up in the mountains a lift can often be arranged with one of the locals. One local, Adnan Ozturk, has taken it upon himself to befriend visiting yachtsmen, and if he has time he may drive you up to the quarries. Only four-wheel-drive vehicles can get up the rough tracks. The drive is spectacular and not for the fainthearted.

PORT MARMARA

Approach

The harbour lies in the SW corner of the island.

Conspicuous The village on the slopes above the harbour is easily identified. The light structure on Aba Burun and a small fort above the village are conspicuous. The harbour lies at the eastern end of the village, and the outer mole and a white light tower on its extremity are easily identified.

By night Use the light on Aba Burun (Fl(2)10s5M) and, closer in, the lights at the harbour entrance (Fl.R.3s6M/Fl.G.3s3M).

Mooring

The harbour is crammed full of large trading *caïques*. A yacht must make the best of it and berth wherever it can. There may be a space between the *caïques*, or a space amongst the fishing boats on the N quay. Care must be taken on the N quay as rubble extends underwater in places. You can often berth alongside the pier at the entrance, taking care of the wreck on the inner half.

Shelter Good all-round shelter.

Facilities

Water In short supply. From a tap in the trees on the N side of the harbour, or from a public fountain in the village, some distance away.
Fuel On the quay.
Provisions Most provisions can be found in the village.
Eating out Numerous restaurants along the waterfront. *Midya tava*, fried mussels, are recommended here.
Other PO. Bank. Ferry to Erdek.

General

The village and wooded valley nestle under the stark rocky slopes of the mountains behind. The village is a small but growing tourist resort, although few foreign tourists have discovered it yet.

The large trading *caïques* and coasters load marble, grapes, sand, whatever must be carried to or from small out-of-the-way harbours in the Marmara Islands. These sickle-shaped craft, called *mavni* in this area, voyage around the Sea of Marmara, the Black Sea, and the Aegean, with one or at most two charts and a compass – no log, radio, radar or other 'sophisticated' aids. One compass I looked at was held in place with two hefty iron nails, and the captain still managed to get safely from one harbour to another.

Recent visitors to the port have reported that the *mavni* are gradually being replaced by small coasters and that there are fewer working *mavni* around.

GUNDOGDU

A village about 2 miles E of Port Marmara. The local trading *caïques* often anchor off here. In the easternmost corner of the bay the shelter is better than it looks on the chart. There are gusts into the bay off the high land.

TOPAGAC

A hamlet about 4 miles ENE of Gundoğdu. If approaching from the E, the hamlets of Topağaç and Asmaliköy are easily confused from the distance, since the two look alike (with conspicuous white minarets) from seaward. Care must be taken of Laz Kayasi, lying about one mile SE of the hamlet.

A yacht can go alongside the quay in the village or anchor off. A small ferry sometimes uses the quay and the locals will let you know if it is due. The bottom slopes gently to the shore and is good holding, on sand. There are gusts off the land, but

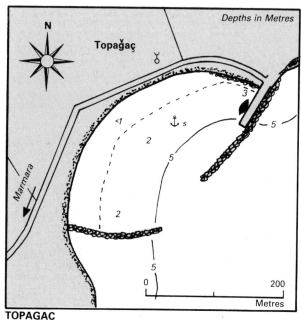

TOPAGAC
40°36'·1N 27°40'E

they are not as frequent or as hard as at other places along the coast.

Some provisions and a restaurant ashore. The beach and wooded coastal flat behind are idyllic.

ASMALIKOY

Approach

The harbour lies at the SE end of Marmara Adasi.

Conspicuous The hamlet of Asmaliköy looks much like the hamlet of Topağaç, 2 miles W of Asmaliköy. Both have conspicuous white minarets. At Asmaliköy the breakwater and some old wooden houses on the waterfront will be seen when closer in. *By night* A F.G.5m3M is exhibited on the extremity of the mole although its range appears to be less. There are street lights along its length. Exercise some caution at night.

Mooring

Go stern or bows-to or alongside the concrete wharf built out from the breakwater. The bottom is sand, rock and weed. A number of fishing boats use the wharf. You may have to move off to make room for them and then berth alongside one of the fishing boats.

Shelter Good shelter from the prevailing winds. The harbour is open W-SW, but this wind is rare in the summer. A few *caïques* winter afloat in the eastern end of the harbour.

Authorities The harbour is administered by the Forestry Authority and a charge may be made. Charge band 2.

Facilities

There is little to be had. Water on the quay or from the mosque. Meagre provisions and a café/restaurant with limited fare. PO.

General

Apart from two villas built on the slopes near the hamlet, there is little to suggest that the outside world has touched life here. The hamlet crouches on a narrow coastal flat under fantastic juts and crags above and behind. The setting is almost eerie in this

Minaret   Entrance   Breakwater

Approach to Asmaliköy, looking N

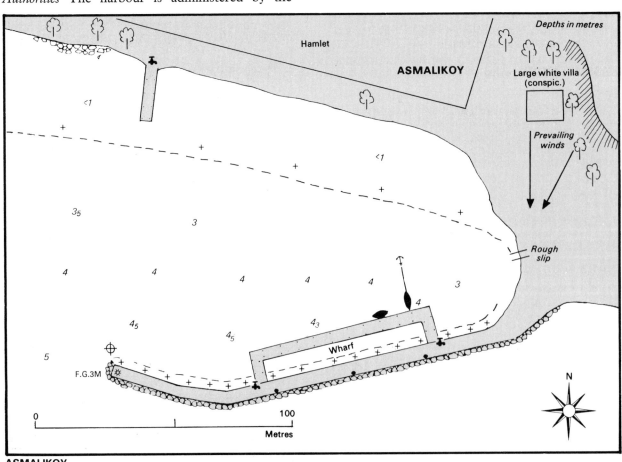

ASMALIKOY
40°37'N 27°42'·4E

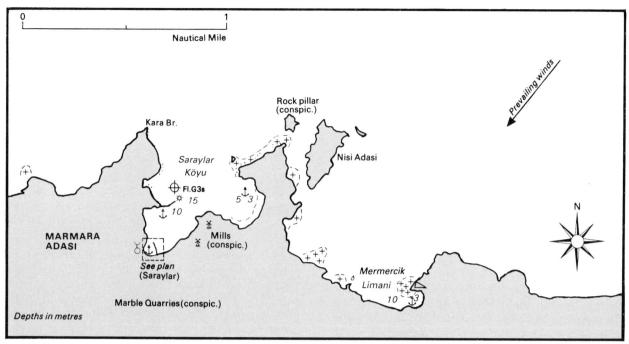

SARAYLAR AND MERMERCIK
40°39'·5N 27°39'·7E

isolated and angry landscape, which is suggestive of
J R R Tolkien's imaginary landscape in his trilogy
The Lord of the Rings.

MERMERCIK LIMANI

A cove in the large bay immediately E of Saraylar.
Care needs to be taken of the reef running out from
the coast immediately N of the cove. Anchor in the
cove in 2–3 metres and take a line ashore to the N
side if necessary. No facilities.

SARAYLAR (Palatia)

Approach

The marble quarries scarring the mountain sides
can be seen from a considerable distance off.

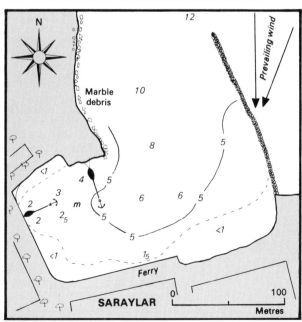

SARAYLAR
40°39'N 27°40'E

Conspicuous rock pillar

Approach to Saraylar, looking W

Conspicuous The end of Kaloeradi, the rocky islet in
the bay, has been eroded to a distinctive rock pillar.
Closer in, the long mole for loading marble and the
light structure at its extremity are conspicuous.

By night Use the light on Domuz Burnu (Fl.10s9M)
and, closer in, the light on the extremity of the mole
(Fl.G.3s.4M). The inner harbour is not lit.

Dangers There are numerous above and below-water
rocks in the approaches (see plan).

Marble mole

Saraylar, looking N from the marble quarries

55

Fishing harbour   Marble mole

Saraylar harbour, looking NNE

Mooring

Large yachts will have to moor alongside the marble-loading mole or anchor in the bay. The former is unpleasant on account of the dust and noise. Small to medium-sized yachts can go bows-to the W quay in the inner harbour. Care must be taken of the depths close in, as the bottom is uneven. The bottom is mud and good holding.

Shelter Good shelter.

Facilities

Water Limited. From private sources in the village.
Fuel From 44-gallon drums. Not always available.
Provisions Some provisions can be found in the village.
Eating out Several restaurants and cafés on the waterfront.
Other PO.

General

Saraylar, once called Palatia when it was Greek in the 19th century, and earlier still the Palatia of the ancient Greeks, exists for marble. It possesses probably the only rough stone breakwater constructed entirely of marble in the Mediterranean.

The village cannot be said to be attractive, being a huddle of mean dwellings cut by dusty tracks. Large trucks and four wheel-drive jeeps lurch about the village and on down to the loading mole, leaving dust clouds and the din of revving diesels behind them. The village is only partially redeemed by a verdigris-green domed mosque and some fine old wooden houses back from the harbour, and by the friendliness of the locals.

You can escape from the noise and dust by anchoring in the cove on the E side of the bay.

Nisis Adasi and rock pillar, looking E

CINARLI

A village on the W coast. A minaret is conspicuous in the village. In calm weather a yacht can anchor off the village in 3–4 metres. With the prevailing northeasterlies there are gusts into the bay, and with strong winds from this direction a swell sets into the bay. The village and hinterland are most attractive.

The N and E coasts of Kapidağ

ILHANKOY

Approach

A small fishing harbour approximately 3 miles N of Narliköy. The white light structure (F.R) on the end of the breakwater is conspicuous. Care must be taken of above and below-water rocks off the coast. The reef off Ilhanköy Burnu, SW of the harbour, should be given a wide berth, and so should Marti Kayasi, a reef extending nearly 300 metres off the point ¾ mile NE of the harbour.

Mooring

Go alongside the W quay or stern or bows-to the N quay. Good all-round shelter.

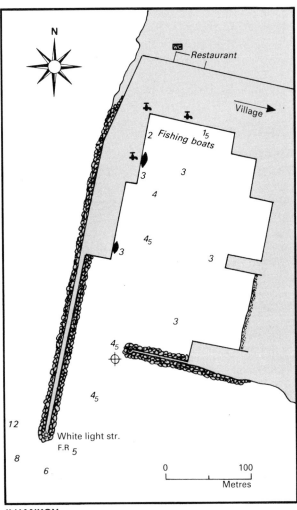

ILHANKOY
40°30'·4N 27°41'·6E

Above Istanbul ferries. *Opposite* Simit - sesame-covered bread rings.
Below The Bosphorus looking out from Bebek. *See page 68.*
Bottom The Bosphorus at Istanbul

Above Asmaliköy looking from the root of the breakwater towards the hamlet. *See page 54. Below Mavnas* in Port Marmara in the Sea of Marmara. *See page 53. Bottom* 'Vege' stall. Candarli. *Opposite* Ayvalik. *See page 86.*

Kuşadasi looking W. *See page 125.*

Dip Burnu anchorage looking ESE. *See page 129.*

Port St Nikolao looking N. *See page 129.*

Port St Paul looking NE over Cil Adasi. *See page 129.*

Altinkum looking NE. *See page 132.*

Above Gökada looking N towards Kuruerik and Talinaki.
Below Kazikli Limani looking NNE over Paradise Bay and Kazikli
Iskelesi. *See page 134.*

Facilities
Water on the quay (recently reported unreliable). Limited provisions. Restaurant and *çay* houses.

General
The fishing harbour and the village are situated in attractive surroundings under wooded slopes. Add to this a safe harbour and friendly locals – the place is a gem.

DOGANLAR (Obus, Drakontas)
A large bay close westwards of Doğanlar Burnu. Anchor in the SE corner off the hamlet, where there is some protection from NE winds. With strong winds from the NE a swell rolls into the bay. The bottom is sand and good holding.

Water in the village. The water on the quay is reported unpotable. The valley and the hamlet are most attractive and well worth a stop in calm weather.

TURAN KOY (Gundogurusu Limani)
The large bay about 2 miles E of Doğanlar. Anchor in 4–5 metres off the E end of the beach, taking care of the reef in the SW corner. With the prevailing NE wind the anchorage can become untenable.

ORMANLI
A large bay 2 miles E of Turan. Suitable in calm weather.

CAYAGZI
A small fishing harbour some 6½ miles E of Ormanli. There are 4·5-metre depths in the entrance and 2–3 metre depths on the N side. The harbour is invariably full of fishing boats, and the only thing to do is to go alongside or bows-to the stern of a fishing boat. However, this may mean that you will have to move if boats on the inside want to get out. Care must also be taken of floating lines from laid moorings. Good shelter from the prevailing NE wind.

Fuel and water nearby. Meagre provisions, a restaurant and *çay* houses.

CAKILKOY
A small fishing harbour ¾ mile SSW of Kapsül Burnu, the NE extremity of Kapidağ. There are 4–5 metre depths in the entrance and 3–4 metres under the E breakwater. Like Cayağzi, the harbour is crowded with fishing boats, and you will have to go alongside or bows-to the stern of a fishing boat. Good shelter from the prevailing NE wind.

Water on the pier in the harbour. Basic provisions and a simple restaurant.

Recent reports indicate the harbour is being enlarged.

KARSIYAKA
A small fishing harbour off the village 2 miles SW of Cakilköy. The harbour is mostly shallow, and the best policy is to anchor off the village W of the harbour. Mediocre shelter. It is reported that the harbour has been extended and dredged and now affords good shelter.

Water and fuel ashore. Supermarkets and good shopping. Restaurants.

KUM LIMANI
A large open bay 2 miles SW of Karşiyaka. Anchor off the two-headed bay where convenient. Mediocre shelter only.

TATLISU
A large open bay 2 miles SW of Kum Limani. Anchor off where convenient. The small harbour on the W side is shallow and unsuitable for yachts.

Bandirma Körfezi
(Gulf of Bandirma)
The small enclosed gulf running approximately NE to SW between the E side of Kapidağ peninsula and the Asiatic coast. Mola Adalari, a group of three islands, lies at the entrance to the gulf. The islands are fringed by above and below-water rocks and a detached reef (Mola Bankasi), just awash, about ¾ of a mile SE of Haliada.

The large commercial harbour of Bandirma lies at the head of the gulf on the S side, and here there is all-round shelter.

BANDIRMA
BA 1006

Approach
Conspicuous A large cement factory and a sulphuric acid factory to the W of the city are conspicuous. Closer in, the harbour breakwaters are easily identified.

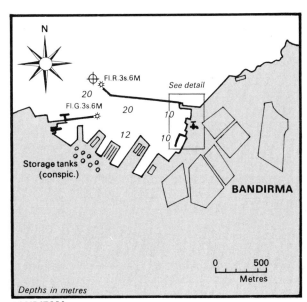

BANDIRMA
40°21'·6N 27°57'·6E

Inner basin Entrance   *Outer breakwater*

Bandirma harbour looking NW

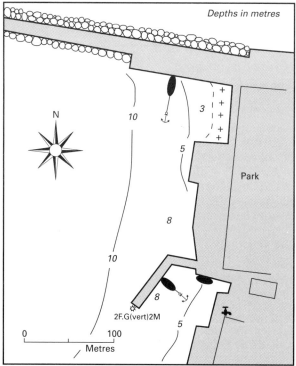

BANDIRMA DETAIL

By night The harbour entrance is lit: Fl.G.3s6M and Fl.R.3s6M. S mole 2F.G(vert)2M

Mooring

Go alongside in the basin on the E side, or stern or bows-to the N quay in the NE corner of the harbour.

Shelter Good all-round shelter.

Authorities A port of entry, hence a full complement of authorities.

Facilities

Water Close to the quay.
Fuel In the town.
Provisions Good shopping for all provisions.
Eating out Restaurants in the town.
Other PO. Banks. Hospital. Turkish gas. Hardware shops. Buses to Istanbul and Izmir.

General

Bandirma is a commercial port that resounds to the clattering and hammering of cranes and trucks all day long and most of the night. There is little to see to justify a special trip here, but it is a useful 'big town' harbour for the facilities to be found. The park near the waterfront, with restaurants and *çay* houses, is as pleasant a place as anywhere to be.

KURSUNLU

A small harbour approximately 15 miles E of Bandirma. The entrance to the harbour has largely silted, with just 1–1·2 metre depths in the entrance. Inside depths are slightly more. Anchor in the middle. The village of Kurşunlu is nearby.

IMRALI ADASI (Kalolimno)

An island lying about 10 miles W of Boz Burun in the approaches to Gemlik Körfezi. The island is a penal colony, and approaching close to it, anchoring, or landing on it is prohibited.

Off the southern tip of the island a reef (Sigburun Resifi or Lena Reef) extends SSW for about 2 miles. There are numerous patches with less than 2 metres of water over them, and consequently it should be given a wide berth. The current hitting the reef creates overfalls which make identification of the reef easy by day. The depths increase abruptly at the extremity of the reef.

Note Local magnetic anomalies have been reported in the vicinity of the island, particularly in the channel S of it.

Gemlik Körfezi
(Indjir Limani, Gulf of Gemlik, Gulf of Mudanya)

The gulf in the SE of the Sea of Marmara enclosed by Boz Burun peninsula and the Asiatic coast. The land about it is mountainous and drops sheer into the sea. Much of it is heavily wooded, but some of the slopes are bare or thinly covered in *maquis*. There are several places where a yacht can find shelter.

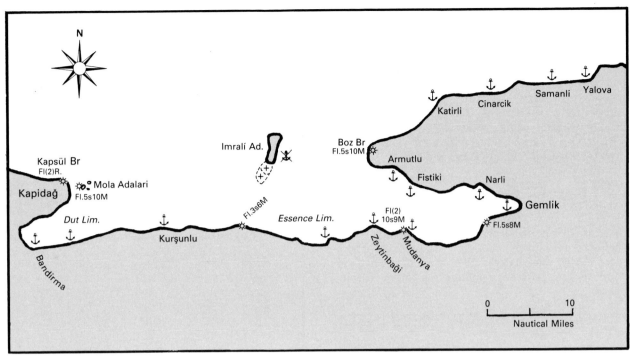

KAPIDAG TO YALOVA

Anchorages in Gemlik Körfezi

ZEYTINBAGI LIMANI

Approach

A harbour situated just inside the southern entrance point to Gemlik Körfezi. The town just W of the harbour is easily identified. The white light tower (unlit) on the extremity of the breakwater will be seen closer in.

Mooring

In calm weather go alongside in the SW corner. The shelter in here is not as good as it looks and easterlies cause a considerable surge. The best policy in this event is to anchor off under the breakwater.

Facilities

Water on the quay. Fuel in the town. Provisions, with a market on Thursdays. Restaurants. PO. Bank. Bus to Bursa.

General

The old town is interesting and worth a visit despite the uncomfortable harbour.

MUDANYA (Mudania) 40°22'·6N 28°53'·5E
BA 1006

An open anchorage suitable only in calm weather. The pier is mostly used by cargo boats and local fishing boats, though you can squeeze in with the fishing boats on a calm day. The town has all amenities, with good shopping for provisions, restaurants, PO and banks.

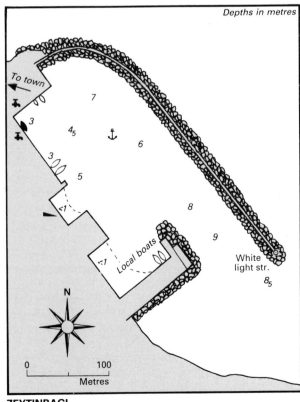

ZEYTINBAGI
40°23'·8N 28°48'·2E

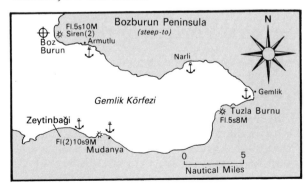

GEMLIK KORFEZI
Boz Burun light 40°32'N 28°47'·1E

GEMLIK 40°26'N 29°09'·1E

Lies at the head of the gulf. The pier is used by cargo boats, but there is usually plenty of room to go alongside. This is complicated by the fact that the pier is very high, but there are several landing stages where you may be able to go alongside. Alternatively, anchor off. The prevailing wind is usually light here, but a residual swell is pushed in. The town has all amenities, with good shopping for provisions, restaurants, PO and banks.

NARLI

A small fishing harbour on the N side of the gulf. Go alongside the S quay in the small harbour, where there are 3–6 metre depths for the most part. Good shelter. Alternatively, anchor off the village, where there is also reasonable shelter from the prevailing wind. Some provisions and a restaurant in the village.

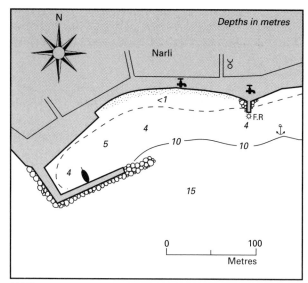

NARLI
40°28'·9N 29°02'·1E

ARMUTLU

An open anchorage off the village of Armutlu. Anchor in 5–10 metres or go alongside the pier. Reasonable shelter from the prevailing wind. Ashore some provisions and several restaurants can be found.

Gemlik Körfezi to the Princes Islands

KATIRLI (Esenköy)

Approach

A small harbour lying approximately 10 miles NE of Boz Burun. Care needs to be taken of an above-water rock approximately 0·2 of a mile S of the entrance.

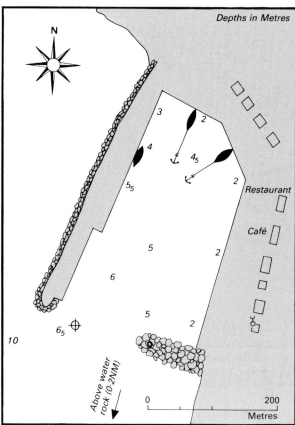

KATIRLI
40°37'·3N 28°57'·1E

Mooring

Go alongside the N quay or stern or bows-to the NE quay at the head of the harbour. Care needs to be taken of floating mooring lines. The bottom is mud and weed, good holding. Good shelter from the prevailing wind.

Facilities

Water on the quay. Most provisions can be found. Restaurants and *çay* houses. PO.

General

The area seems to be developing into a small resort, and there has been a fair amount of building going on in recent years.

CINARCIK

A fairly large harbour approximately 6 miles E of Katirli. The end of the breakwater is lit: F.G.3M. The S side of the harbour is shallow, but there are good depths under the breakwater. Go stern or bows-to the quay where shown. Reasonable shelter from the prevailing NE wind.

Water on the quay. Fuel in the town. Good shopping for provisions. Restaurants. PO. Banks. Fast catamaran ferry to Istanbul. A charge is made for berthing and water.

Immediately N of the harbour it is possible to anchor under Deveboynu Burun, where there is some shelter from the prevailing wind. Anchor in 3–5 metres under the headland. The holding is reported to be bad.

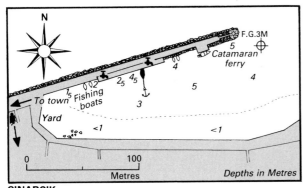

CINARCIK
40°39'·1N 29°07'·8E

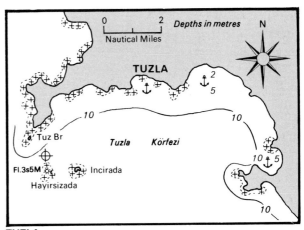

TUZLA
Hayirsizada light 40°47'·5N 29°15'·8E

SAMANLI

A small fishing harbour approximately 7 miles E of Cinarcik. There are reported to be 2–4 metre depths for the most part.

YALOVA

A commercial harbour, and not really a place for yachts. It is possible to go stern or bows-to on the E side of the harbour, but it may be difficult to get out of or back into the enclosed and locked customs area.

Izmit Körfezi

(Gulf of Ismit)

Much of this gulf is used by the Turkish navy and yachts should exercise caution when in the vicinity of naval installations. A large part of the gulf is also taken up by industrial estates so there is little point for a yacht to enter the gulf apart from Atabay Boatyard mentioned below. It is not certain whether the old regulations concerning entry and navigation to the gulf still obtain, but in any event a yacht should proceed with caution and obey any signals from the shore. On no account should photographs be taken in the gulf.

ATABAY BOATYARD

40°46'·27N 29°26'·4E
At Gebze. This boatyard has been recommended as giving good service and providing good repair facilities. It is much used by the racing fraternity from Istanbul. 20 ton travel hoist. Hard standing. Most yacht repairs can be made.

Contact Atabay Turizm ☎ (262) 655 5854
Fax (262) 655 5616

Tuzla Körfezi

A yacht can find good shelter from the prevailing wind in Tuzla Körfezi. The eastern side of the large bay is mostly taken up with factories and related service industries, so it is best to anchor off Tuzla town on the N side of the bay. Anchor in 3–8 metres off the town on mud and weed.

Good shopping for provisions, and restaurants, in Tuzla town. Buses to Istanbul.

AYDINLI

A large harbour on the N side of Tuzla Burnu. With the prevailing N–NE winds off the land the best place to be is not in the harbour, but anchored off the beach N of the harbour. With southerlies the harbour affords good shelter. A yard in the harbour.

PENDIK

The large bay 2 miles NE of Aydinli. On the S side of the bay there is a commercial harbour, but a yacht is better off heading for the N of the bay and anchoring off Pendik town. Anchor in 6–8 metres off the town. Good shelter from the prevailing wind.

Good shopping for provisions, and restaurants, in Pendik. Buses to Istanbul.

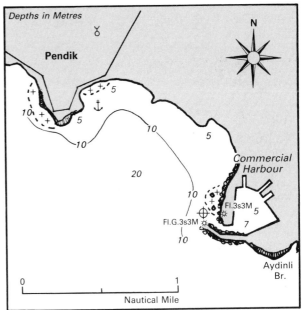

PENDIK
40°51'·6N 29°15'·2E

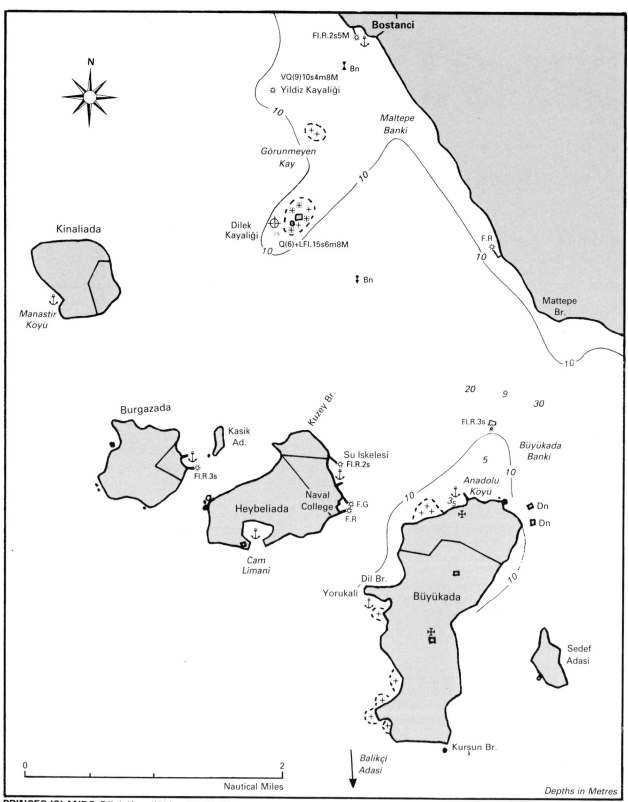

PRINCES ISLANDS Dilek Kayaliği bn 40°54'·9N 29°05'·4E

Princes Islands
(Prenses Adalari, Kizil Adalar)

An archipelago of four major islands and several smaller ones, lying 2 to 3 miles off the Asiatic coast in the eastern approaches to the Bosphorus. The islands are a popular weekend spot for Stamboulites looking for a breath of fresh air. The larger islands are wooded with dwarf pine, and there are numerous delightful old Levantine villas on Büyükada and Heybeliada. Cars are prohibited.

Note In the summer the islands are popular with local yachts from Istanbul, and at weekends the anchorages can be very crowded. Small bunker tankers are moored in several of the bays and do a roaring trade at weekends.

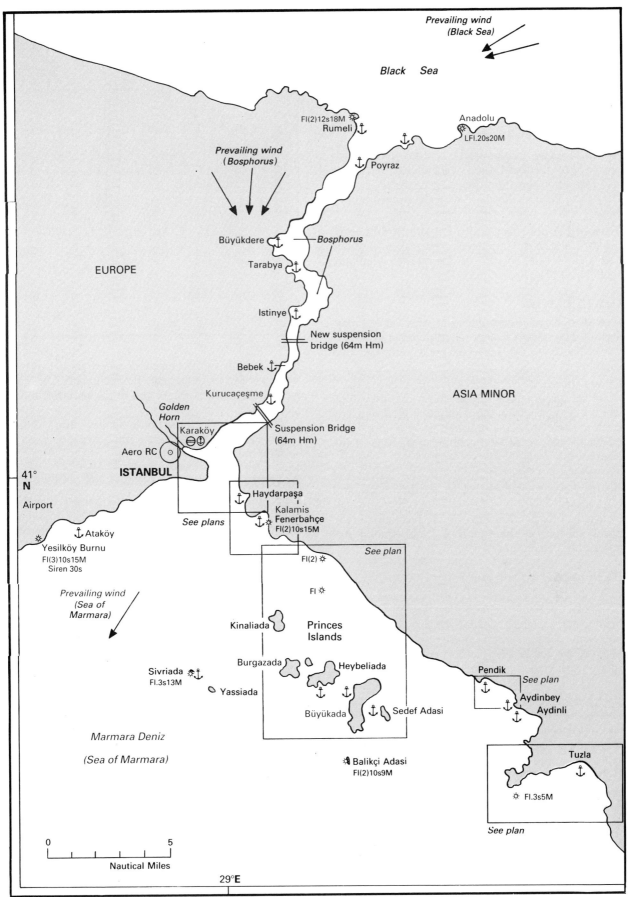

Prevailing wind
(Black Sea)

Black Sea

Fl(2)12s18M
Rumeli

Anadolu
LFl.20s20M

Poyraz

Prevailing wind
(*Bosphorus*)

Büyükdere

Bosphorus

EUROPE

Tarabya

Istinye

New suspension
bridge (64m Hm)

Bebek

Kurucaçeşme

Golden
Horn

Karaköy

Suspension Bridge
(64m Hm)

ASIA MINOR

Aero RC

ISTANBUL

41°
N

Airport

See plans

Haydarpaşa

Kalamis
Fenerbahçe
Fl(2)10s15M

Ataköy
Yesilköy Burnu
Fl(3)10s15M
Siren 30s

Fl(2)

See plan

Fl

Prevailing wind
(Sea of
Marmara)

Kinaliada

Princes
Islands

Burgazada

Heybeliada

Pendik
See plan

Sivriada
Fl.3s13M

Yassiada

Aydinbey
Aydinli

Büyükada

Sedef Adasi

Marmara Deniz

(Sea of Marmara)

Tuzla

Balikçi Adasi
Fl(2)10s9M

Fl.3s5M

See plan

0   5

Nautical Miles

29°E

PRINCES ISLANDS AND THE BOSPHORUS
Sivriada light 40°52'·6N 28°58'·2E

BUYUKADA (Prinkipo)

The largest of the group, it has a permanent population and numerous hotels and restaurants. Shoal water extends for ½ a mile to the N of the island, with a N cardinal buoy (lit: Fl.R.3s) marking the extremity of the shoal water. Care must also be taken of two dolphins off the NE side of the island. There are no good anchorages, but in settled weather there are two possibilities:

Anadolu Köyu Anchor off the NW side of the town on the N of the island. Care needs to be taken of the reef extending out from the coast to the SW of the ferry pier. Poor shelter here with the prevailing NE wind.

Yorukali A cove just under Dil Burnu on the W side of the island. Care needs to be taken of above and below-water rocks off the coast. Mediocre shelter.

HEYBELIADA

Lies close W of Büyükada, from which it is separated by Heybeliada Kanali (good depths in the fairway). There are two places where a yacht can find shelter:

Cam Limani 40°52'·2N 29°04'·97E A bay on the S coast affording good shelter from the prevailing wind. Open only from the S although if there is any swell outside it seems to work its way into here. Clean enough to swim! Facilities in the NE of the island.

Su Iskelesi A small harbour on the NE of the island. Poor shelter but close to the shops and restaurants.

Just S of Su Iskelesi there is the harbour for the naval college on the shore. A yacht should not attempt to berth here.

BURGAZADA (Antigone)

Lies close W of Heybeliada. On the E side a short breakwater protects the ferry pier. Anchor under the breakwater, leaving room for the ferry to manoeuvre. Some facilities ashore. Between Burgazada and Heybeliada lies Kaşik (Pide) Adasi, a small rocky islet.

KINALIADA (Proti)

Lies about one mile N of Burgazadasi. On the SW end of the island it is possible to anchor in Manistir Köyu. Poor shelter.

BALIKCI ADASI

A small island lying about one mile S of Büyükada. A light is exhibited on it: Fl(2)10s9M.

SIVRIADA (Oxia) and YASSIADA (Plati)

Two small islands lying about 3 miles W of the main group. The two islands are easily identified and are useful marks in the approaches to Istanbul. A light is exhibited on Sivriada: Fl.3s13M.

On the E side of the island there is a small harbour that can be used by small to medium sized yachts.

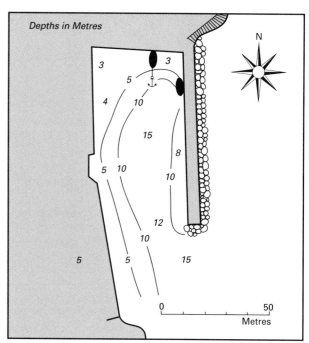

SIVRIADA

Care is needed at the entrance where there can be a considerable cross-current. Berth alongside or stern or bow-to towards the N end of the harbour. Good protection.

There are no facilities and no water ashore. There is however wonderful peace and quiet after the din of Istanbul.

MALTEPE BANKI

Opposite Kinaliada, shoal water (peppered with a number of reefs) extends out from the mainland coast for 1½ miles. The extremity of the shoal water is marked by two beacons: Dilek (lit: Q(6)+LFl.15s8M ‡ topmark) and Yildiz (lit: VQ(9)10s8M ‡ topmark). Although it is possible to pass inside the beacons, the prudent course is to keep to seawards.

Istanbul

Approaches to Istanbul

From the W, following the northern shore of the Sea of Marmara, a large hangar and the airport control tower near Yesilköy are easily identified. In the roadstead off Ahirkapi Burnu there are always a large number of ships at anchor. From the SW the islands of Sivriada and Yassiada are easily identified. Closer in, the skyline of old Stamboul is one of a kind: the Sultan Ahmet Mosque (the Blue Mosque), Ayasofya Museum (Hagia Sofia), and the Topkapi Palace (the Old Seraglio) are all easily identified. The wreck of the supertanker that was formerly so conspicuous in the southern approaches to the Bosphorus has largely been cleared. The wreck is marked by yellow conical buoys (W and E cardinal marks) at either end. On the Asiatic side the hospital buildings and Haydarpaşa railway station are easily identified.

Caution Ferries are constantly crossing the Bosphorus between Haydarpaşa and the Golden Horn. Yachts should keep an eye on them and be prepared to give way at all times. They have one speed only: full ahead.

Harbours and anchorages close to Istanbul

ATAKOY MARINA

This new marina with an associated hotel complex ashore has recently been completed on the northern shores of the Sea of Marmara, approximately 6 miles W of the entrance to the Bosphorus.

Approach

The marina is situated just to the E of Yesilköy Burnu and Istanbul International Airport. From the W the planes landing at the airport provide the best clue to the general whereabouts of the marina. The buildings and control tower at the airport are conspicuous and closer in the marina breakwater and shopping complex will be seen. To the W of the marina the tall Holiday Inn hotel is conspicuous. From the W the entrance cannot be seen until you are right up to it. From the E the marina and its entrance are easily identified.

By night Use the light at the airport (Aero AlFl.WG. 10M) and the light on Yesilköy (Fl.10s15M). The harbour entrance is lit: F.G/F.R and F.R.

VHF The port office listens out on Ch 73 (call sign *Ataköy Marina*).

Mooring

Data 700 berths. Visitors berths. Max LOA 70m (sic.). Depths 4·5–7·5m.

Berth Where directed. There are short finger pontoons which you tie alongside. Large yachts go stern-to on the outer wall.

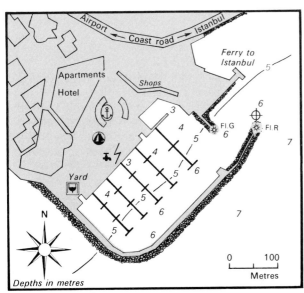

ATAKOY MARINA
40°58'·3N 28°53'E

Shelter Good all-round shelter.

Authorities Harbourmaster and marina staff. Charge band 2/3. Long-term stays are negotiable and good winter rates can be obtained. Any formalities must be carried out at Karaköy.

Facilities

Services Water and electricity (220V) at or near every berth. Telephone connections possible. A small shower and toilet block in the marina.

Fuel On the quay.

Repairs A yard in the marina with a 50-ton travel-lift. Covered workshop area. Chandler in the marina.

Provisions Provisions and ice at the marina. Good market about 10 minutes' walk away or take a taxi to the *Migros* supermarket.

Eating out Restaurant and snack bars in the marina complex.

Other Turkish gas and *Camping Gaz* can be ordered. Laundry service. Hire cars. Train, buses, *dolmuş* and taxis to Istanbul. Ferry service to Istanbul. Internal and international flights from Istanbul Airport nearby.

General

The marina is now up and running, with fashionable boutiques in the marina complex and a 'Yacht Club' complete with bar and swimming pool. Unfortunately the marina is fairly noisy at night with loud music from the bars and some crews have been driven away by the din. The marina has an unfortunate architectural fault in that the entrance faces NE and the prevailing current running along the coast carries any flotsam and jetsam right into it. The marina staff do their best to keep it clean, but there is still a significant amount of rubbish floating around in it. The management is working on a solution to the problem and recent reports indicate that things are getting better.

Situated close to the airport, the marina is handy for crew changes or to leave the boat for a while should you need to return home. It is about 20 minutes into Istanbul along the coast road and about 15 minutes by ferry, so it is reasonably handy for the attractions and sights in Istanbul proper.

Ataköy Marina ☎ (212) 560 4270 *Fax* (212) 560 7270.

KUMKAPI

A small fishing harbour tucked under the W side of the entrance to the Bosphorus. It is usually packed with fishing boats, but you may be able to find a berth alongside under the breakwater. Shelter is adequate from the prevailing NE wind, but there is a lot of wash inside from the ferries and other boats churning up and down and across the Bosphorus.

Water nearby. Good shopping for provisions, and restaurants nearby. And of course you are not too far away from old Stamboul.

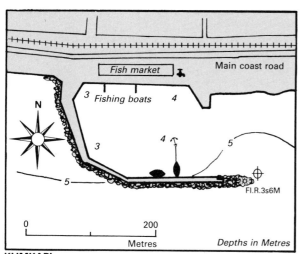

KUMKAPI
41°00'·1N 28°58'E

KALAMIS MARINA
(Kalamis ve Fenerbahçe Marmara Turizm)

A new marina in the NE corner of Kalamis Köyu.

Approach

Once into Kalamis Köyu the breakwaters of the marina and the light towers at the entrance are easily identified. The breakwater sheltering the new harbour of the Fenerbahçe Yacht Club will also be seen immediately S of the marina.

By night The entrance is lit: Fl(2)G.10s3M and Fl(2)R.10s3M. The entrance to Fenerbahçe marina is also to be lit.

VHF Ch 16.

Mooring

Data 540 berths. Limited visitors berths. Max LOA 22m. Depths 2–5m.

Berths Stern or bows-to where directed or where convenient and report to the marina office. Laid moorings with lines tailed to the quay.

Shelter Good all-round shelter. The marina is rapidly filling up with yachts permanently based in Istanbul.

Authorities Harbourmaster and marina staff. Charge band 2/3. A number of yachts have been asked to take the yacht's papers to the authorities at Karaköy.

Facilities

Services Water and electricity (220V) at or near all berths. Shower and toilet block in the marina. The water is reported to be turned off at times. The showers and toilets are not always the cleanest.

Fuel Can be delivered by mini-tanker to the marina.

Repairs There is an area for hard standing, and workshop space. A mobile crane can haul yachts out and a travel hoist is planned in the near future. Most mechanical and engineering work can be carried out in the marina or nearby. Some GRP and wood repairs can be made. Several chandlers in the marina or nearby, and most engine spares can be ordered.

Provisions Good shopping for provisions nearby. At

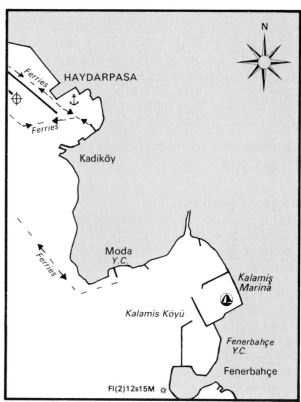

HAYDARPASA TO FENERBAHCE
Haydarşa 40°59'·8N 29°00'·6E

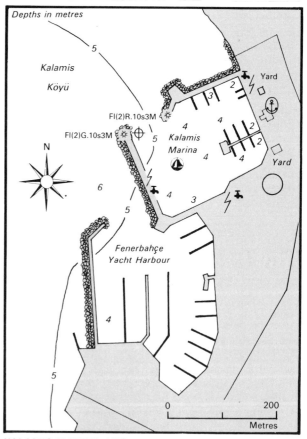

KALAMIS MARINA AND
FENERBAHCE YACHT HARBOUR   40°58'·3N 29°02'·1E

Kadiköy there is an excellent market, one of my favourites in Istanbul, where you can buy just about everything including fresh fish, shellfish, dried fruits and nuts, herbs and spices and, of course, fruit and vegetables. Wander around it just for the sheer delight of looking, smelling and tasting.

Eating out Several restaurants nearby and more in Kadiköy. Get a taxi or *dolmuş* to Kadiköy and a ferry across to Istanbul, where you will be spoilt for choice.

Other PO and banks in Kadiköy. Turkish gas and *Camping Gaz* can be ordered. Taxis and *dolmuş* to Kadiköy.

General

The marina is the nearest safe place to Istanbul itself. Unfortunately the late night amplification of music takes away some of its charms for some visitors.

The shortest route to old Stamboul is to take a taxi or *dolmuş* to Kadiköy and get one of the delightfully old-fashioned ferries across to Galata from there. To take a taxi all the way means a long and perilous trip through the congested streets of the Asiatic side to the suspension bridge, and then through the even more congested streets of the European side.

The suburb of Fenerbahçe, nearby, is known more for its football team, always near the top of the Turkish league, than for things to see and do in the vicinity, but there are some pleasant and interesting walks around some of the old streets if you just want to get the feel of suburban life on the Asian side.

Admiral Fahri Koruturk Marinasi ☎ (216) 346 2346/ 346 1477 *Fax* (216) 346 1656.

FENERBAHCE YACHT CLUB

Adjacent to Kalamis Marina is the harbour of the Fenerbahçe Yacht Club. This yacht harbour is now virtually complete and you may be allotted a berth here instead of Kalamis Marina if the latter is full. It will be an attractive and well equipped yacht harbour with some 1250 berths when complete, but suffers from the same noise pollution as Kalamis.

The Bosphorus
(Istanbul Boğazi, Karadeniz Boğazi)

Like the Dardanelles, the Bosphorus is a narrow strait somewhat resembling a large river. A considerable current flows from the Black Sea down the Bosphorus to the Sea of Marmara. The current can run at up to 4–5 knots in places. A yacht must contend not only with the contrary current but also with the prevailing wind, which blows from the NE down the strait. By day, passage in the Bosphorus is straightforward. At night, although it is well lit, the lights of the many buildings along its shores make identification of the lights difficult, and a night transit is not recommended.

Admiralty chart 1198, a large-scale chart of the Bosphorus showing the currents and counter-currents, is essential for low-powered yachts pro-

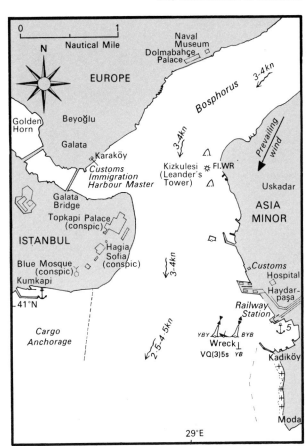

APPROACHES TO ISTANBUL AND THE BOSPHORUS

ceeding up the Bosphorus to the Black Sea.

Note Buoyage and lights in the Bosphorus are arranged for passage from the Black Sea to the Sea of Marmara in a southerly direction. That is, starboard-hand buoys and lights are on the west side and port-hand buoys and lights on the east side. All buoys now conform to IALA System 'A' cardinal markings.

KARAKOY

All formalities are carried out at Karaköy, but it is not a safe place to berth in a yacht. Go to Ataköy, Kalamis or any of the harbours around the Bosphorus and then get a bus or taxi to Karaköy.

HAYDARPASA

BA 1198

A yacht can anchor S of the station at Haydarpaşa, out of the way of the ferries. It is mostly too shallow to go stern-to anywhere. The bottom is soft mud, and not everywhere good holding. This anchorage is dirty and smelly and disturbed by the wash from the constant coming and going of the ferries, but is the closest to Istanbul. The ferry to Galata is close by. Provisions and restaurants in Kadiköy.

KURUCACESME

A quayed area on the W side of the Bosphorus, just past the first suspension bridge. It sits opposite Galatsaray, an islet squared off and built up by man. Go stern or bows-to where possible. There are

Haydarpaşa

mostly 2–3 metre depths under the short pier.

It is very uncomfortable under here, with the continuous wash from ferries and ships in the Bosphorus, and is not really to be recommended. Water on the quay. Fuel ashore. Shops and restaurants nearby.

BEBEK

A bay on the European side of the Bosphorus, about 2 miles N of the old suspension bridge and a mile S of the new bridge. The shelter in here is better than it looks on the chart, and local yachts are kept here all year round. In fact, there are so many yachts in here that it can be difficult for a visiting yacht to find a berth.

Mooring

Go stern or bows-to wherever you can, although it is likely that you will have to move at least once before you find a space that is free. Care needs to be taken of rocks just under the water in some places, especially on the S side, so it pays to go bows-to if possible. The alternative is to anchor in the middle

Bebek: the anchorage in the 'middle'

amongst the yachts on permanent moorings, and this is what many visiting yachts will have to do, although once again it can be crowded in the middle.

Note There is a counter-current in the bay running in a northerly direction around the shore, and this can make manoeuvring difficult.

Shelter Good shelter in here, although the wash from passing ships and from the ferries can be uncomfortable and you should keep pulled well off the quay.

Facilities

Water From local sources.
Fuel From a petrol station in jerry cans, or a mini-tanker can deliver larger amounts.
Repairs Limited repairs can be carried out.
Provisions Good shopping for all provisions nearby.
Eating out Numerous restaurants nearby.
Other PO. Banks. Turkish gas and *Camping Gaz*. Buses and *dolmuş* to Istanbul. Taxis.

General

If you can find a free berth, or a spot to anchor in the middle of the bay, Bebek is as pleasant a place as anywhere to stop while in Istanbul. It is about twenty minutes to half an hour to Galata Bridge and old Stamboul, depending on how congested the roads are. Buses and *dolmuş* run regularly.

ISTINIYE

A narrow inlet just over 2 miles N of Bebek. Floating docks take up most of the inlet, but local boats are kept on the N quay. If there is space available, go stern or bows-to. There are laid moorings tailed to buoys. Good shelter.

Water on the quay. Fuel nearby. Provisions and restaurants nearby.

TARABYA

An inlet approximately 4 miles N of Bebek on the European side. The inlet is jammed full of local yachts and you must berth wherever you can squeeze in. Good shelter out of the current.

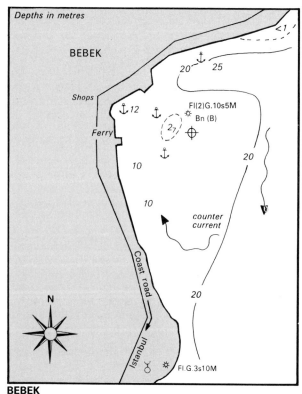

Depths in metres

BEBEK

Shops

Ferry

Fl(2)G.10s5M
Bn (B)

counter current

Coast road

İstanbul

N

Fl.G.3s10M

BEBEK
41°04'·7N 29°02'·9E

Tarabya

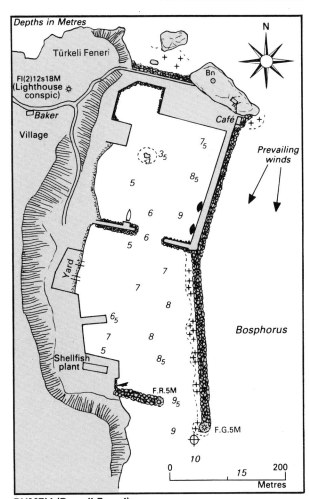

RUMELI (Rumeli Feneri)
41°13′·8N 29°06′·9E

Provisions and restaurants ashore. Bus and *dolmuş* to Istanbul.

BUYUKDERE

A bay just over a mile NW of Tarabya. There are numerous mooring buoys in the bay. Anchor on the N side of the bay, where there is some protection from the swell pushed down by the prevailing wind. It can sometimes be very rolly at anchor in here, and the bay is not really suitable as an overnight anchorage.

Turkish Hydrographic Office

About 1¼ miles N of the new suspension bridge on the Asian side of the Bosphorus is the Turkish Hydrographic Office. It is possible to go alongside the quay off the office while obtaining charts here. If you are proceeding up into the Black Sea, this is a good place to obtain charts for this stretch of coast at significantly less cost than equivalent British Admiralty charts.

RUMELI (Rumeli Feneri, Büyük Limani)

A fishing harbour, sitting directly under the western entrance point to the Bosphorus from the Black Sea.

Approach

The harbour breakwater under the small islet is easily identified from the S, though not from the N, when it will not be seen until you are into the Bosphorus. A white beacon on the islet and the lighthouse on the W side of the northern entrance to the Bosphorus are conspicuous.

By night Use the light at the N entrance to the Bosphorus (Fl(2)12s18M) and the lights at the entrance to the harbour (Fl.G.3·6s3M and F.R.5M).

Mooring

The harbour is very crowded with fishing boats, so fit in where you can. You can usually go alongside in the inner basin. Good all-round shelter.

Facilities

Limited provisions only, and a simple restaurant.

General

The harbour is a proper working harbour, much removed from the tourism of Istanbul, and the village a simple place with not a boutique or trinket shop in sight. Its location, situated at the northern entrance to the Bosphorus, is spectacular and well worth a stop.

POYRAZ

A fishing harbour just SW of the E side of the northern entrance to the Bosphorus.

Approach

The fort on the bluff above the harbour and the breakwater are easily identified.

Mooring

Anchor where convenient under the breakwater, and take a line ashore to it if necessary. The harbour gets very crowded with local yachts at weekends.

Facilities

Restaurant and several cafés.

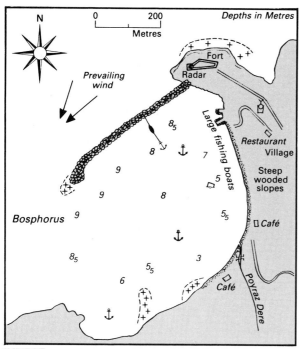

POYRAZ
41°12′·4N 29°07′·6E

General

The bay is an attractive place, and the locals are a friendly lot. It is a popular destination for local boats on summer weekends, the end of the line in the Bosphorus, with the only alternative the swell of the Black Sea.

The Black Sea

(Karadeniz)

See Chapter VIII

FORMALITIES

If you are visiting Istanbul and intend to return to Canakkale, whether or not you need to take your boat's papers to Karaköy to clear in and out of Istanbul is a moot point. In years past it was unnecessary, indeed well nigh impossible, to clear in and out of Istanbul unless you were bound for the Black Sea. However, in recent years yachts have been advised to clear in and out of Istanbul, and it is now prudent to take the boat's papers to Karaköy. All the offices are in the same block by the water at Karaköy, and there is also a tourist office there to help if necessary. It is easy enough to get to Karaköy from any of the marinas and anchorages mentioned in the previous section.

If you are entering Turkey for the first time you must, of course, get a Transit Log at Karaköy. If you are proceeding up into the Black Sea you must also clear in and out of Karaköy, even if you are only going to the Turkish Black Sea coast.

A word of warning. There are sometimes one or two agents at Karaköy, softly spoken and very polite gentlemen, who will offer to help you clear in and out of the various offices. I suggest you enquire in advance how much the fee for their services will be. Although it can take a while to get papers processed, there are no real difficulties to doing this yourself without the aid of an agent. Incidentally, you may also come across agents offering help elsewhere, at Canakkale and Izmir, to name two other places and, again, I suggest you enquire in advance how much the fee will be, should you decide that you need their services.

Istanbul

General

This city is one of my favourites. From seaward the skyline of old Stamboul is miraculously intact and has not been obliterated by high-rise buildings, as has happened in too many other major cities in the world. Closer in, there is evidence of more modern construction in Old Stamboul and Galata, but the architectural heritage of Byzantium and the Ottomans still remains. Everywhere pencil-slim minarets remind us that, while this is technically Europe, it is not wholly so. Asia Minor and Islam beckon from across the Bosphorus.

There are many parts to the city, and I will not attempt the impossible task (for which I am not qualified) of outlining what there is to see and do in Istanbul. Whole guide books are devoted to it, and I recommend *Strolling through Istanbul* (John Freely and Hilary Sumner-Boyd), and afterwards John Freely's informal sketches of life in Istanbul, *Stamboul Sketches*.

But don't miss: a ride on the delightfully old-fashioned ferries plying the Bosphorus – they are gradually being replaced by modern ferries, with not a bit of the charm of the creaky old originals. A fish meal on Galata Bridge. The Harem at Topkapi Palace. A picnic lunch in the gardens of Topkapi Palace. The covered Bazaar. The Byzantine grandeur of Hagia Sofia. The gentle wash of blue tiles in the Blue Mosque. The accumulated wealth of proto-Greek and Hellenistic art in the Museum of Antiquities. A walk around the back streets of the old Latin quarter in Galata. A ferry ride up the Bosphorus (excursions, including lunch, run every day). Another fish meal on Galata Bridge.

Many people have bewailed the loss of Istanbul as it once was, the grand old cosmopolitan city in a superb natural sitting astride the Bosphorus, but for a newcomer like me it still has immense charm and great beauty. Andrew Mango captures the spirit of modern Istanbul well:

'Istanbul has more natural advantages than almost any other great city. And if the recent boom has destroyed the fine balance between man and the environment which Ottoman civilization had achieved, the loss need not be permanent, nor is it complete. There are still a few quarters of the old city where the old east can be felt. Parts of the Bosphorus and the islands are as attractive as ever. If parks and public gardens are inadequate, there are scores of waterside restaurants, where the view, the air, the food and the drink meet in a unique and euphoric combination. The city walls, churches and above all the mosques stand in all their glory. Although no longer cosmopolitan, Istanbul is vigorous and thrusting. Like the rest of Turkey which it represents as it never did before, and whose problems and possibilities, experiences and inadequacies, pride and impatience it concentrates, it will probably have to sustain many shocks before it settles down in a technological world. Like all great cities, Istanbul demands discrimination, knowledge, patience and sympathy. A visitor who can muster these qualities will not be disappointed by it.'

Andrew Mango *Discovering Turkey*

The northern shores of the Sea of Marmara

The northern coast is bordered by low cliffs, and is somewhat bare in comparison to the southern shores. The prevailing winds blowing from the NE–NNE make for a fast passage along these shores, in relatively flat water. The harbours described along this coast are all small commercial harbours, and for the most part do not have the charm of those along the southern coast.

YESILKOY (40°57'·4N 28°49'·8E)
A fishing harbour situated approximately 2 miles W of Ataköy Marina and ½ a mile W of Yesilköy signal station. There are 5–6 metre depths in the entrance, shelving gradually. Anchor in the basin on the E side, or anchor and take a line ashore to the breakwater on the W side.

Diesel nearby. Provisions and restaurants ashore. PO. Bank. Train to Istanbul (about 30 minutes).

The harbour is directly under the flight path of aircraft taking off and landing at the airport, and is consequently very noisy. The local fishermen appear not to be the friendliest souls around, and this,

Baba Burun (W side of Büyükçekmece), looking NW

combined with the aircraft noise, diminishes the charms of the place.

BUYUKCEKMECE (Mimarsinan)

Approach
The large bay is easily identified.

Conspicuous There are always numerous coasters anchored off the harbour in the NW corner of the bay. Behind the harbour a large cement factory is prominent, and closer in the harbour breakwater, with a white light tower on the extremity, is easily spotted.

By night Use the light on Değirmen Burnu (Fl.5s10M) and the harbour light (F.R.3M).

Dangers Care must be taken of the reef fringing the coast between Değirmen Burnu and the eastern entrance to the bay.

Mooring
The harbour is always full of coasters and large *caïques*. A yacht must make the best of it and berth wherever it can. The best spot is stern or bows-to between the *caïques* with a long line to the breakwater. Alternatively, a berth may be found alongside the fishing boats on the quay on the S side.

Shelter Good shelter in the harbour.

Anchorage Good shelter from the prevailing winds

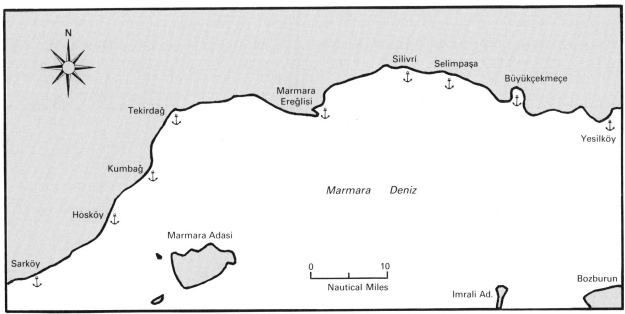

YESILKOY TO SARKOY

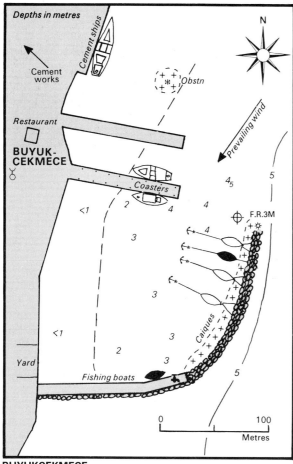

BUYUKCEKMECE
41°00'·9N 28°34'E

can be found in the NE corner of the bay. Anchor in 5–10 metres on mud – good holding.

Facilities

Water A tap on the quay.
Fuel Some distance away to the N.
Provisions In the village by the harbour.
Eating out A restaurant by the harbour.

General

Büyükçekmece is a cement-loading port. Nobody could call it attractive, but it is a useful port of call close to Istanbul.

SELIMPASA (41°03'·2N 28°22'·2E)

A very small fishing harbour about 9 miles W of Kaba Burun. Care is needed of an isolated reef lying approximately half a mile SE of the harbour. There are 3–4 metre depths in the entrance to the harbour and 1·5–3 metre depths inside the outer half of the

Kaba Burun, looking E

harbour. It is usually crowded with fishing boats, but a berth may be found alongside the quay on the breakwater. The inner half of the harbour gets progressively more shallow.

Water on the quay or in the fish market. Fuel about a mile away. Some provisions and restaurants ashore.

SILIVRI

Approach

The harbour lies close W of Kaba Burun, whose brown steep cliffs hide the town and the harbour if you are approaching from the E.

Conspicuous A tall brick chimney and a pylon are conspicuous. Closer in, the breakwaters are easily seen.

By night The entrance is lit Fl.G.5s5M/ Fl.R.5s5M. The pier head is lit F.R.2M. The lights are not always to be relied upon.

Note In the approach, you may find a line of four buoys in a SW direction from the side of the harbour. They mark a sewerage outfall.

Mooring

Go alongside or stern or bows-to the W quay, where there is usually room, or stern or bows-to the central pier. The bottom is sand and good holding.

Shelter Good all-round shelter. The harbour is open to the NW across the bay.

Authorities Harbourmaster. A modest charge may be made.

Anchorage If a berth cannot be found in the harbour, a yacht can find good protection from the prevailing

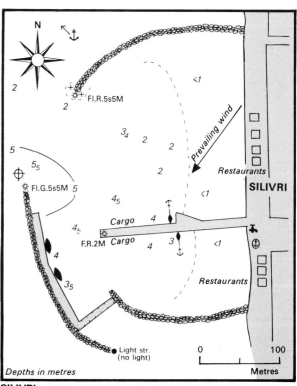

SILIVRI
41°04'·4N 28°14'·3E

Approach to Silivri looking E

Approach to Silivri, looking E

winds anchored out in the N of the bay. Anchor in 3–5 metres on sand.

Facilities

Water At the root of the pier.
Fuel Fuel station close to the harbour.
Repairs Minor mechanical repairs only.
Provisions Good shopping for provisions in the town. A small fruit, vegetable and fish market.
Eating out Good restaurants around the harbour.
Other PO. Bank. Turkish gas. Hardware shops. Bus to Istanbul.

General

The harbour is a noisy spot, with coasters loading and unloading, but otherwise it is a pleasant enough place.

MARMARA EREGLISI

BA 1006

A large bay close N of Adaardi Burun, offering only poor shelter from the prevailing winds. The white lighthouse and dwelling on Adaardi Burun are conspicuous, and closer in a number of large oil storage tanks on the end of Adaardi Burun will be seen.

Caution Care must be taken of the reef fringing Adaardi Burun, and of the remains of the breakwater between the cape and the light tower at the entrance to the bay. The breakwater is only partially above water.

The best shelter in Marmara Ereğlisi is found in the cove at the northern end of the bay. Anchor in 5 metres where there is a partial lee from the NE wind. Local boats are on moorings at the southern end of the bay, but it is most uncomfortable here. The swell rolling into the bay makes it dangerous to go on the quay. Provisions and a restaurant ashore.

Note Approaching Marmara Ereğlisi from the W, a radio mast on Karga Burun is conspicuous by day and night. At night it is lit by two Aero Oc.R.2·5s20/16M disposed vertically. One and a

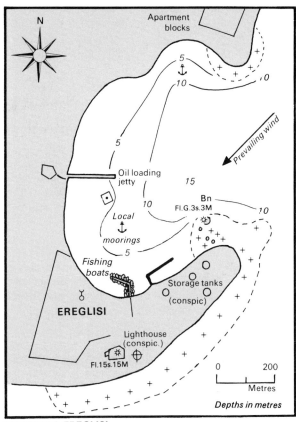

MARMARA EREGLISI
40°58'·1N 27°57'·7E

Marmara Ereğlisi: S side of the bay

half miles ESE of Karga Burun lies a reef, Orencikkayasi, marked by a white light tower (Fl.R.3s5M).

TEKIRDAG (Rodosto)

BA 1006

A bay with a long pier for cargo ships. Tucked under the pier is a small harbour where you can find good shelter from the prevailing wind. Go alongside the S quay or stern or bows-to the E quay. Customs office near the harbour.

Provisions and restaurants ashore. A tourist office near the harbour.

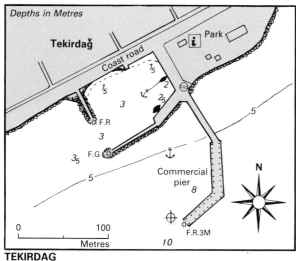

TEKIRDAG
40°58'·4N 27°31'·1E

The pier is used by coasters and *mavni*, and some of the *mavni* encountered around the Marmara Islands will be running across to here. Most of the grapes from Paşalimani Adasi are brought here for wine-making.

KUMBAG (40°52'N 27°27'·6E)
A very small and mostly shallow harbour 9 miles S of Tekirdağ. Small yachts can squeeze inside and anchor with a long line to the breakwater just inside the entrance. Provisions and restaurants ashore.

HOSKOY
A small fishing harbour 9 miles SW of Kumbağ. The entrance is prone to silting, and a substantial sandbar has already built up. With the prevailing wind there is a confused swell at the entrance and care is needed. With even a moderate onshore breeze entrance may not be possible.

Go stern or bows-to the E quay. Good shelter

from the prevailing wind once inside.

Fuel near the harbour. Provisions and restaurants in the town. PO.

SARKOY
Approximately 20 miles NE of Gelibolu and 12 miles SW of Hoşköy is the small harbour of Sarköy. Go alongside the quay on the N or bows-to the E quay. Good shelter from the prevailing wind. The harbour is run by a fishermen's co-operative, which makes a charge for the use of the harbour.

Water on the quay. Provisions and restaurants in the village.

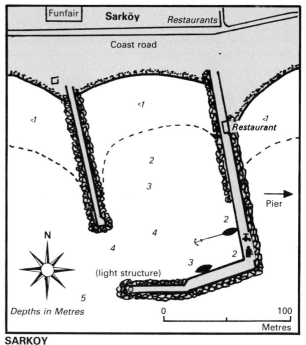

SARKOY
40°36'·5N 27°07'E

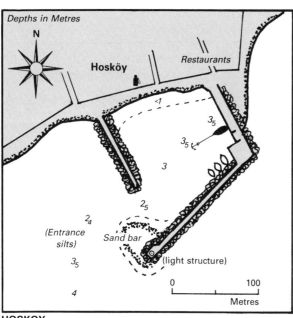

HOSKOY
40°42'·6N 27°18'·8E

II. The Aeolian coast

The Dardanelles to Ceşme

This chapter covers the northern Aegean coast between the Dardanelles and Ildir Körfezi as far as Ceşme. I call it the Aeolian coast, although in fact Aeolis proper encompassed only the region between Ayvalik and Izmir. Nor did the great city-state of Pergamon belong to Aeolis, being a Hellenised Anatolian city brought to prominence by a politic ruler who changed allegiances at a propitious time during the wrangles over Asia Minor after Alexander's death. But the label serves a useful purpose in defining the greater part of the coast as Aeolian.

The Aeolians were pushed out of their home in Thessaly and Boetia in the north by a Doric invasion from still further north around 1000 BC. Unlike their neighbours the Ionians, in the south, the Aeolians were farmers, and the fertile land of the region suited them well. Today it is still a rich agricultural region. The olives grown around Ayvalik are reputedly the best in Turkey, and tobacco and grain crops are also much in evidence.

The Aeolians are not as well remembered as the other confederacies, and little remains of their cities. There were 12 major cities founded in all, and the ruins of several lie along the coast. The capital was Cyme, near Nemrut Limani (Nimrod's Harbour) on the south side of Candarli Körfezi. Around the same gulf stood three other Aeolian cities: Pitane, Gryneum, and Myrina. Further to the south stood Larissa, and Izmir was originally Aeolian. Little or nothing remains of these ancient cities, which were once as prosperous and well known as other more familiar names to the south.

At Eskifoça we find an Ionian colony within what was strictly Aeolis. Izmir later became an Ionian city, and south and west of here belonged wholly to the Ionian Confederacy. Compared to the ancient remains further south, there is little here to remind us of these ancient farmers. Alexandria Troas, Assos, and Pergamon have a different lineage. But although nothing remains of their cities, they are remembered by the humorist Athenaeus as being much given '. . . to wine, women, and luxurious living'. They need no other memorials.

Weather patterns

In the summer the prevailing wind is the *meltemi*, which usually gets up at midday and blows through the afternoon until sunset. The *meltemi* begins to blow in early summer, blows most strongly in late July and August, when it can get up to Force 5–6 and sometimes more, and blows less frequently again in later summer. In August it may continue to blow day and night for several days. The wind tends to follow the contours of the coast, blowing from the N or NW, and to blow into the gulfs from the W. At night a NE breeze, the *poyraz*, may blow off the land, sometimes with considerable strength. The *poyraz* is strongest around Ayvalik, where it will sometimes blow throughout the day in the spring and autumn. There is some room for confusion here, as the prevailing northerlies will sometimes be called the *poyraz* and sometimes the *meltemi*.

As with the Greek islands nearby, the *meltemi* tends to gust off the high land more strongly than it blows out to sea. The gusts are particularly bad around Baba Burnu and Eskifoça, and off the Karaburun peninsula.

Gales are almost equally from the N and S, although gales from the N seem to be strongest.

Note In Izmir Körfezi the *meltemi* is called the *imbat*.

Data

PORTS OF ENTRY
Ayvalik (exit)
Dikili
Izmir
Ceşme

PROHIBITED AREAS
1. Landing is prohibited around Sivrice Burnu on the N side of Müslim Kanali, and also on Bozcaada and Tavşan Adasi. (But see the notes for Bozcaada and Sivrice.)
2. In Izmir Körfezi the following are military areas where anchoring and landing are prohibited: Hacilar Limani, Yenikale, the naval installations in the N of the Bay of Izmir, and the Karaburun peninsula between Dalyan Burnu and Eğri Limani. A yacht should keep well clear of obvious military installations, and refrain from displaying cameras.
3. Anchoring, approaching near and landing on the coast of Uzun Ada (38°28'N 26°43'E) and Hekim Adasi are prohibited.

MAJOR LIGHTS
Tavşan Adasi Fl.WR.5s14/10M

BOZCAADA
Bati Burnu Fl(2)15s15M
Eşek Adalari Fl.3s8M
Beşiğe Burnu Fl.3s7M

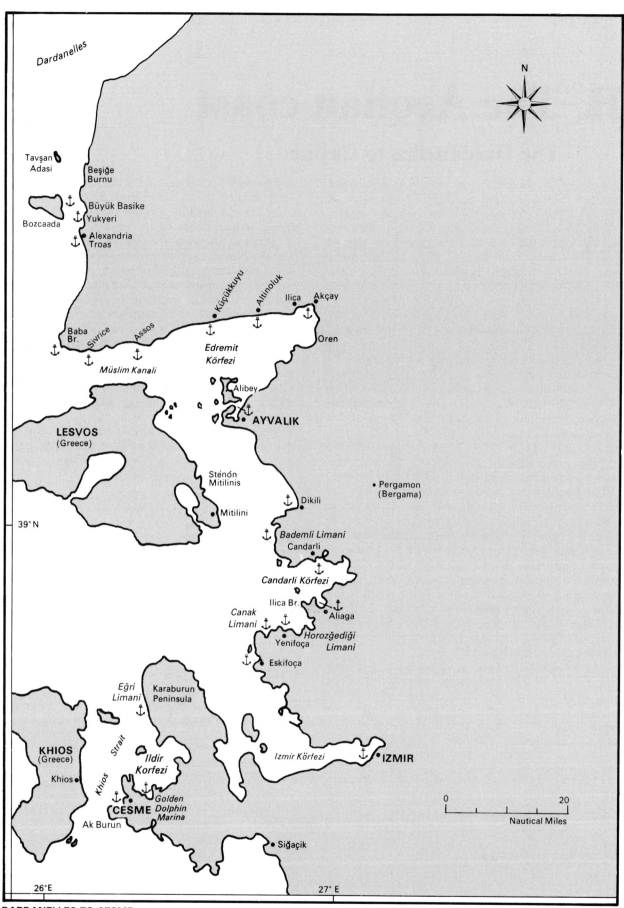

DARDANELLES TO CESME

THE COAST
Baba Burnu Fl(4)20s15M
Sivrice Burnu Fl(2)10s10M
Karaburnu Fl(3)10s10M
Boz Burun Fl.5s10M
Günes Adasi Fl.3s8M
Ciplak Ada, Ali Burnu Fl.R.3s8M
Ayvalik Limani (Korkut Burnu) Fl.3s7M
Bademli Limani Fl.WR.3s7/4M 102°-R-120°,
140°-R-156°
Tavşan Ada Fl(3)10s15M
Fener Adasi (Eski Foça) Fl.5s12M
Saip Adasi Fl(2)10s10M
Uzanada Fl(3)15s12M
Cigli Airfield Aero AlFl.WG.10s10M
Karaburun Fl(4)20s12M
Toprak Ada Fl.10s7M
Kizil Burnu Fl.3s8M

Quick reference guide

	Shelter	Mooring	Fuel	Water	Provisions	Eating out	Plan	Charge band
Bozcaada	B	BC	B	B	C	B	•	1
Yukyeri	C	C	O	O	O	O		
Baba Burnu	C	C	O	B	C	C		
Sivrice	C	C	O	O	O	O		
Assos	O	C	O	O	C	C	•	
Küçükkuyu	B	AB	B	B	C	C	•	1
Altinoluk	A	AB	B	B	C	B	•	1
Akcay	C	C	O	B	C	C		
Oren	C	C	O	O	O	C		
Poroselene	B	C	O	O	O	O	•	
Patrica Limani	C	C	O	O	O	O	•	
Kumru Köyü	C	C	O	O	O	O	•	
Camlik Köyü	B	C	O	O	O	O	•	
Alibey	A	AC	O	B	C	B	•	1
Ayvalik	B	AB	B	A	A	A	•	1/2
Dikili	A	AB	B	B	B	B	•	1
Bademli Limani	A	C	O	O	C	C	•	
Mardaliç Adasi	C	C	O	O	O	O	•	
Candarli	B	C	B	B	B	C	•	1
Kadirğa Limani	C	C	O	O	O	O	•	
Akça Limani	B	C	B	B	C	C	•	
Aliaga	B	C	O	O	O	O	•	
Nemrut Limani	O	C	O	O	O	O		
Yenifoça	B	C	B	B	C	C	•	
Canak Limani	C	C	O	O	O	O	•	
Eskifoça	B	AC	A	A	B	B	•	1/2
Izmir	B	A	B	A	A	A	•	1/2
Levent Marina	A	A	A	A	O	C	•	2
Urla Iskelesi	A	A	O	B	B	C	•	1
Akkum	A	A	O	O	O	C	•	
Balikiliova Limani	C	C	O	B	C	C	•	
Gerence Köyü	B	C	O	B	C	C	•	
Mordogan	C	AC	B	B	C	C	•	
Kaynarpinar	B	AB	O	B	C	C	•	1
Port Saip	B	A	O	B	O	O	•	1
Karaburun Iskelesi	C	A	O	B	C	C	•	
Yeniliman	B	AB	O	B	C	C	•	1
Eğri Limani	B	C	O	O	O	O	•	
Kara Adasi	C	C	O	O	O	O		
Gerence Körfezi	C	C	O	O	O	O		
Ildir	B	C	O	O	O	O	•	
Ilica	C	C	O	B	C	C	•	
Golden Dolphin Marina	A	A	A	A	C	C	•	3
Hoteleratan	C	C	O	O	O	C		
Dalyan	A	A	O	B	O	C	•	2
Ceşme	A	AC	B	B	B	A	•	1/2

BOZCAADA LIMANI

BA 1608

Approach

The harbour lies on the NE corner of the island.

Conspicuous From the N, the white lighthouse and dwelling on Tavşan Adasi and the light tower on Eşek Adalari are conspicuous. Closer in, the castle behind the harbour and a large outline of a soldier in white on the slopes above the town are conspicuous. From the S, Goz Tepe, a conical peak on the NE corner of the island, and the light structure on the SE corner of the island, are easily identified. Closer in, the rough rock breakwaters and the harbour entrance will be seen.

By night The approaches and channel are well lit. From the N use the lights on Tavşan Adasi (Fl.WR.5s14/10M), Beşiğe Burnu (Fl.3s7M) and Eşek Adalari (Fl.3s8M). From the S use the lights on Mermer Burnu (Fl.5s10M) and Eşek Adalari. The harbour entrance is lit: Fl.R.3s3M and Fl.G.3s5M.

Dangers
1. Care must be taken of the currents N of Bozcaada, which set SW and then W towards the reefs and shoal water around Tavşan Adasi and N of Bozcaada.
2. Reefs and shoal water surround Tavşan Adasi and Bozcaada. An approach from the W to Bozcaada should be made with considerable caution.
3. With southerlies when the wind is against the current a confused sea is raised along this coast.

Mooring

The best place to be when the *meltemi* is blowing is under the N breakwater with a long line ashore. Underwater rocks extend out from the quay and the breakwater, making it impossible to get close enough to step on and off, so you will have to use your dinghy to get ashore. In calm weather or out of the *meltemi* season you may be able to squeeze in alongside the pier or go bows-to the S quay. Care is needed off much of the quayed area because ballasting extends out underwater. The bottom is mud and weed, good holding.

Shelter Good shelter from the prevailing winds. The harbour is open E, but the wind rarely blows from this direction.

Authorities Port police and customs.

Note The former military restrictions on Bozcaada seem to have been much relaxed in recent years. Nonetheless restrictions apply to parts of the island

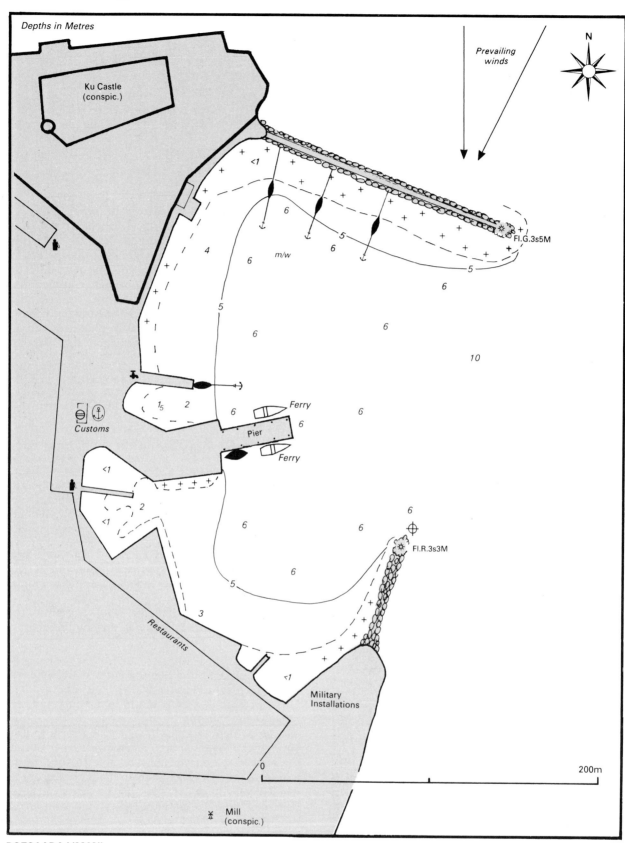

Depths in Metres

Ku Castle
(conspic.)

Prevailing
winds

N

<1

6

m/w

4

6

5

6

Fl.G.3s5M

5

6

5

6

6

10

Customs

1.5

2

6

Ferry

6

Pier

6

Ferry

<1

2

6

6

6

<1

5

Restaurants

3

6

Fl.R.3s3M

<1

Military
Installations

0

200m

Mill
(conspic.)

BOZCAADA LIMANI
39°50'·2N 26°04'·5E

S breakwater Entrance N breakwater

Approach to Bozcaada, looking SW

and it would be prudent to confine your photography to Bozcaada Limani and to civilian subjects at that.

Facilities

Water Public tap near the quay.
Fuel Fuel station near the quay.
Repairs Minor mechanical repairs only.
Provisions Most provisions can be obtained, but the locals are somewhat dependent on supplies brought in by ferry from the mainland.
Eating out Several pleasant restaurants around the harbour.
Other PO. Bank. Ferry to the mainland.

General

Bozcaada is the ancient Ténedos, home of Apollo the Mouse God, and the Greek base for the attack on Troy. In Byzantine times, during the reign of Justinian, huge granaries were built so that ships carrying grain to Constantinople could be unloaded here and the grain ferried up the Dardanelles by small freighters. Nothing remains of the granaries, but the Genoese castle built to protect the harbour in the last days of western trade is in excellent repair.

The locals nurture a budding tourist industry. There are several hotels and pleasant restaurants

Bozcaada: mooring under the N breakwater with a long line ashore, looking E from the castle

shaded by trees on the waterfront. The vineyards on Bozcaada, once famous for the quality of their grapes, are much diminished, but a drinkable red is still made and is available in the village.

BOZCAADA ANCHORAGES

On the S of the island there are several bays and coves which are reported to afford shelter from the *meltemi*. Care is needed of off-lying rocks and reefs, and it would be prudent to move on if the military object to your presence.

BUYUK BASIKE LIMANI (Yukyeri Köyu)

Close under Kum Burnu a yacht can anchor in 5–10 metres on sand. Good protection from northerlies but open to the S. A loading pier on Kum Burnu is used by coasters, and there is often a ship loading here. Bright spotlights in the vicinity of the pier are easily identified at night.

YUKYERI LIMANI

S of Büyük Basike a yacht can anchor off the coast at Odun Iskelesi or Dalyanköy. These are open roadsteads and should not be used except in calm weather. Care is needed of shoal water off the coast.

Alexandria Troas

The ruins of the ancient city and port lie immediately SE of Tuzla Burnu (Eski Istanbul Burnu). In calm weather a yacht can anchor close S of Tuzla Burnu and you can row ashore to inspect the site.

The city was founded by Antigonus the One-Eyed, in the 4th century BC. He named it Antigonia after himself and populated it from the surrounding Troad towns. Lysimachus, King of Macedonia, defeated Antigonus in 301 BC and renamed the city Alexandria Troas. It grew to become a prosperous and powerful city-state in Hellenistic times, and continued to be important through the Roman period. Its importance declined when Constantinople was made the capital of the Roman Empire. By the Middle Ages it was but a small village amongst the ruins of a once grand city. Most of the ruins and the harbour date from the Roman period.

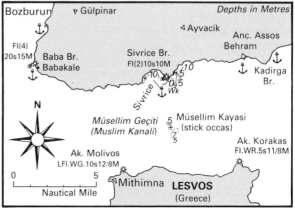

MUSELLIM GECITI (Muslim Kanali)

AKLIMANI

Under Bozburun there is a bight in the coast that can be used in calm weather or a light *meltemi*. Care is needed of the reef fringing Bozburun.

BABA BURUN

The high and steep-to cape on the N side of the entrance to the channel between Turkey and the Greek island of Lésvos. This channel is called Müsellim Geçiti or Müslim Kanali by the Turks and Dhiavlos Mouselim by the Greeks. At Baba Burnu there is a small village in which a fort and a minaret are conspicuous. The light structure on the cape is also conspicuous.

There is now a large fishng harbour here with the entrance on the S side. There are 6–7m depths in the entrance and 2–5m depths inside. Anchor in the NW corner with a long line to the breakwater. There are no quayed areas and the loading pier is used by large trawlers. Good protection inside from the *meltemi* although it can blow strongly from the E off the mountains at night. Limited provisions and a restaurant ashore.

Note This is a military area and landing is theoretically prohibited. However, the military did not seem to object here.

SIVRICE

A large bay, immediately W of Sivrice Burnu, on which the tall white lighthouse (Fl(2)10s10M) and dwelling are conspicuous from some distance off. Care is needed of the reef fringing Sivrice Burnu for some distance off, and of a wreck with 0·9 metres least depth reported over it. There is also a reef extending out from the coast for approximately 1000m NE of Sivrice Burnu.

A yacht can anchor on the W or E side of the bay.

1. On the W side anchor in 5–10 metres off the hamlet. Care is needed of the above-water rock just NNE of Dut Burnu. A rocky ledge with less than 1 metre is reported to run out 200 metres from the shore off the hamlet. Reasonable shelter from the *meltemi*.
2. On the E side anchor in 4–8 metres off the hamlet. Care is needed of the above and below-water rocks extending out from Dokuntu Burnu on the S side of the bay. Reasonable shelter from the ·*meltemi*.

MUSLIM KAYA

A reef, Müslim Kaya, lies 3 miles S of Sivrice Burnu and 4½ miles NE of Ak Mólivos on Lésvos. It is just awash, but is difficult to see even in calm weather. It is occasionally marked by a stick, but this cannot be relied upon. Give it a wide berth. There is shoal water N and S of the reef, with least depths of 5·5 metres over the shoals just NNW of the reef.

BEHRAM KALE (ancient **Assos**)

The village of Behram Kale, the site of ancient Assos, lies about 5 miles E of Sivrice Burnu and

close W of Kadirğa Burnu. It is unmarked on most charts.

Sivrice Burnu is easily identified by the tall white lighthouse and dwelling on it. The site of Assos on the gently rounded summit of an extinct volcano cone can be identified from the distance by a mosque and large square tower. Closer in, the hamlet by the sea at the base of the cone will be seen.

Off the village the ancient harbour is easily identified. It is mostly shallow, and the entrance is rock-bound with slabs of the partially destroyed ancient mole (see plan). With care a very small yacht could go bows-to the short jetty. Most yachts will have to anchor to the E of the hamlet in 10 metres. Poor holding, on rock and boulders, and indifferent shelter. Even with winds from the N a swell rolls into the bay. Ashore there are several restaurants and a small hotel in a delightful setting. This would be the perfect spot for a land-based holiday in a hotel, should you ever swallow the anchor.

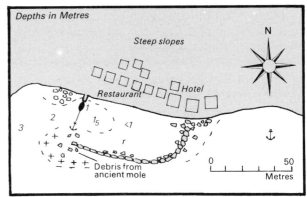

ASSOS
39°30′N 26°20′E

Approach to Assos, looking NW

Lighthouse on Sivrice Burnu

Assos

The site remains mostly unexcavated, and therefore you will need some time and considerable effort to find your way around. The position of the site, atop the extinct volcanic cone, with fine sea views across to Lésvos, is magnificent. The walls of Assos, three kilometres long, were said to be the most impressive Hellenistic walls in Asia Minor.

Assos was founded by colonists from Mithimna (Methymna), just across the channel in Lésvos, early in the 1st millennium BC. The city soon prospered as a landing place for cargo that were then ferried overland to avoid the perils of the passage through the Dardanelles and the Bosphorus.

Its greatest period was in the 4th century BC, under the tyrant Hermeias. He was a fond student of Plato, and invited Erastas and Coriscus, two of Plato's assistants, to come to Assos and turn it into an ideal city-state along Plato's principles. He also invited such notables as Theophrastus and Aristotle to study here. Aristotle carried out much of his research into the life sciences at Assos, and formulated a basis for biology that endured right up until the research of European naturalists in the 16th and 17th centuries. He must have liked Assos, for he married the tyrant's niece, Pythia, who bore him a child while he was there.

Alexander the Great freed the city from tyrannical rule in 334 BC, and subsequently it became part of the kingdom of Pergamon, and later part of Rome.

The ruined city at one time stretched from the sea to the top of the cone. Here a temple to Athena, built in the 6th century BC along both Doric and Ionic lines, was the central attraction of the city. Little remains today of the ancient ruins. Numerous other remains can be seen, including the Byzantine city wall and a conspicuous watch tower, the ruins of a gymnasium, stoa, agora and theatre of Hellenistic times, and the ancient harbour, which is in surprisingly good repair given that it is well over 2000 years old.

EDREMIT KORFEZI

The gulf running E from Müslim Kanali. On the N side there are two small fishing harbours and several anchorages.

KUCUKKUYU

About twelve miles E of Assos is the small fishing village of Küçükkuyu. The entrance is lit F.G.3M/F.R.3M. A night entrance is possible with care. Go bows-to the rough stone pier inside, or anchor and take a long line ashore to the outer breakwater. Good shelter from the *meltemi*.

Water tap near the harbour. Fuel nearby. Provisions and restaurants in the village. PO. Buses to Canakkale and Ayvalik.

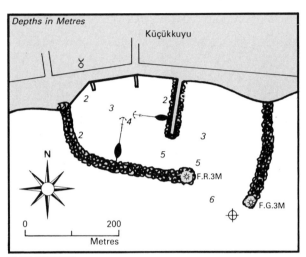

KUCUKKUYU
39°32'·7N 26°36'·5E

ALTINOLUK

Eight miles E of Küçükkuyu is the fishing harbour of Altinoluk. An L-shaped mole with another short breakwater at the entrance provides good shelter inside. Hotel and apartment developments stretch a considerable distance E of the original village and there is now considerable tourism in the area. There are 3-metre depths at the entrance, decreasing to 1 metre off the village quay. Anchor and take a long line to the breakwater, or go bows-to the N quay with care.

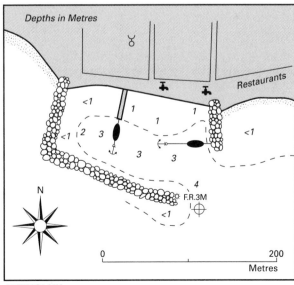

ALTINOLUK
39°33'·9N 26°44'·7E

Ciplak Adasi   *Channel*   *Eğribuçak Burnu*

Ayvalik: S channel between Ciplak Adasi and Ayvalik peninsula,
looking NNW

Alibey Adasi   *Lighthouse (Körkut Burnu)*

Entrance to Ayvalik channel (Dalyan Boğazi), looking NE

Ayvalik channel (Dalyan Boğazi), looking E (seaward beacons)

Water nearby. Provisions and good restaurants close to the harbour. PO. Bank.

The harbour and village are attractively situated, and the locals are a friendly lot who rarely see a yacht. The outer breakwater is lit F.R.3M, but a night entrance is not recommended.

AKCAY

In the NE corner of the gulf it is possible to anchor off the hamlet of Akcay. Anchor off in 4–6 metres. Reasonable shelter from the *meltemi*. Limited provisions and several restaurants ashore.

OREN

At the head of the gulf, the village of Ilica has hot springs nearby. In the SE corner at Oren the locals keep their boats anchored out over the summer, so presumably it should be tenable for a yacht to anchor here with care in settled weather.

Ayvalik archipelago
BA 1675

Ayvalik and its off-lying islands lie opposite Lésvos on the southern side of Edremit Körfezi. From the N and W the large square tower on the summit of Maden Adasi is conspicuous. Closer in, the light structures on Yumurta Adasi and Günes Adasi are easily distinguished. From the S the numerous hotels behind the beach on the S side of Ayvalik peninsula and the cliffs of Eğribuçak Burnu (which are so eroded as to look like man-made fortifications) are conspicuous. Closer in, the light structure and a stone dwelling on Ali Burnu (Ciplak Adasi) are easily spotted.

Approach

The approach to Dalyan Boğazi, the channel leading into Ayvalik Limani or 'the lake', is straightforward by day and night. By day, the small white lighthouse on Körkut Burnu (Rowley Point) is conspicuous. Once up to it the beacons marking the channel are easily identified. A small rusty red conical buoy (▾ topmark) marks the shoal water on the N side of the entrance to the channel.

By night Use Rowley Point (Fl.3s7M) and the channel beacon lights: the westernmost to be left to port is VQ(6)+LFl.15s7M; then three pairs of Fl.R. 3s5M and Fl.G.3s5M.

0   2
Nautical miles
N

Kiz Ad.

Tr (Ruin)

Deveboynu
Bu.

Balik Ad.

3
10
Poroselene

Maden
Adasi

<1

2
5   10

Kuthu Ad.

Güverçin
Ad.   10   *Patrica
Limani*   20
20

Hasir Ad.

Alibey
Adasi

<1

Poyraz
Ad.

<1
<1

Kamis
Ad.

4

*Holiday
village*

Mosko
Ad.

Alibey   *Holiday villages*

<1   *Causeway*
<1

Storage tanks
(conspic)

AYVALIK

VQ(6)+LFl.15s7M
Fl.R.3s
Fl.R.3s

Fl.R.3s5M
Fl.G.3s5M

4₅

<1

*Ayvalik Limani
('The Lake')*

4₅

Fl.G.3s
Fl.G.3s

<1

4₅

Fl.3s7M

*Dalyan
Boğazi*

Körkut Br. (Rowley Pt)
Small Lt Ho
(conspic)   Wooded

<1

See plan

Yassi
Tepe

Kucuk
Köy

Hotel

<1
<1

*Kumru
Köyü*

Wooded   *Canak
Tepe*

*Camlik
Köyü*

<1

Ciplak
Ad.

Fener
Br.

Fl.R.3s8M

Cliffs
(conspic)

Cave   *Hotels*

*Prevailing
winds*

<1   *Long sandy beach*   <1

AYVALIK LIMANI AND APPROACHES
(Körkut Br light 39°19'N 26°37'·8E)

Anchorages in the archipelago

1. **Poroselene (Gumus Köyü)** The large bay formed where Maden Adasi and Alibey Adasi almost meet. A sand bar just under water and marked by stakes blocks the channel between the two islands. Anchor in 3–4 metres on a gently shelving bottom. The holding, on hard sand and weed, is uncertain in places, but the water is very clear and you can row over your anchor and see if it is set. The setting is quite lovely, with just a fisherman's house ashore, although some visitors have reported a plague of flies in the anchorage.

   This bay is the Poroselene of Greek and Roman times, of which Pausanias wrote: 'I have seen with my own eyes, at Poroselene, a dolphin, filled with gratitude towards a child who had saved his life; he had been wounded by fishermen and the child had taken care of him. I have seen this dolphin answer the child's call and carry him on its back wheresoever the child wishes to be taken.' Modern writers have expressed doubts about this story. But in Opononi, a small township by the sea in New Zealand where I spent a summer holiday as a teenager, there are numerous photographs and accounts of Opo the dolphin. Opo used to come to the beach and take young children for short rides on its back, until it died in March 1956.

   Caution Care must be taken of two shoal patches in the bay. Neither of them is marked.

   Note There is no mole or quayed area in the N of the bay, although these are shown in earlier plans.

2. **Patrica Limani (Gokçeliman)** The large bay on the E side of Alibey Adasi. Anchor on the N side of the bay where convenient in 3–6 metres. Reasonable shelter from the prevailing wind if you are tucked right up close under the northern shore, although a brisk *meltemi* sends in a swell. Near Karagoz Burnu is the abandoned monastery of Ay Dhimitrios.

3. **Poyraz Adasi** A good lee from northerlies can be found in a bay on the SW corner of this island.

4. **Mosko Adasi** Anchor at the southern end of the shallow channel between Mosko Adasi and Alibey Adasi. Good shelter from northerlies in pleasant surroundings. There is a hotel and a village on Alibey a little further up the channel.

5. **On the S side of Ayvalik peninsula** A yacht can anchor off the beach lined with hotels. An indifferent lee from northerlies, as there is usually a swell running here.

6. **Kumru Köyü (Cennet Köyü)** On the SW side of the 'lake' is the large bay of Kumru Köyü. Anchor in 3–5 metres under the northern entrance point, where there is reasonable shelter from the *meltemi*.

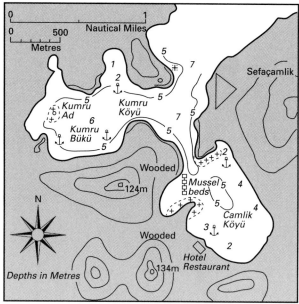

KUMRU KOYU AND CAMLIK KOYU

7. **Camlik Köyü (Pasa Köyü)** Another almost land-locked bay just SE of Kumru. Anchor in the cove in the N, in 3–4 metres on mud. Good shelter. Alternatively, anchor further S in the bay in 3–5 metres. A hotel on the W side of the bay. The surroundings are magnificent, under steep wooded slopes, although it is now reported that the road around the E side is busy with traffic taking away some of the charm. The steep-to basalt cone (Canak Tepe) dividing Kumru and Camlik is known as 'The Devil's Table' from local folklore describing how the devils used to meet here and wine, dine, and make merry.

ALIBEY

Approach

The harbour is situated on the N side of the channel between Alibey Adasi and the mainland.

Harbour

Approach to Alibey, looking N

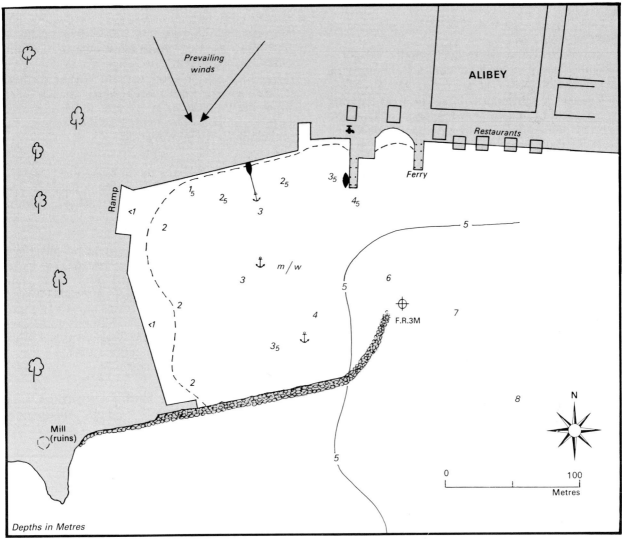

ALIBEY
39°19'·9N 26°39'·4E

By night The end of the breakwater is lit F.R.3M but should not be relied upon. A night entrance is possible with care.

Mooring

Go bows-to the quay on the N side of the harbour, taking care close in where it is shallow just off the

Alibey harbour, looking ENE

quay. If there is room it may be possible to go alongside the pier closer to the village. Alternatively, anchor off in the harbour. The bottom is mud and weed, good holding.

Shelter Good shelter, although strong SE winds might make it uncomfortable. With SE winds it may be better to anchor off under the breakwater.

Facilities

Water A tap near the pier.
Provisions Most provisions available. Good shopping in Ayvalik, a short ferry ride away.
Eating out Good restaurants along the waterfront, including good fish restaurants, all with splendid views over the 'lake'.
Other PO. Regular ferries to Ayvalik.

General

Alibey is a crumbling old Greek village complete with a large disused church. Its aspect is grand and it has a tangible if faded elegance. It is now enjoying some prosperity in Turkish hands as a local tourist resort. East of the village a number of holiday villages and hotels sprawl along the coast.

AYVALIK

Approach

Once through Dalyan Boğazi and into the 'lake' it is difficult at first to spot the harbour. It lies at the S end of Ayvalik town.

Conspicuous A high brick chimney near the harbour is conspicuous. Closer in, the large white light towers at the entrance to the harbour and the outer breakwater are easily identified.

By night The entrance is lit Fl.G.3s5M/ Fl.R.3s5M.

Mooring

Go stern or bows-to or alongside the quay where shown. The harbour is often crowded with fishing boats and local craft, though a berth can usually be found. A foul area is reported in the position shown on the plan.

Entrance to Ayvalik harbour, looking SW

Shelter Moderate shelter, although the *meltemi/poyraz* blowing into the harbour makes it uncomfortable. Ensure that your anchor is well in before leaving the boat.

Authorities A port of entry, with the full complement of authorities. For some reason it has been impossible to clear in at Ayvalik and it has been necessary to go to Dikili either by road or sea. It is possible to clear out of Ayvalik.

Note

1. A yacht can also moor on the town quay in settled weather. Open to the N and W. It is noisy here, being close to the restaurants and cafés on the waterfront, but conveniently close to the town centre.

2. At the time of publication it is reported that there is much construction under progress with the intention of turning the harbour into a yacht marina. Four floating pontoons are to be installed off the breakwater with berths for 100 yachts. Water and electricity points. Showers and toilets ashore. A fuel station will be installed later. Completion is envisaged for late 1997.

Facilities

Water On the quay. You may have to negotiate with the coastguard to obtain water here. Alternatively

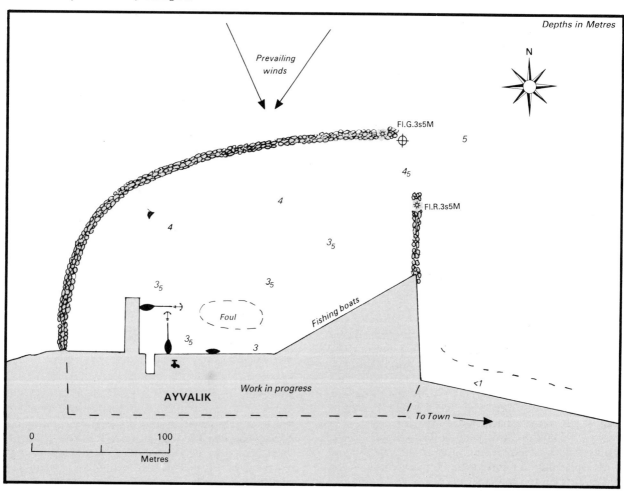

AYVALIK 39°18'·9N 26°41'·3E

Ayvalik harbour, looking E towards the town

The old customs quay at Ayvalik, looking E

there is water on the Mobil fuel jetty (see below).

Fuel A mini-tanker can deliver to the harbour. There is also a fuel jetty N of the town. Head for the conspicuous tanks and warehouse where you will see a restaurant and a boatyard. Close by is a jetty with a Mobil sign with 2-metre depths reported off the outer end of the jetty. Water also available.

Repairs Some mechanical repairs can be carried out in the town. A yard N of the town hauls out large *caïques*, and might be able to haul small yachts, depending on draught.

Provisions Good shopping for all provisions in the town. A small fruit, vegetable and fish market off the main street running back from the seafront. Ice from a factory N of the town (you will need a taxi).

Eating out Excellent restaurants of all types. It is worth splashing out and having a meal in one of the restaurants on the old customs pier with wonderful views out over the 'lake'.

Other PO. Hospital. Turkish gas. Hardware shops. Buses to Istanbul and Pergamon (Bergama). Ayvalik is a good place to leave your yacht for a visit to Pergamon – buses run regularly to the site. Ferry to Lésvos.

General

Situated on the edge of the 'lake', Ayvalik is an attractive working town rapidly becoming a tourist resort. The town is a pleasing mix of 19th- and early 20th-century architecture, set under gentle slopes clad in olive and pine. The site was occupied in Hellenistic and Roman times, but there are few remains.

Contemporary Ayvalik dates from the early 1700s, and prospered in the 19th century, producing olive oil, soap, wine and salt. There were many tanneries, and a number of mills grinding imported wheat. Smuggling was also rife in this archipelago, ready made for smugglers. In 1923 the Greek population was exchanged for Turks from Crete, Lésvos and Macedonia. Today, fine olive oil is still produced here and tourism continues to grow.

Unfortunately the ubiquitous Turkish holiday villages have sprouted on Alibey Adasi opposite, partially obliterating what was once a fine view, but avert your eyes and Ayvalik is still a gem.

DIKILI

Approach

The town, nestling at the head of the gulf, is easily located.

Conspicuous A number of large apartment blocks on the hillside above the harbour are conspicuous, and closer in a number of large hotels on the waterfront will be seen. The harbour breakwaters will be seen, but it is difficult to determine where the harbour

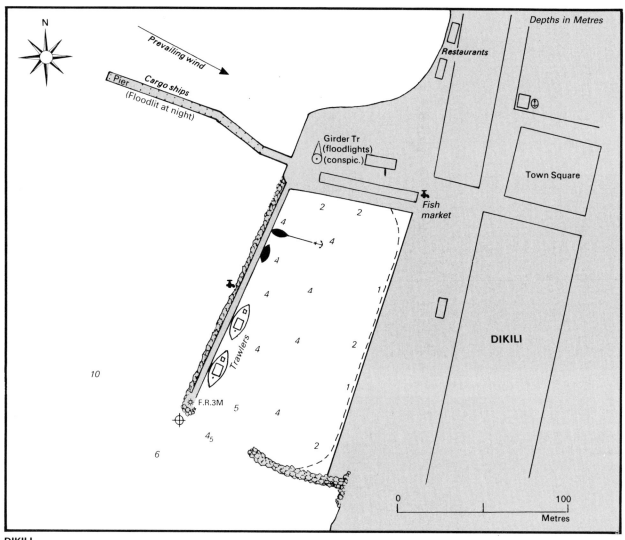

DIKILI
39°04'·2N 26°53'·2E

Harbour

Approach to Dikili, looking E. Note cruise liner anchored off

entrance is until close up. There is often a cruise ship anchored in the roads dropping people off to visit Pergamon.

By night The entrance is lit by a single F.R.3M. The long loading pier is usually floodlit at night, these lights having a good range.

Mooring

Go stern or bows-to or alongside the breakwater quay. The harbour is usually crowded with fishing boats and you may have difficulty finding a berth, but persevere and a space will usually be found. The bottom is mud and good holding.

Shelter Good all-round shelter.

Authorities A port of entry, with a full complement of authorities. Charge band 1/2.

Facilities

Water On the quay.
Fuel In the town.
Repairs Some mechanical repairs can be carried out.
Provisions Good shopping for all provisions. Small fish market at the harbour. Bazaar on Tuesdays with a good choice of fresh fruit and vegetables.
Eating out Restaurants on the waterfront.
Other PO. Banks. Turkish gas. Buses to Izmir and Pergamon (Bergama). Taxis.

Asin Limani looking NE over to Isene Bükü. *See page 136.*

Below Güllük looking ESE. *See page 138.*

Passage between Salih Adasi E end and the mainland coast looking E. *See page 139.*

Torba looking WSW. *See page 139.*
Below Turk Bükü looking SSE over Kesir Burnu and Büyük Ada. *See page 140.*

Gundogan (Farilya) looking SW over Küçük Farilya Bükü to Büyük Farilya Bükü. *See page 141.*

Above Yalikavak. Good *meltemi* anchorage on N side of Yalikavak Bay.
Below Yalikavak harbour and village looking south. *See page 142.*

Below Gümüşlük looking E. *See page 146.*

Left Bitez looking NW. *See page 150*

Above Akyarlar looking NW. *See page 148.*

Below Bodrum looking NNE. *See page 151.*

General

Pergamon is just 28km away, and Dikili is a safe harbour in which to leave a yacht if planning a visit to the site. Bus and *dolmuş* services to Bergama are frequent and cheap. The harbour is a pleasant little workaday place, with friendly and inquisitive locals. Occasionally coal is loaded here, and if the wind is in the wrong direction you may find your yacht covered in coal dust.

Pergamon

The site of this ancient city lies atop a majestic hill some 335 metres (1100ft) high in the middle of a large plain. The hill and the ruins of the city can be seen from afar as you approach the modern city of Bergama built below. If you have arrived here by bus or *dolmuş*, I recommend that you get a taxi to the summit and, after exploring the ruins, walk down the hillside following the ancient road as best you can. You will miss some interesting parts of the lower city if you explore only the summit.

The site has been occupied since Thracian times. Alexander took it in 334 BC, and it was under his successors that it rose to fame. Lysimachus unwisely left a hoard of 9000 gold talents with the eunuch Philetaerus, who, as soon as Lysimachus was gone, allied himself with another of Alexander's generals, Seleucus. He used the treasure to enlarge and enrich Pergamon, and the city began its rise to fame and prosperity. Pergamon became important as the intermediary link between Syria and Macedonia, a link which continued into the Roman era after the city was left to the Romans by Attalus III in 143 BC. It became the second city of Roman Asia and was an important fortress until the decline of Byzantium.

As an important city, Pergamon attracted artists and philosophers. It produced a distinctive school of sculpture, of which numerous beautiful pieces have survived. Some lesser known pieces are exhibited in the local museum in the town. Under Eumenes II (197–159 BC) the famous library of Pergamon was established. The word 'parchment' is said to come from Pergamon. The Ptolemies, jealous of the size of the Pergamon library, banned the export of papyrus to Anatolia, and the city was forced to refine the manufacture of parchment from animal hides.

On a low plateau about a mile from the lower city are the ruins of the ancient Aesculapium. Galen the physician (AD 130–200) was born in Pergamon, and developed the principles laid down by Hippocrates in Kos. He was to exercise a profound influence on medicine and medical practice until as late as the 17th century. Galen stressed the beneficial effects of a good diet, mineral baths and cold dips. He also wrote on a sort of psychotherapy, formulating an analysis of dreams some 1800 years before Freud.

The site of Pergamon is impressive. There are numerous ruins, some of which are undergoing reconstruction, and the commanding view from the summit is grand. The theatre (seating for 15,000 on a precarious slope), the library (it housed 200,000 volumes), the palaces, the altar of Zeus, the temples and the agora are well worth seeing, but in the end it is the magnificent site atop the steep hill that leaves the lasting impression.

In Bergama the local museum houses some finds from the site, as well as a collection of Turkish costumes and crafts. Just opposite the bus station, it is well worth a visit.

BADEMLI LIMANI

Approach

A yacht can enter the anchorage through the North or South Channel.

Conspicuous From the N, Güverçin Kayasi and Garipadasi and Kalemadasi islands are easily identified. The light structure (a white steel girder tower) on Pisa Burun and a white house on the northern tip of Kalemadasi are conspicuous. From the S, the white cliffs of the islands show up well in contrast to the reddish-brown cliffs of the mainland.

By night With care a yacht could enter through the N channel in calm weather, using the light on Pisa

Kalemadasi   *Garipadasi*   *Güverçin Kayasi*

Bademli Limani approach from the north

Garipadasi   *Kalemadasi*   *Mainland*

Bademli Limani the approach from the S. Note the conspicuous white cliffs of the islands

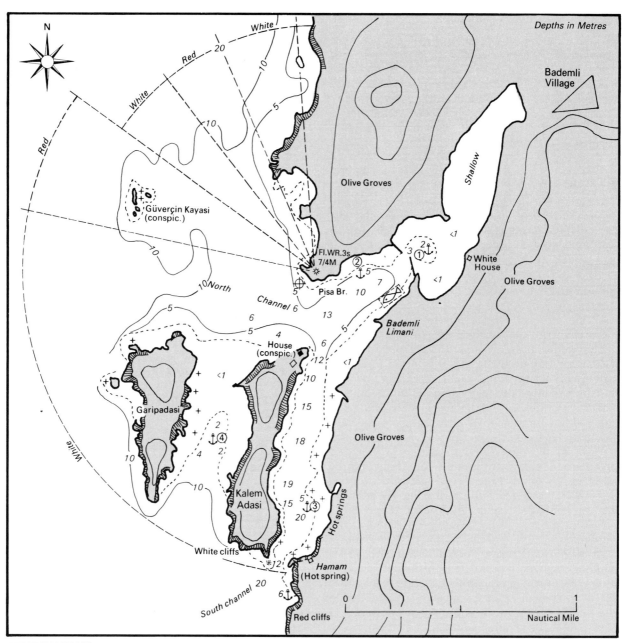

BADEMLI LIMANI
39°01'·2N 26°47'·9E

Burun (Fl.WR.3s7/4M – the red sectors cover the mainland and Güverçin Kayasi). A yacht should not attempt to navigate the South Channel at night.

Dangers

1. The channel between Garipadasi and Kalemadasi is shallow and not navigable.
2. Care must be taken of a reef with an above-water rock off the SE end of Kalemadasi.

Mooring

A yacht can find good shelter in one of four places.

1. In Bademli Limani itself. A rough breakwater has been built out from either side of the first narrows (see plan). The depths shoal rapidly NE of the breakwaters, and a yacht must proceed with care.
2. Anchor just under Pisa Burun, where there is good shelter from the *meltemi*.
3. Anchor at the end of the South Channel in 3–6

metres and take a line ashore if necessary. The bottom is uneven and care is needed. Good holding on sand. Good shelter.
4. Anchor between Garipadasi and Kalemadasi in 2–4 metres. Good holding on a sandy bottom. Open only to the S.

Facilities

Some provisions and several restaurants in Bademli village, about one mile from Bademli Limani anchorage. A fish restaurant here has been recommended.

General

The water is clear blue over a sandy bottom, and the surrounding country wooded or cultivated with olives. The anchorages are altogether delightful and, what is more, have hot water in abundance. Along

Bademli Iskelesi, inside the shallow lagoon

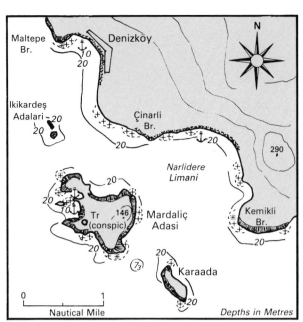

MARDALIC ADASI AND ADJACENT COAST

the eastern shore of the South Channel there are numerous hot springs. There are also hot springs on Kalemadasi and on the mainland shore.

In the SE corner of the South Channel anchorage there is a shelter over the biggest spring – a sort of ready-made *hamam*. Up the beach a little way is a natural rock pool, about bath size, that some hedonistic god has heated to bath temperature and provided with a view across the bay to Kalemadasi island. At sunset I bathed here in the most glorious bathroom a god could devise. Ancient masonry in the shallow water and near to the *hamam* indicates that the ancients enjoyed these natural springs too.

Mardaliç Adasi and adjacent coast

BA 1618

Just before you turn the corner into Candarli Körfezi there are several islands opposite the steep-to coast. The largest, Mardaliç Adasi, is easily recognised by a large tower on the summit. There are several places where a yacht can anchor on Mardaliç and the coast opposite.

1. ***Mardaliç Adasi*** On the NW side of the island there are two coves where a yacht can anchor. Anchor in 3–6 metres and take a line ashore if necessary. Reasonable shelter from the *meltemi*. The anchorage is wonderfully isolated, and could someone climb up to the tower and find out something about it, please.
2. ***Denizköy*** The bay N of Mardaliç under Maltepe Burnu on the mainland coast. There is a small settlement ashore, and a holiday village is under construction high up on the slopes above. Anchor in 4–10 metres off the beach. Although there is a lee from the *meltemi*, a swell rolls in, making it uncomfortable.
3. ***Narlidere Limani*** A large bay opposite Mardaliç Adasi. With the *meltemi* a swell is pushed in here, but in calm weather you can anchor off the beach in 8–15 metres.

Candarli Körfezi

CANDARLI

BA 1618

Approach

Conspicuous The town on the headland is easily identified from some distance off. The castle and a minaret in the town are conspicuous.

By night There are no lights, but in calm weather a yacht could approach the anchorage with caution.

Dangers The small harbour on the W side of the town should not be approached at night, on account of the above and below-water rocks near the entrance (see plan).

Mooring

Anchor in the bay on the E side of the town in 4–6 metres. The bottom is black mud and excellent holding. A small yacht can anchor in the harbour with a line ashore to the rough stone breakwater, but there seems little to gain from this. The locals only use the inner basin, and perhaps they know something about shelter in here during gales.

Shelter Good shelter in the bay on the E side from the prevailing northerlies. Open only to the S. Good shelter in the harbour on the W side, but see note above.

Facilities

Water In the town.
Fuel In the town.
Repairs Some mechanical repairs only.
Provisions Good shopping for provisions. Market on Fridays.
Eating out Restaurants in the town.
Other PO. Bank. Bus to Izmir and Istanbul.

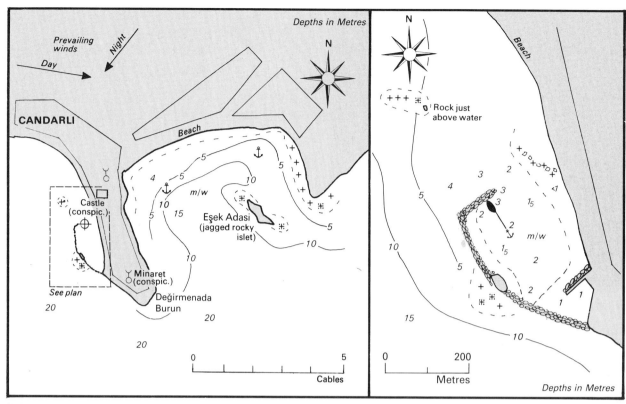

CANDARLI 38°56'N 26°56'E

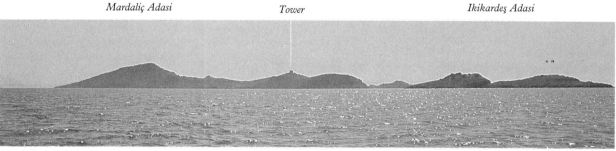

Mardaliç Adasi   *Tower*   *Ikikardeş Adasi*

Mardaliç Adasi, looking S. Note conspicuous ruined tower on
summit

Castle   *Small harbour*   *Değirmenada Br*

Candarli: headland, looking E

Castle   *Small harbour*

Approach to Candarli, looking ENE

Candarli: inner basin of the fishing harbour

General

The town, formerly Greek, is a thriving centre for the surrounding farmland. The restored 14th-century Genoese castle is stark when close to, but with two pencil-thin minarets on either side it looks, in silhouette, like something out of Disneyland.

Candarli stands on the site of the ancient Aeolian city of Pitane, though the only remains to be found are built into the castle and the village houses. Recently a 4th-century BC drainage system and walls have been found within the castle.

KADIRGA LIMANI (Dema Limani)

This large and mostly shallow bay lies about 5 miles E of Candarli. The bay is bordered by low sandbanks. A yacht should anchor in 3–5 metres on the eastern side of the bay. The bottom is sand and good holding. This is the site of ancient Elaea, the sea port of Pergamon, and scattered stone blocks from the ancient harbour can be seen on the sea bed. There is nothing to be seen ashore.

AKCA LIMANI (Glimi Limani)

A large bay lying one mile S of Kadirǧa Limani. The entrance is obstructed by above and below-water rocks, and a yacht should not attempt to enter the bay at night. By day it can be entered through the N or S passage (see plan). Anchor where convenient. The buildings of Yenisakran and Caltilidere line the shores of the bay. Some provisions and several restaurants can be found inland.

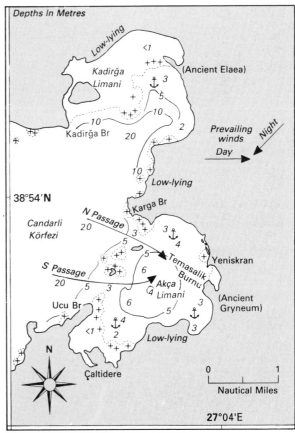

KADIRGA LIMANI AND AKCA LIMANI

On a short headland, Temaşalik Burnu, near Yenisakran, is the site of the Acolian city of Gryneum. There are only a few mounds and assorted masonry remaining.

ALIAGA LIMANI

BA 1618

A large bay on the S side of the gulf of Candarli. The tall chimneys, storage tanks and piers of an oil refinery on the W side of the bay are conspicuous. This ugly industrial installation blots out any other attractions Aliaga might have, except as a port of refuge. Entry by day or by night is straightforward. The entrance to the bay is lit: Q.G.5M and Q.R.5M. The lights of the oil refinery and a flare are also easily picked out.

Anchor in the NE corner or in the SW corner. The former gives good protection from most winds. Aliaga town was largely built from the ruins of ancient Myrina and Cyme.

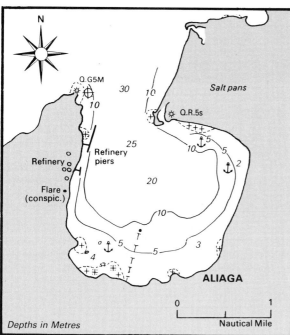

ALIAGA LIMANI
38°50'·2N 26°56'·7E

SHIPBREAKING AREA

Anchoring is restricted in an area from Ilica Burnu to Tavşan Adasi and from Pirasa Adasi across to Kalabakhisari. This area is for ships waiting to go to the shipbreakers. You will often encounter rusty old coasters and ferries anchored or run aground in the bay immediately E of Ilica Burun.

NEMRUT LIMANI

BA 1618

A bay on the W side of Ilica peninsula. It is easily recognised by the large PETKIM refinery on its eastern shores. Here four large white chimneys with red tops and a flare are conspicuous from a considerable distance off. There are numerous loading jetties around the bay. There is little to

attract a yacht to such an industrial wasteland, and in any case the bay offers indifferent shelter from the prevailing winds. This is, or was, the site of ancient Cyme and the harbour of Nimrod.

HOROZGEDIGI LIMANI

A large bay about 2M SW of Nemrut Limani. Indifferent shelter only.

YENIFOCA (Yenice, New Foça)

A large bay immediately W of Horozgediği. From the distance the chimneys of the PETKIM refinery at Nemrut Limani are conspicuous, and closer in the villas on the E side of Yildirimkaya Burun are easily identified.

Caution The reef, with isolated rock, extending from the W side of the bay in a northeasterly direction, shown on Admiralty chart 1618 as above water, is in fact just under the water and can be difficult to pick out. A good lookout must be kept for it. Another reef extends a short distance from the E side of the bay in a westerly direction.

Once into the bay, a small yacht may find room on the end of the short mole in the SE corner of the bay. There are 5-metre depths in the entrance and 2–4 metre depths off the outer part of the mole. There is usually room to anchor and take a line ashore to the outer end of the mole. Alternatively, anchor off the town, or in the NW corner under the short spit. The bottom is mud and good holding.

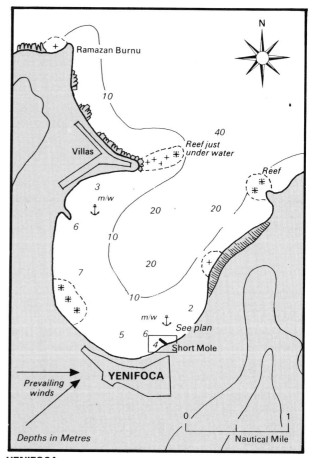

YENIFOCA
38°45'N 26°51'E

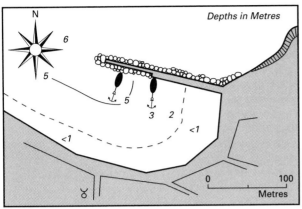

YENIFOCA HARBOUR

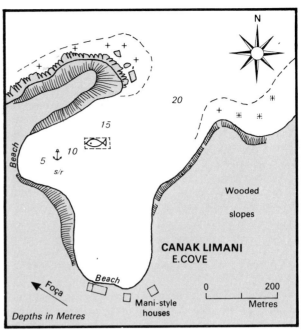

CANAK LIMANI – E COVE
38°44'N 26°46'E

Restaurant at the root of the mole and others along the waterfront. Most provisions available in the village. The village of Yenifoça is attractive enough, but much of the new building around the shores is not.

CANAK LIMANI

Two small bays 3 miles W of Yenifoça. The western cove has a short pier on the E side, with a small army post nearby. The eastern cove is the more attractive, with just a few ruined houses at its head.

In the E cove care must be taken of a reef on the W side of the entrance. Anchor at the head or in the cove on the W side of the bay. In the latter, anchor in 5–10 metres on a gently shelving bottom. The holding is not the best, on gravel and weed, but the water is exceptionally clear and you can choose a good spot in which to drop the hook.

The shores are pleasantly wooded, and the bay is deserted at night after the local fishermen, amateur and professional, have gone home.

Yenifoça

Yenifoça: approach to the bay, looking S

Harbour   *Yenifoça*

Yenifoça, looking SSE

Note It is reported that a fish farm now obstructs much of this anchorage.

ESKIFOCA (Old Foça)

BA 1618

Approach

The approach, through the islands fringing the harbour proper, is delightful.

Conspicuous The islands in the approaches are easily identified from the N. Closer in, the white light structure on Fener Adasi and a military observation tower on the S side of South Harbour are conspicuous. Once into South Harbour, a number of buildings around the head of the bay and some old fortifications (including several large arches at sea level) on Değirmen Burnu are conspicuous.

By night A yacht should keep well off the coast until the approach can be made from the W. Use the light on Fener Adasi (Fl.5s12M), and closer in the light on Değirmen Burnu (Fl.R.3s8M).

Dangers The islands and coasts are fringed by above and below-water rocks. Special care should be taken of the shoal water extending N of Değirmen Burnu.

Mooring

A yacht should make for Büyükdeniz Limani. Go stern or bows-to the quay, or anchor in the SW corner of the harbour. On the quay care must be taken of rubble, which extends a short distance underwater in places. The bottom shelves steeply here, and your anchor will be in 15 metres of water a short distance off. In the SW corner anchor in 6–10 metres on mud and weed – bad holding in places.

A yacht can berth in Küçükdeniz, but it is usually crowded with fishing boats, and the shelter is no better than that of Büyükdeniz.

Shelter Shelter on the quay is better than it looks with the prevailing wind. The wind is northerly

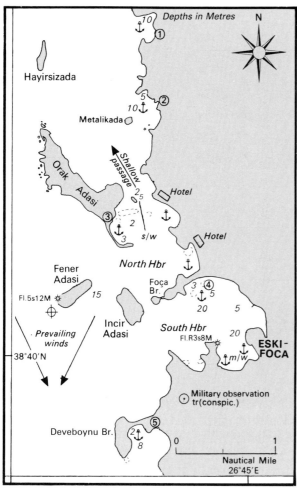

ESKIFOCA – APPROACHES AND ANCHORAGES
38°40'·6N 26°42'·7E

during the day, veering to the NE in the evening. The W side of Büyükdeniz is most uncomfortable in the evening, when the wind goes to NE.

Authorities Customs near the quay in Büyükdeniz, who will want to see your papers. Charge band 1/2.

Facilities

Water On the quay, but normally closed. There is a public water fountain nearby.
Fuel On the quay. You will have to locate the 'fuelman'.
Repairs Minor mechanical repairs only. On the W

side of the peninsula is a small boatyard which hauls fishing boats and *gulets* and could probably haul small yachts.
Provisions Good shopping for all provisions in the town.
Eating out Good restaurants on the waterfront at Küçükdeniz.
Other PO. Banks. Laundry. Turkish gas. Bus to Izmir.

General

The town and hinterland are most attractive. Even the large military camp nearby does not intrude on Foça. The locals go about their business as if the army didn't exist, although soldiers are always in evidence, doing PE or sweating over the assault course on the slopes behind the town.

Nothing remains of ancient Phocaea, the Ionian settlement that existed here. The Phocaeans were great navigators, and founded numerous colonies, in the Black Sea, in the Bosphorus, in Italy and at Massalia (Marseille). Herodotus wrote in *Book One* of his *Historaii*: 'The Phocaeans were pioneer navigators of the Greeks, and it was they who showed their countrymen the way to the Adriatic, Tyrrhenia and the Spanish peninsula as far as Tartessus. They used to sail not in deep, broad beamed merchant vessels but in fifty-oared galleys.'

Foça continued to be of importance during the Hellenistic and Roman periods, but then declined for a time until the Genoese revived it in the 13th and 14th centuries. The fortifications around Büyükdeniz were originally Genoese. The attraction for the Genoese was alum, used in the dyeing and tanning industries, which was mined locally and shipped to Europe. The Genoese also founded Yenifoça at this time. The Ottomans took the city in AD 1455, and thereafter its fortunes declined.

Yenifoça, looking SSE

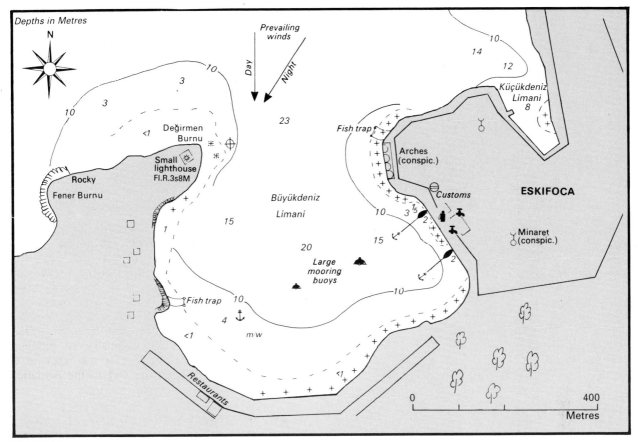

ESKIFOCA
38°40'·2N 26°44'·7E

NEARBY ANCHORAGES

1. In the bay E of Hayirsizada. Anchor in 5–6 metres on sand. Some shelter from the prevailing wind. Attractive surroundings.

2. In the bay E of Metalikada Islet. Anchor in 5–6 metres on sand. Reasonable shelter from the prevailing wind. A fine sandy beach runs around the bay, with a holiday village behind it in a pleasant wooded location.

3. *North Harbour* Anchor inside the low rocky spit off the southern end of Orak Adasi in 4–6 metres. Alternatively, anchor in either of the coves opposite on the coast. The holding is reported to be bad here. There is a Club Méditerranée holiday village on the mainland coast and another holiday village just S of it.

4. On the N side of South Harbour behind the narrow isthmus connecting Foça Burnu to the mainland. Care must be taken of underwater rocks here. Anchor in 4–8 metres on a weedy bottom, mediocre holding. Reasonable shelter.

5. In the bay in the southern approaches to South Harbour. There are several bungalow complexes around the shore. Shelter from the prevailing northerlies looks good.

Izmir Körfezi

This large gulf extends for some 22 miles in a southeasterly direction to Yenikale, and thence inland for about 7½ miles in an easterly direction to the port of Izmir. The western side of the gulf formed by the Karaburun peninsula is mountainous and steep-to, spectacularly so. The Peak of Mimas (Asarçik Kaya), a steep-to sugarloaf peak at the northern end of this mountain ridge, is easily recognised from the distance. The eastern side of the gulf, after Eskifoça, is low-lying. There are numerous lagoons and sandbanks, with shoal water extending some distance to seaward. A yacht sailing along this coast should keep a careful eye on the depths.

At Yenikale the waist of the gulf widens again into the Bay of Izmir. The bay is backed by high hills, but the shores are mostly flat and flanked by sandbanks and shoal water. The waters of the bay are much polluted. Once past Yenikale, the colour of the water changes to a putrid brown-green and the local tourist office advises that swimming is prohibited.

WINDS

The prevailing winds blow from the NW directly into Izmir Körfezi, raising a short, troublesome sea. This can make getting out of the gulf a bothersome business. The best policy is to leave early in the morning, hoping to motor as far as possible before the wind gets up at about midday. The *meltemi* is known locally as the *imbat*.

97

IZMIR KORFEZI

PROHIBITED AREAS

In the Izmir Körfezi there are several places where it is prohibited to navigate, anchor or land. Izmir is the headquarters of NATO land forces, and consequently prohibited zones are rigidly enforced.

1. **Haçilar Limani** It is prohibited to anchor or land in Haçilar Limani S of Eskifoça.
2. **Uzun Ada and Hekim Ada** It is prohibited to approach, navigate, anchor or land on these two islands.
3. **Yenikale Geçiti** It is prohibited to anchor or land in Yenikale Geçiti.

IZMIR (Smyrna)

BA 1522

Approach

The city and harbour of Izmir are approached through the buoyed channel leading into the Bay of Izmir.

Conspicuous The channel buoys are large and easily located. At the narrowest point of the channel, the short headland of Yenikale, with earthworks on it, shows up well from the distance. Once into the bay, the city of Izmir will be seen spread around both shores. It is difficult to locate the old harbour, although there are usually cargo ships anchored off. Closer in, the outer breakwater and the white light towers at the extremities will be seen. Enter at either end of the harbour.

By night Straightforward. The buoys marking the

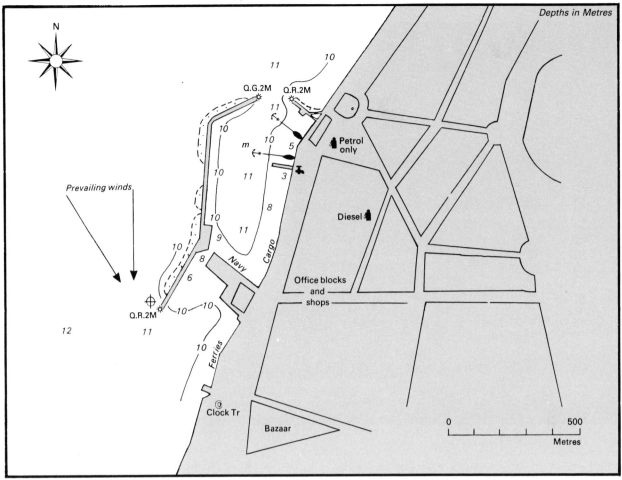

IZMIR OLD HARBOUR
38°25'·4N 27°07'·6E

channel are lit (Fl.R.3s5M and Fl.G.3s4M). The harbour entrances are lit, but the lights do not have a good range and are difficult to make out against the bright lights of the city. (Harbour lights, S entrance: Q.R.2M. N entrance: Q.G.2M and Q.R. 2M. Pier F.R.2M.)

Dangers Ferries run regularly between Izmir and Karşiyaka on the opposite shore. These large ferries come inside the breakwater on part of their route, so special care must be taken when manoeuvring inside the harbour.

Mooring

Go stern or bows-to in the NE corner of the harbour. The bottom is revolting black mud – good holding, but very messy.

Shelter With the *imbat* there is a slop in the harbour, uncomfortable but not normally dangerous.

Authorities A port of entry. The officials are all located near the new commercial harbour, but will come to the old harbour to carry out the necessary formalities. Charge band 1/2.

Facilities

Water On the quay. Its purity has been reported to be suspect.
Fuel In the town, but quite near the harbour. There are petrol pumps close to the quay.

Repairs Mechanical, engineering and electrical repairs can be carried out in the town. (See Levent Marina.)

Provisions Excellent shopping for all provisions. Excellent fruit and vegetables from the bazaar in Konak.

Eating out Good restaurants of all categories close to the waterfront.

Other PO. Banks. Hospital. Turkish gas and *Camping Gaz*. Buses to all parts of Turkey. Internal and international flights.

General

The location of Izmir, on the slopes around the bay, has been praised since ancient times. But for the yachtsman Izmir is not a pleasant place to be: the waters of the bay are a poisonous polluted brown (the local tourist board says that swimming is prohibited), the harbour is grubby and uncomfortable, and the city is an unattractive sprawl of reinforced concrete.

The site was occupied in Aeolian times, and later by the Ionians, until it was destroyed by the Lydians in the 6th century BC. It is commonly believed to be the birthplace of Homer (along with Khios), but there is no definite proof either way. Smyrna was founded by Lysimachus, one of Alexander's generals, but not until the Roman occupation did it become important. It was then one of the three most

99

Izmir harbour, looking NW

important cities in Asia, along with Pergamon and Ephesus.

Its continued importance under Byzantium, the Latins (mostly Genoese), the Turcomans and the Ottomans can largely be attributed to the fact that the harbours for Pergamon and Ephesus (the Cayster estuary) silted up in Roman times. Silting has taken place in the Gulf of Izmir as well, and in the 19th century the approaches to it were becoming so shallow that action was called for. In 1886 the Gediz Cay (ancient Hermus) was diverted from its original course to its present channel south of Eskifoça. Thus Izmir escaped the fate of its ancient sister ports, although the narrow channel must be continually dredged for modern deep-draught ships.

In the 19th and early 20th centuries Smyrna was an important commercial port for Europe, with a cosmopolitan population and ships of all nations waiting for cargo in the bay. After the First World War the Greeks, encouraged by certain European countries, including Britain, landed an army here, intending to annex some of western Asia into a greater Greece. The Turkish army, rallied by Ataturk, soon routed the Greek army, which fell back in confusion to Smyrna. The evacuation of Greeks and foreigners from Smyrna in September 1922 was a catastrophe. The town was set on fire, adding to the panic, and although many were rescued, it is estimated that at least 100,000 died.

After the Second World War Izmir was largely rebuilt, and the city has spread in recent years right around the shores of the bay. It is now the third largest city in Turkey, and was succinctly described by a local architect I met as 'a city of merchants, a city of money'.

LEVENT MARINA

A new marina in the SW corner of the bay, near Güzelyali.

Approach

The harbour should be approached on a SW course to avoid shoal water extending out from the coast NW of it. Close in the breakwaters and the masts of yachts in the harbour will be seen.

By night The entrance is lit: Fl.G/Fl.R.

VHF Ch 16, 73.

Mooring

Berth where directed. Yachts of over 20 metres need to take care because of the restricted room inside. There are finger pontoons and laid moorings. Good all-round shelter. Charge band 2.

Facilities

Services Water and electricity near every berth. Toilets and showers. Laundry.

Fuel On the quay.

Repairs A slipway with a reported capacity of 250 tons. Limited hard standing. Workshops where most repairs can be arranged, including electronic repairs. Chandlers.

Provisions None nearby.

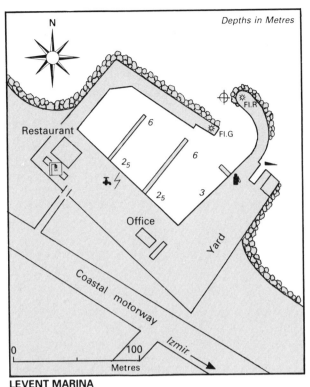

LEVENT MARINA
38°24'25N 27°04'04E

Eating out Restaurant within the marina.
Other Izmir is about 15 minutes away by taxi. Bus and *dolmuş* services are infrequent.

General

This new mini-marina (total 70 berths) provides the only secure berths close to Izmir. The management is reported to be friendly and helpful, but the siting of the marina close to the coastal motorway and its associated noise is unfortunate. The marina is also poorly served by bus and *dolmuş*, although it is reported that a ferry terminal (operating to Izmir old harbour?) is to be built. Nonetheless, it is rapidly filling up.

Address: Levent Marina, 1880 Sokak No. 72, Cakalburnu, Izmir ☎ (232) 277 1111/259 7794 *Fax* (232) 259 9049

GUZELBAHCE

Between Izmir and Urla there are two small fishing harbours at Güzelbahçe, about 3 and 4 miles E of Karantina Adasi. Of these, the easternmost harbour has better depths – mostly 1·5–2·5 metres inside. Both harbours are usually packed with fishing boats, and it is difficult to find anywhere to berth. Moreover, the main coast road runs right beside the harbours, and they are not the most pleasant places to be.

URLA ISKELESI

BA 1522

Approach

The approach can be hair-raising with the afternoon *imbat* pushing you down into the dead end bay, but

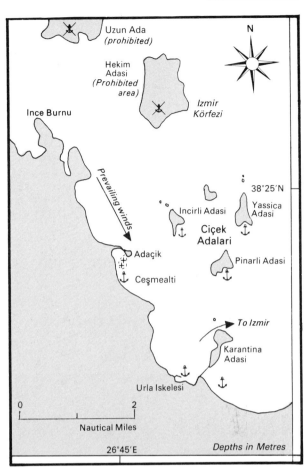

URLA LIMANı- APPROACHES TO URLA ISKELESI

the harbour is easily identified, and once inside the breakwater you are out of the sea and wind.

Conspicuous The twin gentle humps of Karantina Adasi are easily identified. A minaret behind the harbour and a stumpy white light tower (unlit) in the middle of the breakwater are conspicuous. Closer in the outer breakwater and the entrance are easily located.

By night A F.G.3M is exhibited at the end of the breakwater. Q on the end of the pier.

Mooring

The harbour is crowded with fishing boats, but the locals are generally helpful in finding you a berth. Go stern or bows-to the N quay. Care is needed of the rock ballasting which extends underwater from the quay, so if possible go bows-to. The bottom is mud and weed, good holding.

Shelter Good all-round shelter.

Facilities

Water At the root of the mole.
Fuel On the outskirts of the village. A mini-tanker can deliver to the harbour.
Repairs Minor mechanical repairs. Several workshops nearby build small wooden *caïques*.
Provisions Good shopping for provisions.
Eating out Several restaurants around the harbour, including some good fish restaurants.
Other PO. Bus to Izmir.

101

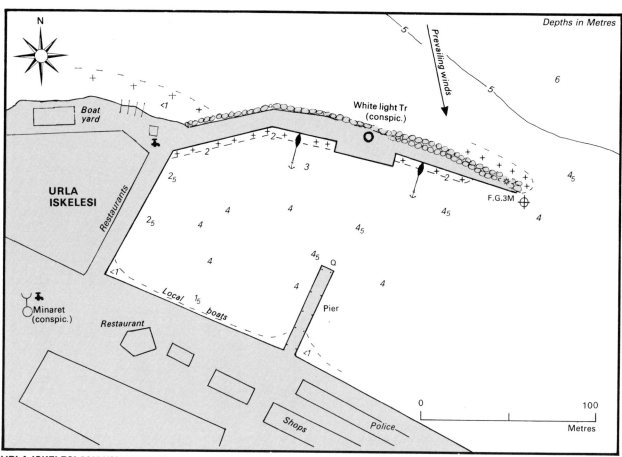

URLA ISKELESI 38°22'N 26°46'·4E

General

Urla Iskelesi, the landing place for Urla, which lies just inland, is a scruffy but not unattractive fishing village. The headland of Karantina Adasi, originally an island but now joined to the mainland by a causeway (by Alexander the Great), was the site of one of the members of the Ionian Confederacy, and is remembered as the birthplace of the philosopher Anaxagoras.

This incredible man attempted, in the 5th century BC, to understand and explain the universe in rational terms. He believed in infinitely divisible 'seeds' (a sort of precursor to the atomic theory, not unlike that of Democritus) which came together to form solids through centrifugal force, directed by a supreme Mind (Nus). He did not believe that the heavenly bodies were divinities, and explained that they were stones torn from the earth, that the sun was a red-hot collection of such stones, and that the moon reflected the light of the sun. Remember, this was nearly 2,500 years ago! For his theories on the heavenly bodies he was charged with crimes against the gods, and exiled to Lampsacus in the Troad.

NEARBY ANCHORAGES

1. On the E side of Karantina Adasi there is a good lee from the *imbat*. Anchor in 5–10 metres in the SW corner.
2. A yacht can anchor under Adacik, where there is a good lee from the *imbat*. A large hotel complex on the short headland is conspicuous. Care must be taken of underwater rocks behind the

Lighthouse   Entrance   Pier

Urla Iskelesi, looking E

headland. Ashore in Çeşmealti there are numerous hotels and restaurants, and provisions can be obtained.

3. Pleasant day anchorages can be found in the small Çiçek Adalari archipelago. There are attractive anchorages on the SE side of Inçirli Adasi and on the S side of Yassica Adasi. The anchorage on the S side of Yassica Adasi affords good shelter from the *imbat*. Anchor in 2–8 metres on sand and weed, good holding once through the weed.

Harbours and anchorages between Urla and Kara Burun

Along the E coast of Karaburun peninsula there are several small fishing harbours and anchorages which are well worth exploring, depending on the weather.

AKKUM

A small harbour tucked down on the E side of Gülbahçe Körfezi. Care is needed in the approach of shoal water extending out from the coast immediately N of the harbour. Make the approach to the harbour from the SW. Go stern or bows-to either side of the central pier. The bottom is sand and weed, good holding. Good shelter from the *imbat*.

Ashore there is only a huddle of fishermen's huts. A restaurant opens in the summer.

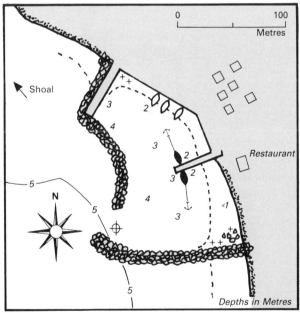

AKKUM
38°22'·5N 26°41'E

GULBAHCE AND YILAN ADASI

In calm weather a yacht can anchor off Gülbahçe, on the W side of the gulf, and under Yilan Adasi, the islet near the head of the gulf. Often the *imbat* does not blow home with any strength into the gulf and there is just a bit of local chop. Provisions and restaurants in Gülbahçe.

BALIKLIOVA LIMANI

A large bay on the W side of the entrance to Gülbahçe Körfezi. There are several places where a yacht can find shelter.

1. At the N end of the bay are two coves where reasonable shelter from the *imbat* can be found. Anchor where convenient. Ashore there is a holiday village, looking something like a concentration camp with its high wire fences and spotlights, and a camping ground.

2. Just S of the village there is a rough stone breakwater providing good shelter. Care is needed of an isolated reef approximately 70 metres NE of the entrance. There are 2·5-metre depths in the entrance and 2–3 metre depths off the breakwater. Most of the harbour on the SW side is shallow, with depths of less than a metre. Anchor under the breakwater and take a line to it. Good shelter from the *imbat*. Ashore in the village, provisions and restaurants will be found.

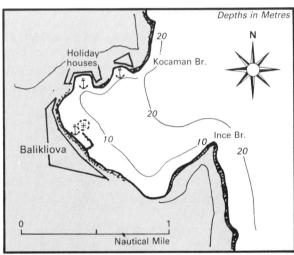

BALIKLIOVA LIMANI
38°25'·5N 26°36'E

GERENCE KOYU

The large bay about 2½ miles N of Balikliova. There are several places where a yacht can anchor around the bay.

1. On either side of the tiny headland jutting out from the N side. Anchor in 5–10 metres off the camping ground on the E side or off the W side. Reasonable shelter from the *imbat*, although some swell may penetrate. Water at the camping ground and a restaurant in the summer.

2. In the N creek at the head of the bay. Anchor in 5–6 metres on mud. Good shelter. Ashore there is the hamlet of Tahta Iskelesi, though little is available here. Along the coast there is a startling splash of green on the narrow strip of land under the steep, barren slopes.

3. In the S creek. Fish farms now clutter the creek, but you can still find convenient depths to anchor in near the head of the creek. A few fishermen's houses ashore, but little else.

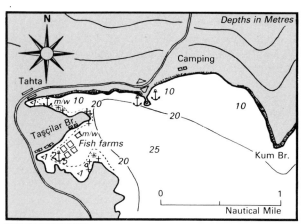

GERENCE KOYU
38°28′N 26°37′E

MORDOGAN

A large village on Karaburun peninsula, about 3 miles N of Kum Burnu. A large apartment block is conspicuous on the SE side of the cove. A fishing harbour has been formed by building a breakwater out from one side of a small cove.

The entrance is fringed by underwater rocks and rubble, so some care is needed. With the prevailing northerlies there is a swell at the entrance, making

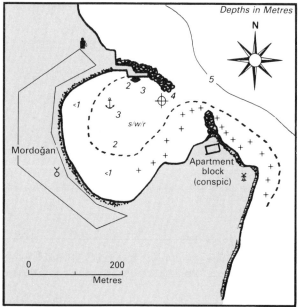

MORDOGAN
38°31′·1N 26°37′·6E

entry a little tricky. Approach from the NE, keeping reasonably close to the end of the breakwater. Anchor in 2–3 metres under the breakwater, or there may be room to go alongside or stern or bows-to the quay. Reasonable shelter from the *imbat*.

Fuel near the harbour. Provisions and restaurants ashore. PO.

KAYNARPINAR

A miniature fishing harbour about 3½ miles N of Ardic Burnu. Care is needed of a set net off the breakwater, supported by two poles, but otherwise the approach is free of dangers. Go alongside or stern or bows-to where possible. The harbour is normally crowded with fishing boats, and you will probably have to go alongside one of them. Good shelter from the *imbat*.

Limited provisions and several *çay* houses. The wooded setting in this little bight in the coast is thoroughly enchanting, and it is well worth squeezing in here if you can.

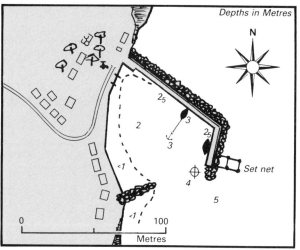

KAYNARPINAR
38°33′·7N 26°34′·3E

ESENDERE

A small and mostly shallow harbour about 3½ miles N of Kaynarpinar. A small yacht might find some shelter under the rough stone breakwater, but for most craft the harbour is too shallow.

Conspicuous building   *Breakwater*

Mordoğan, looking SW

104

PORT SAIP

Approach

The harbour is situated in the S corner of the bay, under Bozdağ Burun.

Conspicuous A hotel on the rocky bluff immediately N of the harbour will be seen. The breakwater is difficult to see from the distance, but a light tower on the extremity will be seen closer in.

By night There are no lights.

Mooring

Go stern or bows-to the N quay. The bottom is mud with some rocks – good holding.

Shelter Good shelter, although there may be a reflected swell off the cliffs opposite the entrance with onshore winds. With N–NE winds there are reported to be gusts off the high land.

Dangers The harbour bottom is uneven, especially near the W quay. I have given minimum depths in the harbour plan.

Facilities

None nearby, except for a water tap on the beach. Provisions in Karaburun village, about 1½km up the steep hill behind.

Harbour

Approach to Port Saip

Port Saip, looking SE

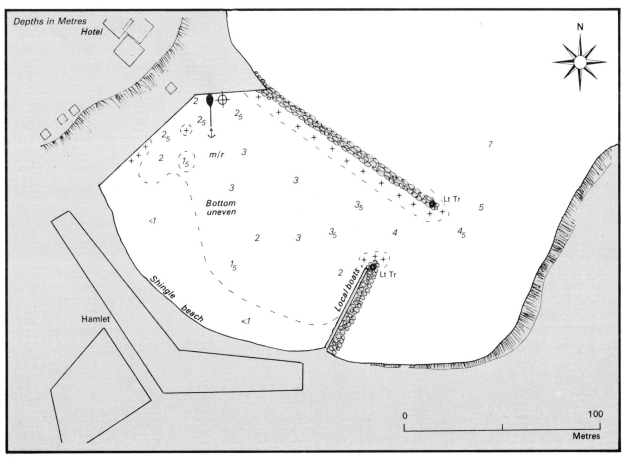

PORT SAIP
38°38'·7N 26°31'·84E

General

The setting is spectacular: the steep rocky slopes of the mountains behind and the wooded valleys and lower slopes are reminiscent of Moorea in Tahiti. Only the palms are missing. The hamlet at the harbour is a poor little place, but not unfriendly.

KARABURUN ISKELESI

This miniature harbour, in the S corner of the bay under Büyük Adasi, has room for one or two small yachts only. The houses around the bay and the breakwater are easily seen once into the bay. Enter the miniature harbour with care and go bows-to the short pier. The sides of the harbour are fringed by

Karaburun lighthouse

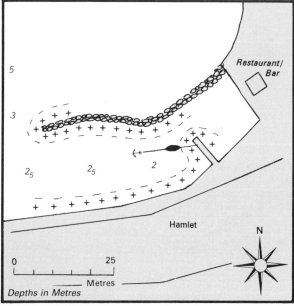

KARABURUN ISKELESI
38°39'N 26°31'E

Karaburun Peninsula, looking NE

underwater rubble. Limited provisions and a restaurant by the harbour. An army observation post broods over the bay atop the ridge behind the hamlet.

Caution Care must be taken of shoal water off the western end of Büyük Adasi. There are least depths of 1·8m (1 fathom). The shoal patch is easily seen in calm weather.

YENILIMANI

A new harbour (*Yeni* = 'new') approximately ½ a mile E of Komur Burnu. Care is needed of the permanent set net off the breakwater. Keep fairly close to the outer breakwater through the entrance and go stern or bows-to the S quay. Good shelter from the *meltemi*.

Some provisions and a restaurant in the village. The village is a pleasant spot, stuck right out on the

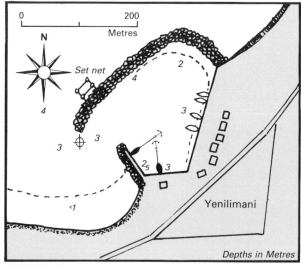

YENILIMANI
38°40'·5N 26°26'·4E

Büyükada Adasi   *Karaburun Iskelesi*

Approach to Karaburun Iskelesi, looking SE. Büyükada Adasi is on the left of the picture

end of Karaburun, and the locals are a friendly bunch.

EGRI LIMANI

Approach

Conspicuous The Uç Adalar rocks off the W side of the Karaburun headland are easily identified. They are evil-looking rocky spurs jutting out of the sea. A small stone cairn on the W side of the entrance cannot be seen until close in.

By night There are no lights, and I would not advise a night entry.

Dangers

1. Care must be taken of the reef extending half a mile off the coast from Denizğiren, a hamlet a little over 1½ miles NNW of the entrance to Eğri Limani. In calm weather the sea breaks on part of

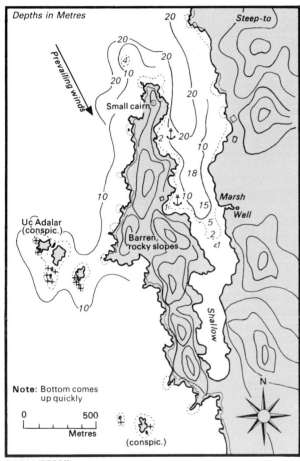

EGRI LIMANI
38°33′N 26°22′E

Uç Adalar   *Entrance*

Approach to Eğri Limani looking NNE

Entrance   *Uç Adalar*

Approach to Eğri Limani looking S

the reef, but with any sea running it would be difficult to pick out. A yacht should keep well off the coast to avoid the reef.
2. The plan on BA 1625 shows a clear passage between the Uç Adalar islets, but it looked shallow and perilous to me. I did not fancy trying it.
3. Off the entrance there is a shoal patch with least depths of 4 metres (13ft). It is difficult to identify.
4. Eğri Limani has silted since earlier plans were made, and care must be taken of the depths.

Mooring

Anchor in one of the coves on the western side. The bottom is mud and weed – mediocre holding only.

Shelter Moderate shelter from the *meltemi*. Although I have sheltered here adequately from the *meltemi* on several occasions, it appears others have not had comfortable nights. Usually the *meltemi* dies down in the evening and a moderate katabatic wind from the N–NE kicks in the late evening. If in doubt set a second anchor here.

Facilities

Fish can sometimes be bought from local fishermen sheltering here. Otherwise there are no facilities.

General

The surroundings are spectacular but bleak. A few small farms are scattered around the coastal flat, but otherwise the bay is deserted.

Ildir Körfezi

Across the mouth of this gulf, between Uç Burunlar and Kiraz Burnu, lie the Kara Islands and the islands of Uzan and Toprak, making it almost landlocked. There are numerous other islands and scattered reefs and shoals in the gulf.

Between Top Burnu and Kalaytas Burnu, around the western shores of the gulf, the coast is heavily built up with large hotels and holiday villages. This area is a booming tourist resort, capitalising on the sandy beaches, clear water and natural hot mineral springs. Just a short distance away at Egri Limani you could be a thousand miles removed from the 'Costa Ceşme'.

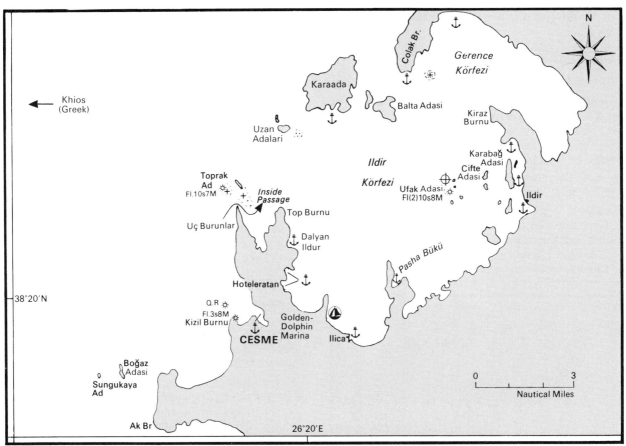

ILDIR KORFEZI
Ufak Adasi light 38°23'·5N 26°25'·7E

GERENCE KORFEZI

A large extension northeastwards of Ildir Körfezi. The rock ¾ of a mile E of Colak Burnu is above water and easily located. Just under Colak Burnu there is a small cove providing some shelter from the *meltemi*. In Gerence Körfezi reasonable shelter from the *meltemi* can be found in the northern corner. There seems to be an afforestation programme under way ashore.

KARAADA

On the S coast of this island there are several inlets which look as if they would provide good shelter from the *meltemi*, although they are quite deep.

ILDIR

The anchorage lies behind Karabağ Adasi, under a small islet. A yacht can enter around the N or S end

Ilidir: the village and knoll, from the anchorage behind the island

of Karabağ Adasi. Unfortunately most of this anchorage is now taken up with a fish farm, and there is little room to anchor. The anchorage off Ildir village is bad holding and subject to gusts, so it should only be used in calm weather.

At Ildir village there are the remains of ancient Erythrae and subsequent fortifications. Little remains of Erythrae, part of the Ionian confederacy, apart from some sections of the city walls. The site is spectacular, though, with a view out over the village (Greek until 1922) and the islands to Ildir Körfezi.

PASA BUKU (Pasha Bay)

A bay on the E side of Kalaytas Burnu, providing good shelter from the *meltemi*. A sandy beach at the head and several hotels and holiday villages on the slopes around the bay.

Caution

Care must be taken of the reef off Kalaytas Burnu. The sea breaks on it, making it easy to identify.

ILICA

A small and mostly shallow harbour one mile SE of Golden Dolphin Marina. The outer breakwater is easily identified. Care must be taken of a reef extending off the coast and a short distance N of the outer breakwater. The southern half of the harbour is obstructed by above and below-water rocks.

Anchor in the northern end under the breakwater

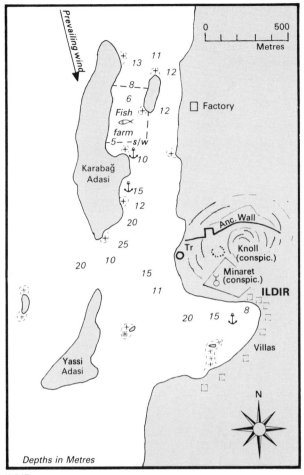

ILDIR
38°24′N 26°28′E

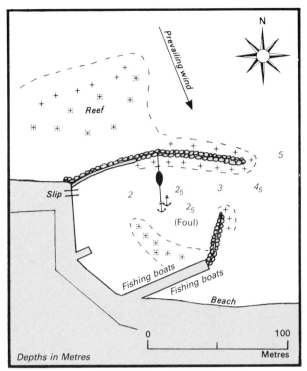

ILICA
38°19N 26°22′E

Approach to Ilica, looking S

Harbour

and take a line to it. The bottom is sand and good holding, but care should be taken of numerous large anchors and chains fouling the bottom. The flukes of several of these large anchors lying on the sea bed stick up and could be dangerous to a yacht. Good shelter from the *meltemi*.

Ashore there are numerous large hotels and restaurants. The area is renowned for its hot springs, which are said to be beneficial to those suffering from skin complaints (the springs are slightly radioactive).

GOLDEN DOLPHIN MARINA (Altin Yunus)

Approach

The marina lies on the S side of Kalem Burnu, which is easily recognised by a tall three-bladed wind generator on it. The marina and the hotel complex associated with it cannot be seen until you have rounded the headland.

Conspicuous The large hotel complex behind the marina and the masts of the yachts in the marina are easily identified.

By night The harbour entrance is lit: F.G and F.R.

VHF The marina listens out on VHF Ch 16.

Mooring

Data 125 berths. Max LOA 35m. Depths 2–5m.

Go stern or bows-to or alongside where directed by a marina attendant. There are laid moorings for most but not all berths. The marina is crowded in the summer and a berth may not be available.

Shelter Good all-round shelter.

Authorities Port captain. The authorities from Cesme can be called for entry formalities. Charge band 3.

Facilities

Services Water and electricity (220V) at or near every berth. A shower and toilet block.

Fuel A fuel quay outside the marina. A trolley is provided for refuelling with jerry cans inside the marina.

Repairs A yard next to the marina hauls out yachts on a slipway. Some repairs can be carried out here.

Provisions Shops nearby.

Eating out Restaurants within the hotel complex.

Other PO. Bank.

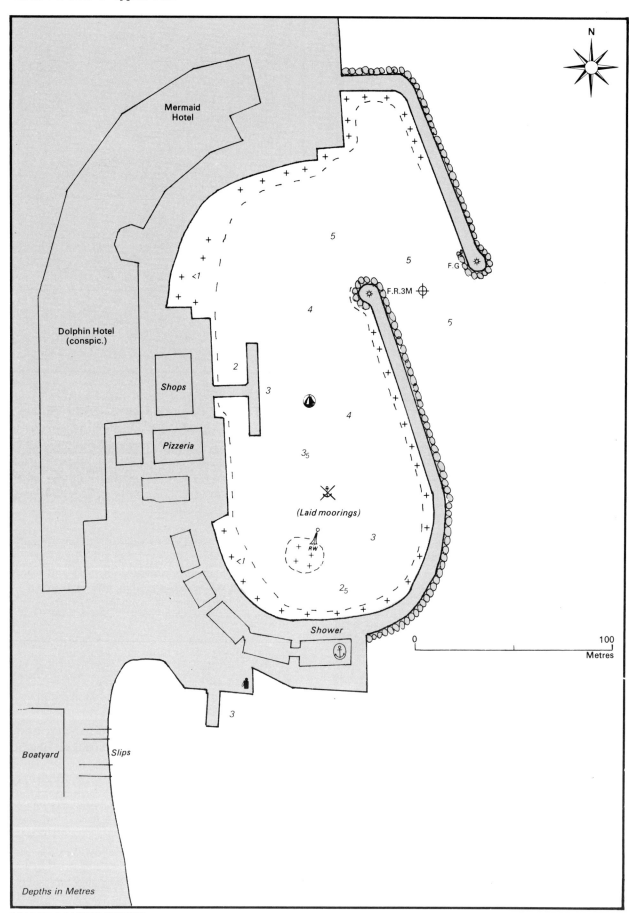

N

Mermaid
Hotel

5

5

F.G

F.R.3M

Dolphin Hotel
(conspic.)

4

5

2

3

4

Shops

3₅

Pizzeria

RW

(Laid moorings)

3

2₅

Shower

Boatyard   Slips   3

Depths in Metres

0   100
                                                  Metres

GOLDEN DOLPHIN MARINA
38'19'·5N 26°20'·8E

Golden Dolphin Marina

Golden Dolphin Marina, approach looking S

General

The marina is an adjunct of the huge hotel complex behind. It is a pleasant enough spot, full of the boats of the rich from Istanbul and Izmir. One gets the feeling that cruising boats that don't have matching fenders and mooring warps, with Avons and bicycles littering the deck, are tolerated rather than welcomed.

Altin Yunus Setur Marina ☎ (232) 723 1434/723 1631 *Fax* (232) 723 4620.

HOTELERATAN BEACH

A cove on the W side of Boyalik Limani, popular with the yachts based at the Golden Dolphin Marina. Anchor in 4–5 metres on a sandy bottom. Good shelter from the *meltemi*. In the summer a small restaurant and a bar open on the beach. The slopes about the cove are pleasantly wooded, with a few villas dotted around the shore.

Immediately N of Hoteleratan Beach there is another bay also affording good shelter from the *meltemi*. In the summer a bar opens on the beach.

DALYAN ILDUR

A small harbour on the E side of Top Burnu. The entrance to the harbour is difficult to discern until close in. Once it has been identified you should get everything ready for berthing, as there is little room for manoeuvring inside. Go stern-to the quay where convenient. The harbour has mostly been dredged to a least depth of 3 metres. The bottom is mud and good holding. Excellent all-round shelter.

Ashore there are several upmarket fish restaurants. Water and electricity on the quay. The small fishing harbour has been turned into something of a mini-marina, but possesses great charm for all that. Charge band 2.

If there is no room on the quay, a yacht can

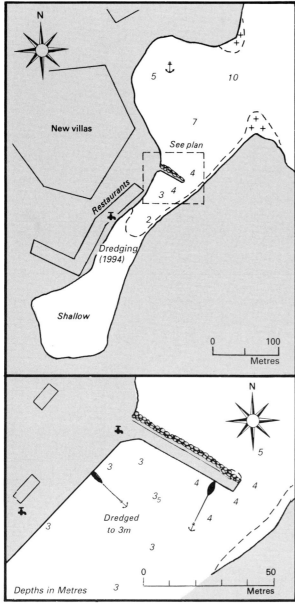

DALYAN ILDUR
38°21′N 26°19′E

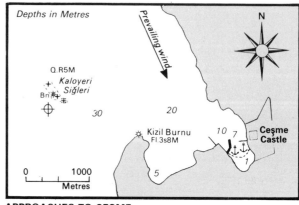

Light structure on Kaloyeri Siğleri

anchor in the cove immediately N of the small harbour. Good holding on sand, but not well sheltered from the *meltemi*.

Note It is reported the inlet has been dredged to the SW for a further 100 metres.

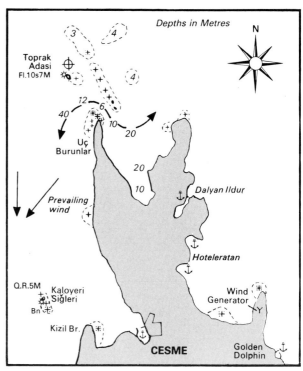

UC BURUNLAR
Toprak (Alev) Adasi light 38°23′·3N 26°16′·4E

UC BURUNLAR PASSAGE

Off Uç Burunlar there are a number of above and below-water rocks and the small but easily identified islet of Toprak Adasi (Alev Ada). Of these, only the rocks shown at the S end of the reef off the thin islet E of Toprak Adasi are actually above water. The thin islet just mentioned and the rocks off Uç Burunlar, shown as above water on BA 1625, are in fact reefs just under the water.

The reefs running out from Uç Burunlar can be difficult to spot, especially when approaching from Çeşme. In calm weather a yacht can pass inside the rocks and reefs with due care. I recorded a least depth of 6 metres in the fairway of the inner passage. With the afternoon breeze whipping up white caps it can be difficult to pick out the reefs, and a yacht is advised to go north of the maze of rocks and reefs (see plan).

APPROACHES TO CESME
Kaloyeri light 38°19′·8N 26°16′·1E

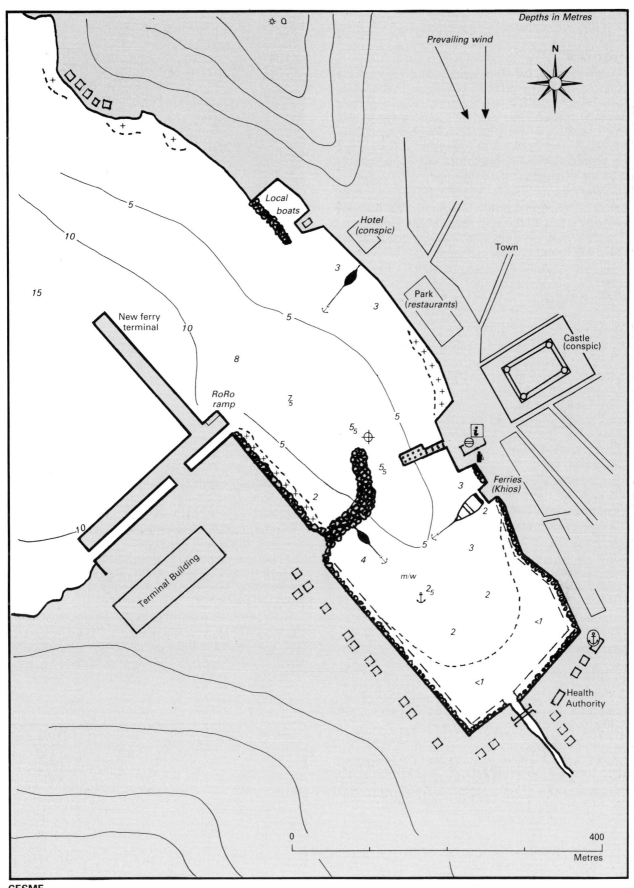

Depths in Metres

Prevailing wind

N

Local
boats

Hotel
(conspic)

Town

Park
(restaurants)

Castle
(conspic)

New ferry
terminal

RoRo
ramp

Ferries
(Khios)

Terminal Building

m/w

Health
Authority

0   400

Metres

CESME
38°19'·2N 26°18'E

CESME

BA 1625

Approach

Conspicuous The white masonry light pillar marking Kaloyeri Siğleri is easily identified, as is the white light tower on Kizil Fener Burnu. The new ferry terminal and new pier running out from the W side of the bay are conspicuous. The Genoese castle does not show up well until closer in. The outer breakwater is easily identified, but it is initially difficult to make out the entrance.

By night Use the lights on Kaloyeri Siğleri (Q.R.5M) and Kizil (Fener) Burnu (Fl.3s8M). The harbour entrance is not lit, but with care a yacht could enter. The pier on the E is floodlit. On the ridge N of the town a Q is occasionally exhibited.

Dangers Care must be taken of the shoal water and reefs extending SE of the light tower marking Kaloyeri Siğleri.

Mooring

At present there is little quayed space for yachts. When the new quayed area around the harbour is complete this will be rectified, and there will eventually be a large number of berths. Anchor behind the breakwater in 3–4 metres. The bottom is mud and weed, and not everywhere good holding. The bay to the west of the harbour marked 'good holding ground' on the Admiralty plan is unsuitable for a yacht, being open to the *meltemi*.

Note In calm weather *gulets* sometimes go stern-to the quay off the town. Care is needed of the rock ballasting which extends underwater in places. With the *meltemi* this is not a good place to be.

Shelter Good all-round shelter in the harbour, although the *meltemi* will cause you to roll around a bit. It usually dies down in the evening so that you get a peaceful night's sleep.

Authorities A port of entry. Customs and immigration are conveniently housed on the ferry quay. The health authorities and harbourmaster are at the southern end of the harbour. Charge band 1/2.

Facilities

Water On the quay, but not potable. Potable water is difficult to find, the nearest source being a tap across the road from the petrol station.

Çeşme: looking towards the castle from the W side of the harbour

Fuel Near the old ferry quay.

Repairs Minor mechanical repairs only.

Provisions Good shopping for all provisions in the town. Supermarket on road to Izmir. Ice available.

Eating out Excellent restaurants in the town and on the waterfront.

Other PO. Banks. Turkish gas. Buses to Izmir. Ferry to Khios.

General

Çeşme is a growing tourist resort, enjoying some measure of prosperity from the ferry link with Khios. The fine castle on the waterfront was built by the Genoese in the 14th century and captured by Beyazit I in 1400. It protected the harbour and the Turkish fleet until they were attacked by three Russian squadrons in 1770, when the Turkish fleet was destroyed and Turkish sea power broken, allowing the Russians access to the Mediterranean from the Black Sea.

The town is a bustling little place, seemingly caught halfway between the new trade in tourists and the old agricultural life. It grows on you, and many of us have some affection for Çeşme.

III. The Ionian coast

Ceşme to Gülük Körfezi

This chapter covers the coast from Ceşme to Güllük Körfezi (the ancient Gulf of Mandalya). The coast is for the most part mountainous, although there are several large plains bordering it, most notably the marshy plain covering part of what was the ancient Gulf of Latmos. The waters of the Menderes river have deposited sufficient silt over 2000 years to build up the coast to some 20 miles westwards of where it once lapped the shores of ancient Herakleia.

Ionia takes its name from Ion, son of Creusa and the sun god Apollo. Later Greek legend tells us that the sons of Codrus, the last king of Athens, colonised the area after invasions from the north forced them to look for land further afield. We know that the first Ionians settled here as early as the 10th century BC, after the Aeolians had colonised the country to the north. The colony grew to become one of the most influential civilisations in Asia Minor, producing great artists and scientists, and paving the way for a civilisation that reached its height in the Hellenistic period.

Ionia produced many notables. It is commonly accepted that Homer was an Ionian; he certainly wrote in the Ionian dialect. Thales of Miletus is looked upon as the father of physical science. Anacreon of Teos was one of the most revered lyric poets of antiquity. And the Ionians accomplished all this, it seems, in great comfort and with some style. Pausanias in his tour of Ionia praised it thus:

'Ionia enjoys the finest of climates and its sanctuaries are unmatched in the world . . . The wonders of Ionia are numerous, and not much short of the wonders of Greece itself.'

About 700 BC the Panionic League was formed. Twelve cities belonged to the league: Samos and Khíos, Phocaea, Clazomenae, Erythrae, Teos, Colophon, Lebedos, Ephesus, Priene, Myus and Miletus. Smyrna was later added to the original twelve. The religious and administrative centre was the Panionium, near Priene. The league was largely formed for religious purposes, and the cities tended to be politically and commercially independent, a factor that was to be their undoing when the Persians arrived on the scene. Internecine bickering over individual contributions undermined the defensive capabilities of the league, and the Persians simply moved in from the south.

The Persians ruled for two centuries, but Greek culture still flourished, and when Alexander the Great came to power he found the Greek cities alive and well. Under Alexander's unification the cities prospered and the Hellenistic period was ushered in.

In 144 BC the Romans established control and Ephesus was made the capital of Roman Asia. Under Roman rule, Ionia continued to prosper, until the decline of Rome and the rise of Byzantium.

Today the Ionian region is just as beautiful as it was in ancient times. It is a fertile region, possessed of a fine climate, although it rains a lot in the winter, if you are contemplating wintering afloat in the region. Bordered by the blue Aegean, the coastline twists and turns to form many lovely bays, with small villages stacked up on the hillsides or huddled at the water's edge. For the most part it is peopled by farmers, so that there are few large fishing ports and little local traffic on the water.

During the Roman era the lyric poet Catullus visited Ionia and was captured by its charms. He was probably tired of the bickering and back-stabbing going on in Rome, much as one tires of the pettiness of London or Paris or Rome, and was eager to return:

'and Catullus will forsake these Phrygian fields
the sun-drenched farmlands of Nicaea
and make for the resorts of Asia Minor, the famous cities.
Now the trepidation of departure, now lust of travel,
feet impatiently urging him to be gone.'

Weather patterns

In the summer the prevailing wind is the *meltemi*. A short distance off the coast it blows from the NW, but closer in it follows the contours of the coast and in the gulfs curves to blow more from the W. The *meltemi* can blow with considerable strength from late July through to September, often getting up to Force 6–7. It blows with less strength in the early summer.

A yacht must be careful of gusts off the mountains, which can be considerably stronger than the wind strength on the open sea. Gusts are particularly violent around Ak Burun and off the peninsula terminating in Teke Burnu, off the high land on the eastern side of Siğaçik Körfezi, off Samos Island and the S side of the Can Dağli mountains (between Dip Burnu and the ancient Gulf of Latmos), and off the northern side of Güllük Körfezi. At night a NE wind may blow off the land.

In the spring and autumn the winds are predominantly northerlies, but some southerlies can be expected. In the winter strong winds are almost equally divided between N and S. Most of the rain in this region falls in the winter.

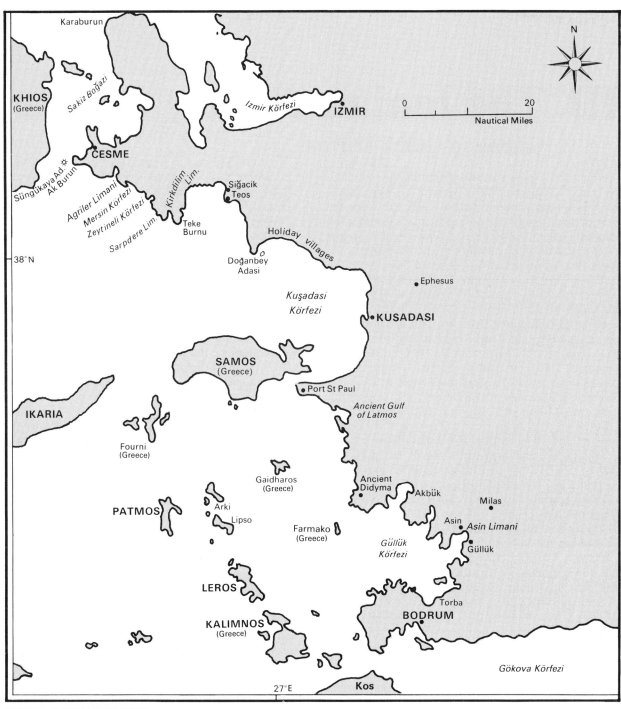

CESME TO GULLUK KORFEZI

Data

PORTS OF ENTRY

Kuşadasi
Güllük

Note Güllük, although designated as a port of entry, is not
commonly used by yachts.

MAJOR LIGHTS

Süngükaya Adasi Fl.5s10M
Bozalan Burnu Fl(2)5s6M
Teke Burnu Fl(3)15s10M
Doğanbey Adasi Fl(2)5s7M
Kuşadasi Fl(2)10s8M
Bayrak Adasi Fl.5s8M
Karaada Fl.5s7M
Tekağaç Burnu Fl.15s10M
Incegöl Burnu Fl.3s5M
Güllük Fl(2)5s7M
Tavşan Ada Fl(2)10s9M

Quick reference guide

	Shelter	Mooring	Fuel	Water	Provisions	Eating out	Plan	Charge band
Agriler Limani	AB	AC	O	B	O	C	•	1/2
Mersin Körfezi	B	C	O	O	O	O	•	
Zeytinelli Körfezi	C	C	O	B	O	C		
Sarpdere Limani	A	C	O	O	O	O	•	
Kirkdilim Limani	B	C	O	O	O	O	•	
Gökkovar Limani	A	C	O	O	O	O	•	
Demircili Limani	C	C	O	O	O	O	•	
Siğaçik	A	A	B	A	B	B	•	2
Teos Limani	C	C	O	O	O	C	•	
Körmen Adasi	C	C	O	O	O	O		
Cam Limani	C	C	O	O	O	O	•	
Kuşadasi	A	A	A	A	A	A	•	2
Dip Burnu	C	C	O	O	O	O		
Port Saint Paul	C	C	O	O	O	O	•	
Port Saint Nikolao	B	C	O	O	O	O	•	
Kovala	O	C	O	O	O	O		
Cukurcuk	B	C	O	O	O	O		
Büyükturnali	C	C	O	O	O	O		
Altinkum	B	C	B	B	C	B	•	
Kuruerik Limani	B	C	O	O	O	C	•	
Akbük Limani	C	C	O	O	C	C	•	
Kazikli Limani	B	C	O	O	O	C	•	
'Paradise Bay'	B	C	O	O	O	O	•	
Cam Limani	C	C	O	O	O	O		
Gök Limani	C	C	O	O	O	O		
Asin Limani	A	AC	B	A	C	B	•	1/2
Güllük	C	AB	O	B	B	B	•	1/2
Varvil Köyü	C	C	O	O	O	O		
Kuyucak	A	C	O	O	O	O	•	
Güvercinlik	C	C	O	O	C	B		
Torba	A	A	O	B	C	C	•	1/2
Denir Limani	C	C	O	O	O	O		
Ilica Bükü	B	C	O	O	O	O		
Türk Bükü	B	AC	O	B	C	B	•	
Gundoğan	B	AC	O	B	C	C	•	
Yalikavak	A	AC	B	A	B	B	•	1/2

SUNGUKAYA AND BOGAZ ADASI

Proceeding through Sakiz Boğazi (Khíos Strait), two small islands lie close to Turkey. The outermost is Süngükaya Adasi, which is easily recognised. The light tower on it, a white masonry tower 8m (26ft) high, is conspicuous (light characteristic Fl.5s10M). Boğazi Adasi is a slightly larger island, closer to the coast. There are good depths in the fairway between Boğazi Adasi and the mainland.

AK BURUN

Approaching from the S, a white cliff on the southern side of the cape stands out well. A yacht can find a lee from the *meltemi* in the large bay on the S side of Ak Burun, but care must be taken of two rocky patches with least depths of 1·8m over them. There are strong gusts into the bay.

AGRILER LIMANI (Alaçati Körfezi)

A large bay lying 7½ miles SE of Ak Burun. From the W, Sharp Peak and Mt St Elias show up well. From the S the white cliffs on the eastern side of the entrance can be seen from some distance off. There are several places where a yacht can anchor:

1. On the W side, in a bight just past some low cliffs. Reasonable shelter from the *meltemi*.
2. In the bay on the E side, off Koçak. Poor shelter from the *meltemi*.
3. Near the head of Agriler Körfezi. Care must be taken of shoal water off the western side and at the head of the bay. The bottom is mud and good holding.
4. *Agriler Harbour* The harbour in the NW corner of the bay. There are 2m depths in the entrance and mostly 3m depths inside. Go stern or bow-to the quay on the N side. Good all-round shelter. Restaurant and *pension* nearby. It is about 3km into Alacati village for provisions. A 45-minute walk or call a taxi from the *pension*. Water and toilets. It is proposed the harbour will be elevated to 'marina' status. Charge band 2.

Note There are gusts into the bay with the *meltemi*.

A few villas have been built around the stony, barren hills surrounding the bay.

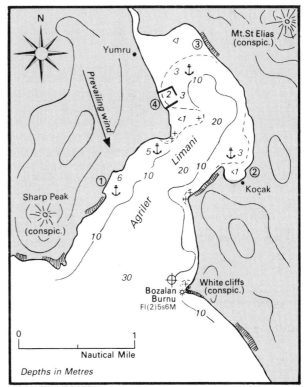

AGRILER LIMANI
38°13′·5N 26°23′·4E

MERSIN KORFEZI

A large enclosed bay lying about 3 miles SE of Agriler Limani. Cigden Adasi, the southernmost island in the approaches, is easily identified from some distance off. At the entrance to the gulf, a

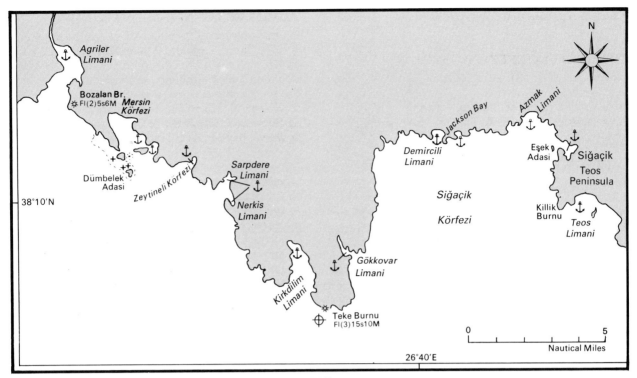

AGRILER KORFEZI TO TEOS Teke Burnu light 38°06'·3N 26°35'·6E

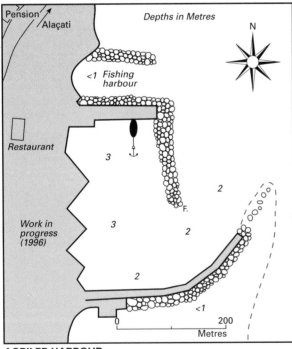

AGRILER HARBOUR

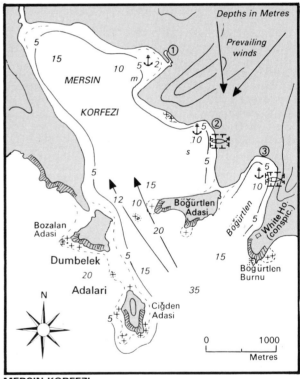

MERSIN KORFEZI
38°13'N 26°26'·5E

white house on the eastern side is conspicuous. Bozalan Adasi and Böğürtlen Adalari, the other two islands in the entrance, are not easily identified against the hills behind. The rock in the middle of the passage between Bozalan and Böğürtlen Adalari has its tip painted white and is easily identified. A yacht can pass on either side of the rock into the large bay beyond. A yacht can anchor in one of three places:

1. In a cove on the E side of the bay near the head of Mersin Körfezi. Anchor in 5–7 metres on mud. There is nothing ashore.

2. In a cove on the E side of Mersin Körfezi, just N of Böğürtlen Adasi. Anchor in 3–5 metres on sand. There is a beach nearby, but nothing else.

3. ***Böğürtlen*** The large bay close E of Böğürtlen Adasi. Anchor in 7–10 metres on sand. There are strong gusts into the bay with the *meltemi*. The white house on Böğürtlen Burnu is a military post, although it is not always manned. Otherwise the bay is deserted.

Note It is reported that fish farms now take up much of anchorages 2 and 3.

ZEYTINELI KORFEZI (38°11'·5N 26°29'·5E)

Lies about 1½ M SE of Böğürtlen Adasi. Anchor near the head, where there is good shelter from the *meltemi*. The resort at the head of the bay is for air force personnel on R & R. The management is reported to be helpful if you go ashore.

SARPDERE LIMANI

A bay lying a little over a mile SE of Zeytinelli Körfezi. Good shelter from the *meltemi* can be found in either of the two coves at the head of the bay. The cove on the E is shallow (2–3 metres), but with care a yacht can anchor here. Nearly all-round shelter in idyllic surroundings.

The cove on the E is situated at the bottom of a wooded ravine, and the small coastal flat is cultivated, providing a welcome splash of green after the barren slopes to the N. In the northern cove a number of villas have been built near the water's edge. Anchor where convenient on a gently shelving bottom. The water is very clear here.

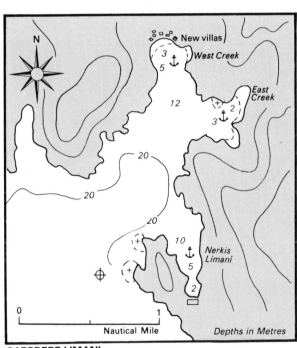

SARPDERE LIMANI
38°10'·15N 26°30'·55E

Fishermen, Sarpdere Limani

NERKIS LIMANI

At the entrance to Sarpdere Limani an inlet curves back to the S, providing nearly all-round shelter within. However, in the summer the prevailing northerlies blow straight in, setting up a bit of a chop – more uncomfortable than dangerous. The bottom shelves gently to a sandy beach at the head. Anchor in 3–5 metres on sand and weed, good holding. The inlet is attractive, with thick *maquis* on the surrounding slopes and crystal-clear water. Pylons now run around the E side of the bay bringing electricity to the building at the head of Nerkis Limani. It is to be hoped this is just a fisherman's co-op and not the start of yet another holiday village.

KIRKDILIM LIMANI

A large bay immediately W of Teke Burnu. Anchor at the head of the bay in 3–6 metres where it curves around to the NW. The bottom is mostly sand, and the water is so clear that you can see exactly where to drop the anchor. Here there is nearly all-round shelter in tranquil surroundings. With the *meltemi* there are gusts into the bay, but no sea enters and so the *meltemi* is not bothersome.

A few fishermen use the bay, but otherwise you have it to yourself.

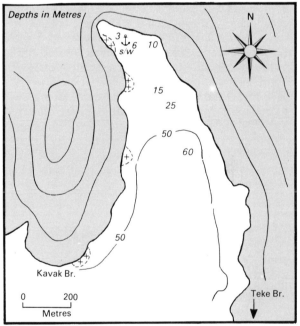

KIRKDILIM LIMAN
38°08'·5N 26°33'·8E

TEKE BURNU

This bold cape is prominent from W and E. The cape slopes evenly at about a 40° angle from a high plateau to the sea. The light structure on the cape will be seen closer in (Fl(3)15s38m10M).

Teke Burnu, looking SE

GOKKOVAR LIMANI (Gokliman Kokar)

A deep fjord lying 2 miles N of Teke Burnu in Siğaçik Körfezi. The entrance is difficult to see until close to it, but the approach is free of dangers and the depths are everywhere considerable. Once at the entrance, the fjord opens up to a large deep bay with two narrow creeks. The fjord is everywhere deep, with the bottom rising abruptly to the shore. Consequently you will have to drop your anchor in 10–20 metres of water and take a line ashore. At the head of the N cove the bottom comes up abruptly from 3–8 metres to a rocky shelf with less than 1 metre over it.

Anchor in either the E creek or N creek. In E creek anchor in 10–12 metres and take a line ashore to the shore. The rocks here are now much despoiled by the graffiti from *gulets*. In N creek there are several indentations along the W side of the creek where you can anchor and take a line ashore. At the head of N creek the bottom comes up quickly and care is needed when approaching the end of the inlet. Anchor and take a line ashore. Nearly all-round shelter in either creek. The whole fjord is a place of breathtaking beauty, quite unlike the bays to the N and S. The sides of the fjord are bordered by rocky pillars weathered into fantastic jagged sculptures. The plateau above is cultivated. There is a farmer on the top of E creek and at dusk N creek echoes to the sound of a hundred goat bells when

the goatherd uses the route around Gökkovar to get his charges back home. Behind, the bare rocky slopes of Kiran Dağ serve only to emphasise the beauty of the lagoon and creeks.

DEMIRCILI LIMANI (Demirali)

Lies near the NW corner of Siğaçik Körfezi. The bay is reasonably easy to identify. Keep well clear of the islets and rocks lying off the coast. Anchor off the beach of the bay in 5–8 metres or in the E cove in 3–6 metres. The E cove shallows fairly quickly towards the head and the bottom is uneven in places, especially around the rocks on the N side. The bottom is sand and weed, good holding once through the weed. Good shelter from the *meltemi* although there are gusts into the bay. Some ground swell works its way around into the bay and it may be a good idea to put a stern anchor to hold the yacht into the swell. The E cove suffers less from the ground swell. Open S.

There is a huddle of houses in the NE corner of the bay and a farmer/fisherman in the E cove.

Immediately E of Demircili Limani is Jackson Bay which also affords some shelter from the *meltemi* although not as good as Demircili.

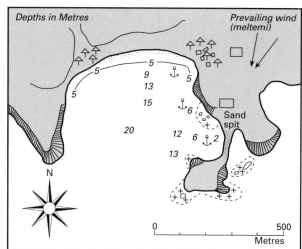

DEMIRCILI LIMANI

AZMAK LIMANI

The large bay in the NE corner of Siğaçik Körfezi. The bay shelves gently in to the shore but shallows up some distance out. Anchor in 2–4 metres off the long beach where the river flows in. Good holding on mud and weed. Good shelter from the *meltemi* although there are gusts into the bay. Some ground swell rolls around making the anchorage a bit rolly. Open S.

The bay is pretty much deserted apart from a few fishermen and is a pleasant spot. The bay immediately W also affords reasonable shelter from the *meltemi*.

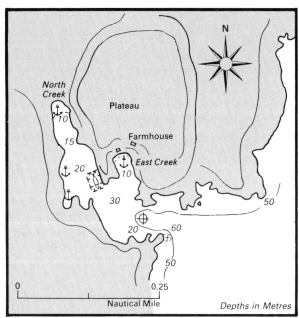

GOKKOVAR LIMANI
38°08'·3N 26°36'·6E

Left Cokertme looking NW from the entrance. *See page 156.*

Below Sehir Adalari looking E. Duck Rock is easily seen in the foreground. *See page 158.*

Below Söğüt looking SSE. *See page 159.*

Above Değirmen Bükü. E creek looking SE. *See page 160.*

Kormen Adasi and
anchorage under the
headland looking SW.
See page 164.

Below Tuzla Köyü looking S at the anchorages on the
southern side near the entrance. *See page 161.*

Above Söğut . The west jetty. *See page 159. Below* Knidos looking south from the ancient city. *See page 166.*

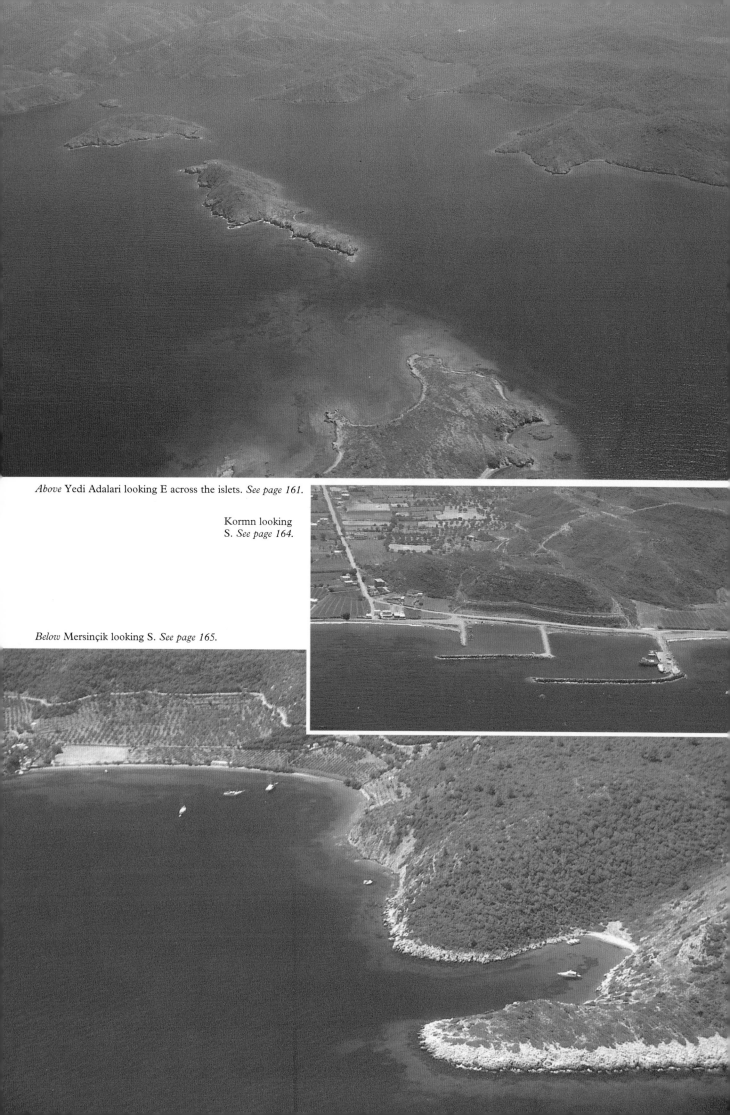

Above Yedi Adalari looking E across the islets. *See page 161.*

Kormn looking S. *See page 164.*

Below Mersinçik looking S. *See page 165.*

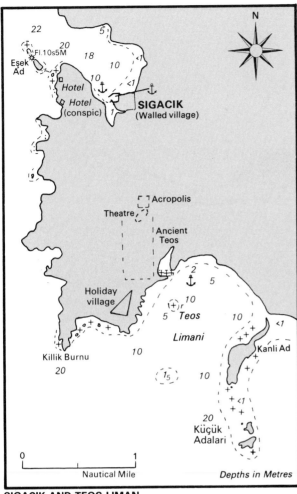

SIGACIK AND TEOS LIMAN

By night Use the light on Eşek Adasi (Fl.10s5M). The harbour entrance is lit (F.R.2M and F.G), though the lights should not be relied upon.

Dangers
1. There are 2–4 metre depths in the channel between Eşek Adasi and Teos peninsula, but a reef obstructs most of the passage. Do not attempt the passage without local knowledge, and even then my advice would be to go around the outside of the islet. Although I have been through here in *Tetra*, it was a hair-raising business which I won't repeat again.
2. A reef, mostly under water, extends in a NW direction from the northern tip of Eşek Adasi. It can be seen in calm weather.

Mooring

Go where directed in the small harbour. There are laid moorings at most berths.

Shelter Good all-round shelter in the old harbour. A number of boats winter afloat here.

Authorities Harbourmaster. Charge band 2.

Facilities

Services Water on the quay. Electricity can be connected.
Fuel Can be delivered by tanker.
Repairs Limited mechanical repairs.
Provisions Most provisions available in the village. Better shopping in Seferihizar, and a market on Fridays – about 5km away via a regular bus service. Ice can be ordered.
Eating out Good restaurants close to the harbour.
Other PO. Bus to Izmir.

General

The old walled village (pronounced 'Saajik') and small fort are in reasonable repair, and it is interesting to walk around a village that has changed little over several centuries. The surrounding wall is virtually intact, and pieces of ancient marble, probably from Teos, can be seen incorporated into it. The fort is of Genoese origin.

Life here is hard and the village is poor. Most of the villagers are engaged in agricultural work on the surrounding farmland. Ancient Teos is about 4km away, and you can get a bus or a taxi to the site – or walk if you are feeling energetic.

SIGACIK

BA 1057

Approach

The old walled village and the small harbour will not be seen until you are well into the bay (Siğaçik Körfezi).

Conspicuous From the W, Eşek Adasi, the small island off the NW tip of Teos peninsula, is difficult to pick out from the land behind. A hotel complex in the bay just S of Eşek Adasi on Teos peninsula is conspicuous, and another to the N will also be seen. From the S, Eşek Adasi can be distinguished when following the coast of Teos peninsula. Once into Siğaçik Bay the walled village and the harbour breakwater are easily identified.

Fort   *Breakwater*   *Entrance*

Approach to Siğaçik, looking SE

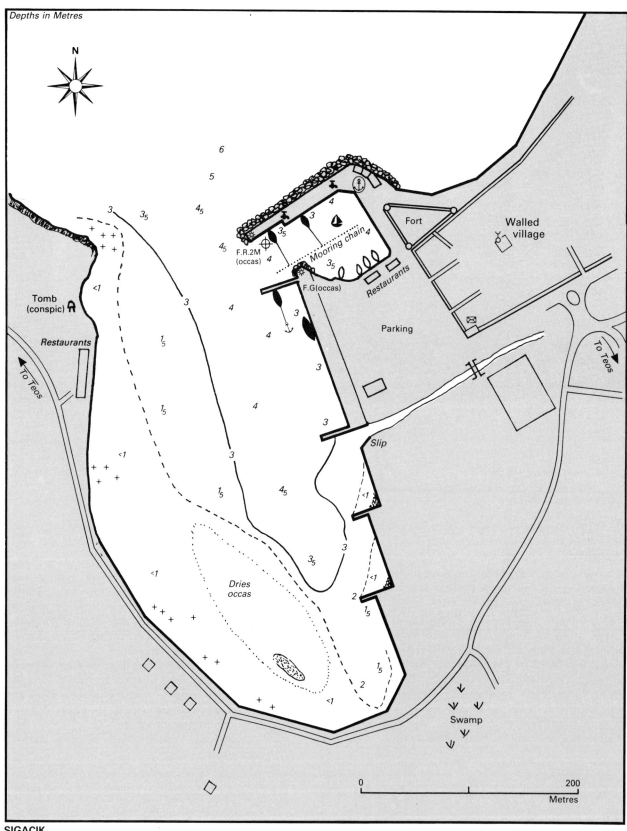

Depths in Metres

N

6

5

4₅

3   3₅

4₅   5

<1

Tomb
(conspic)

Restaurants

To Teos

1₅

1₅

<1

<1

3

3

3

4

4

4

4₅

1₅

Dries
occas

<1

2

1₅

4

4₅

3₅

<1

<1

3

2

1₅

Slip

3

3

3

Parking

Restaurants

F.R.2M
(occas)

3₅

3₅

4

Mooring chain   4

3₅

F.G(occas)

4

3

3

4

4₅

4

Fort

Walled
village

To Teos

Swamp

0   200

Metres

SIGACIK
38°11'·66N 26°46'·93E

Siğaçik harbour, looking E from the coast opposite

Note Work on the marina and associated facilities in the bay has stopped for the time being and will be resumed when more money becomes available. The proposed development is shown in the plan. Siğaçik Marina ☎ (232) 743 1386

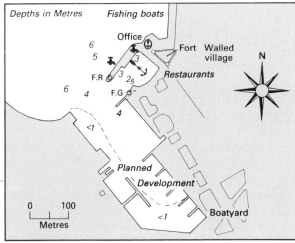

SIGACIK

TEOS LIMANI

A yacht can anchor in Teos Limani, on the S side of the isthmus connecting Teos peninsula to the mainland. A large brummagem holiday village is conspicuous on the slopes nearby.

Care is needed of an isolated reef in the entrance to the bay, and of another reef with less than 1 metre depths over it, further into the bay. This reef is not shown on the charts. Local fishermen suggest keeping about 400 metres off Kanli Adasi. There are variable depths closer in and care is needed.

Anchor in 5–6 metres. The holding is reported to be uncertain SW of the mole. Good shelter from northerlies, but open to the S.

Ancient Teos

The ancient Ionian city lies in a delightful setting amongst olive groves, across the fields from the anchorage. The city was established by the Minyans, and later became Ionian and an important centre of the Actors' Guild of Ionia. These artists of Dionysus were as much a religious order as a band of actors. They travelled widely throughout Ionia and enjoyed great fame and a certain amount of notoriety. The lyric poet Anacreon was born in Teos, and carried on the traditions of the Actors' Guild by means of an admirably sybaritic lifestyle. John Freely describes it thus:

'The most famous son of Teos was Anacreon, one of the greatest lyric poets in the ancient Greek world. Anacreon was born in Teos about 572 BC and died there eighty-five years later after a rich and varied life, drawing his last breath at a banquet where he choked upon a grape-pip. As Critias of Athens wrote of Anacreon after the old poet had sung his last poem of love: "Teos bore thee, thou sweet old weaver of womanish song, rouser of revels, cousener of dames, rival of the flute, lover of the lyre, the delightful, the anodyne; and never shall love of thee, Anacreon, grow

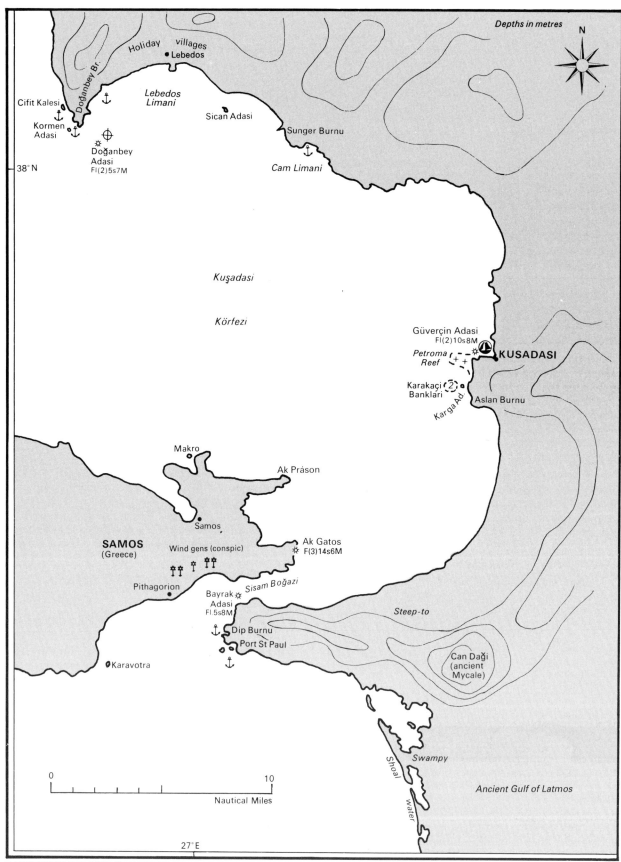

DOGANBEY BURNU TO PORT ST PAUL
Doğanbey Adasi light 38°01'·3N 26°52'·9E

old and die, as long as serving lads bear round bumpers above board, so long as a band of maidens does holy night-long service of the dance. . ." '

The Companion Guide to Turkey

Most of the ancient city is in poor repair, but the Temple of Dionysus, the fortified walls, parts of the Acropolis, the theatre, and the ancient harbour are easily found.

The Concrete Coast

From Teos right down past Kuşadasi, many of the beaches have had vast concrete holiday villages built around them. This wholesale reconstruction of the landscape may give the impression that there are numerous places where a yacht can bring up, but in fact there are mercifully few harbours and bays a yacht can use, and consequently the yachtsman will be spared seeing these man-made edifices close up.

CIFIT KALESI

(Mouse Island, ancient Myonneus)

A slab-sided island looking something like a slice of cake. A cleft nearly splits it in two. A yacht can anchor on the S side, off the causeway joining the island to the coast, but there is indifferent shelter only. Strong gusts off the high land when northerlies are blowing make it most uncomfortable.

KORMEN ADASI

Lies about one mile S of Cifit Kalesi. Kormen Adasi is a ragged pitted red island nearly joined to the shore. A yacht can find shelter in an inlet sheltered on the W by the island. Good shelter from the *meltemi* although there are gusts into the anchorage. A road runs down to the head of the bay but otherwise it is deserted. A hot spring is reported to issue from a cave halfway along the E side of the island.

Kormen Adasi   *Doğanbey Adasi*

Kormen Adasi and Doğanbey Adasi, looking NE

DOGANBEY ADASI

Lies about one mile SE of Kormen Adasi. The slab-sided island is easily identified from some distance off. A light is exhibited on it: Fl(2)5s7M.

LEBEDOS

In settled weather a yacht can anchor on the E side of Kisik Yarmimadasi so that you can go ashore and

Doğanbey Adasi looking E

look at the ruins. Lebedos was never an important city, and there is little to see.

CAM LIMANI

Close E of Sunger Burnu, a yacht can find good shelter from the *meltemi* in a bay to the E of Camlimani Adasi. Cam Limani itself is a military zone, and anchoring here is prohibited. However recent reports indicate it may be possible to anchor here where shelter is better than in the bay to the E. Anchor in the bay to the E, in 5–10 metres off the hotel, where there is reasonable shelter from the *meltemi*. A taxi can be arranged to visit the ruins of Claros and Notium. However, it is better to arrange a visit from the security of Kuşadasi marina, where your yacht can be left in perfect safety.

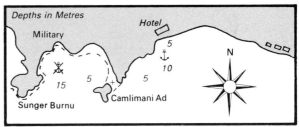

CAM LIMANI
38°01'N 27°05'E

KUSADASI

BA 1057
Imray-Tetra chart G32

Approach

The marina lies at the northern end of Kuşadasi town.

Conspicuous From the NW the town, spreading up the slopes behind Kuşadasi Roads, can be seen from some distance off. From the S a tall white tower (part of a hotel complex) on Aslan Burnu is conspicuous. A large hotel and apartment complex looking like the radiator of a large American car is conspicuous on the slopes just N of Aslan Burnu. Hotel and apartment blocks stretch from Aslan Burnu to Kuşadasi proper. Closer in, the fort on Güvercin Adasi and the marina breakwaters are easily identified. A large hotel and apartment complex behind the marina is conspicuous. There are often a number of large cruise ships anchored out, or berthed at the piers in the S of the bay.

By night Use the light on Güvercin Adasi (Fl(2)10s 8M) and the lights at the entrance to the marina (Fl.R.3s5M and Fl.G.3s5M).

VHF Ch 16, 72 (Call sign *Kuşadasi Marina*).

125

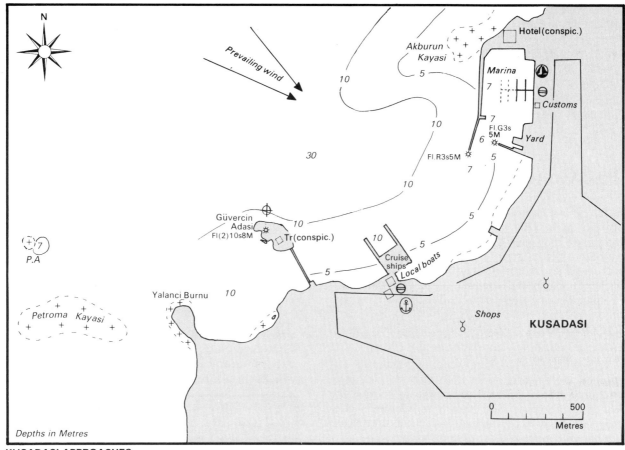

KUSADASI APPROACHES
37°51'·9N 27°14'·9E

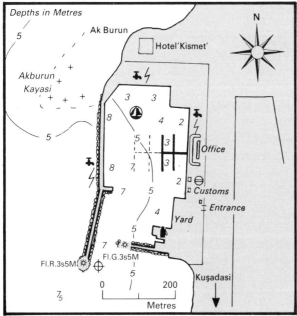

KUSADASI MARINA
37°52'·1N 27°15'·6E
Dangers

1. *Karakaçi Banklari* A reef with least depths of 2·1m (7ft) over parts of it extends in a NW direction for nearly a mile from Karga Adasi. (Karga Adasi lies about one mile N of Aslan Burnu.)
2. *Petroma Kayasi* A reef with some rocky patches just submerged extends in a westerly direction for just over half a mile from Yalanci Burnu. The latter lies close SW of Güvercin Adasi. Both reefs are difficult to spot and should be given a wide berth.
3. *Akburun Kayasi* extends 200 metres in a westerly direction from the root of the outer mole of the marina.
4. On the Turkish chart a reef and shoal patch is shown approximately 500 metres N of Petroma Kayasi. In 1996 this was marked by a very small red buoy and a patch of discoloured water was visible. The prudent course would be to avoid the area and make the approach from a westerly direction.

Mooring

Data 474 berths. Visitors berths. Max LOA 55m. Depths 2-7m. Once into the marina an attendant will direct you to a berth. There are laid moorings at most berths. Large yachts go stern-to the outer breakwater.

Shelter Excellent all-round shelter. A large number of yachts winter afloat here.

Authorities A port of entry. Customs in the marina. Health, immigration, and harbourmaster in the town close to the town pier. Charge band 2.

Facilities

Services Water (low pressure in the summer) and electricity (220V) at or near every berth. Shower (brackish water) and toilet block. Telephone connections can be made.

Kuşadasi. Approach to the marina, looking NNE

Fuel On the quay.

Repairs A 60-ton travel-hoist hauls yachts onto hard standing in the marina. Mechanical repairs at the marina. Gardiennage and routine maintenance afloat. Engineering, electrical and mechanical repairs in the town. Full engineering facilities in Soke and Izmir.

Note All repairs in the marina must be carried out through the offices of the marina, and this can add to the basic repair bill.

Provisions Small grocery shop in the marina. Excellent shopping for all provisions in Kuşadasi. Market on Fridays.

Eating out Bar and restaurant in the marina. Excellent restaurants of all categories along the waterfront and in Kuşadasi.

Other PO (24 hours). Turkish gas and *Camping Gaz*. Banks. Laundry. Hospital. Hire cars. Bus to Izmir, where there are internal and international flights. Ferries to Samos.

Marina services

Weather forecast Weather forecasts can be obtained from the marina, with a day's notice. Normally they are posted, in English, every day in the summer.

Address Turban Kuşadasi Marina, Kuşadasi, Aydin, Turkey ☎ (256) 614 1752/4/6 *Fax* (256) 614 1758.

General

Kuşadasi is a booming tourist town. There can be as many as eight cruise ships anchored in the roadstead, bringing tourists to visit Ephesus. Numerous hotels and *pensions* line the waterfront, to accommodate those who want to relax on the beaches as well as sample the ancient ruins of Ephesus and other nearby sites. The number of souvenir shops, carpet shops, and restaurants has increased dramatically to provide for all the tourists' needs, and it is difficult to walk very far in any direction without being asked to 'look at a carpet mister'.

The marina is a popular spot for yachts to winter afloat, and is often crammed to capacity. It is located about 1 kilometre from the town proper, but it is a pleasant walk along the waterfront. Kuşadasi (it means 'Isle of Birds') is built on the site of ancient Neapolis, of which nothing remains.

Ephesus

Ephesus lies near the modern town of Selçuk, a short distance from Kuşadasi. *Dolmuş* run regularly from Kuşadasi to Selçuk, and stop at Ephesus, so it is an easy matter to visit some of the most impressive ruins in Turkey. Alternatively, take one of the many organised tours available.

Ephesus lies on the Plain of Cayster, where at one time it had an outlet to the sea. The silt carried down by the river Cayster caused the site to be moved further and further westwards as the sea receded from the original site. The ruins you see today are Hellenistic, with a Roman overlay acquired after Rome made Ephesus the capital of the province.

The original site, occupied by Lydians and Carians, was on the northern slope of ancient Mt Pion (Paniyir Daği). The Ionians arrived in 1000 BC and occupied the site. The new settlers modified an existing shrine to Cybele, the Anatolian mother goddess, and made it a shrine to Artemis, the Greek fertility goddess. The town prospered until King Croesus of Lydia destroyed it, in 550 BC, and forcibly moved the Ionians to the plain below.

Ephesus survived Alexander's conquest and the squabbling that went on amongst his successors. Its greatest period of prosperity began when it was made capital of the Roman province of Asia.

As the Roman capital, it became the principal commercial city of Asia, supported by its excellent harbour. In it was erected one of the two wonders of the world to stand in Asia Minor, the temple of Artemis (the other was the mausoleum in Halicarnassus). The temple was rebuilt many times, the most famous occasion being after 365 BC, when Herostratus burnt it down in order that he might achieve immortality. (He did – his name is remembered to this day.) The rebuilt temple was enormous, four times the size of the Parthenon, and was ranked among the seven wonders of the world by Philo of Byzantium. It was destroyed by the Goths when they sacked Ephesus in AD 263.

The site today is impressive for its size and for the clarity with which you can picture the ancient city. You can walk down the marble street and see the ruins of the theatre, agora, library, odeon, stadium, gymnasium, and even the so-called brothel. The bones of the ancient city are laid bare, and it takes little to visualise what life was like in this once great city.

But Ephesus is something more, in as much as it encompasses the evolution from the ancient Anatolian mother goddess, through Artemis the Greek fertility goddess and Diana the Roman equivalent, to the Christian era. Not far away is the Church of Haghia Maria, the church where the Mother of God is supposed to have ended her days on earth. The evolution from paganism to Christianity figured prominently in the Acts of the Apostles, for Ephesus was one of the earliest places where Christianity began to supplant the old gods and the old ways. Saint Paul visited here in AD 53, and '. . . entered into the synagogue, and spake boldly for the space of three months, reasoning and persuading as to things concerning the Kingdom of God.' This caused something of a stir amongst the local population, particularly the silversmiths, who carried on a good business selling silver shrines of Diana to pilgrims. They could see the demise of their business if this new religion became popular: '. . . Sirs, ye know that by this business we have our wealth. And ye see and hear, that not alone at Ephesus, but almost throughout all Asia, this Paul hath persuaded and turned away much people, saying that they be no gods which are made with hands: and not only is there danger that this our trade come into disrepute; but also the temple of the great goddess Diana be made of no account, and that she should even be deposed from her magnificence, whom all Asia and the world worshippeth.' Paul eventually departed, but he continued to snipe at the Ephesians from afar, exhorting them to follow the path of righteousness and rid Ephesus of the pagan Diana. An astute man, he knew that he must convert these very ancient centres of worship to the new way or else Christianity would not flourish. A tough man he must have been too, to travel the distances he did and to endure so much hardship.

Ephesus declined not through Paul's exhortations but when its harbour finally silted up for good. By then the new order was well established and Byzantium was the new power in the region. Monotheism had supplanted the old values of pantheism.

SISAM BOGAZI (Samos Strait)

The narrow strait between Samos and the high mountains of Can Daği (ancient Mykale) on the Turkish side. The strait is slightly less than a mile across at the narrowest part – the closest Turkey and Greece get to each other. Bayrak Adasi, a low island, lies at the western end of the strait close to the Turkish coast. A white light structure (Fl.5s8M) and dwelling on it are conspicuous. A line of tall wind generators on the slopes behind Pithagorion on Samos are also conspicuous.

There are good depths in the fairway between Bayrak Adasi and the Turkish coast. A current of up to 3–4 knots, though usually less, sets to the E, causing tide-rips N of Bayrak Adasi. If you pass S of the island there is little in the way of disturbed water. There are also strong gusts down into the strait off Samos when the *meltemi* is blowing.

SISAM BOGAZI (SAMOS STRAIT) AND NEARBY ANCHORAGES Cil (Tavşan) Adasi light 37°39'·1N 27°00'·1E

Lighthouse

Bayrak Adasi, Sisam Boğazi (Samos Strait), looking W

DIP BURNU

A small bay lying about 1½ miles S of Bayrak Adasi. From the N a distinctive conical peak close to the coast is conspicuous, and Dip Burnu lies about ¾ of a mile S of it. A white hut on the S side of the bay and an army post in a grey house on the N side can be seen from closer in. Anchor in 4–5 metres on sand. Some shelter from the *meltemi*, although there are gusts into the bay. The small islet on the NW side provides some protection from the W, but winds from the S–SW send a swell in.

Conical peak

Approach to Dip Burnu from Sisam Boğazi (Samos Strait)

Samos   *Conical peak*

Approach to Dip Burnu, looking NE

PORT SAINT PAUL

A bay lying S of Dip Burnu and immediately E of Cil Adasi. The latter, a barren rocky island fringed by above and below-water rocks, is easily identified. Sy Ada and Sandal Ada are difficult to make out in the approach from the S as they blend into the hills behind. Proceed between Cil Adasi and Sy Adasi (Nero Island), and anchor in 2–5 metres. Care is needed of uneven depths under Sy Adasi and of the shallow water off the coast. The bottom is sand and weed, but not everywhere good holding. Good shelter from the *meltemi*, although there are gusts into the bay, and some ground swell works its way around, making it uncomfortable.

Cil Adasi   *Entrance*

Cil Adasi and the entrance to Port St Paul, looking NNE

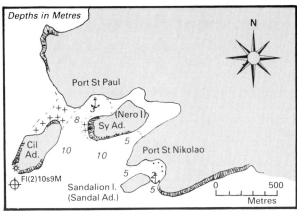

PORT ST PAUL AND PORT ST NIKOLAO
37°39'·1N 27°00'·1E
(Cil Adasi light)

Saint Paul, on one of his voyages up the Anatolian coast, is supposed to have put in here for the night, to rest his oarsmen from the back-breaking slog against the *meltemi*.

PORT SAINT NIKOLAO (Nikolo)

A small bay lying on the eastern side of Port Saint Paul. Sandal Ada (Sandalion Islet) lies in the entrance to the bay. Proceed on the E side of the islet and anchor in 2–4 metres. The bottom is sand with some rock and weed, and not everywhere good holding. The bay shallows rapidly to 2 metres and less in the middle. Good shelter from the *meltemi*, although there are gusts.

The soldiers stationed at the *gendarmerie* in Dip Burnu will often walk around to the bay, not so much to inspect papers as to collect cigarettes and whisky.

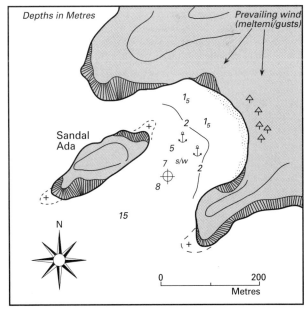

PORT ST NIKOLAO
37°39'N 27°01'E

The ancient Gulf of Latmos

From seaward it is impossible to visualise the coastline as it was before the time of Christ. It appears uniformly flat and monotonous. Not until you take a trip inland, and survey from on high what is now a great plain criss-crossed with ditches to keep it drained, do you get any idea of what the ancient coastline was like. At the eastern end of the plain, Bafa Lake is all that remains of the Latmian Gulf, and even its salty waters are receding as more silt is brought down by the ancient Menderes or Meander river (Turkish: Menderes Nehri). At one time this river emptied into the sea some 15 miles further east.

Around the ancient gulf stood a number of great Ionian cities, including the greatest of them all, Miletus. Silting was taking place in ancient times and is not a modern phenomenon. Strabo tells us that the channel to the harbour at Priene had to be kept dredged in his day. It should be remembered that ships of this period drew little more than a metre or two at the most for the largest. (John Morrison gives the dimensions of a large trireme as: length 35m, breadth 4·65m, draught 1·1m. Trading vessels would have been appreciably smaller, though of deeper draught.)

The cities

Priene Occupies a spectacular site on a rocky shelf on the side of the ancient Mykale Mountains. The city was moved here from a site further inland when silting forced abandonment of the harbour. In Roman times the harbour at this new site had also silted. Consequently, Priene was never considered an important city during the Roman occupation, and its architecture was never adulterated by Roman modifications. It remains an excellent example of what an Ionian city was like, with few additions from Rome cluttering the site.

Myus Was situated on the banks of the Menderes in the NE of the ancient gulf. It was never a great city, and little of interest remains today.

Herakleia (Herakleia-under-Latmos) Was in fact a Carian city on the border with Ionia. You can get to the ancient city by hiring a boat from the camp-site on the southern side of Bafa Lake, or you

The Menderes River (anc. Meander) that completely changed the coastline and filled in most of the ancient Gulf of Latmos

can drive there. Although it was never an important city, the ruins are picturesque on the stark slopes of Mount Latmos, and it is perhaps the most dramatic site around the gulf. The waters of the lake below help one to visualise what the city must once have looked like.

A legend associated with the site adds to its romance. Endymion, variously described as a king, a shepherd or a mystic, was apparently a beautiful young man with whom the moon goddess, Selene, fell in love. She caused him to fall asleep forever so that she might look upon his beauty whenever she wished.

While he slept he evidently retained some of his faculties, for Selene lay with him and in time bore him fifty daughters. John Freely adds an interesting footnote:

'Apparently the myth lingered on into Christian times, when Endymion was venerated locally as a mystic saint. According to tradition, the Christian anchorites who took refuge on Mount Latmos in early Byzantine times discovered an ancient tomb which they took to be Endymion's and made it into a sanctuary. Each year the anchorites would open the lid of the sarcophagus inside the tomb, whereupon the skeleton within invariably emitted a strange humming sound. This they interpreted as Endymion's attempt to communicate to man the name of God, which he had learned from Selene while they slept together on Latmos. And indeed a very interesting and unique tomb-sanctuary has been found in Heracleia about three hundred metres to the south-east of the Temple of Athena; it has been tentatively identified as Endymion's sanctuary, though no sepulchral humming has been heard from the sarcophagus within.'

The Companion Guide to Turkey

The legend of Endymion endured into the Middle Ages, when the phrase 'the moon sleeps with Endymion' was commonly used to mean a mystical communion with God.

Miletus This, the greatest of the Ionian cities although not the best preserved, was situated on the SW shores of the Latmian Gulf. It was the principal port and the richest and most powerful city. It established colonies all over the Mediterranean and the Black Sea.

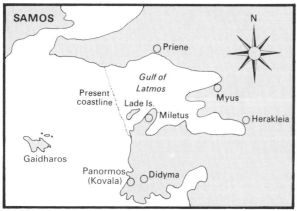

THE ANCIENT GULF OF LATMOS IN 500 BC

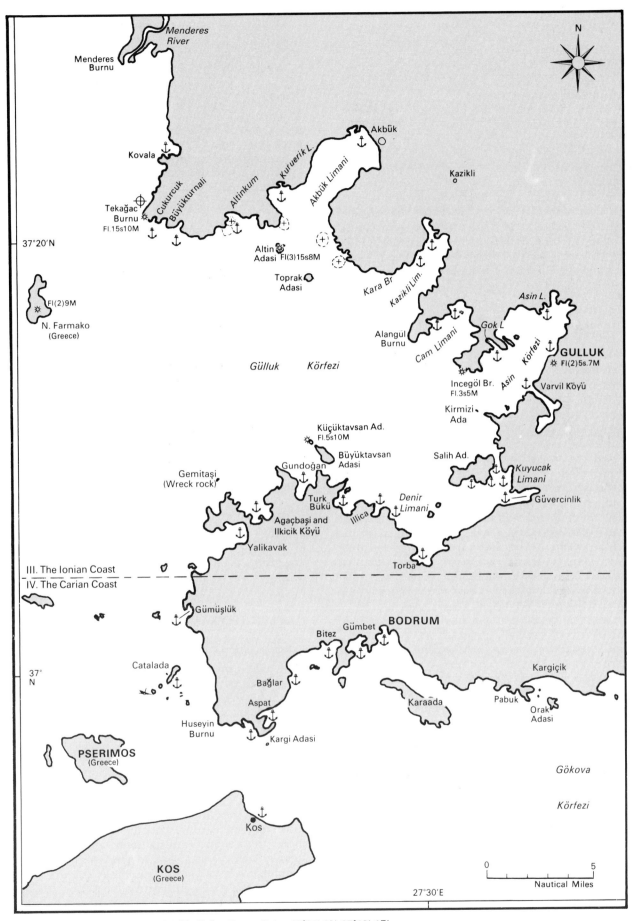

N

Menderes River

Menderes Burnu

Kovala

Akbük ○

Kazikli ○

Kuruerik L.

Akbük Limani

Tekağac Burnu
Fl.15s10M

Cukurcuk
Büyükturnali

Altinkum

37°20′N

Altin Adasi Fl(3)15s8M

Toprak Adasi

Kara Br

Kazikli Lim.

Asin L.

Fl(2)9M

N. Farmako
(Greece)

Alangül Burnu

Cam Limani

Gok L.

Asin Körfezi

GULLUK
Fl(2)5s.7M

Gülluk   Körfezi

Incegöl Br.
Fl.3s5M

Varvil Köyü

Kirmizi Ada

Küçüktavsan Ad.
Fl.5s10M

Büyüktavsan Adasi

Salih Ad.

Kuyucak Limani

Gemitaşi
(Wreck rock)

Gundoğan

Turk Bükü

Denir Limani

Güvercinlik

Agaçbaşi and
Ilkicik Köyü

Illica

Yalikavak

Torba

III. The Ionian Coast
IV. The Carian Coast

Gümüşlük

BODRUM

Bitez   Gümbet

Catalada

37°
N

Kargiçik

Bağlar

Aspat

Karaada

Pabuk

Orak Adasi

Huseyin Burnu

Kargi Adasi

PSERIMOS
(Greece)

Gökova

Körfezi

Kos

0   5
Nautical Miles

KOS
(Greece)

27°30′E

GULLUK KORFEZI TO BODRUM (Te Kağaç Burnu light 37°21′·3N 27°13′·1E)

Numerous ruins remain, including those of the largest theatre in Asia Minor, several temples, the agora, public baths, council chambers, and a Delphinium. The city was destroyed by the Persians in 494 BC, and although it again prospered, it never regained its former greatness.

Miletus was one of the birthplaces of western science and philosophy. Thales of Miletus, who lived in the late 7th century BC, was the first of the Ionian physical scientists. He attempted to determine the material basis of the world, finally determining it to be ultimately water. He is credited (by Herodotus) with having determined to within a year the solar eclipse of 585 BC. He studied the cause of the Nile floods and devised a method to measure the height of the Pyramids. He is traditionally remembered as the archetypal absent-minded professor who fell down a well while mulling over a problem.

Güllük Körfezi

(ancient **Gulf of Mandalya**)

This deeply indented gulf has a large number of well sheltered anchorages. Apart from those mentioned here, there are many more offering some shelter in settled weather when the *meltemi* is not blowing strongly. A glance at the chart will quickly convince you that several weeks is not too long to spend here if you are to potter around every bay and creek bordering the shores of the gulf.

Mountains border the gulf on the eastern and southern sides, while the northern side is flatter. The coast on the northern side is mostly bare or covered in low *maquis*, whereas the slopes on the southern and eastern sides are thickly wooded in pine, with cultivated valleys. In recent years vast swathes of the coast have been built on, to such an extent that the gulf is now very nearly ringed by the ubiquitous holiday villages. These concrete boxes arranged in grid patterns have destroyed much of the charm of the gulf, especially on the northern side, though fortunately there are still a few places left for the yachtsman to escape to.

Numerous ancient sites are dotted about the gulf. The two best known are Didyma and Iassus, the former a short taxi ride from Altinkum and the latter easily visited from Asin Limani.

A yacht going into the gulf will need to stock up on provisions, water, diesel, etc, as little can be obtained in most of the places in the gulf. There is no diesel conveniently available, although it can be

Light tower

Tekağac Burnu and light tower, looking N

brought by mini-tanker to Asin, and is also available near Altinkum. Some provisions are available in Güllük, or again from Bodrum via Torba, but otherwise only basic items can be found.

Winds

In the summer the *meltemi* blows into the gulf from the W and WNW. On the northern side there are gusts into some of the bays. On the southern side and particularly in the SE corner the wind follows the contours of the coast, so that in places it may blow from the SW and in others from the NW. At night there may be a NE wind off the mountains inland.

KOVALA

This bay, close to the ruins of Didyma, is open to the *meltemi* in the summer. A yacht wishing to visit the ruins should make for Altinkum.

CUKURCUK

A bay lying close under Tekağaç Burnu. The cape is a long low spit with a white light structure on it that is conspicuous from some distance off. The small W creek is now blocked off by a fish farm. Proceed slowly towards the entrance of the E creek and the point between the two creeks. The bottom shoals very gradually into the shore from 4m at the entrance to 1·75–2m in the middle. Nose into 2–3 metre depths (you can go closer than you think in the clear water) to drop anchor. The bottom is sand and mud, good holding. The *meltemi* gusts out of the bay but the holding is good. Open S.

The bottom is everywhere sand and good holding. The water in the area is crystal clear, and there is good underwater fishing along the nearby coast.

Note Immediately SSE of Tekağac Br lies a shoal patch, Tekağac Bankasi, with least depths of 5 metres over it.

ALTINKUM (Karakuyu Iskele, Skrophes Bay)

A large bay about 4½ miles E of Tekağac Burnu. Care is needed of the reef and shoal water running right across the entrance to Altinkum (see plan). The reef is occasionally marked by a pole beacon, but this should not be relied upon. The reef is easily identified by day, but an approach should not be made by night. Make the approach to the anchorage around the E side of the bay. Although there is a passage on the W side of the reef, much used by local boats, the prudent course is to approach from the SE.

Anchor in 3–6 metres on sand, good holding. Good shelter from the *meltemi*.

Ashore there is good shopping for provisions, and there are numerous restaurants and bars. The former fishing village has metamorphosed into a booming resort barely recognisable as its former self. The bars and discos can elevate the decibel level in the anchorage to considerable levels.

Altinkum is the best place from which to visit the ruins of ancient Didyma, about 3 miles away, and

W entrance point   Gulet quay   W water tower   Reef

Altinkum, looking NNW

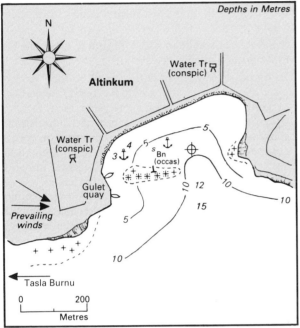

ALTINKUM (Skrophes Bay)
37°21′N 27°16′·8E

taxis can be arranged in the town (determine the price beforehand).

Note Local *gulets* shelter under Tasla Burnu just west of Altinkum, but this is not so much for the shelter as to be convenient to the holiday village for ferrying tourists around.

Didyma

Didyma was not one of the Ionian cities, but a religious sanctuary to Apollo, famed for its oracle long before that at Delphi became prominent. Oracles were issued as early as 600 BC, and one of the earliest oracles inscribed here regarding piracy instructs the suppliant that 'It is right to do as your fathers did.'

Didyma was famed for its huge temple. The original temple to Apollo was destroyed by the Persian Darius in 494 BC, and lay in ruins until Alexander the Great arrived. The remains of the huge temple that can be seen today date from 300 BC, and although work continued on it for two hundred years, it was never finished. Some of the roughly hewn stonework and numerous unfluted columns can be seen. This is the largest Ionic temple in the world, measuring approximately 120

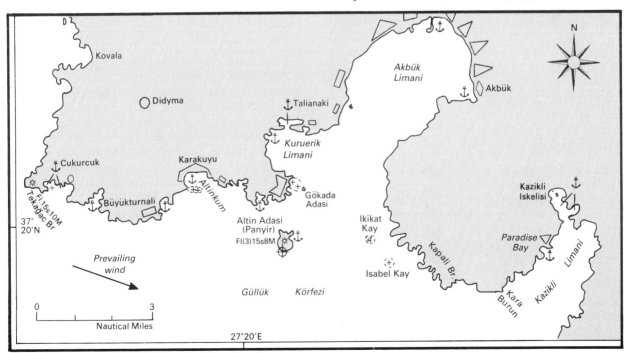

NORTHERN SIDE OF GULLUK KORFEZI Altin Ada light 37°19′·7N 27°19′·7E

metres by 60 metres. It was largely destroyed by an earthquake in the 15th century, but sufficient columns remain in place to give a powerful impression of its size.

KURUERIK LIMANI (Chiovraki)

A large bay lying about three miles E of Altinkum, on the western side of the entrance to Akbük Limani. A yacht should not attempt to pass inside Gökada Island (St Kyriaki Island), which is connected by a reef to the mainland.

Anchor in the NW corner of the large bay or enter Talianaki, the enclosed bay on the N side of Kuruerik Limani. In Talianaki, anchor in 3–4 metres at the N end, in mud. Excellent holding and good shelter from the *meltemi*. The E end of Talianaki is shallow.

Kuruerik literally means 'dry plum', but I don't know if that is a proper translation of the name. The general area has recently been developed as a major holiday resort, diminishing its charm for the yachtsman seeking a solitary anchorage. Bars and restaurant ashore.

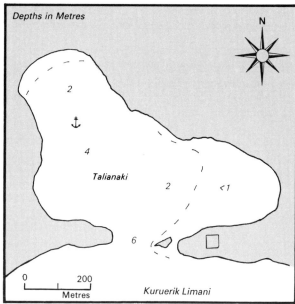

KURUERIK LIMANI (TALIANAKI)
37°22'·6N 27°19'·8E

AKBUK LIMANI

The large bay on the N side of Güllük Körfezi. A yacht should make for the E side of the spit at the N end of the bay. Anchor in 3–4 metres on mud. Good holding and good shelter from the *meltemi*. The anchorage is open S and E. In the E corner there is a short mole used by tripper boats.

The slopes right around Akbük Limani have been extensively developed, and it is ringed by huge holiday villages and hotels.

Note Care should be taken of Ikikat Kayasi and Isabel Kayasi, lying about half a mile offshore in the southern approaches to Akbük Limani. There is some confusion about the depths over the reefs.

Turkish chart 224 gives a least depth of 4 metres over Ikikat and 2·2 metres (7·2ft) over Isabel Rock. The old Admiralty chart 1546 gives least depths of 1 fathom (1·8 metres) over Ikikat and ½ a fathom (0·9 metres) over Isabel. There are good depths close inshore, or a yacht should keep well offshore, to avoid these two reefs.

KAZIKLI LIMANI

The large bay lying between Alangül Burnu on the S and Kara Burun on the N. The bay narrows towards the head. When approaching from the W and S, the high land rising up from the relatively low-lying land of the northern coast of the bay is easily identified. There are several places for a yacht to anchor.

Note At the entrance to Kazikli Limani, there can be strong gusts with the *meltemi*.

1. **Paradise Bay** An unnamed cove on the Turkish and Admiralty charts, which has been (inevitably) called 'Paradise Bay' by some yachtsmen. It is on the W side, about 2 miles NE of Kara Burun. There is a mussel farm off the S entrance point. Anchor in 3–5 metres on sand. Good holding and good shelter from the *meltemi*. The bay is open to the E.

   The slopes about are thickly wooded in pine, and there is a small beach at the head. It is a wonderful spot, and even the mussel farm fits in. The only question must be, 'How long will it be before they build a holiday village here?'.

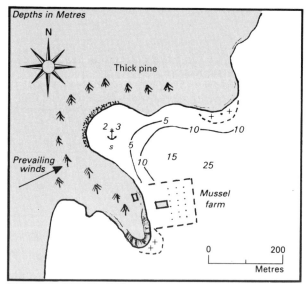

PARADISE BAY (Kazikli)

2. Just up from 'Paradise Bay' there are several coves which provide shelter from the *meltemi*. In one of them there is a small holiday village and a restaurant.
3. Near the head of Kazikli a yacht can anchor in one of several places (see plan). Several mussel farms obstruct the head of the inlet, but there is still plenty of space to anchor. The bottom is mud, good holding. Good shelter. Restaurant ashore.

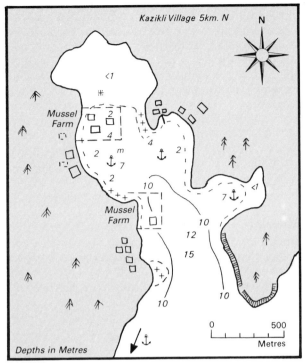

KAZIKLI
37°20′N 27°28′·7E

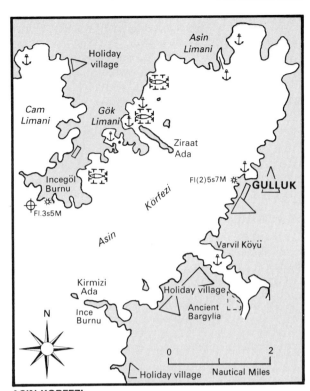

ASIN KORFEZI
Incegöl Burnu light 37°13′·8N 27°30′·6E

CAM LIMANI (Alangül Körfezi)

The large bay on the S side of Teke (Alangül) Burnu. There are several bays on the N side which provide some shelter from the *meltemi*. The inlet just under Teke Burnu is attractive, with suitable depths for anchoring. The bay at the head of the gulf also provides some shelter, although a strong *meltemi* pushes some swell in.

Incegöl Burnu and light structure, looking NW

ASIN KORFEZI

This small gulf at the eastern end of Güllük Körfezi has several anchorages, including Asin Limani, with the ruins of ancient Iassus close by. Opposite Asin

Limani is Güllük, the only town of any size in the gulf if you take away the holiday villages.

The light structure on Incegöl Burnu (Fenerburnu/Karaburun) can be seen from some distance off, and the islet off the southern entrance, Kirmizi Ada, is easily identified. There are good depths in the fairway between Kirmizi Ada and Incegöl Burnu.

GOK LIMANI (Shiero Bay)

A long squiggly bay lying about halfway along the western side of Asin Körfezi. The entrance is not easy to discern, but if you are coasting you will see the rocky islet on the N side of the entrance. Leave the rocky islet to starboard and proceed to the NW side of the bay. Care should be taken of a reef on the eastern side, a short distance inside the entrance.

Anchor in 6–8 metres off the beach of the western side. It becomes shallow towards the northern end. The bottom is mud and good holding. Good shelter from the *meltemi*, although a little swell may be pushed up into the bay at times.

The slopes about the bay are covered in pine and

Minaret   Byzantine tower

Approaches to Port Asin, looking N

135

maquis and, inevitably, a holiday village, which now spreads across the lower slopes.

Just N of Gök Limani on the other side of the headland are several coves, which also provide shelter from the *meltemi* and suitable depths to anchor in.

Note In Gök Limani and the coves along the coast between Gök Limani and Asin Limani there are now numerous fish farms choking the sheltered areas. There are still sufficient places to anchor although not the choice there once was.

ASIN LIMANI

(Port Isene, Kurin, ancient Iassus)
BA 1644

Approach

This almost landlocked inlet, the ancient harbour of Iassus, lies at the N end of Asin Körfezi.

Conspicuous The large abandoned hotel complex on the western side of the cove is conspicuous from the entrance to Asin Körfezi. Closer in, the fort on the eastern side of the bay and a white minaret in the

village will be seen. Near the entrance, the ruins of a Byzantine tower on the E side of the entrance are easily identified. The remains of the ancient break-water extend, just underwater, from the western side, leaving a comparatively small entrance. The extremity of the sunken breakwater is sometimes marked by a stick or a small buoy. A yacht should keep about 15–20 metres W of the tower to pass through the entrance where there are 9-metre depths. A transit of 350° (true) on the white mina-ret in the village leads clear through the entrance.

Note Although only just underwater, the sunken breakwater does not always show up well.

Mooring

Anchor on the W side just inside the entrance and take a long line ashore. Alternatively, go stern or bows-to the new quay, if you can find a space amongst the clutter of *gulets* on it. Care is needed off the quay as the rock ballasting extends a short distance underwater, and it may be best to go bows-to. There are mostly 1·5–2 metre depths immedi-

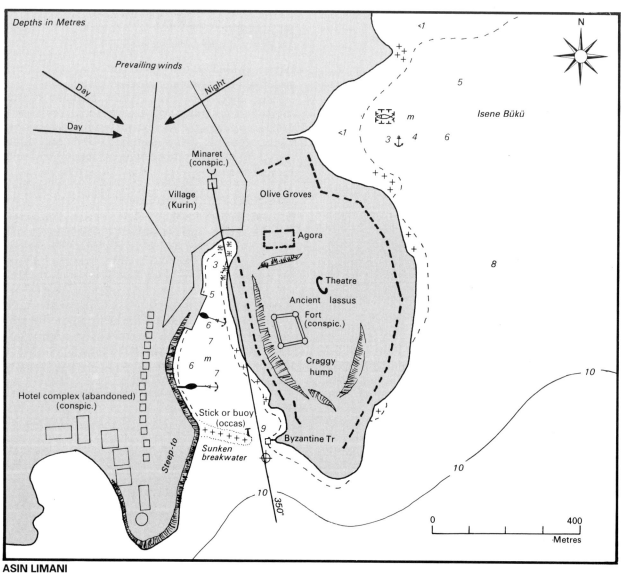

ASIN LIMANI
37°16′·7N 27°34′·7E

Byzantine tower   End of sunken breakwater

Asin Limani looking SSE towards the entrance

ately off the quay. The bottom is mud and weed and good holding.

Shelter Good all-round shelter, although strong southerlies make the anchorage uncomfortable.

Facilities

Water On the quay.
Electricity Can be connected on the quay.
Fuel A mini-tanker can deliver to the quay.
Provisions Limited provisions only. It is a short trip across to Güllük to get provisions.
Eating out Several restaurants in the summer.
Other Taxi or *dolmuş* to Milas. Local boat to Güllük.

General

The anchorage, under the craggy slopes with the fort atop the eastern side and the small village at the head, is delightful. The ruins of ancient Iassus lie amongst olive groves, with donkeys and cows grazing in the ancient agora and temple. It is well worth the short walk to the ruins (which lie beside the craggy hump and not on top), as much for the setting and the shady glen as for edification. The ugly blot of the modern hotel complex on the western side, sited and executed without an iota of good taste, contrasts badly with the overgrown ruins of Iassus.

ISENE BUKU

The anchorage immediately N of Asin Limani. There is now a fish farm here, but still sufficient room to anchor. It affords good shelter from the *meltemi*. Anchor in 3–5 metres on mud and weed, good holding. It is about 20 minutes' walk across the isthmus to the village.

Iassus

(Iassos)

The mythical origins of the city say that it was founded by Peloponnesians from Argos, and artefacts recovered from the site indicate that it was indeed occupied in Mycenean times, and later colonised from the Argive in about 900 BC. Don't always doubt the myth-makers. Later it had a close association with the Milesians and became Carian in character. In the 5th century BC it became part of the Delian confederacy. It sided with Athens against the Spartans and Persians on numerous occasions, each time to its cost. It was sacked by the Spartans in 412 BC, sacked again by Lysander a little later, and made a Persian satrapy in 387 BC.

George Bean relates a story told by Strabo of the inhabitants: 'Most of the wealth of Iassus came from fish, particularly the export of salted fish. One day the inhabitants were watching a performance in the theatre when the gong signalling the start of the fish market was sounded and all but one of the audience rushed off to do business there. An actor came up to thank the old man who had remained behind and he, cupping his hand to his ear, exclaimed he had not heard the signal and promptly shuffled off to join his fellow citizens at the market.'

After siding with Athens, Iassus sided with Mithridates against the Romans, and so Sulla let pirates sack it to teach the inhabitants a lesson. They seem to have had an uncanny knack of teaming up with the losing side. Iassus declined after this, but was the seat of a bishopric during Byzantine rule. The fort on the top of the craggy hump was built by the Knights of St John.

The ruins have been partly excavated by the Italian school, who return each summer to continue the excavations. The Temple of Zeus, the city wall, the agora and a small theatre, the theatre proper, and parts of the land wall for the city can be seen today amid the olive groves. The site is enchanting.

GULLUK (Küllük)

BA 1644

Approach

The port lies about halfway along the eastern side of Asin Körfezi.

Conspicuous A large white hotel above the village and the red tile roofs of the houses of the village can be made out from the clutter of apartments and holiday villages around it. The white light structure on the S side of the harbour entrance is also easily identified.

By night Use the light on the S side (Fl(2)5s7M), and a weak F.R on the pierhead.

Mooring

The harbour doesn't have a lot of space for visiting yachts. You may find a berth on the T-pier off the shore, or a space under the short breakwater with a long line ashore. In the morning if it is calm you may be able to go alongside the bottom half of the cargo pier, although it is inconveniently high for getting on and off unless you are on the lower landing stage. The latter berth is not a good one when the *meltemi* is blowing.

Shelter Good shelter from the *meltemi* under the breakwater, but uncomfortable and at times even untenable on the cargo pier. The small T-pier is uncomfortable but not dangerous with the *meltemi*.

Authorities A port of entry. The offices for customs, immigration, health, and the harbourmaster are all on the waterfront. Try to arrive early in the morning, when it should be calmer, and go onto the cargo pier to clear in. Then you can move to the inner basin or another anchorage.

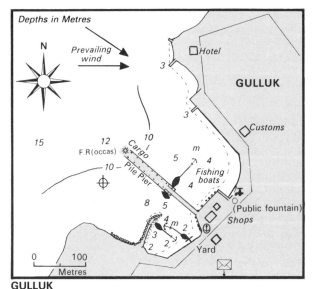

GULLUK
37°14'·4N 27° 35'·8E

Facilities

Water Public water fountain near the harbour. Water on the T-pier. (The water has been reported to be suspect.)

Fuel The nearest place is on the main road to Milas, about 15km away. Take a taxi or *dolmuş*.

Repairs A yard in the harbour can haul yachts and carry out wood repairs. Local *gulets* with an attractive underwater shape are built here. In Milas there are excellent engineering and mechanical workshops.

Provisions Good shopping for provisions.

Eating out Several good restaurants around the waterfront.

Other PO. Taxi and *dolmuş* to Milas.

General

Güllük is in a sleepy little hollow, a scruffy but likable village. Even the port officials seem little concerned when you arrive. It is the port for Milas, and emery ore is loaded here. Recently the constructors seem to have gone mad, and apartments and holiday villages are going up around Güllük at a frenzied pace.

VARVIL KOYU (Ulelibük, ancient Bargylia)

A large deep bay two miles SW of Güllük. The cleft between the hills on either side is not difficult to identify. A large holiday village has been built on the S side. The bay has silted since earlier surveys, and the bottom comes up quickly to one metre and less just inside the entrance. Anchor in 5–6 metres, taking care of underwater rocks fringing the S side. The bottom is mud and good holding. The bay does not offer good shelter from the *meltemi*, which sends in some swell and makes it uncomfortable.

The ruins of ancient Bargylia lie about one mile away (as the crow flies) and are much overgrown. The agora, temple, and theatre can be found.

INCE BURUN

On the S side of this cape a small private harbour has been built. It is associated with the holiday village on the headland.

KUYUCAK (Konjakhi)

An inlet opposite the SE side of Salih Adasi. A stone building standing at the head of the T-shaped projection in the bay is conspicuous when approaching from the SW, and a fish farm will be seen on the N and S sides of the entrance. A large hotel has been built on the N side of the lagoon, but it will not be seen until you are into the entrance.

The SE creek has mostly silted. The NW creek has also silted since earlier surveys. In the latter, the bottom comes up quickly from 8 metres to 2–3 metres and then shelves gradually to the shore. Anchor just inside the NW creek in 2·5–3 metres. The bottom is gooey mud, excellent holding. Excellent shelter from the *meltemi*, and nearly all-round shelter (SW winds do not blow home).

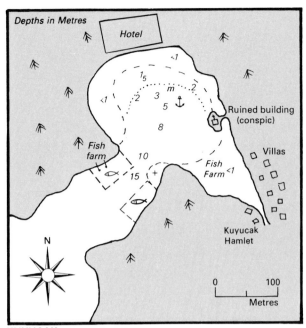

KUYUCAK
37°09′N 27°33′E

Despite the construction of the hotel and a number of villas, the lagoon remains a lovely spot. The houses of the hamlet of Kuyucak are scattered around the head of the SE creek. The abandoned stone building is a ghostly reminder of the Greek colony which once lived in this isolated place.

SALIH ADASI

The large island in the SE corner of the gulf, separated from the mainland by a narrow channel. There are good depths in the fairway.

Unfortunately all the sheltered anchorages around the island and on the N side of Guverncilik are occupied by rafts of fish farms.

GUVERCINLIK (ancient **Port Haryanda**)

A large, deep bay, one mile S of Kuyucak. Once the entrance has been opened the hotels and restaurants at the head of the bay will be seen, as well as a village on the hillside behind. The cove on the N side

immediately inside the entrance is now obstructed by a fish farm, so you will have to anchor off the village. Anchor in 5–10 metres where convenient. The *meltemi* does not blow home with its full force here, but it is still very uncomfortable and may become untenable. The bottom is mud and weed, reasonable holding.

Provisions and restaurants ashore. The main road runs around the coast to Milas and Bodrum. Buses and *dolmuş* run regularly.

TORBA (Torbali)

Approach

The small harbour lies in the SW corner of Torba Limani (Turfanda Bükü). From the W, the harbour and hamlet cannot be seen until you are well into the bay. From the N a large holiday village to the E of the harbour is conspicuous, and closer in the harbour breakwater and entrance are easily identified.

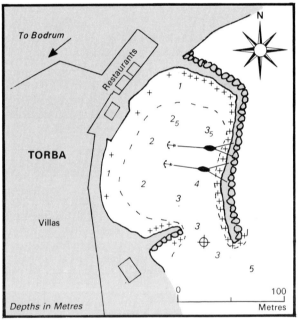

TORBA
37°08′·1N 27°22′·6E

Entrance

Outer breakwater

Torba: approach, looking SW

Mooring

Go stern or bows-to the outer breakwater. There is no quayed area, and you must moor the boat a little distance off, with long lines ashore to convenient rocks, to avoid the rubble extending a short distance underwater. Use a dinghy to get ashore. The bottom is mud and sand and good holding. Good all-round shelter.

Facilities

Limited provisions. Several restaurants open in the summer. A regular *dolmuş* service runs to Bodrum (about 8 kilometres away) in the summer.

General

Torba has become a fairly upmarket summer villa resort, but still has great charm. It is a peaceful spot, despite the large holiday village to the east, and the harbour is a useful alternative to Bodrum, which can be very crowded in the height of summer.

DENIR LIMANI

A small bay, offering reasonable shelter from the *meltemi*. The shoal off the entrance (least depth 3·7 metres) is easily spotted in calm weather.

Anchor near the head of the bay. There is a jetty at the end used by *gulets* and yachts. The *meltemi* tends to blow across the mouth of the bay but sends some swell in. Some development ashore.

ILICA BUKU (Karasi)

A long inlet just over one mile E of the entrance to Türk Bükü. A large hotel on the W side of the entrance is conspicuous. At the head of the bay there are now fish farms on the W and S sides, but it is still possible to anchor here. Anchor near the head of the bay in 5–8 metres and take a line ashore. The bottom is mud and weed and good holding. The anchorage is not the most comfortable with the

GULLUK KORFEZI – SOUTH COAST
Küçüktavşan (Fener) Adasi light 37°10'·7N 27°23'·1E

meltemi, but the surroundings are spectacular.

The slopes about are thickly wooded in pine, while at the water's edge there are stands of deciduous trees. The inlet with the hooked peak of Kara Dağ (Black Mountain) towering over it has now had a road built around it, eroding something of the majesty and solitude of the place.

TURK BUKU (Ghiul)

Approach

The large villa and apartment complex on the western slopes of the bay is conspicuous. Once up to the entrance, the houses strung all around the large bay are visible. From the NE, the line of windmills on the ridge above the western bay is conspicuous.

Turk Bükü: anchorage on the W side

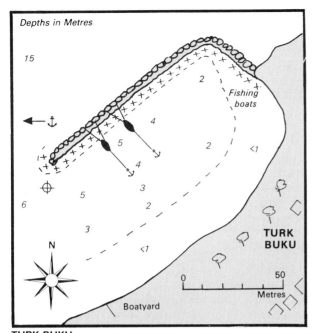

TURK BUKU
37°08′N 27°25′E

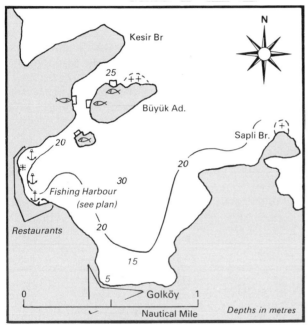

TURK BUKU APPROACHES

Note There is a deep-water passage inside the two islands on the NW side of the bay, but care should be taken sailing through here during the *meltemi*, when there are fierce gusts.

Mooring

Anchor in the W bay, in the NW corner, or immediately W of the entrance to the small harbour. A reef runs out for about 100 metres from the W side of the bay. Anchor in 6–15 metres just N of the reef. In places it is possible to take a long line ashore. The bottom is sand and weed, and patchy holding in places. A yacht can also go stern or bows-to inside the harbour, with a long line ashore to the breakwater. Rubble extends some distance underwater, so that you cannot go close-to, but must use a dinghy to get ashore.

Shelter Shelter from the *meltemi* is good in the bay, although there can be strong gusts. Shelter in the harbour is nearly all-round.

Facilities

Some provisions ashore. Several restaurants open in the summer around the shores of the bay. *Dolmuş* to Bodrum.

General

The bay is surrounded by steep rocky slopes, with splashes of green in the valleys and white houses scattered higgledy-piggledy around the bay. The bay was originally called Rum Bükü. Rum was the Turkish name for the Byzantine Empire (it is a corruption of Rome), which was later generalised to include all Greeks. The locals changed the name to Türk Bükü after the exchange of populations between Greece and Turkey in the 1920s.

GUNDOGAN (Farilya, Phariah, Pharillah)

Approach

This large bay lies close SSW of Tavşan Adalari (Küçüktavsan Adasi and Büyüktavsan Adasi). The white light structure on Küçüktavsan Adasi is conspicuous from some distance away. What looks like an old Greek church will be seen on the summit of Büyüktavsan. A large holiday village now almost totally encircles the bay. Once the entrance to the bay has been opened the village at the head will be seen.

Mooring

Anchor off the village in 5–8 metres, or in the NW corner of the bay in 5–6 metres, where shelter is better from the *meltemi*. The bottom is thick weed

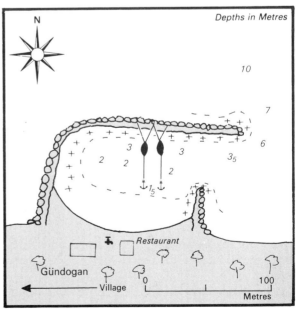

GUNDOGAN
37°08′N 27°23′E

and sand, and the holding is not always the best. Alternatively, go stern or bows-to in the small harbour, with long lines ashore to the breakwater. Rubble extends some distance underwater, so that you cannot go close to the breakwater, but must use a dinghy to get ashore. The harbour is usually full of local fishing boats. Good all-round shelter in the harbour. Reasonable shelter from the *meltemi* in the NW corner of the bay.

Facilities

Water from a tap near the harbour. Provisions and restaurants. *Dolmuş* to Bodrum.

General

The setting about the bay is spectacular, or at least it once was. The bay is now almost entirely encircled by a barracks-like holiday village that obliterates the landscape.

AGACBASI KOYU AND ILKICIK KOYU

These two bays are open to the *meltemi*, but in calm weather can be used. The bays are encircled by holiday villages and hotels which make the place look much like other blank concrete ghettos around the Bodrum peninsula. Watersports activities at several of the hotels.

GEMITASI (Wreck Rock)

This rock pillar (6·4m/21ft high), lying off the southern entrance to Gülluk Körfezi, is more conspicuous than its modest height might suggest. It is easily identified, and a handy reference point when entering the gulf on the southern side.

Gemitaşi (Wreck Rock)

YALIKAVAK

Approach

In the large bay on the S side of Yalikavak Yarimadasi there are a number of anchorages and a small harbour off the village. Once the entrance is opened, the houses of the village and the development around the bay will be seen.

Note The *meltemi* tends to curve around the headland and blow into the bay from a westerly direction.

Dangers Care must be taken of above- and below-water rocks fringing the coast. On the S side of the

AGACBASI KOYU AND ILKICIK KOYU

These two bays are open to the *meltemi*, but in calm weather can be used. The bays are encircled by holiday villages and hotels which make the place look much like other blank concrete ghettos around the Bodrum peninsula. Watersports activities at several of the hotels.

GEMITASI (Wreck Rock)

This rock pillar (6·4m/21ft high), lying off the southern entrance to Gülluk Körfezi, is more conspicuous than its modest height might suggest. It is easily identified, and a handy reference point when entering the gulf on the southern side.

YALIKAVAK

Approach

In the large bay on the S side of Yalikavak Yarimadasi there are a number of anchorages and a small harbour off the village. Once the entrance is opened, the houses of the village and the development around the bay will be seen.

Note The *meltemi* tends to curve around the headland and blow into the bay from a westerly direction.

Dangers Care must be taken of above- and below-water rocks fringing the coast. On the S side of the bay a reef extends in a NW direction to nearly halfway across the bay. A yacht must keep to the N side of the bay when approaching the village and harbour.

Mooring

There are a number of anchorages and a small harbour.

1. In the cove just inside the northern entrance. Reasonable shelter from the *meltemi*.
2. In the large bay on the N side. Anchor in 5–8 metres on sand, mud and weed, good holding

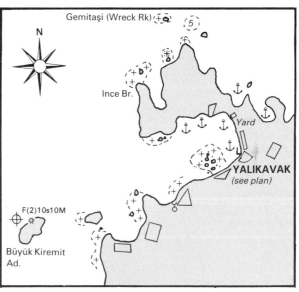

APPROACHES TO YALIKAVAK
Büyük Kiremit Adasi light 37°05'N 27°14'E

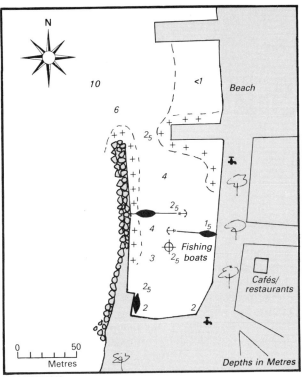

YALIKAVAK
37°06'·4N 27°17'·5E

Yalikavak, looking S from the entrance into the small harbour

once through the weed. Good shelter from the *meltemi* although there are gusts into the bay.

3. In the small harbour. Depths are irregular inside, but are mostly 2·5–4 metres on the W and in the middle. Go stern or bows-to or alongside wherever you can squeeze in. Nearly all-round shelter. A charge is sometimes made.

Facilities

Water On the quay.

Fuel On the outskirts of the village.

Repairs A boatyard in the NE corner of Yalikavak bay. It hauls yachts, and appears to specialise in catamarans, for some reason.

Provisions Good shopping for all provisions in the village. Ice available.

Eating out Good restaurants on or near the waterfront.

Other PO. *Dolmuş* and minibus to Bodrum.

General

The village is a rapidly growing tourist resort, and a number of hotels and villas have been built around the coast, yet it retains much charm, and is well worth the attempt to squeeze into the small harbour.

IV. The Carian coast

Gümüşlük to Marmaris

The Carian coast between Gümüşlük and Marmaris is a wild mountainous area which until recently was largely dependent on the sea for transportation and communication. Today you can reach Milas from Bodrum by a fast highway in half an hour, but fifteen years ago the journey took four hours on the old road.

The Carians were an indigenous people in this southwest corner of Anatolia, living here before the first Aeolian and Ionian colonists arrived at the beginning of the first millennium BC. After the Ionians, the Dorians arrived and colonised much of the area as well as the Greek islands opposite. The Dorian league thus formed was composed of Knidos, Kos, Kamirus, Lindos, Rhodes and Halicarnassus (until it was expelled for its Carian tendencies). When the Persians arrived the area was allowed a considerable degree of autonomy, with local satraps keeping order but owing allegiance to the Persians.

In the 4th century BC Mausolos was made satrap of the region and he set about making Caria great.

He modelled the cities along Greek lines and expanded the Carian fleet, and soon Halicarnassus was the thriving centre of Caria. We know much about Caria from Herodotus, the father of written history, who was born in Halicarnassus in 430 BC. He recorded in detail the life and times not only of Caria, but of most of the known world, in his history of the conflict between the Greeks and the Persians.

When Alexander the Great swept through Asia Minor he left the Carians their independence, although they owed allegiance to him. In the struggles that followed Alexander's death, and under Roman and Byzantine rule, the region declined, and until recently it was considered pretty much a remote part of Turkey. In the early part of this century dissident writers and artists were exiled to Bodrum from the delights of Istanbul.

Over the last fifteen years tourism has brought prosperity to the area, and large numbers of holiday villages have been built around some of the more accessible coast. This concrete saturation has without doubt obliterated the charm of some parts of the

GOKOVA KORFEZI

area, including Bodrum peninsula, but fortunately there are still remote and wild areas enough in the deep gulfs along the coast.

Bodrum and Marmaris are the two major centres for charter yachts in Turkey, and in early May there is an 'agents' week' in Marmaris. Around the Carian coast and extending along the Lycian coast you will find the greatest concentration of yachts in Turkey. Many are based in Turkey, but many also come across from Greece to explore this rugged coast.

Weather patterns

In the summer the normal wind is the *meltemi*, blowing from the NW to WNW. It is strongest in July and August, when it can get up to Force 6–7 and cause a considerable sea which becomes confused in the channels and off headlands. In the early and late summer the *meltemi* blows less strongly, and there are more days of little or no wind at all. Sometimes the *meltemi* will die at night and then resume the next day, about midday, but it can also blow day and night for a week or more. In the gulfs the wind follows the coast and curves around to blow from the west. Towards the heads of the gulfs, it tends to weaken and become more variable.

Close to the N side of a gulf there will often be gusts from a northerly direction off the high land, but this is local, and a few miles off the wind will be more constant from a W–NW direction. Gusts are particularly violent off the N coasts of Gökova Körfezi and Hisarönü Körfezi. There can be extremely violent gusts with the *meltemi* in the channel between the Catal Islands and the coast, off Deveboynu Burnu (Cape Krio), off Datça and Karaburun (where you turn the corner to go up to Marmaris).

In the spring and autumn there are thunderstorms, often accompanied by strong squalls, but these seldom last for long. Winds in the spring and autumn are almost equally divided between N and S. In winter, winds are from the N and S and gales in the winter can be from N or S.

Data

PORTS OF ENTRY
Bodrum
Datça
Marmaris

MAJOR LIGHTS
Büyük Kiremit Adasi Fl(2)10s10M
Catalada Fl(4)20s6M
Hüseyin Burnu Fl(3)10s8M
Kargi Ada Fl.5s8M
Karaada Fl(2)5s7M
Oren (Sancak) Burnu Fl.3s8M
Orta Ada (Snake Island) Fl.10s9M
Koyun (Balisu) Burnu Fl(3)10s7M
Ince Burnu (Shuyun) Fl(2)5s7M
Deveboynu Burnu (Cape Krio) Fl(2)10s14M
Mersinçik Burnu Fl.WR.3s7/5M 154°-R-270°

Ince Burun (Injah Pt) Fl(3)15s8M
Karaburun Fl(2)10s10M
Kadirğa Burnu Fl(3)15s12M
Keçi Adasi Fl.R.2s5M
Nimara Adasi (Ince Burnu) Fl.3s5M

Quick reference guide

	Shelter	Mooring	Fuel	Water	Provisions	Eating out	Plan	Charge band
Gümüşlük to Bodrum								
Gümüşlük	B	AC	O	B	C	B	•	1
Catalada	O	C	O	O	O	O		
Karatoprak	B	A	O	B	C	C		
Akyarlar	C	C	O	O	C	C	•	
Aspat	B	C	O	O	O	C	•	
Kargi Bükü	C	C	O	O	O	O	•	
Bağlar	C	C	O	O	O	C		
Bitez	B	C	O	B	C	B	•	
Gümbet	B	C	O	B	C	B	•	
Bodrum	A	A	A	A	A	A	•	2
Gökova Körfezi								
Pabuç	C	C	O	O	O	O		
Orak Adasi	C	C	O	O	O	O	•	
Kargiçik Bükü	C	C	O	O	O	O		
Alakişla Bükü	C	C	O	O	O	O		
Cökertme	B	C	O	O	C	C	•	
Oren	O	C	O	O	C	C		
Akbük	B	C	O	O	O	C		
Gökova	C	C	B	B	C	C		
Gelibolu	C	C	O	O	O	O		
Sehir Adalari	B	C	O	O	O	C	•	2
Söğüt	B	AC	O	A	C	C	•	1/2
Kesr	B	C	O	O	O	O	•	
Değirmen Bükü	A	C	O	B	O	C	•	
Kargilibük	B	C	O	O	O	O	•	
Tuzla Köyu	B	C	O	O	O	O		
Yedi Adalari	B	C	O	O	O	O	•	
Amazon Creek	B	C	O	B	C	C		
Gökçeler Bükü	B	C	O	O	O	O	•	
Çati	A	C	O	O	O	O	•	
Körmen	A	AC	O	B	C	C	•	
Mersinçik	B	C	O	O	O	O		
Hisarönü Körfezi								
Knidos	C	C	O	O	O	C	•	
Echo Bay	O	C	O	O	O	O		
Palamut	A	A	O	B	C	B	•	2
Kalaboshi	C	C	O	O	O	C		
Parmak Bükü	C	C	O	O	O	O		
Kargi Köyu	B	C	O	O	O	O		
Datça	B	AC	B	A	B	B	•	2
Değirman Bükü	B	C	O	O	O	O		
Kuruca Bükü	B	C	O	C	C	C	•	
Bençik	B	C	O	B	O	C	•	
Keyif Bükü	B	C	O	O	O	O	•	
Keçi Bükü	A	C	O	A	C	B	•	
Turgut	B	C	O	O	O	O		
Selimiye	B	AC	O	B	C	C	•	
Dirsek	B	C	O	O	O	C	•	
Sömbeki Körfezi to Marmaris								
Bozburun	A	AC	B	A	C	B	•	2
Söğüt	C	C	O	O	O	C		
Bozuk Bükü	B	C	O	O	O	C	•	
Serçe Limani	B	C	O	O	O	C	•	

Arap Adasi	C	C	O	O	O	O		
Gerbekse Creek	C	C	O	O	O	O	•	
Ciftlik	C	C	O	O	O	C	•	
Kadirğa Limani	C	C	O	O	O	O	•	
Kumlu Bükü	C	C	O	O	O	C	•	
Turunç Bükü	B	C	O	O	O	C	•	
Marmaris	B	AC	A	A	A	A	•	2
Marmaris Marina	A	A	A	A	A	A	•	2
Berk Marina	A	AB	B	A	O	C		

GUMUSLUK

Approach

The islands in the approaches are easily identified, but the bay cannot be seen until close in.

Conspicuous From the S–SW, a holiday village on the slopes N of the anchorage can be seen. The village of Gümüşlük will be seen across the narrow isthmus from the N, and across the islet from the S. A military observation tower on a rocky escarpment on the W side of the entrance is conspicuous.

By night There are no lights.

Dangers

1. The remains of the ancient breakwater (totally submerged), extending about 35 metres in a southeasterly direction, must be avoided. A yacht should keep close to the small islet in the entrance.
2. There are strong gusts off the land around the entrance. A yacht should proceed into the bay under power.
3. In the approach from the S care is needed of the reef running out from Karabakla Burnu. It is easily identified even with a few whitecaps around.

Mooring

Anchor in 5–15 metres where convenient. The bottom is mud and weed, good holding once through the weed, though this can take some doing. Alternatively, anchor off the W side of the bay and take a long line ashore.

Note

1 The northern half of the bay which was formerly cordoned off is now open to yachts.
2 The rock shown on the old Admiralty chart 1546 has 5 metres least depth over it.

Shelter Good shelter tucked into the N end of the bay. Reasonable shelter in the S end of the bay. The *meltemi* gusts over the low isthmus, so make sure your anchor is holding properly. With the *meltemi*, a

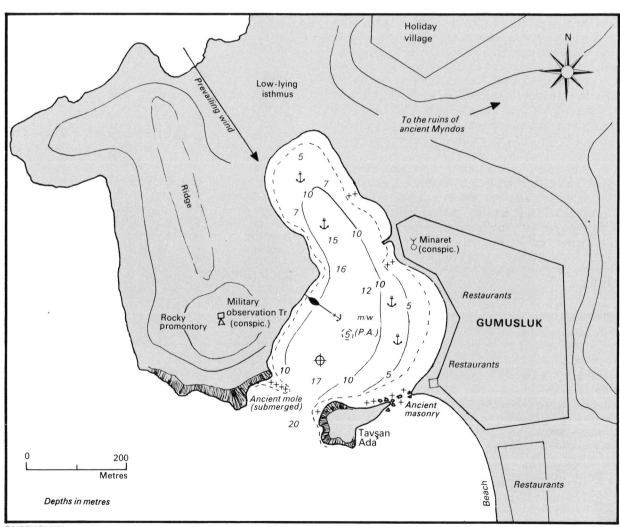

GUMUSLUK
37°03'·5N 27°13'·85E

Military observation tower   *Entrance*   *Islet*

Approach to Gümüşlük, looking E

reflected swell is pushed into the S end, and it can get very rolly at anchor.

Facilities

Water in the village. Most provisions can be found in the village. Numerous restaurants and bars, including several good fish restaurants. *Dolmuş* to Bodrum.

General

The bay and village are most attractive. The beach S of the village has been developed for tourism, but there is not too much; nor are there too many tourists, and the place still has the feel and atmosphere of a village.

A short walk away are the ruins of ancient Myndus. The city enclosed the harbour by means of a wall on the ridge forming the western side of the bay, and continued in an almost perfect square inland to the E. Much of the wall can be traced, but little else remains. The wines of Myndus were said by Athenaeus to be salty in taste because they were mixed with salt water, a practice believed to eliminate hangovers and aid digestion.

The islet in the entrance is called Tavşan Ada, Rabbit Island, after the rabbits that used to live on it. I'm not sure whether or not they were bred for eating, as I don't recall ever seeing rabbit in the butcher's or on a menu.

Gümüşlük to Gökova Körfezi

The coast between Gümüşlük and Paşa Rock, where you turn the corner to enter Gökova Körfezi, is fringed by above and below-water rocks, with a number of islands lying a short distance off. The channel between the coast and the islands is easily negotiated, with good depths in the fairway. The islands off the coast are easily identified, as is Hüseyin Burnu, by its prominent white lighthouse and dwelling. Paşa Rock has a beacon on it which is also conspicuous.

When the *meltemi* is blowing, you either whoosh down this channel or have a struggle to get up it. When heading N, it can be better to anchor at Akyar or Aspat and wait for the *meltemi* to die down so

that you can motor up the channel in the morning.

In former times, before there were adequate charts of the region, this maze of islands and reefs was a lethal trap for trading ships coasting to and from Halicarnassus and other ancient ports along the coast. Numerous wrecks litter the islands, and local fishermen are constantly hauling up old amphorae in their nets. Peter Throckmorton, who did much of the early work locating wrecks around the nearby coast, astutely sums up the trap these islands presented to ancient seafarers:

'From the big island's peak I could see Yassi Ada, where our wrecks lay. Watching the boil of waves on the west reef, I came to a clearer understanding of why shipwrecks lay there. Yassi Ada was the westernmost of the group. One hundred yards to the west of it was the reef, its top just below the surface. A prudent seaman would want to clear the whole Chattal group, thinking, "Why pick your way among those rocks if you don't have to?" He would be running, at this time of year, before the *meltemi*, if he were headed from the north toward Rhodes, seventy miles away, or Halicarnassus, fifteen miles away from Yassi Ada. He would want to stay away from the lee shore of Pserimos or Kos, six miles downwind. So he would stay close to Yassi Ada, then sail on a broad reach: twelve miles to go with a lee shore under him all the way until he was free of the easternmost point of Kos and ready to stand away for Rhodes or Knidos or Kos harbour. Not wanting

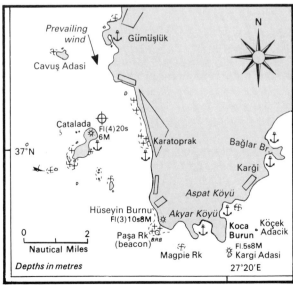

GUMUSLUK TO ASPAT
Catalada light 37°00'·7N 27°13'·4E

to go too close to the outermost island, and knowing that almost all Aegean islands are steep-to, he would stand a cable length off and running before the strong *meltemii* in fairly heavy seas, would be on the reef before he could do a thing about it. Yassi Ada was, and is, a very subtle ship trap.'

Peter Throckmorton *The Lost Ships*

Coda The reefs off Catalada claimed yet another victim when a cargo ship used for transporting sheep to the Middle East cut the W end of the island too finely and is now prominently perched on the end of the reef.

CATALADA

The island lying 1¾ miles off the coast and about 3 miles NW of Paşa Rock. It is easily recognised, being nearly divided in two except for a narrow isthmus joining the two halves. In settled weather a yacht can find a reasonable lee from the *meltemi* under the isthmus where the expedition boat from Bodrum was based during the underwater excavation of a Roman ship that hit the reef. (See above.)

Anchor in 4–6 metres on a sandy bottom. There are above and below-water rocks near the shore. Gusts with the *meltemi*. A light is exhibited on the NE tip of the island. Characteristic: Fl(4)20s6M.

KARATOPRAK (Turgutreis)

A small fishing harbour opposite Catalada. The harbour is partially rock-bound, and there are barely 1·5-metre depths at the entrance. With the *meltemi* blowing down the channel there are breaking waves at the entrance. A small yacht could investigate in calm weather.

Concrete holiday villages now obliterate much of this bit of coast, so that it is difficult to identify where the original villages begin and end.

HUYSEYIN BURNU (Hussein Point)

The low-lying cape before you turn into Gökova Körfezi. The lighthouse is conspicuous, Fl(3)10s 8M. A yacht should keep to seaward of Paşa Rock, lying off Hüseyin Burnu, as a reef connects it to the cape. A beacon (BRB but in need of paint, with ⁝ topmark) on Paşa Rock is conspicuous.

Caution

There is an error on the pre-1983 Admiralty chart 1604, which shows a beacon on Magpie Rock (Bekci Kayasi), lying about ¾ mile SE of Hüseyin Burnu, where there is none. It does not show the beacon on Paşa Rock as it should. This error has been corrected on subsequent charts. Magpie Rock (Bekci Kayasi) is difficult to see, and I have never satisfied myself as to its exact position despite looking for it. The situation is confused because the old Admiralty charts give a least depth of 4·5 fathoms (incorrectly amended to 4ft/1·2 metres from my earlier information) and the Turkish chart a depth of 8·2 metres. I have not ascertained the depth with any exactness, and waves do not break on it. The prudent course is to keep well clear of it. Kargi Adasi on a transit of 080° or less will keep you well clear of Magpie Rock.

Note A line of white buoys running out from Akyarlar Burun marks a sewage disposal pipe.

AKYARLAR

The bay close W of Koca Burun (Cape Petera). The small harbour in the NW corner is usually full of

Hüyseyin Burnu (lighthouse)   *Paşa Rk (beacon)*

Paşa Rock (with beacon) and the lighthouse on Hüyseyin Burnu, looking NE

Karği Adasi, looking NE

Holiday village *Fort*

Aspat Koyu looking N

gulets and local boats, but a small yacht may find room to squeeze in on occasion. Anchor in NE corner of the bay in 3–5 metres on sand and weed. Good shelter from the *meltemi* although there are gusts into the bay off the land. Restaurants and some provisions ashore.

KARGI ADASI

The jagged rocky islet off Koca Burun. A light is exhibited on the islet: Fl.5s8M.

ASPAT KOYU

The large bay lying about one mile N of Koca Burun. It is easily identified by the large hotel complex stretching around the shore. Anchor in the N or S end of the bay on a sandy bottom. Good shelter from the *meltemi*, although there are gusts into the bay. The S bay is the more popular with restaurants ashore. The N bay is more tranquil. In the N bay anchor off the creek running into the bay in 3–6 metres, mud or sand and weed, good holding. On the top of the conical hill on the E side of the bay there are the remains of what look like ancient masonry and some more recent remains. Despite good intentions it has always seemed a bit too hot to climb to the summit when I have been here.

KOCEK ADACIK

The thin jagged thread of above-water rocks off the entrance to Aspat Köyü. The rocks are easily recognised by day.

KARGI BUKU

The bay lying directly under Bağlar Burun. Reasonable shelter from the *meltemi* here, though there are gusts off the land.

The bleak, rubble-strewn peaks inland, bereft of vegetation, are in stark contrast to the wooded foreshore and the holiday villages that have now been built around the lower slopes.

BAGLAR KOYU

The large bay on the N side of Bağlar Burun. In calm weather, or with a light *meltemi*, anchor off the beach where convenient. Restaurants ashore. Tripper boats from Bodrum often come here in the summer.

Gökova Körfezi
Gulf of Gökova, Kerme Körfezi, Gulf of Kos, ancient **Gulf of Keramos**
Admiralty chart 1055
Turkish chart 311
Imray-Tetra chart G35

This long and much-indented gulf is a popular cruising ground, especially for charterers from Bodrum. There are many beautiful anchorages on both sides of the gulf and, despite the numbers of yachts cruising around this area, you will seldom fail to find a deserted bay if you look hard enough. In spring or autumn you will have it virtually to yourself. Although easily accessible by sea, the hamlets around the gulf are quite isolated, and there are few places for provisioning. Consequently, you should stock up well in Bodrum before setting off into the gulf.

In ancient times, when most travelling was done by sea, this gulf boasted numerous great cities near the water. From Myndus, there was a chain of cities around the shores: Halicarnassus, Keramos, Kedreai, and Knidos. The waters about Keramos have silted so that it now stands about a mile from the sea. In later centuries, the inaccessibility by land of many of these sites meant that they were left pretty much alone. The sites of Kedreai and Knidos, at opposite ends of the gulf, may have succumbed to nature's interminable forces, but they have been little touched by the locals for building materials, and the over-zealous amateur archaeologists of the 19th century have not vandalised them too much. Even the most cynical of us cannot escape the romance of a Kedreai or a Knidos, and cannot but marvel at the skill of these ancient architects.

A local yachtsman, Sadun Boro, is attempting to have part of this area between Gökova and Knidos on the southern side of the gulf established as a nature reserve. Sadun, a celebrity in Turkey since he was the first Turkish national to sail around the world, hopes to restrict hotel development in order to keep this remote area in its present natural state – a sentiment I cannot help but share, having spent many pleasant days pottering in and out of the bays and coves along this coast.

Unfortunately, the government has decided to site a low-grade coal-burning power station near Oren,

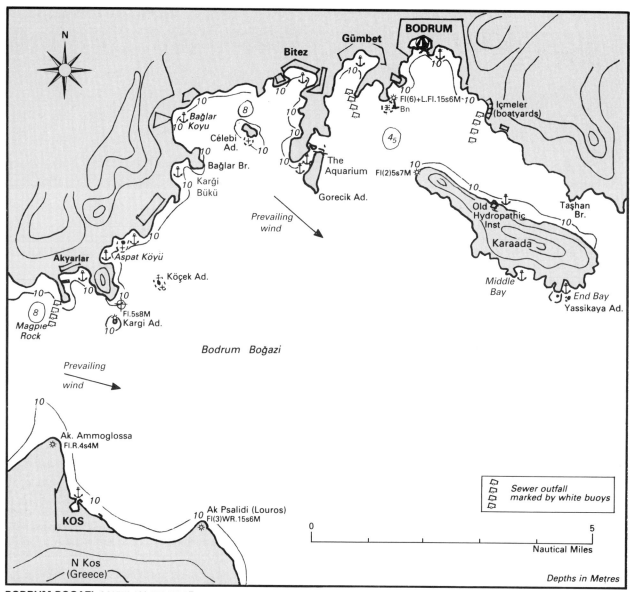

BODRUM BOGAZI 36°57'·6N 27°18'·3E

and this has caused much anger in Bodrum over the ecological damage it will do. At present the anger of the locals has caused the government to delay the start-up date for the power station indefinitely, though cynical souls in Bodrum suspect that this delay will last only for as long as the power station is an issue. Let us hope that this is for some time to come, and that the locals will also object to the building of other concrete abominations along the coast like the ubiquitous holiday villages around Bodrum Peninsula.

Winds

In the summer the *meltemi* curves around into the gulf to blow along it from the W. The wind loses strength towards the head of the gulf, but gusts over the mountains on the northern side, often with considerable force. At night a NE wind may blow for a period, but it generally dies off before dawn.

Note When making for Bodrum from Cape Krio against the meltemi, a yacht should keep on a port tack, when it will find that it can gradually head higher and higher, fetching Bodrum in a great semi-circle, as it were.

BITEZ (Agacli Köyü, Petasa Bay)

The long enclosed bay lying NE of Celebi Adasi (Parthena Island). In the bay itself care needs to be taken of several buoys laid as marks for the sailing holiday centres. Anchor in 3–5 metres in the eastern half of the bay. The bottom is sand and weed, good holding. The central pier has 2–2·5 metre depths off the end and a yacht can go stern or bows-to it if there is room. Good shelter from the *meltemi*, though there are gusts down into the bay. With strong southerlies a considerable swell rolls into the bay, and it can be dangerous in southerly gales.

Water available on the pier. Limited provisions available. Numerous restaurants and bars. *Dolmuş* and taxi into Bodrum.

The hinterland is attractive, being largely planted with citrus orchards, for which the area was once renowned. The appearance of clusters of villas on

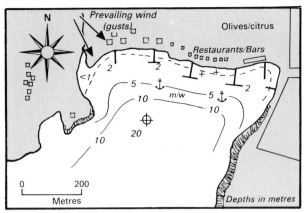

BITEZ
37°01'·45N 27°23'E

the slopes at either end of the bay and numerous hotels along the foreshore has obliterated some of the charm of the place, but it is still recognisable as Bitez. Several of the hotels along the shore house a number of sailing holiday centres. As a consequence, the bay is crowded with windsurfers, sailing dinghies, and speedboats towing water-skiers. Several discos assail the night air with the latest dance music, to keep the novice sailors happy into the late evening. A lively spot rather than a quiet alternative to Bodrum.

ADA BOGAZI ('The Aquarium')

Between Ada Burun and the SE side of the island of Gorecik Adasi is an anchorage popularly known as 'The Aquarium'. It is much visited by tripper boats in the summer, though they all depart for the night. With the *meltemi*, a yacht can anchor in here with a line ashore to Ada Burun. The approach must be made from the W. As you enter the anchorage, the depths remain constant around 8–9 metres before suddenly coming up to 2–3 metres on the NE side. Anchor here with a long line ashore to Ada Burun. Remember that the *gulets* anchored further inside draw very little compared to a yacht, though you can explore further in with care.

In southerlies or calm weather, yachts can also anchor in the bight on Gorecik Adasi, just inside the W entrance.

Note On the charts, the shallow area in the inner part of 'The Aquarium' is not shown. The gap on the E side between Gorecik Adasi and Ada Burun, partially obstructed by a small islet, has depths of 1 metre and less, and should not be attempted. Again, the small local boats using this gap draw comparatively little compared to yachts and most displacement motorboats.

GUMBET (Kümbet)

The bay immediately E of Bitez, between Ada Burun and Ince Burun. The line of white buoys running out from the shore marks a sewage disposal pipe. Anchor near the head of the bay in 5–10 metres on sand and mud. Good shelter from the *meltemi*.

Restaurants and provisions ashore. *Dolmuş* or taxi to Bodrum. The shores around the bay have been considerably developed, and Gumbet has now become a suburb of Bodrum. There are numerous hotels, and at night numerous discos to entertain the holiday-makers, so it is not a quiet place. Yachts sometimes prefer to anchor here in the summer, where there is a cooling breeze, rather than go into Bodrum, where it can get stuffy and dusty.

DIKILITAS KAYASI (Haremten)

Lying close off Harem Burnu is a reef marked by a beacon (YBY) with a S cardinal ⍖ topmark. An area of shoal water spreads mostly NE from the beacon. A yacht should keep well to seaward of the beacon. Local boats often cut between the reef and Harem Burnu, where there are least depths of 7–8 metres in the fairway, but the prudent course is to go outside the beacon. It is lit: Q(6)+LFl.15s6m6M.

The beacon on Dikilitas Kayasi in the approaches to Bodrum

'CLUB M' QUAY

Off Değirmen Burnu, there is now a quay under the sprawling complex of 'Club M', on the slopes of the point. *Gulets* are often berthed here in the summer when the prevailing wind blows off the land. It is untenable in southerlies, even moderate ones.

BODRUM (ancient Halicarnassus)

BA 1644
Turkish chart 3111
Imray-Tetra chart 35

Approach

Straightforward by day and night.

Conspicuous The cluster of white buildings around the slopes behind Bodrum is easily distinguished from the distance. From Gümbet to Bodrum, holiday villages, large hotels and villa/apartment complexes extend in an almost unbroken line to the town. Closer in the castle of St Peter will be seen. The harbour lies immediately W of the castle, and the breakwaters are easily identified. Although the entrance cannot be seen until close to, it is obvious where it is, especially in the summer, when *gulets* and yachts are constantly coming and going.

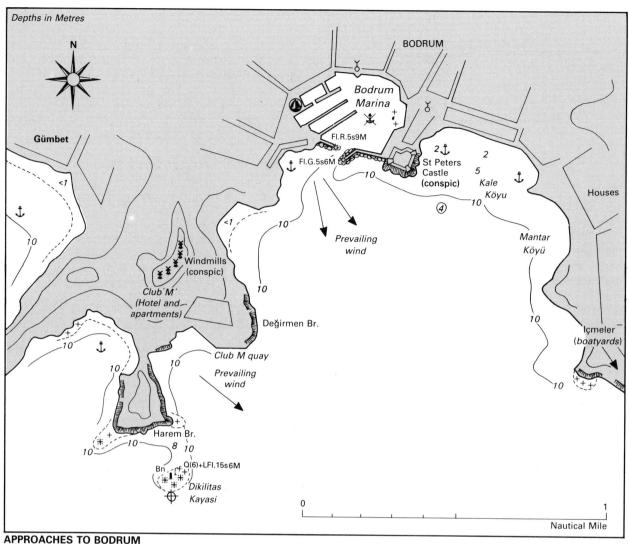

APPROACHES TO BODRUM
Dikilitas Beacon 37°00'·9N 27°24'·9E

By night Use the lights on Kargi Adasi (Fl.5s8M) and Karaada (Fl(2)5s7M). Dikilitas Reef is lit Q(6)+LFl.15s. Closer in, use the lights on the extremities of the breakwaters (Fl.R.5s9M and Fl.G.5s6M). The castle is spotlit on summer nights.

VHF Ch 11, 16 (summer 0600–1900, winter 0700–1600 except Sunday). Call sign *Bodrum Marina*.

Dangers
1. Care must be taken of Dikilitas Reef, a short distance off Harem Burnu.
2. Care must be taken of *gulets*, tripper boats, small ferries and yachts in the comparatively narrow entrance to the harbour. *Gulets* nearly always leave or arrive at full throttle, and have little idea of internationally accepted rules of the road.

Mooring

Data 275 berths. Visitors' berths. Max LOA 30m. Depths 2–5m.

Once into the harbour, a yacht must head for the marina. Anchoring off in the harbour is now prohibited, and a sign to that effect is displayed at the harbour entrance. All the rest of the quayed

space outside the marina is reserved for Turkish flag boats and is jealously guarded. An attendant will direct you to a berth in the marina. There are laid moorings on the inner berths and laid moorings are also to be installed for the two new outer pontoons. When they have been installed, a yacht should not use its own anchor, except in the case of large yachts going on the outside of the outer pontoon.

Shelter Good all-round shelter. With strong southerlies, berths on the S side of the outer pontoons can get uncomfortable, though not dangerous, with the slop across the harbour. Yachts are wintered afloat in the marina.

Authorities A port of entry. Customs and immigration are in offices near the extremity of the eastern breakwater. The health officer and harbourmaster are nearby in the town. However, you must obtain your Transit Log in the marina. After collecting the Transit Log, it is usually permissible to walk round to the relevant offices:

1. Health authorities
2. Immigration
3. Customs
4. Harbourmaster
5. Coastguard

Above Knidos looking NE. *See page 166.*

Palamut looking NE.
See page 168..

Below Datça looking N. *See page 169.*

Above Bençik. Hotel bay immediately E of
Bençik looking NE. *See page 171.*

Selimiye looking
ESE. *See page 173.*

Below Keçi Bükü looking ENE. *See page 172.*

Above Bozburun harbour
looking SE. *See page 176.*

Below Kizil Adasi passage
and anchorage looking E.
See page 177.

Above Serce looking S.
See page 179.

Ciftlik looking W. See page 180.

Below Marmaris town and marina looking N. See page 182.

Below Turunc Bükü looking W. *See page 181.*

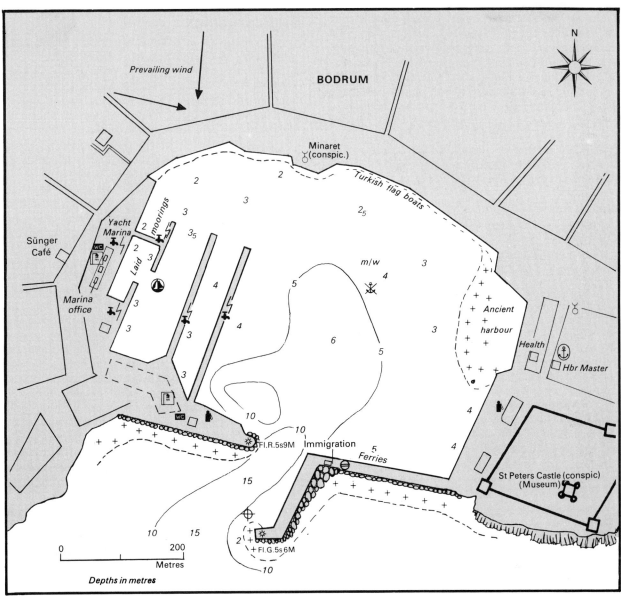

BODRUM
37°02'·1N 27°25'·5E

Occasionally you may be required to take your yacht over to the customs and immigration quay.
Charge band 2.

Anchorages

1. You can anchor in the bight immediately W of the entrance to the harbour. It is always a bit rolly here, as much from the wash of craft as from the ground swell.
2. Kale Köyu. Local craft anchor here throughout most of the summer. Reasonable protection from the *meltemi*. Untenable in southerlies. The only drawback to Kale Köyu is the deafening noise from the bars and discos that turn this bay into a churning decibel hell.

Facilities

Services Water and electricity (220V) at or near every berth. Recently there have been water shortages, and the water has only been on for an hour or two in the morning and evening. Shower and toilet block in the marina complex.

Fuel On the western breakwater.

Repairs Gardiennage and routine maintenance afloat. Engineering, electrical and mechanical repairs in the town. For major engineering and mechanical repairs, the engine will have to go to Milas or Izmir. Several chandlers close by.

Sailmaker Seagull Sailmakers. ☎ (office answerphone and *fax*) (252) 316 2611 (loft) (252) 316 5726. Address: Loft 'Saray', Saray sk No. 12, Tepeçik, Bodrum 48400, or PO Box PK14, Bodrum.

Provisions Mini-market in the marina. Excellent shopping for all provisions in the town. Migros supermarket on the main road NNW of the marina is open 24 hours in the summer. Excellent and colourful market on Thursdays and Fridays, in the stadium near the old village, when the local produce is brought from the outlying areas into Bodrum. Ice available in the marina.

153

Eating out An excellent choice of restaurants, from the simple to the sophisticated, in the town and around the waterfront. Allegiances change from year to year as cooks and favourite waiters come and go. *Other* PO. Banks. Local gas and *Camping Gaz*. Doctors and dentists. Laundry in the marina, or there are several others close by. International telephone calls, fax and telex services available in the marina. Buses to Izmir and Marmaris. Ferries to Kos. Ferry to Datça. Internal and international flights from Bodrum Airport. International flights from Dalaman (in the summer) and Izmir.

Marina services

Weather forecast Daily weather forecasts posted (in English).
Address Turban Bodrum Marina, 48400 Bodrum, Muğla, Turkey ☎ (252) 316 1860 *Fax* (252) 316 1406.

General

Bodrum is an enchanting and thoroughly likable town, if a little hot and dusty in the height of summer. It has something of a reputation as a Bohemian town, a reputation it acquired when a number of dissident artists and writers were exiled here. The most famous of these was Cevat Sakir Kabaagac, who became known as the Fisherman of Halicarnassus, after his many stories of the locals and the town. Cevat was exiled here in 1908, and remained in Bodrum until his death. Bodrum must be one of the most beautiful places that exiles have been banished to – no Siberia this.

It is currently enjoying a tourist boom as foreigners discover what the rich from Istanbul and Ankara have known for some time, though some locals wish it had remained unknown to the 'hordes from the north'.

Wandering around the town, you should make a point of seeing the Castle of St Peter, which houses the excellent Hall of Underwater Archaeology. This is one of the best museums of its type in the Mediterranean, with finds from wrecks around the coast dating from the Bronze Age to the Ottoman period, excavated (if that is the right word) by Dr George Bass and his team.

BODRUM CUP

Every year the Bodrum Cup Regatta for traditional wooden boats is held around the second or third week of October. A few foreign yachts participate, and there is now a division for boats of modern construction. In 1995 over 80 boats took part, and the sight of all those *gulets* sailing is as spectacular as it is unexpected. Different legs are sailed each day, with a new route around Gökova Körfezi adding to its appeal. It is to be much recommended. If you are interested, contact ERA Yachting in Bodrum ☎ (252) 316 2310/ 316 2054 *Fax* (252) 316 5338 *E-mail* era-f@servis2.net.tr.

Halicarnassus

Little remains today to remind us that this was once a great and powerful city, at one time the centre of Caria. Early on the city was part of the Dorian Confederacy that included Knidos, Kos, Kamirus, Lindos and Rhodes. Halicarnassus was dropped from the union when it made overtures to Caria. In the early 6th century it came under the control of the Lydian kings. Under Xerxes, Lygdamis II was made tyrant, and he was succeeded by his remarkable daughter, Artemisia I. She was so successful a leader that she was made admiral of the Halicarnassian fleet that formed part of Xerxes' invasion fleet against Athens, though in the battle she managed to ram and sink one of the boats on the Persian side. In 377 BC Mausolos became ruler. Under his administration the city prospered, and the Halicarnassian fleet quickly expanded to become one of the most powerful in the Aegean.

After the death of Mausolos, his sister-wife Artemisia II ruled, and it was in this period that the massive tomb of Mausolos was built. One of the seven wonders of the world, it also bequeathed the word 'mausoleum' to the English language. The tomb apparently stood fifty metres high and was some twenty metres long, with the whole edifice adorned with magnificent friezes. It was still standing in the 12th century, but was reportedly destroyed by an earthquake in the 15th century.

Halicarnassus was largely destroyed by Alexander the Great, and little remains today of the ancient city. Parts of the city wall, the site of the tomb of Mausolos, and the theatre (just behind the marina on the hillside) can be seen, and much ancient masonry has been incorporated into the Castle of St Peter. Around the town you will find odd columns, capitals and scraps of masonry built into the houses, or serving as doorsteps, cornerstones, parts of walls or supports for water troughs, or just lying around.

We know a great deal about Halicarnassus from Herodotus (482–24 BC), the father of written history, who was a native of the city. From Halicarnassus he travelled widely in Egypt, eastern Europe, and Asia to gather the material for his nine-book history of the wars between Greece and Persia. Herodotus is remarkable for his curiosity about various personalities and his lack of partisanship towards his own race – he treats all equally, in a wholly readable manner. He died far from his home, in Thurii in southern Italy, after disagreeing with the Dynasts ruling his own city.

NEW BODRUM HARBOUR

Plans have been drawn up for a new harbour situated at Içmeler. The harbour is planned for the burgeoning number of *gulets* based at Bodrum. At the time of publication work had yet to begin on the new harbour and like many of these projects it remains to be seen if it goes ahead at all.

BOATYARDS

In the vicinity of Bodrum there are a number of boatyards accustomed to hauling out yachts. Most of them lie at Içmeler, about three kilometres SE of the town. Several of the yards have travel-hoists (between 30–60 tons); larger craft can be hauled on a cradle and sledge.

A regular *dolmuş* service runs from Bodrum centre to Içmeler and back, approximately on the half hour. At Içmeler there are a small chandler's and a paint shop, engineering shops, including several which can carry out stainless steel work, wood-working shops, and engine repair shops. There are also a small provisions shop and café/restaurants.

With the large numbers of local boats based in Bodrum, it is worth booking early to get a place at one of the boatyards, as demand already outstrips capacity.

One of the yards is Yat Lift PK 424, 48400 Bodrum ☎ (252) 316 7842 *Fax* (252) 316 7620. VHF Ch 69. Betas Agency can also arrange hauling and repairs. Murat Toprak ☎ (252) 316 1697 *Fax* (252) 316 4898

At Ortakent a new boatyard has been established. Hauling is by cradle and sledge; ☎ ERA Yachting (252) 358 5574/358 5237.

Karaada

(Black Island)

The large island lying in the SE approaches to Bodrum.

On the N coast, the white buildings of the old hydropathic institute are conspicuous. Local boats run tourists across for the hot mineral springs ashore. In calm weather you can anchor off here to go ashore for the springs. These are said to be beneficial to those suffering from rheumatism and arthritis.

On the S side, there are two bays that can be used with the prevailing NW–W wind:
Middle Bay Lies approximately ⅔ of the way down Karaada. Anchor where convenient and take a line ashore. There are strong gusts down into the bay with the *meltemi*.
End Bay Lies at the SE end of the island and is the better anchorage of the two. Anchor and take a line ashore to the W side of the bay. The gusts are less severe here, and the surroundings are attractive, with pine-clad slopes around the bay.

Both bays are popular with the tripper boats, and with local boats out for the day from Bodrum.

NOTE FOR GOKOVA KORFEZI

With the *meltemi*, there are extremely strong gusts down off the high land on the N side onto the sea for up to 2 miles off. The direction of the gusts off the land varies, but is generally between NW–N.

PABUC

A small bay 4 miles E of Karaada. Anchor in 6–10 metres off the beach, and take a long line ashore if possible. There are strong gusts out of the bay with the *meltemi*.

ORAK ADASI

The bare, rocky island lying in the approaches to Kargiçik Bükü. There is a light on the island characteristic Fl.10s17m7M. There are two coves on the island where a small yacht can find some shelter.

On the N side there is a cove with a jetty at the head. Anchor in 3–8 metres on a sand and stony bottom and take a line to the jetty. Fair shelter only.

On the E side there is a small cove opposite an islet. Care must be taken of a reef to the N of the islet, and of another reef immediately W of it. Anchor in the cove in 4–10 metres on a sand and shingle bottom, and take a line ashore.

When the *meltemi* is blowing there are strong gusts down onto the islands – care needed. There have been reports of big and bold rats here, so take precautions if you have a line ashore.

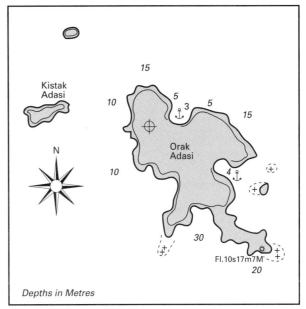

ORAK ADASI
36°58′·5N 27°35′·1E

KARGICIK BUKU (Kishle)

A large bay N of Orak Adasi. Anchor on the western side of the bay in 5–6 metres. The bottom is sand and rock, bad holding. Good shelter, although there are strong gusts with the *meltemi*. A beach ashore, and exceptionally clear water in the bay. There is now a holiday village on the shores with restaurants.

ALAKISLA BUKU (36°59′·8N 27°39′E)

A large bay some 3 miles NE of Orak Adasi. Yildiz Adasi (Prasa, Hermo Islet) lies off the southern arm of the bay. A detached shoal lies between the northern tip of Yildiz and the southern point of the bay. A yacht should keep closer to the point to avoid this shoal when passing between the islet and the point. Anchor at the head of the bay, where there is shelter from the *meltemi*, although there are strong gusts off the mountains. Open S and E.

COKERTME (Fesiliyen Köyü, Vasilika)

Approach

The entrance to the bay is difficult to pick out from the distance. From the E–SE the huge power station near Oren is easily identified, but when coasting from the W the top of the chimney of the power station will only be seen above the E entrance to the bay when closer to. In the summer, small motor-boats often come out to the entrance to tout for business in one or other of the restaurants here. The hamlet cannot be seen until you are up to the entrance of the bay.

Mooring

The best place to be is in the W cove, with a long line ashore to the N side. Alternatively, anchor in the N cove with a line ashore to the W side, or closer in with a line ashore to the beach. There are a number of laid moorings which can be used if free. The *meltemi* tends to gust in off the high land, and at times there can be violent gusts into the anchorage. The bottom is mud, sand and weed, poor holding in places. In calm weather it is possible to anchor off the hamlet, though depths drop off quickly.

Note A tout in a motorboat usually helps you to get a long line ashore, but do not be pressured for a promise to go to his particular restaurant that night.

Facilities

Several restaurants. The roguish Captain Ibrahim's offers a sort of floor show, while the Rose Mary has excellent home-cooked food and a quieter family atmosphere. Limited provisions.

General

The bay is popular as the first night stop for yachts and *gulets* heading down into the gulf, and can get crowded at the height of summer. It is an attractive spot, hemmed in by high precipitous slopes clad in pine, and in olives on the lower slopes. The hamlet perched precariously on a sand spit under the slopes is a convivial spot, and usually draws people back to it on their way out of the gulf. One of the locals is usually around with his camel, offering rides for a fee – usually negotiable, depending on the time of year. Carpets are made in the village; if you enquire in one of the restaurants you can see them being woven, and buy one if you think the price is right.

OREN (Camalti, Keramos) 37°01'·3N 27°58'·4E

The bay on the E side of Oren Burnu. The power station and tall chimney just W of Oren are conspicuous from a considerable distance off. Closer in, the light structure on the point (Fl.3s8M) is conspicuous, as is the village on the shore to the W of the point. Oren offers indifferent shelter, and is in any case very deep for anchoring. There is a pier off the power station. The ruins of ancient Keramos are about one mile from the anchorage.

Note The large coal-fired power station and a village for the workers have been constructed just W of Oren. The power station is to run on low-grade coal, mined on the other side of the coastal mountain range. Siting the power station on this once tranquil spot has generated much local anger, especially in Bodrum, and caused the government in Ankara to delay operation of the power station, although it is apparently ready to go. How long this delay lasts remains to be seen.

AKBUK LIMANI (37°01'·9N 28°06'·5E)

Between Oren and Gökova, the high mountains drop almost vertically into the sea from a considerable height. About 6 miles E of Oren lies Akbük Burun, a short peninsula which is easily identified against the high mountains behind.

Anchor in the W corner of the long bay behind the peninsula, off the restaurant prominent on the shore. The bottom shelves steeply from 10–15 metres close to the shore. Anchor and take a line ashore, or go stern or bows-to one of the jetties if there is room – in the summer *gulets* take up most of the space. On the SW side of the bay the bottom shelves less steeply. The bottom is sand and weed and not everywhere good holding. Because of the depths you must anchor in and the fierce gusts off the mountains when the *meltemi* is blowing, you are strongly advised to take a line ashore.

In the event of SE–E winds, it is reported that there is a bight on the N side, just E of a white house, that affords shelter from these winds. Anchor in 2–3 metres on sand, with a line ashore.

Restaurant ashore but little else. The surroundings here are magnificent, with steep rugged slopes clad in pine dropping down to the sea.

GOKOVA ISKELE (37°03'N 28°18'·7E)

The village of Gökova, from which the gulf takes its name, lies at the head of the gulf. Here the high

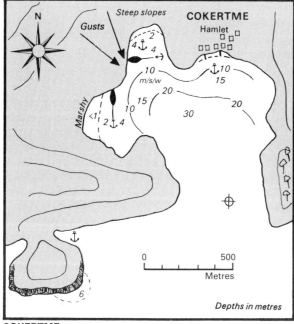

COKERTME
36°59'·9N 27°47'·6E

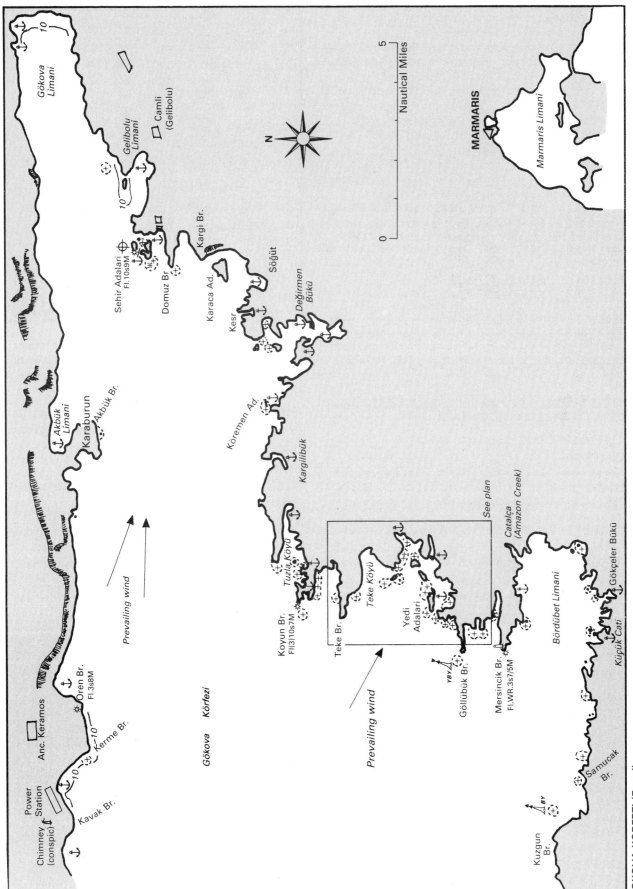

The Carian coast

MARMARIS

Marmaris Limani

Nautical Miles

5

0

N

Gökova Limani

Gelibolu Limani

Camli (Gelibolu)

Kargi Br.

Sehir Adalari ⊕ Fl.10s9M

Domuz Br.

Karaca Ad.

Söğüt

Kesr

Değirmen Bükü

Akbük Br.

Akbük Limani

Karaburun

Köremen Ad.

Kargilibük

Tuzla Köyü

Koyun Br. Fl(3)10s7M

Teke Köyü

Teke Br.

See plan

Yedi Adalari

YBY

Göllübük Br.

Catalça (Amazon Creek)

Mersincik Br. Fl.WR.3s7/5M

Bördübet Limani

Gökçeler Bükü

Küçük Cati

Oren Br. Fl.3s8M

Power Station

Chimney (conspic) Ad.

Anc. Keramos

Kerme Br.

Kavak Br.

Gökova Körfezi

Prevailing wind

Prevailing wind

Samucak Br.

BY

Kuzgun Br.

10

10

~10

10

10

GOKOVA KORFEZI (E end)
Orta Ada light 37°00'N 28°12'·3E

157

mountains plummet down to the flat land of the river delta around the Igriazmak river.

Anchor off the village and small harbour in the NE corner in 5 metres on a mud bottom – excellent holding. Indifferent shelter. Depths behind the new mole are one metre and less, though very small yachts and shallow-draught motorboats have squeezed in here to find good shelter. Care is needed, as the channel into the harbour is tricky and probably silts and changes.

Water in the village and fuel from a petrol station about 8km away. Provisions and a restaurant in the village. Bus or taxi to Bodrum and Marmaris.

Just to the W of Gökova Iskele there is a small cove used by local fishing boats, which may be a useful anchorage, depending on the wind. Good restaurant ashore.

GELIBOLU BUKU (Camli)

Turkish chart 3111

A large bay just E of Sehir Adalari. A yacht can anchor near the head of the bay, although depths are considerable. With the *meltemi* some swell is pushed into the bay, but in calm weather it would be worth exploring.

SEHIR ADALARI (Shehir Oghlan, Snake and Castle Islands, ancient Kedreai)

Turkish chart 3111

Approach

Conspicuous The cluster of white buildings of the holiday village in Taş Bükü shows up well from the NW. The islands themselves are difficult to make out from the land behind. Closer in, the white light structure on the W end of Snake Island will be seen.

By night There is only the light on Snake Island (Fl.10s9M). A night approach is not recommended.

Dangers Care must be taken of Duck Rock, lying about 400 metres W of Castle Island. It is now marked by a metal pole beacon with a W cardinal ⨉ topmark.

Mooring

A yacht will normally proceed into the anchorage off Castle Island between Castle and Snake Islands, or between Castle Island and the mainland. By day either of these passages is straightforward. The shoal water is easily identified, but it is useful to have someone up front conning you in. Anchor in 5–10 metres in the middle of the bay, or better still, proceed further into the bay, anchor in 2·5–3 metres and take a line ashore. The bottom is sand and weed, good holding. A yacht can also anchor off the eastern side of Castle Island, under the remnants of the ancient mole, or in Taş Bükü.

In the summer the anchorage at Castle Island gets very crowded, and is also churned up by tripper boats coming and going.

Shelter Shelter is good from the prevailing wind, except in the outer part of the anchorage, which gets a reflected swell, making it uncomfortable. In the

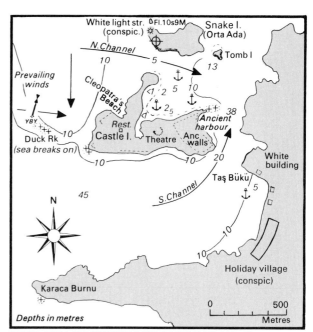

SEHIR ADALARI (SNAKE AND CASTLE ISLANDS)
Snake Island light (Orta Ada) 37°00'N 28°12'·3E

evening the westerly day breeze will often turn around to blow from the NE, and this should be taken into account when anchoring.

Dangers Care must be taken of the remains of the ancient mole, now underwater, off the NE point of Castle Island.

Facilities

A restaurant/café in the summer. There are several restaurants in Taş Bükü, and from here a *dolmuş* runs to Marmaris in the summer. A custodian now patrols the island and keeps it clean. A modest charge is levied on anyone coming ashore, to pay for the custodian and for cleaning up the island. Yachts using the anchorage may also be charged, even if their crews do not go ashore.

Anchorage at Castle Island, looking E

General

The islands are enchanting and mysterious, but not in summer. Between the harsh clatter of the generator at the restaurant and the noisy throngs on Cleopatra's Beach, there is no enchantment and little mystery, and at times one can be forgiven for wishing that Cleopatra was still around to issue an imperial edict banning day-trippers. The latter are usually only interested in the place as a location for sunning themselves on the beach and buying cold ice cream. I will go as far as saying that I recommend you stop here only briefly for lunch in the summer. In the spring and autumn the island is a different place altogether.

On Castle Island there are many ruins, dating from early Carian to the last Byzantine occupation. This is the site of ancient Kedreai, part of the Rhodian Confederacy and later part of Roman Asia Minor (it was occupied by the Romans in 129 BC). The small beach on the west of the island is known as Cleopatra's Beach, and the tale behind the name is interesting. Cleopatra is believed to have taken up residence on the island, and one of her many extravagant gestures was to have galleys of sand shipped from North Africa to create the beach for her lover, Antony, to sunbathe on. According to Professor Tom Goedike (in H M Denham), the sand is not of this region, and is indeed typical of African sand.

The ruins on the island are romantically situated amid olive groves, and the small theatre, seating about 1500 by my reckoning, is sited (with all the skill and flair we have come to associate with these ancient planners) with a fine view across the bay between Castle and Snake Islands to the mountains on the north side of the gulf. Today we get glimpses of the view between mature olive trees growing in and around the theatre. There are numerous other remains close by, and the outer defensive wall around the eastern half of the island can be followed for most of its length. Part of a defensive wall on Snake Island and on the coast across the narrow

channel can also be seen. Tomb Island is so named from an ancient sarcophagus found on it.

SOGUT (Söyüt, Karaca)

Approach

The large bay lying S of Karaca Adasi. Coasting from Sehir Adalari, Karaca Adasi is easily identified, and you should potter through the channel between the island and the mainland just for the sights alone. The entrance to the bay is difficult to identify from the distance, and the houses at the head of the bay will not be seen until you are up to the entrance.

Mooring

Go stern or bows-to one of the jetties off the village where shown, or anchor and take a long line ashore to the W side of the bay. The depths are considerable and come up quickly to the shore, so you will usually be dropping your anchor in 10–20 metres. Off the jetties the depths decrease abruptly from 10 metres or so to 2–3 metres.

Shelter Nearly all-round shelter in the bay, and some yachts have wintered here. The prevailing wind tends to go around in circles in the bay, and any gusts are usually brief and not of any force.

Facilities

Fresh spring water from either of the jetties. The water here is renowned for its purity, so much so that the bay has been dubbed 'honey water bay' by some. Several restaurants and limited provisions. Ice available. *Dolmuş* to Marmaris.

General

The bay is a wonderful, serene spot, and even the small holiday village on the river flat does not overly intrude on the place. The slopes around the bay are densely wooded with pine, which somehow hangs on to the steep rocky slopes. You might think it a good place for trekking, but in my experience it pays to stick to the tracks and the road, as the terrain is so steep and the rock so crumbly that you make little

Soğut . The W jetty

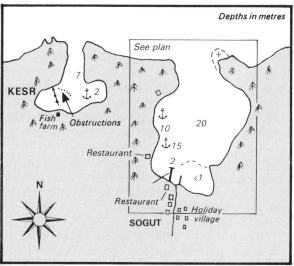

SOGUT AND KESR

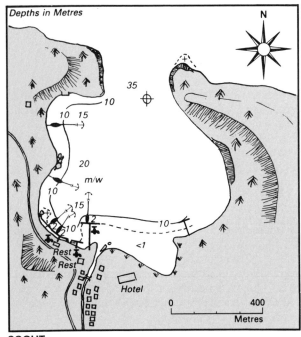

SOGUT
36°57′N 28°11′·4E

progress, although, to compensate, the views from the tops of the slopes are stupendous.

KESR (Canak Limani)

A fjord-like inlet lying immediately W of Sögüt. The entrance is difficult to make out from seaward, but once you are in line with the entrance a white house will be seen at the head. The inlet forks at the bottom and the western creek is obstructed by a fish farm.

Anchor in the eastern arm. There are 6–7 metre depths in the entrance to the creeks, but only 2 metres and less in the eastern arm. Anchor and take a line ashore. Good all-round shelter under thickly wooded slopes.

DEGIRMEN BUKU (Deremen, English Harbour)

Turkish chart 3111

Approach

The entrance is difficult to identify positively from the distance. From the N–NW the jagged outlines of Koremen Adalari (Kem Rocks) stand out, and closer in Karaada (Pelit Adasi) will be seen.

Dangers Care needs to be taken of the underwater rock lying approximately 300 metres S of the E end of Karaada (Pelit Adasi). It is difficult to spot, and should be given a wide berth.

Mooring

The large, much indented bay has numerous safe anchorages around its shores. A yacht will normally make for one of three places:

1. The southernmost part of the bay. Anchor in the NE corner in 10–12 metres, on mud and weed. A villa rumoured to belong to the president has been built here; if anyone important is in

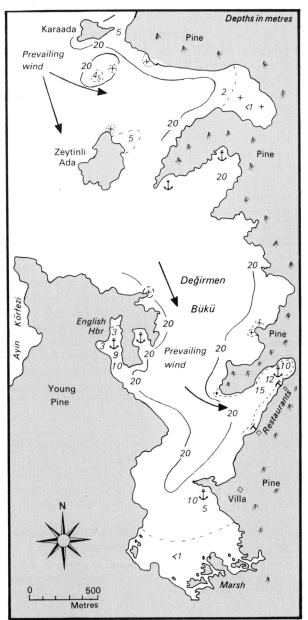

DEGIRMEN BUKU
36°56′N 28°10′E

residence there will often be gunboats anchored off, and you will be dissuaded from anchoring anywhere in the vicinity.

2. In the arm on the eastern side that curves back up to the NE. Anchor and take a line ashore to the N side. Alternatively, go bows-to the wooden jetty off the northernmost restaurant. There are 2-metre depths close to the end. The bottom everywhere comes up quickly from 10 metres or more to a shallow rocky ledge fringing the bay. The ledge is easily seen by day. The day breeze tends to curve around and blow up into the inlet, but is generally not bothersome. Excellent all-round shelter at the head of the inlet. Water from a hose on the jetty of the northernmost restaurant. Simple fare from the restaurant, which often has fresh fish.

3. ***English Harbour (Ingilizi Limani)*** The arm on the western side that curves back up to the N.

Anchor in the middle in 6–7 metres and take a line ashore. The bottom is mud and good holding. The end of the inlet has silted. Excellent all-round shelter. The inlet gets its name from the time when English torpedo boats used it as a base during the second world war.

General

The slopes on the eastern side are covered in a magnificent pine forest. Near the head of the bay there are many deciduous trees, mostly fragrant amber, which grow only in a few places in the eastern Mediterranean. It is worth every effort to go for a ramble ashore through forest and fields more like the country in the Balkans than that in the Aegean. On the western side of the bay a fire has destroyed the pine forest that once covered the slopes, but a reafforestation programme has again covered it in young pine.

The denuded slopes around the coast are a sombre reminder of the disastrous consequences of a careless cigarette end or a barbecue fire left untended. Yachtsmen should take every care in this beautiful place, and for that matter anywhere – all the more so because fingers have been pointed at careless yachtsmen as the cause of this and other fires.

KARGILIBUK (Guzlemek)

An inlet lying 1½ miles W of Koremen Adalari (Kem Rocks). This group of rocks is easily identified, but the entrance of Kargilibük is difficult to see until close in.

Anchor at the elbow of the inlet in 5–8 metres. The head has silted. Good shelter from the day breeze blowing down the gulf. The inlet is attractive, with thick pine right down to the water's edge, and has a remote, almost spooky feel to it.

TUZLA KOYU (Balisu Bay)

(36°55'·6N 28°01'·3E Koyun Burun light)

A long inlet running E from Koyun Burun (Balisu Burnu). The light structure on Koyun Burun (Fl(3)10s7M) is conspicuous, and closer in the islet in the outer part of the bay is easily identified.

Anchor in either of the coves on the S side inside the entrance with a long line ashore. Care is needed of rocks and reefs off the coast, but these are easily spotted in calm weather. Good shelter from the *meltemi* which tends to blow across the mouth of the

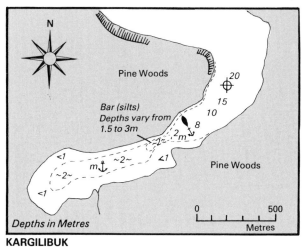

KARGILIBUK
36°56'·1N 28°05'·8E

large bay. There are some gusts from the W-SW with the *meltemi*. The water is clear and the swimming good. No facilities.

Caution

Care must be taken of the isolated reef about ¼ mile W of Koyun (Balisu) Burun. The isolated reef is difficult to spot, although the sea occasionally breaks over one of the rocks. Although there is a safe passage between the cape and the reef, the prudent course is to keep to seaward of the reef.

Note On the old Admiralty chart 1604, the cape below Balisu is called Koyun. On Turkish chart 311, Balisu is called Koyun, and the cape below it Teke Burnu.

YEDI ADALARI (Seven Islands)

BA 1644

Turkish chart 3111

Yedi Adalari are a chain of small islands close off the coast. There are numerous above and below-water rocks in the vicinity of the islands and adjacent coast. Some care is needed by day, and a yacht should not on any account approach the islands by night. The day breeze blows with some strength onto this coast, setting up a considerable sea. There are several places where a yacht can find shelter:

1. *North Cove* In the small cove at the northeastern end of the islands. Care must be taken of a rocky patch just underwater near the head of the cove. Anchor in 10–14 metres on the western side and take a line ashore to a tree. Good shelter.

2. *East Creek* In the long inlet on the eastern side. Anchor just inside the southern arm and take a line ashore. Alternatively, proceed further into the inlet. The tip of the southern entrance point in line (090°) with the extremity of the northern side (see plan) leads clear of the shoal water on either side of the entrance to the inner lagoon. The depths drop to 3 metres as you cross the bar, but increase quickly again to 7 metres. Anchor in 6–7 metres on mud and take a line ashore. Excellent all-round shelter in attractive surroundings. The only inhabitants, apart from

Koyun Burun, looking SW

Yedi Adalari: the anchorage at the N end looking down from the slopes on the W side. *Nigel Patten*

YEDI ADALARI ANCHORAGES

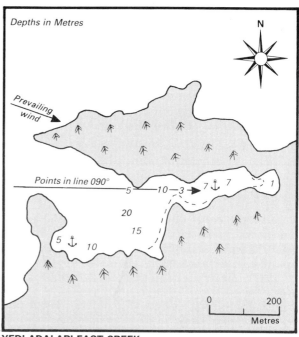

YEDI ADALARI EAST CREEK
36°52'·2N 28°03'·5E

vivid blue kingfishers and several herons, are two fishermen who have a camp at the head of the lagoon.

3. **Gokağac** Anchor at the SW end, inside the western entrance to the islands. Shelter from the westerlies here.

Yedi Adalari: the creek, looking W from the anchorage

The surroundings are more rugged and wild than the country further E. The pines are twisted and bent by the prevailing westerlies, and the outlying islands are bereft of vegetation and surrounded by menacing rock pinnacles.

GOLLUBUK BURUN

The reef off the end of this cape (Gollubuk Kayasi) is now marked by a W cardinal(YBY ☓ topmark) buoy. (Note: the buoy was not in place 1995.)

AMAZON CREEK (Catalca)

36°51'·5N 28°05'E

The long inlet lying approximately 2½ miles ESE of Mersinçik Burnu. The white light structure on Mersinçik Burnu is easily identified. Light characteristic Fl.WR.3s30m7/5M 154°-R-270°-W-154°. The entrance to Amazon Creek is not easy to make out from the distance.

The depths decrease quickly from 3m in the entrance to 1–1·5m. Only shallow draught craft should attempt to edge there way in. The bottom is mud. Deeper draught boats can find some shelter anchored under the headland in a number of coves W of Amazon Creek. Shelter is adequate under the headland depending on the strength of the *meltemi* and good in Amazon Creek if you can tuck up inside.

The facilities extended to yachtsmen from the camping ground include: water, ice, showers, bar, restaurant, and provisioning from Marmaris. The creek is an enchanting spot with dense pine growing out over the water's edge, giving it the appearance, I suppose, of jungle of sorts – hence the name. In recent years the amount of rubbish blown into here by the prevailing wind has besmirched some of it's jungle-like charm.

GOKCELER BUKU AND KUCUK CATI

In the southeasternmost part of the gulf, on the S side of Bördübet Limani, there are a number of deserted anchorages. These lie at the narrowest part of Datça Yarimadasi (the Dorian Promontory). Care must be taken in the vicinity of these anchorages, as there are numerous above and below-water rocks and shoal patches that the sketch plan can show only approximately. There are two useful anchorages, although several other small coves can be used with care.

GOKCELER BUKU

The entrance is difficult to pick out from the distance. Care must be taken of a 4 metre shoal patch in the entrance, and of a reef with less than 2 metres over it off the E entrance point. Underwater rocks fringe the sides of the bay.

Anchor on the W side in 5–10 metre depths and take a line ashore. Reasonable protection from the prevailing winds. On the E side of the bay there is a cove into which a yacht could squeeze with care, in order to tuck itself out of the prevailing wind. The slopes about are thickly covered in pine and the water is wonderfully clear.

KUCUK CATI

A dogleg bay lying approximately half a mile W of Gökçeler Bükü. Two-Tree Island, the small islet off the western entrance point, can be identified, and closer in a couple of stunted trees will be seen growing on it.

Proceed into the bay and anchor in 3–5 metres, taking a line to the N side. The bottom is mud, sand, and weed, good holding. Nearly all-round shelter. Ashore there is a depot for boat gash. You can walk up to the road to Datça, just above, and flag down a *dolmuş* to get into Datça for provisions.

Amazon Creek. *Nigel Patten*

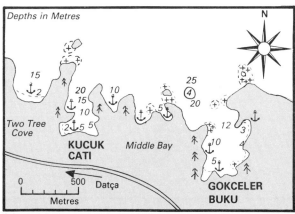

GOKCELER BUKU AND KUCUK CATI

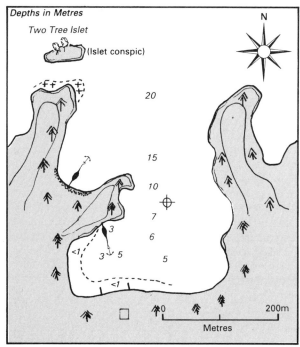

KUCUK CATI
36°47'·7N 28°00'·9E

OTHER ANCHORAGES

In the vicinity of Küçük Cati and Gökçeler there are several coves which can be used in calm weather or a light *meltemi*.

1. ***Küçük Cati Beach*** In the entrance to Küçük Cati there is a sandy beach, on the W side. In calm weather or light W–NW winds a yacht can anchor off here and take a long line ashore. The surroundings are idyllic.

2. ***Two-Tree Cove*** Immediately W of Küçük Cati there is a bay which can be used in calm weather. Anchor off at the head of the bay.

3. ***Middle Bay*** Between Küçük Cati and Gökçeler are several coves, suitable in calm weather or light W winds if you tuck right inside.

4. ***Gerence Cove*** Approximately 1 mile W of Two-Tree Island there is a bay, under Gerence Burnu, which looks as if it would afford some shelter from westerlies.

KUZGUN BURNU

The isolated reef lying just E of Kuzgun Burnu is now marked by a N cardinal (⬆ topmark) buoy.

KORMEN (Gormen, Korköy)

Approach

The harbour lies on the S side of the large bay under Ince Burnu (Cape Shuyun).

Conspicuous The low coastal flat between high mountains to the W and E is easily identified. Closer in, a white building near to the harbour, and the rough stone breakwaters, will be seen.

By night Ince Burnu is lit Fl(2)5s7M. The harbour entrance is not lit.

Dangers The *meltemi*, blowing from the NW, sends in a considerable sea which piles up in a confused swell at the entrance. Care is needed at the entrance, where you must turn side on to the swell.

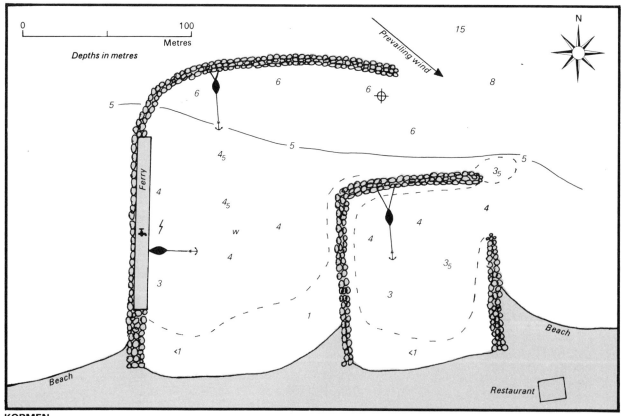

KORMEN
36°46'·2N 27°37'E

Mooring

Go stern or bows-to the quay or the rough breakwater on the N side. The northern half of the quay is used by a car ferry and should be left free. The bottom is sand and weed and mostly good holding.

Shelter Good all-round shelter.

Facilities

Water and electricity on the quay. Restaurants and *pension* nearby. Limited provisions can sometimes be obtained.

General

I find the location between the towering mountains of the Dorian promontory spectacular, but most people think the place a bit dull. The coastal flat is intensively cultivated, mostly in market garden produce. I am told that one of the restaurant owners speaks French, self taught by reading Barbara Cartland in the French translation! I imagine that the conversation would have some quaint idioms, and certainly, certainly, no uncouth utterances.

MERSINCIK (Mersinjik)

(36°45'·55N 27°28'·35E)

An enclosed bay lying close under the cape S of Akçali Adasi and Mersinçik Adasi (Mordala Island). The islands are easily identified from seaward.

The best place to be is in the cove on the NW tip of the bay. Anchor in the bay in 10 metres, on sand and weed. The holding is bad in places, so make sure that your anchor is well in and take a line ashore to the N side. Once you are securely tied up there is good shelter from the prevailing winds, in attractive surroundings. The small hamlet of Mersinçik sits near the shore to the S of the cove.

Hisarönü Körfezi

(Gulf of Hisarönü, ancient Gulf of Doris)

Hisarönü Körfezi means the Gulf of Fortresses, referring to the many ancient and medieval forts dotting the hilltops about the gulf. This long, thin gulf runs in an east-west direction, bordered by the high, craggy mountains of the Dorian promontory on the north, and by the Greek island of Simi and

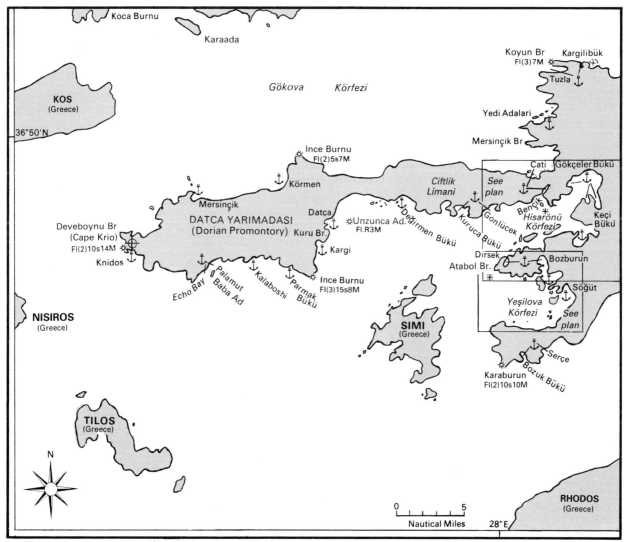

GOKOVA KORFEZI TO KARABURUN Deveboynu Br Light 36°41'·3N 27°21'·8E

Yeşilova Körfezi on the south. The western end of the Dorian promontory is mostly bare rock covered in low *maquis*, with some cultivation in the valleys, but at the head of the gulf there are extensive pine forests down to the water's edge.

Datça is the only town of any size in the gulf, and you should stock up on provisions here if dallying. Limited provisions can be obtained in some of the other hamlets, and there are simple restaurants in a few other places.

KNIDOS (Cnidus, Büyük Limani)

Approach

The bold promontory of Deveboynu Burnu (Cape Krio) is easily identified from the N and S, but will not be seen until you are closer to when coasting from the E.

Conspicuous Deveboynu Burnu stands out well from the N and W; the white lighthouse and dwelling on it are conspicuous from some distance off. It cannot be seen from the S and E, but the few white houses in Büyük Limani show up well. The SW breakwater is easily identified from off the entrance, but the sunken NE breakwater can only be seen as a greenish-brown smudge under the water.

By night Deveboynu Burnu is lit Fl(2)10s104m14M. A night entrance is not recommended.

Dangers
1. The sunken breakwater on the NE side can be difficult to see if there is a chop from gusts into the harbour. A yacht should keep 10–20 metres off the extremity of the SW breakwater, where there are considerable depths through the entrance.
2. When the *meltemi* is blowing, there are severe gusts and a considerable sea in the vicinity of Deveboynu Burnu. In the harbour, the wind gusts over the isthmus and off the slopes from the N with some violence.

Note The old trireme harbour on the N side of the isthmus has silted, and is too shallow even for small yachts.

Deveboynu Burnu (Cape Krio), looking NE

Mooring

Anchor in 5–10 metres near the head of the bay. The bottom is sand and thick weed, and the holding is uncertain in places. Some yachts take a line to one of the rickety jetties off the shore as a precaution against the uncertain holding. When the anchorage is crowded, there is nothing for it but to make sure that your anchor is well dug in.

Shelter Good shelter from the *meltemi*, which blows into the bay from the NW–N, although the violent gusts can cause problems. Open to the S, and with winds from this direction, a swell rolls into the bay and the anchorage can be untenable. With southerlies the best place to be is under the breakwater with a line to it.

Authorities There is a military post ashore; the military will sometimes want to see your papers, and will ask for a crew list. If you visit the ruins of Knidos, they will sometimes search your bags when you return.

Deveboynu Burnu (Cape Krio)   *Anchorage (Büyük Lim)*   *Anc Knidos*

Deveboynu Burnu (Cape Krio): approach to the anchorage, looking NW

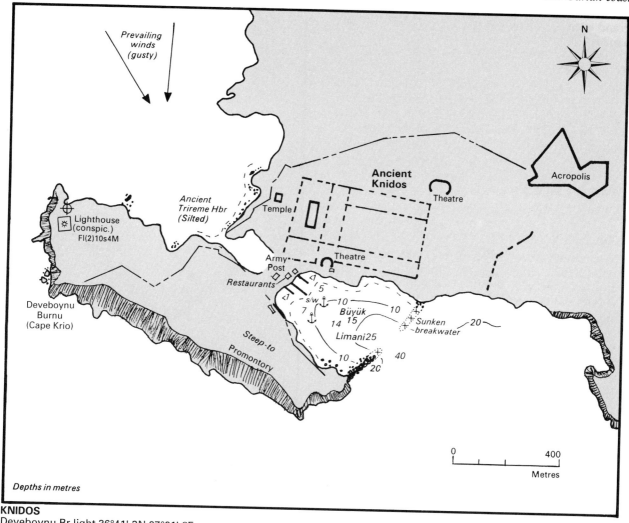

KNIDOS
Deveboynu Br light 36°41'·3N 27°21'·8E

Facilities

A restaurant and small *pension* ashore. The restaurant often has fish caught locally.

General

The solitary ruins of Knidos are scattered about the slopes above the ancient harbour in which you are anchored. The setting is delightful and the ruins, only partly excavated, are a romantic overgrown jumble of huge rock blocks and pottery sherds. Unfortunately, you will rarely contemplate the ruins alone in the summer, when the harbour is full of yachts and *gulets* bringing charterers to this lovely place.

Knidos

This was one of the Dorian hexapolis, the six cities of the Dorian Confederacy. The city was a prosperous one, its inhabitants being industrious and the harbour well placed to handle passing trade.

Knidos was renowned for two things: its statue of Aphrodite and the scientist Eudoxos.

The statue of Aphrodite was by Praxiteles, one of the greatest Greek sculptors. In the 4th century BC, the statue was one of the first of a naked woman, only male statues having been naked until this time. The sexy Aphrodite was believed to bring good fortune to seafarers – it certainly brought large numbers of tourists in this early age to view it. Several stories are told of the statue. One relates how an admirer, enamoured of the statue, crept into the shrine and passionately kissed it on the thigh. Thereafter it was said to bear a dark stain on the inner thigh. Another relates how the shrine had a back door, so that admirers could view Aphrodite's shapely posterior.

The scientist Eudoxos of Knidos was an astronomer and mathematician, who lived in the 4th century BC and is considered one of the founding fathers of Greek geometry. He built an observatory at Knidos in his declining years, and spent his time here watching and mapping the night sky. The architect Sostratus, who designed the Pharos lighthouse of Alexandria, one of the Seven Wonders of the World, was also a native of the city.

Although the ruins have not been systematically excavated, it is easy to pick out the skeleton of the city and identify its parts. The two theatres (the smaller one close by the harbour), the temples, the agora, the city walls and gates, and the ancient harbours can all be identified. Although overgrown, the ruins are impressive because of their size and the

167

...ung, solitary but for the few houses of the ...mlet.

ECHO BAY

The steep-sided bay close S of Palamut. The entrance is difficult to see, but Palamutbükü Ada (Baba Ada) is easily identified. There is a red rocky patch on the cliffs immediately SW of the entrance. Anchor off on the S side and take a long line ashore. Reasonable shelter from the *meltemi*, although a swell creeps into the bay. There is better shelter at Palamut, a short distance NE.

PALAMUT

Approach

Palamutbükü Adasi (a bit of a clumsy name – I prefer Baba Adasi), the long thin island in the approaches, is easily identified. The harbour lies at the SW end of a white beach that shows up well. The houses of the hamlet and a few restaurants and *pensions* along the beach are easily seen. The outer breakwater can be identified when closer in but the entrance will not be seen until close to. There are no lights, and a night entry is not recommended.

Caution With southerlies there is a confused swell at the entrance, making entry difficult. The entrance is narrow, with rubble extending a short distance underwater off the S side, and a shallow patch on the N side. The entrance also appears to be silting, with less depths than it had in my earlier survey. Entry is recommended only in calm weather, when these dangers can be seen.

Mooring

Go stern or bows-to the quayed area on the inner breakwater, or on the catwalk on the SW. The bottom is sand and mud, with some loose rubble on the bottom which can foul anchors – generally good holding. Good all-round shelter, although with strong southerlies there is a bit of a surge inside – more uncomfortable than dangerous.

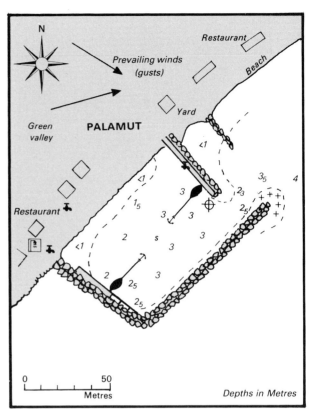

PALAMUT
36°40'·17N 27°30'·19E

Facilities

Water on the quay. Several restaurants close to the harbour open in the summer. Limited provisions. *Dolmuş* to Datça.

General

The green valley behind the harbour is a pleasant contrast to the bare rocky slopes further back. The dusty hamlet is a relaxed place, not overburdened by the few tourists who come here for the fine beach and the crystal-clear water.

About 220 metres SSW of Palamut, a reef extends some distance from the coast. It is likely that this is part of the harbour of ancient Triopium, which probably stood on the flat land where Palamut now

Breakwater *Entrance*

Approach to Palamut, looking WNW

168

is. Thucydides mentions a large harbour at Triopium, and George Bean theorises that a mole may have extended from Baba Adasi, leaving a narrow entrance between the mole and the shore. While the depths do not preclude such an engineering feat, it is likely that such a huge harbour (look at the vast area it would have enclosed) would have attracted more interest and comment from the ancients than that shown. It seems more likely that a much smaller harbour existed on the shore only.

KURUBUKU

A bay lying under Kürübuku Burnu. There is mediocre shelter from the *meltemi* tucked under the headland – some swell is usually pushed in.

KALABOSHI (Ova Bükü)

A small cove lying on the E side of Adatepe Burnu (Kalaboshi Point), offering good shelter from the *meltemi*. The craggy Adatepe Burnu is easily identified. Anchor in 4–5 metres on the W side of the bay. Care must be taken of a reef extending about 100 metres from the middle of the shore. Open to the S.
  Restaurant ashore.

PARMAK BUKU (Domuz)

The bay lying about 2 miles WNW of Ince Burnu (Injah Point). The bay is most attractive, with pine down to the beach. A small hotel in the bay has laid moorings which you can pick up. Shelter from the *meltemi*, but open to the S. Water and a bar and restaurant in the hotel.

INCE BURUN

The cape where you turn the corner to Datça is a long, low finger of a cape that stands out well. The light structure on it (Fl(3)15s8M) will be seen when closer to it.

KARGI KOYU (Miliontes Bay)

The large bay 2½ miles N of Ince Burnu and 1½ miles S of Datça. Anchor off the beach in 5–8 metres on a sand and mud bottom. Good holding and reasonable shelter from the *meltemi*, although there are strong gusts off the high land and some swell penetrates.

DATCA (Datcha)

BA 1644

Approach

The harbour lies close N of Kuru Burnu, and opposite Uzunca Ada (Ata Island).
Conspicuous From the E the buildings of the village

are easily identified, but from the S the village and harbour will not be seen until you are up to the entrance of the bay. The buildings of a hotel complex and holiday village along the coast N of the town will be seen before the buildings of the town proper. Uzunca Ada, a low rocky islet in the approaches with a light structure on it, is easily identified. Once into the S bay the harbour breakwater is easily identified.

By night Use the light on Uzunca Ada (Fl.R.3s3M). From the SE it is difficult to make out the light, as there are several red lights in the town with a better range! The breakwater is lit only by streetlights.

Dangers
1. With the *meltemi* there are fierce gusts into Datça Bay off the land.
2. Care is needed of the reef and islet (Topanca Ada) off the southern entrance to the S bay.

Mooring

Go stern or bows-to the quay where possible. Care is needed, as there are numerous rocky shallow patches off the quay, so that you cannot go close to everywhere and must take a long line ashore. The harbour is crowded in the summer, and you may have to anchor off in the S bay or in the N bay. *Gulets* go on the quay in the N bay, though care is needed in places. The bottom is mud and weed, patchy holding in places.

Shelter Good shelter from the *meltemi*. Southerlies cause a surge, and southerly gales make most berths untenable.

Authorities A port of entry. The customs and harbourmaster are close by the harbour. Charge band 2.

Facilities

Water On the quay, though it appears to be of variable quality in the summer.
Fuel A mini-tanker can deliver to the quay.
Repairs Limited mechanical repairs only. Limited chandlery.
Provisions Good shopping for provisions. Ice available. On the outskirts of the town near the post office there is sometimes a small market for fresh produce.
Eating out Numerous restaurants around the harbour. They often have good fresh fish.
Other Bank. PO. Local gas. Bus and minibus to Marmaris and Muğla (where you can get a connection to Bodrum). Ferry to Bodrum.

General

Datça is a pleasant, sleepy little spot, despite the considerable number of yachts that stop here. It is the place to stock up on provisions if heading into the gulf, as there is little chance to do so again until Marmaris.

Datça is near the site of old Knidos, the ancient capital of the peninsula until the strategic position of (new) Knidos was realised and the population moved to the end of the peninsula. There are a few

Ince Burun, looking NE

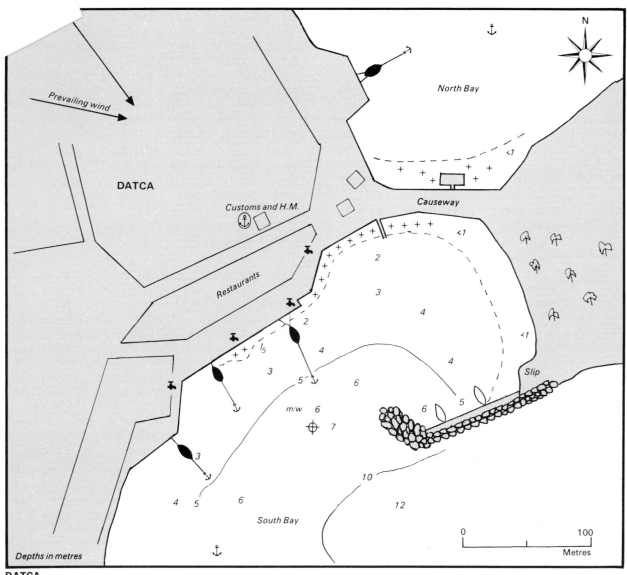

DATCA
36°43'·4N 27°41'·3E

Datça: approach to the harbour, looking NW

ruins of the ancient city to the north of the present village, but these are only really of interest to dedicated rock-hounds.

DEGIRMAN BUKU (Emajik)

Under the islet of Karaincir in the NE of Datça Limani, the long open bay E of Datça itself, there is a cove offering some shelter from the *meltemi*. (It lies on the W side of the peninsula marked 'ancient ruins' on the old Admiralty chart 1604). The village on the slopes behind and a small holiday village on the W side of the peninsula are easily identified. Anchor off the beach, where there is good shelter from the *meltemi*, in attractive surroundings.

On the E side of the same peninsula, under Sarilifman Adasi, there is also a bay affording some shelter from the *meltemi*.

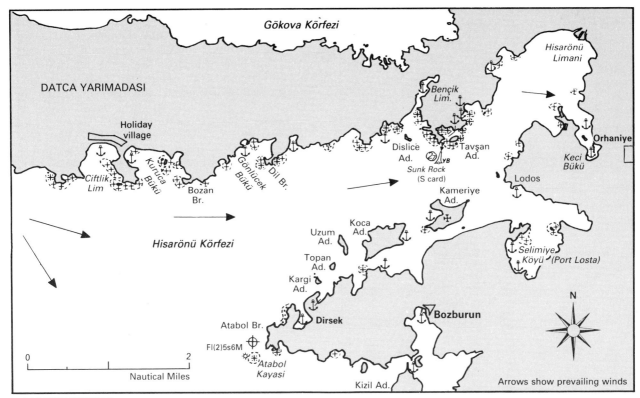

HISARONU KORFEZI
Atabol Kayasi light 36°40'·4N 27°57'·5E

Around this group of islets and the coast caution is required, as there are numerous above and below-water rocks. You should have someone up front conning you in – preferably in calm weather, when the sea bottom is easily seen.

CIFTLIK LIMANI and KURUCA BUKU
(Kuruca Bükü 36°45'·3N 27°53'·5E)

Kuruca Bükü (Kochini Bay) is the large bay on the E side of Adatepe Burnu (Kuruca Burnu, Kara Point). Ciftlik Limani (Ano Armakitha Bay), on the W side of the point, is not as well sheltered from the *meltemi* as Kuruca Bükü. The two bays are easily recognised by the large holiday village extending around their shores.

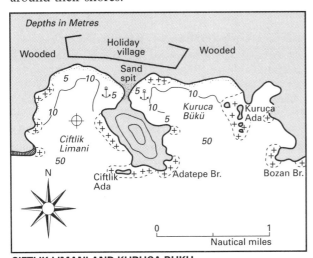

CIFTLIK LIMANI AND KURUCA BUKU
36°45'·N 27°52'·8E

Anchor in Kuruca Bükü, in the NW corner off the beach, in 4–5 metres. The bottom is sand and weed, and good holding once through the weed. Good shelter from the *meltemi*. Open S.

A short walk across the isthmus between the bays several restaurants open in the summer. A small provisions shop, and water from a tap at the camping ground. The coastal flat behind the development is covered in thick pine forest.

GONLUCEK BUKU (Göktas, Vathis Bay)

The large bay immediately E of Kuruca. Attractive setting under steep-to slopes. Anchor in the NW cove. Reasonable shelter from the *meltemi*.

BENCIK (Penzik)

From Kuruca Bükü, the steep-to slopes of the Dorian Peninsula drop sheer into the sea until Bençik, where the rubbly red landscape resembles the scenery around the Grand Canyon, albeit on a smaller scale.

Approach

A large hotel on the E entrance point is conspicuous. Closer in, knobbly Dişlice Adasi, the island in the entrance to the bay, is easily identified. Care should be taken of the reef off the NW tip of Dişlice and of another off the point opposite. Sunk Rock lies in the SE approaches to the entrance (least depth 1·8m) and is now marked by a S cardinal (⍦ topmark) buoy.

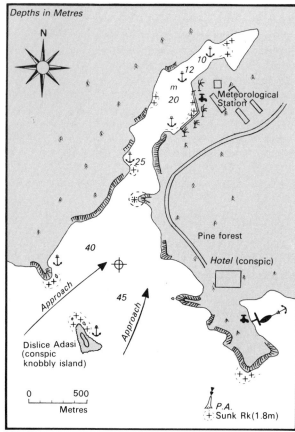

Depths in Metres

N

Meteorological
Station

m
20

25

40

Approach

45

Approach

Dislice Adasi
(conspic
knobbly island)

Pine forest

Hotel (conspic)

0   500
Metres

P.A.
+ Sunk Rk(1.8m)

BENCIK
36°47'N 28°02'·5E

Mooring

The depths are considerable for anchoring. The best place is near the head, where it narrows and depths are 10–12 metres. Take a long line ashore. The bottom is mud. Good shelter from the prevailing winds, but open S. Yachts are sometimes discouraged from using the quay on the E side of the inlet, which belongs to the Meteorological and Solar Research station, although a number have reported no difficulty.

Note With care a yacht can anchor around the elbow at the head of the bay in 2 metres on mud. You will need to sound your way in with a dinghy, as there is a reef obstructing the passage. Here there is all-round shelter, which might be useful in the event of southerlies.

Facilities

A water tap on the quay (reported potable).

General

The red rock landscape, mostly covered in pine, is quite unusual. There have been reports of mosquitoes and sharks. I can only vouch for the mosquitoes, but apparently the hot water discharged into the bay from the solar research station has encouraged sharks to breed here.

At the head of Bençik the Dorian peninsula is at its narrowest, with Büyük Cati on the other side in Gökova Körfezi. Herodotus tells us that when the Knidians were threatened by the Persians they set to

work to dig a canal across here as a defensive measure. The red rock was evidently hard going, and on consulting the oracle at Delphi they heard what they wanted to hear: that if the peninsula had been meant to be an island then Zeus would have made it so. Work was abandoned, and when the Persians invaded, the Knidians were forced to surrender. Herodotus doesn't tell us what the Knidians had to say about the oracle after that. H M Denham notes that when Commander Graves was surveying the region in 1844 he discovered the traces of ancient cuttings in the rock, perhaps the work begun on the ancient canal reported by Herodotus.

BENCIK HOTEL JETTY

In the cove immediately E of Bencik entrance a small T-jetty has been built for the hotel on the slopes above. Good shelter from the *meltemi*. It should be possible to obtain a berth here, assuming you patronise the restaurant and bar at the hotel. Water obtainable.

TAVSAN ADA

With care a yacht can anchor in the cove N of Tavşan Ada. Above and below-water rocks fringe the coast and islet, so every care is needed. Good shelter from the *meltemi* tucked under here.

Just E of this anchorage there are several other coves that can be used with care, and which also afford good shelter from the prevailing wind, although there are gusts off the land.

KUYULU BUKU

The bay immediately N of Kuyulu Burnu. Care is needed of the reef on the N side. Good shelter from the *meltemi*, although there are gusts.

HISARONU LIMANI

At the end of the gulf there is a flat plain, deposited by the silt from the river flowing into the sea here. The small village of Hisarönü stands near the sea. As the prevailing wind blows straight up into here it is not normally tenable, but in the morning calm a yacht can anchor off the beach.

KECI BUKU (Orhaniye, Kiervasili)

At the end of Hisarönü Körfezi on the S side is the large bay of Keçi Bükü.

Approach

The new hotel on Catalca Burnu (near the W entrance point) and another hotel further in will be seen, and once up to the entrance the buildings and yard of Bay Marina are easily identified. Once at the entrance, the ruins of the Byzantine church on the E side of the entrance will be seen, and then the islet, with a small Byzantine fort atop it. Keep to the E of the islet, where there are good depths.

Near the head there is a sand bar, just under water, which does not always show up well. In calm weather it can be seen as a reddy-brown smudge. It lies in a N–S direction, dividing the head of the bay nearly in two.

Mooring

Anchor in the cove on the W side in 6–10 metres, with a long line ashore. Alternatively, go stern or bows-to off the wooden pier at the head, off Kadir's restaurant, which has mostly 2-metre depths along it. It is also possible to anchor behind the sand bar in 3–5 metres or go stern or bow-to the jetty off the Palmiye Restaurant where there are electricity and water connections on the jetty. The bottom is mud and excellent holding. Good all-round protection, although easterly winds (rare in the summer) gust down the valley. The quay off Bay Marina gets bumpy with the *meltemi*, so it is best to go further into the bay.

Note A yacht can also anchor off the W side of the islet with the fort on it, but the prevailing wind gusts down into this area. Care should be taken of the passage between the islet and the W side of the bay, as shoal water extends from the middle of the islet and from the coast, leaving a narrow passage with 3 metre least depths in the fairway.

Facilities

Water at Bay Marina and from Kadir's restaurant. Several restaurants ashore. Kadir runs the original restaurant with the wooden jetty and the 'concrete boat' at the head of the bay. Limited provisions are available in Orhaniye, the small village about 2km away. *Dolmuş* to Marmaris.

Bay Marina On the E side of the bay, the newly completed Bay Marina offers the following facilities. Fuel and water on the quay. Limited provisions. A 50-ton travel-hoist, although there is limited hard standing. Above the yard is an upmarket hotel, complete with heli-pad.

General

Keçi Bükü is a gem. The slopes about are covered in pine. The small village of Orhaniye is shut in by a bookend of steep rocky slopes. A stream keeps the enclosed valley well watered, and the small coastal flat green through the summer. Inevitably, this has attracted the developers, and there are now three hotels – that at Bay Marina and the two in the adjacent bay just west.

TURGUT (Pedalo Bay)

The bay immediately W of Keçi Bükü. In calm weather it is a delightful anchorage, but with the prevailing westerlies into the gulf there is a swell in here, making it uncomfortable. There are now two hotels on the E side of the bay, and more are planned.

DELIKLIYOL LIMANI and SELIMIYE KOYU (Port Losta)

This magnificent, huge bay, the slopes about it thickly wooded in pine, is mostly too deep to anchor conveniently. Care needs to be taken of the reef, with 1·8-metre depths off it, extending off the N entrance to the bay proper. The reef extends further than is shown on the chart. There are a number of places a yacht can anchor in.

1. *Lodos* On the NE side of the entrance to Delikliyol Limani, an upmarket villa/hotel and restaurant/bar, Lodos, has been built. Off the restaurant-bar a quay has been built, with room for up to a dozen or so yachts. Only on one part of the quay, on the W, can a few yachts go bows-to with care. For most of the quay you will have to take a long line ashore, as underwater rocks fringe the quay. There is reasonable protection from the prevailing westerlies, though it is open to the SW. In recent years the restaurant/bar has appeared not to be open for business.
2. In the NW corner of Selimiye Köyü. Anchor and take a long line ashore.
3. *Selimiye* Go stern or bow-to the quay off the hamlet. There are 8–10metre depths about 50 metres off and good depths close to in the middle of the quay. Depths are shallower at either end of the quay. Several restaurants which often have fresh fish and limited provisions. There is also a jetty off the restaurant to the E of the quay.
4. *Kucuven Burnu* Under this headland, on the S side of the entrance, there is a bay which looks interesting, although a swell will probably be pushed in by the prevailing wind.

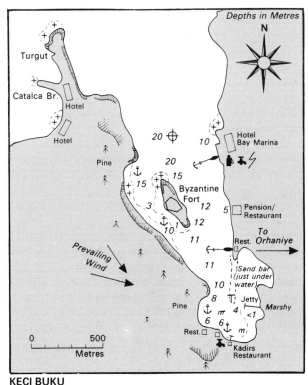

KEÇI BUKU
36°46'N 28°07'·5E

Keçi Bükü looking N from the slopes at the head of the bay

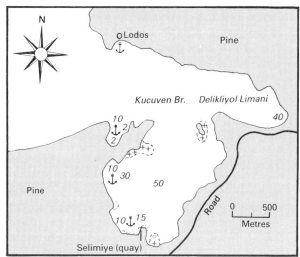

DELIKLIOYOL AND SELIMIYE
36°42'·5N 28°05'·3E

The islands between Selimiye and Dirsek

Along the southern side of the gulf there are a number of small islands. There are no really safe anchorages off them, it being either too deep or too exposed, although there are several places where a

yacht could anchor in calm weather. There is deep water in the passage between all of the islands and the adjacent coast, though care is needed of the odd reef fringing the coast.

Kameriye Ada In calm weather, anchor off in the bay on the W side of the island. This is totally exposed to the prevailing wind blowing into the gulf, so do not dally. It is also possible to anchor off on the N side in calm weather.

On the S side there is an old Greek church, or perhaps a monastery, that would be worth exploring.

Koca Ada On the SE corner there is a bight, with suitable depths for anchoring in, and affording a little shelter from the prevailing wind. On the mainland coast opposite the SW tip of the island there is a bight, useful in calm weather.

In the fjord-like bay running into the mainland coast from the SE tip of the island, local fishing boats are moored. Some swell enters with the prevailing wind, and it doesn't really look suitable for yachts.

Kargi Ada On the mainland coast opposite there is a bay that looks useful.

DIRSEK

The long inlet immediately E of Agil Burnu which forms the W entrance point. The approach and entrance is straightforward. At the head of the bay in the N cove there is a jetty to which yachts can go bow-to with care. There are around 2m depths at the S end of the jetty decreasing to 1m at the N end. Care is needed of a rocky ledge around it and the best policy is to anchor and take a long line to it. Good shelter from the *meltemi*. Alternatively anchor in the S cove in 5–10 metres. Good shelter although the evening NE wind can make it a little bumpy.

In the N cove there is a restaurant and it is at least politic to have a drink and perhaps a meal here if you use their jetty. Showers and toilets at the restaurant. Water from a well.

Yeşilova Körfezi
(Sömbeki Körfezi, Gulf of Simi)

This small gulf, really a very large bay, lies a short distance across from the Greek island of Simi. The port of Bozburun lies at the northern head of the gulf, sheltered by several small islands. The slopes about Yeşilova Körfezi are bare and rocky, with the craggy, steep-to slopes of Karaburun, the ancient

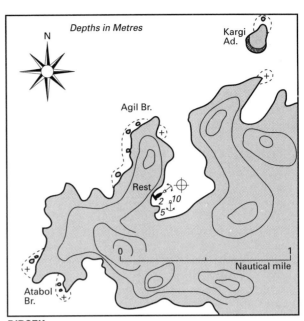

DIRSEK
36°41'·1N 27°58'·75E

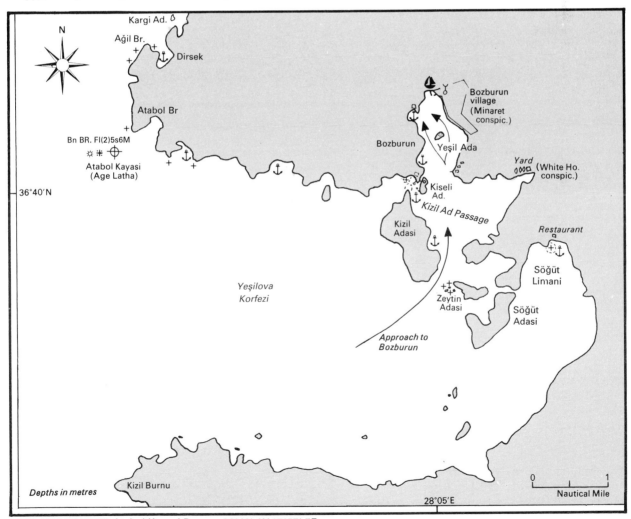

YESILOVA KORFEZI Atabol Kayasi Beacon 36°40'·4N 27°57'·5E

175

Kinossima promontory, bordering its southern side. Only recently has there been a comparatively good road opened up to Marmaris (it still takes some three hours to get from Bozburun to Marmaris, when the distance as the crow flies is only fifteen miles) so that the villages in this remote area are no longer dependent on the old sea routes for communications.

ATABOL KAYASI

Care should be taken of Atabol Kayasi (Age Latha), a group of rocks, just awash, approximately one third of a mile SW of Atabol Burun (Cape Apostoli). A beacon (black with red bands and ⦙ topmark) now stands on the reef. It is lit Fl(2)5s5m6M. Prior to the beacon being installed the reef had a reputation as a notorious yacht-trap. The depths off the reef drop off quickly to 40–50 metres and yachts scudding downwind on the *meltemi* would cut the corner and rip their bottom out on the reef with just enough momentum to slide over the edge and sink in deeper water.

BOZBURUN (Yesilova)

Approach

The harbour lies at the head of the bay at the northern end of the gulf, sheltered on the western side by Kizil Adasi (Vunos Island), and on the S by Zeytin Adasi (Lebunia) and Söğüt Adasi (Kamari). A yacht should enter the bay around the southern end of Kizil Adasi and then proceed up the bay, passing eastwards of Kiseli Ada (Agia Varvarah – a windmill is conspicuous on its northern tip), and on either side of the islet (Yesil Ada) near the head of the bay.

Conspicuous Kizil Adasi is not easily identified from the distance, but closer in it will be recognised. Once into the bay, a white house at the boatyard in the E bay will be seen. The islet obscures many of the buildings of Bozburun, but the houses around the eastern shore of the bay can be seen, and once up to the islet the harbour breakwaters are easily identified.

By night The entrance is lit: Fl.G and Fl.R.

Dangers

1. With the *meltemi* there are strong gusts off Kizil Adasi.

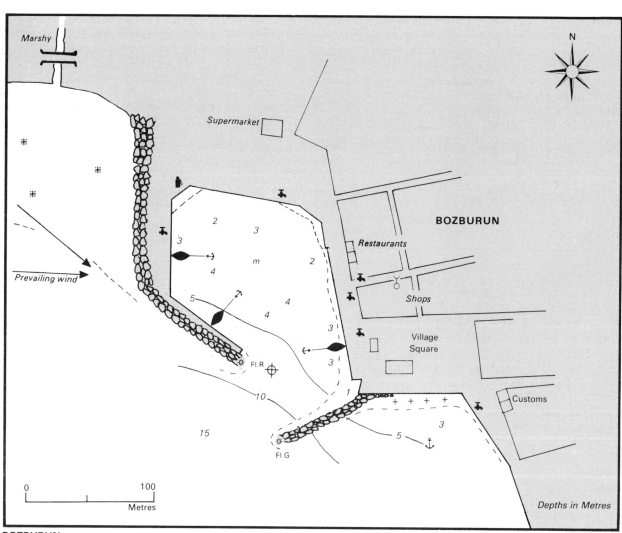

BOZBURUN
36°41'·4N 28°02'·6E

Entrance   E breakwater   Anchorage off the village square

Bozburun: approach, looking N

2. Care is needed of the shoal water off the coast on the eastern side past Yesil Ada.

Note The passage at the northern end of Kizil Adasi is used by the local fishing boats. There are depths of 3·7–5·5 metres, but a yacht should only attempt it with local knowledge, or in a dead flat calm for the first time. It is quite hair-raising on the first occasion, and you should have someone up front conning you through. When the *meltemi* is blowing a considerable sea piles up in the entrance to the passage.

Mooring

Go stern or bows-to where convenient. There are a few shallow patches around the quay, but on the whole there are sufficient depths. The bottom is mud and sand – good holding.

Alternatively, anchor off the square close eastwards of the harbour and take a line ashore. The bottom of sand and mud is good holding.

Shelter Good all-round shelter in the harbour, although you may have to move under the eastern breakwater in strong southerlies.

Authorities Customs and a military post. Charge band 2

Facilities

Water On the quay, but it is brackish. Drinking water is delivered by tanker.
Fuel On the quay.
Electricity 220V can be connected.
Repairs Yachts can be hauled in one of the yards around the bay. Some mechanical repairs can be made, and it is reported that there are an electrician and a sailmaker in Bozburun. A small hardware shop-cum-chandler's in the village.
Provisions Most provisions can be found.
Eating out Numerous restaurants on the waterfront.
Other PO. *Dolmuş* to Marmaris.

General

Bozburun was the Turkish equivalent of the Greek sponge fishing centre of Simi. Now most of the boats built here are *gulets* for the tourist trade in Bodrum and Marmaris, and a modest income from tourism, mostly visiting yachts, has replaced the

sponge fishing industry in Bozburun itself. The village is attractively sited, at the head of the bay, and an hour or two can easily be lost sipping a cold beer in the village square and gazing out over the waters of the bay.

OTHER ANCHORAGES IN THE BAY

1. *Kizil Adasi* A yacht can anchor between the northern end of Kizil Adasi and Kiseli Adasi. It should not attempt to pass between the N end of Kiseli and the coast, as the passage is shallow and rock-bound. Anchor in 5–10 metres on a sandy bottom. Good shelter from the *meltemi*. The anchorage is most appealing, with exceptionally clear water over a sandy bottom, and Byzantine ruins ashore.
2. Anchor in the cove on the E side of Kizil Adasi. Drop the anchor in 10 metres and take a line ashore. Good protection from the *meltemi*, although there are gusts into the bay.

KARABURUN TO MARMARIS
Karaburun light 36°33'·3N 27°58'·7E

177

Karaburun, looking ESE

SOGUT LIMANI

Near the head of this large bay on the eastern side of Sögüt Adasi is the small village of Sögüt. Anchor in the NE cove, in 5 metres. The bottom is sand and weed, and not everywhere good holding. Good shelter from the *meltemi*, although some swell may roll in for a while, more uncomfortable than dangerous. A small restaurant opens in the summer.

The craggy, burnt slopes about the bay have a savage, rugged, wild aspect. The ruins of an ancient fortress (shown on the old Admiralty chart 1604) are nearby, atop a rocky knoll. It was probably ancient Thyssanus.

From Karaburun to Marmaris

Along this steep-to mountainous coast there are few obvious signs of human habitation, yet in ancient times, up until the end of Byzantium, this peninsula supported some sizeable towns. A quick glance at the old Admiralty chart 1604 shows numerous ancient and medieval ruins dotted over the mountains. The barren mountains are grand, in a bleak, threatening manner, and when you turn the corner towards Marmaris the pine-clad slopes are a welcome relief from the burnt mountain slopes.

BOZUK BUKU (Bozukale, Port Apolotheka, ancient Loryma)

This large bay lies 2 miles ENE of Karaburun (Alobi Burnu, Cape Alupo). Karaburun terminates in a low rocky finger. The light structure on it is easily recognised. Approaching Bozuk Bükü, the ancient citadel on the W side of the entrance can be seen from about a mile off, but otherwise it blends into the rocky headland. Inside the bay, a yacht can anchor in one of several places:

1. Just inside the entrance, anchor in the cove under the citadel. Anchor in 8–10 metres and take a line ashore.
2. In one of the two coves on the western side, in 5–8 metres. There are mooring buoys off the restaurants here which a yacht can pick up.

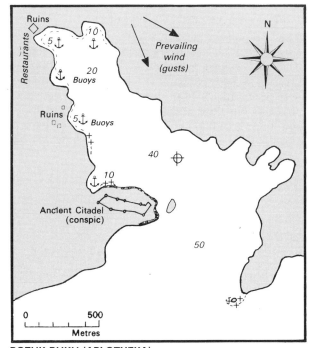

BOZUK BUKU (APLOTHEKA)
36°34′N 28°01′E

Bozuk Bükü: view from the ancient acropolis, looking NW onto the anchorage under it

3. Anchor in one of the two coves near the head of the bay, in 5–10 metres, and take a line ashore.

The bottom is everywhere sand and weed, indifferent holding. Good shelter from the *meltemi*, with the best shelter being under the citadel, just inside the entrance.

The surroundings are grand, with the ruins of ancient Loryma scattered about the bay, and the ancient citadel of Hellenistic origin which has been preserved nearly intact.

The restaurants around the bay seem to come and go, and there were as many as four at one time. At the head of the bay, it is reported that a hotel complex and an associated marina/yacht harbour are to be constructed. At the time of publication work had not begun.

CATAL ADALARI

The two islets off the coast just E of the entrance to Bozuk Bükü. A yacht can pass between the two islets, keeping about one third off the N islet, where there are least depths of 10–12 metres. The closer you go to the S islet, the shallower it becomes, although one third of the way off the S islet there are still 3–4 metre depths.

SERCE LIMANI (Sertchech)

A large fjord-like bay 1½ miles NE of Bozuk Bükü. Catal Adalari, the two small islets between Bozuk Bükü and Serçe, are easily identified. The narrow entrance to the bay itself is difficult to make out until close to. A knobbly rock close to the coast in the entrance will be seen. In the entrance, keep to the N side to avoid a reef off the S entrance point.

Once through the entrance the bay opens out dramatically. Anchor at the SW end in 5–15 metres, or at the N end in 5–10 metres. Off both restaurants there are a number of moorings which can be picked up if one is free. Take a line ashore. The bottom is covered in thick weed, but a sandy patch can usually be found to drop your anchor in.

At either end there is a restaurant, and someone will usually come out to give you a hand to take a line ashore. In the summer the bay is very popular, and can get so crowded that you must simply moor wherever there is space. Good, nearly all-round shelter, but strong E–SE winds send in a swell. In the SW corner southerly gales can make it untenable. Inside the bay the prevailing wind goes around in circles, but at the S end it gusts down the valley when the *meltemi* is blowing.

In the SW corner there is Osman's restaurant although he is no longer here himself. In the N

Serçe, looking E   *Nigel Patten*

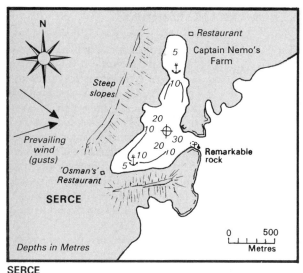

SERCE
36°34'·75N 28°02'·9E

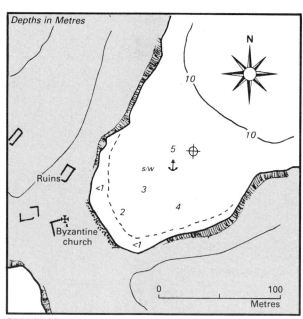

GERBEKSE
36°42'·1N 28°13'·6E

corner there is Captain Nemo's Farm which has good village bread and seafood.

At Serçe the underwater archaeology team led by Dr George Bass recovered many artefacts, including glass objects from an 11th-century Byzantine wreck. These finds are on display in the 'glass wreck' room of the Medieval Age Hall in Bodrum Castle. The story goes that the ship was sailing to Loryma from a Fatimite port when the *meltemi* caused it to look for a harbour of refuge. Attempting to enter Serçe, the ship hit a rock and sank in 32 metres. By a strange coincidence, the first time I entered Serçe my motor was out of action, and so I had to sail into the bay. The winds at the entrance and inside the bay go around in circles, so that even in a modern yacht that responds well and can go to windward I had difficulty negotiating the narrow entrance. Apparently the unhandy craft of Byzantine times, full of glassware, was not as lucky, and foundered off the N side of the entrance.

ARAP ADASI (Arabah Island)

You can approach the anchorage behind the island from the N or S, but the N channel is narrow, with 4–5 metres least depths. Behind the island you can anchor in 10–12 metres, but strong gusts off the land when the *meltemi* is blowing make it uncomfortable, and there is always some ground swell. The setting is attractive, in a solitary and bleak way.

GERBEKSE COVE (Ince Creek, Byzantine Creek)

On the N side of Gerbekse Burun (about ¾ mile S of Ciftlik Adasi), where the rocky promontory is joined to the coast by a low isthmus, there is an attractive anchorage affording good shelter from the *meltemi*. Anchor in 5–7 metres off the beach, where some ruins will be seen. The bottom is sand and weed, and good holding.

The ruins around the shore are probably those of a Byzantine trading post.

CIFTLIK (Chiftlik, ancient Phalarus)

Behind Ciftlik Adasi there is an anchorage described by the Admiralty Pilot as 'small but snug'. The *meltemi* blowing up the coast sends a swell into here, making it uncomfortable, and although not dangerous, it is not what I would describe as snug.

The white buildings of a holiday village are conspicuous in the bay. Anchor off the beach on the W

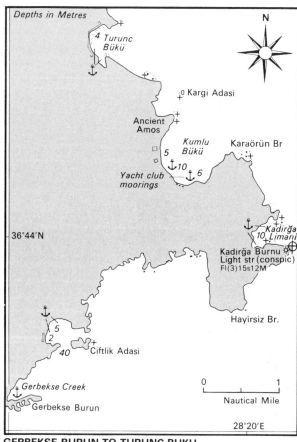

GERBEKSE BURUN TO TURUNC BUKU
Kadirga Br light 36°43'·9N 28°18'·1E

Kadirğa Limani looking W from the entrance

side, in 5 metres. There are a number of jetties off the hotels on the W side where a yacht can go stern or bow-to. It is not always the most comfortable to be on one of the jetties if some swell is running into the bay. The bottom is sand and weed, and good holding once through the weed. Good shelter from the *meltemi*, although there are gusts into the bay, and some ground swell enters. Ashore there are several restaurants.

KADIRGA LIMANI

A small bay lying close N of Kadirğa Burnu (Cape Marmarice). The dwelling and light structure on the cape are conspicuous (light characteristic Fl(3)15s12M). Anchor in the NW or SW corner of the bay, in 8 metres. Easterlies often blow into this bay, making it uncomfortable, but in the event of contrary winds on passage to Rhodos or down the coast it can be useful to wait for favourable winds.

Kadirğa Burun, looking N

Keçi Adasi	Channel	Nimara Adasi

Sark Boğazi, looking N

KUMLU BUKU (Kumlubek Bay)

A large bay lying one mile N of Kadirğa Limani. Anchor off the beach in the SW corner, in 5 metres. The bottom is sand and gravel, and not good holding. Easterlies blow into the bay, causing an uncomfortable chop.

In the SW corner there is a 'yacht club', where there are a number of laid moorings which can be picked up. Ashore there are showers, and a restaurant which one is encouraged to use. Tap ashore, but the water is undrinkable, and good water must come from the restaurant.

Development is beginning around the slopes of the bay, and already a small hotel has been built and more are planned. The ruins of ancient Amos stand atop the cliffs on the N side of the bay.

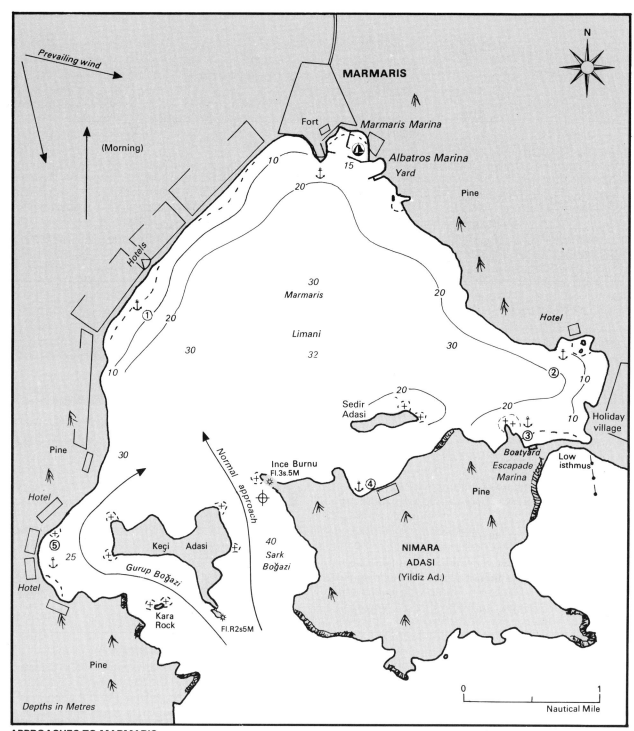

APPROACHES TO MARMARIS
Ince Burnu light 36°48'·9N 28°15'·E

TURUNC BUKU

A small bay lying nearly 1½ miles NW of Kumlu Bükü. There are a considerable number of buildings around the shores of the bay. Anchor off the beach on the W side, in 5 metres, on sand and weed. At the S end of the bay there is a cove offering nearly all-round shelter, being open only to the N. Several restaurants ashore.

MARMARIS (ancient **Physkos**)

BA 1644
Turkish chart 3121
Imray-Tetra chart G36

Approach

There are two passages into the bay of Marmaris around Keçi Adasi (Passage Island). A yacht can pass on either side of Keçi Adasi, through Sark Boğazi (the eastern and preferred channel) or Gurup Boğazi (the western channel). Both channels have good depths in the fairway and are free of dangers.

Marmaris   Ince Burnu

Light structure on the E side of the channel between Nimara adasi and Keçi Adasi, looking NNE

Conspicuous The dwelling and light structure on the southern end of Keçi Adasi are easily identified, as is Kaia Rock in the western channel. The light structure on the NW tip of Nimara Adasi (Yildiz Adazi) is also easily identified. Once into the bay of Marmaris, the town will be seen at the northern end. Closer in, the town quay and yachts berthed there are easily identified.

By night Use the light on Kadirğa Burnu (Fl(3)15s 12M), and those on Keçi Adasi (Fl.R.2s5M) and Nimara Adasi (Fl.3s5M). There are lights at Marmaris Marina (F.G.4m2M/F.R.4m2M) and the town harbour entrance (Fl.R). These last lights are difficult to make out against the loom of the town lights until you are close to. Care is also needed of yachts and *gulets* anchored off the S breakwater of the marina, as they do not always display anchor lights.

Dangers With strong southerlies there are gusts into Sark Boğazi.

Mooring

Go stern or bows-to in the marina or the town harbour. There are laid moorings tailed to the quay in the marina and an assistant will normally help you to berth. In the town harbour use your own anchor.

Shelter Good all-round shelter in the marina and in the town harbour.

Authorities A port of entry. Customs, immigration, health and harbourmaster are all on the waterfront. Charge band 2.

Anchorage It is possible to anchor off the southern breakwater of the marina. It is deep here and you will have to anchor in 18–20 metres. Good holding in mud once the anchor is through the weed on the bottom. Make sure when you are anchoring that you do not obstruct the approach channel to the marina. Shelter here is adequate although it can get uncomfortable with moderate southerlies and is untenable in southerly gales. The constant coming and going of ferries and other craft also sets up a lot of messy wash which make it uncomfortable.

Facilities

Services Water and electricity (220V) at the marina and town quay.

Fuel On the W mole of the marina.

Repairs There are several boatyards in the bay that can haul yachts. Most mechanical and engineering work can be carried out. Several agencies which have their own staff or arrange technical services. Several sailmakers. Several chandlers and hardware shops. See also Marmaris Marina section.

Sunmarina Not actually a marina, but a boatyard. On Nimara Adasi, close to the isthmus that joins it to the mainland, a boatyard has been established. 20-ton hoist. Mechanical, GRP, and wood repairs can be carried out. Other services, such as sail repairs, antifouling, and general winter maintenance, are also offered. Sunmarina, Yalanci Bogaz Mevkil, 48700, Marmaris ☎ (252) 422 0035 *Fax* (252) 422 0036. VHF Ch 69.

Marmarin Next to Sunmarina. 40-ton travel-hoist and slipway. Water and electricity. Some repairs.

Albatros Marina Again not really a marina, more of a boatyard. Just S of Marmaris Marina there is a pier where Albatros Yachting keep their boats. Ashore there is a large yard, with travel-hoist, where some private boats are hauled. Contact Albatros Yachting, Adaköy, Kirlik Mevki, Marmaris.

Marmaris Marina See separate section.

Provisions Good shopping for all provisions in the marina or in town. Market on Fridays at the W end of town. Ice available.

Eating out Numerous restaurants of all types on the waterfront and in the town. Eating out on the waterfront the view across the bay is superb.

Other PO. Banks. Turkish gas and *Camping Gaz.* Bus to Muğla and Fethiye. Ferry to Rhodes. International flights (charter flights) from Dalaman Airport, about 40 minutes' drive away.

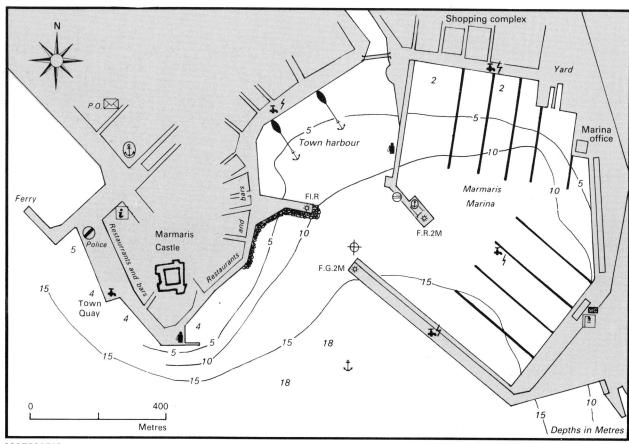

MARMARIS
36°51'·2N 28°16'·6E

General

Marmaris is a booming tourist resort. The setting in the pine-clad triangular bay is magnificent, and provides sheltered waters for dinghy and board sailing. It is one of the principal yacht charter bases in Turkey, and an Agents' Week is staged here in late April/early May. It's a good time to avoid Marmaris if you are not involved in the charter game, as the quay and bay are crammed full of yachts.

The town of Marmaris was devastated by an earthquake in 1958, so that most of the buildings date from reconstruction after that time. What little remains of the old village and a medieval fortress built around a rocky knoll is picturesque, but the same cannot be said of the new hotels that line the foreshore.

MARMARIS MARINA

The marina is located immediately E of Marmaris village.

Approach

The outer breakwater and the entrance are easily located E of Marmaris village. A member of the marina staff will come out in a dory to guide you to a berth and help you tie up.

By night The entrance is lit: F.G.2M/F.R.2M.
VHF Ch 06. Call sign *Port Marmaris*.

Mooring

Data 700 berths. Visitors berths. Max LOA 40m. Depths 2–15m.

Berth Where directed. There are laid moorings tailed to the quay.

Shelter Excellent all-round shelter.

Authorities Customs, immigration, health and harbour authorities within the marina. Marina staff. The marina office is open 24 hours. Charge band 2.

Facilities

Services Water and electricity (220V) at every berth. Telephone connection possible. Shower and toilet block (acclaimed as one of the best in the eastern Mediterranean). 24-hour security.
Fuel On the quay.
Repairs A 100-ton travel-hoist and a 12-ton hydraulic trailer. Workshops for mechanical, electrical, GRP, wood and general engineering repairs. Agents for technical services. Agents for Cummins, Volvo Penta and Perkins. Agent for Autohelm. Sailmakers. Eichler Sail Service ☎ (252) 413 0838 *Fax* (252) 412 0689. Also an agent for North Sails in the marina. Liferaft servicing. Chandlers within the marina complex.
Provisions A mini-market within the marina.
Eating out Restaurants and bars within the marina.
Other International telephone and fax services. Exchange office. Hire cars.

Above Boatyards near the causeway joining Nimara Adasi to the coast looking ENE. *See page 183.*

Above Dalyan. Looking NE to the entrance to the Dalyan River. *See page 190.*

Above Ekinçik. Anchorage in the SE corner looking N. *See page 188.*

Below Kizilkuyruk Köyü looking NNW. *See page 193.*

Above Kapi Creek looking S across the peninsula to Ragged Bay. *See page 193.*

Below Tomb Bay looking NW. *See page 196.*

Boynuz Bükü looking NW.
See page 198.

Above Göçek looking NW across to Göçek town piers and anchorage. *See page 198.*

Below Fethiye Marina and town looking SE. *See page 200.*

Above Gemiler Adasi (top of picture) and mainland looking SE. *See page 203.*

Karacaören and Karacaören Adalari looking E. *See page 203.*

Olü Deniz. Anchorage under Yorgun Burnu looking NNE across to the enclosed waters of Olü Deniz (prohibited to yachts). *See page 205.*

Below Kalkan looking NE. *See page 206.*

General

Marmaris Marina is now fully open for business; the service and facilities are as good as those anywhere in the Mediterranean, and better than many. Numerous berths are occupied by charter boats, but there are also a significant number of cruising boats based here. In addition to the straight yacht facilities, there are cafés and restaurants around the marina, a yacht club, travel agents and a swimming pool – it is possible to entertain yourself entirely within the marina, though I recommend you don't insulate yourself, but venture out to the town and its delights.

Marmaris Marina: 48700 Marmaris, Muğla, Turkey, or PO Box 231/232, Marmaris ☎ (252) 412 2708/412 1439 *Fax* (252) 412 5351.

OTHER ANCHORAGES AROUND MARMARIS LIMANI (See plan page 183)

1. On the NW side of the bay. Anchor in 2–5 metres on a weedy bottom, good holding once your anchor is through the weed. Some of the hotels have wooden jetties, where you may be able to go stern or bows-to – enquire first. Good shelter from the prevailing wind, which blows from the W here. Bars and restaurants ashore, and *dolmuş* and taxis to Marmaris town.
2. Off the hotel in the cove in the eastern corner. Anchor in 2–5 metres and take a line ashore. Restaurant in the hotel.
3. *Berk Marina* A small harbour next to Escapade Marina. An L-shaped mole protects the harbour from northerlies. Berthing is alongside or stern or bow-to. The harbour is often full so enquire beforehand for berths. Water and fuel available. Escapade Marina is nearby with its yard facilities. Restaurant nearby.
4. *Nimara Adasi* Anchor in the cove opposite Bedir Adasi. It is very deep here, and you will have to drop your anchor in 15–25 metres and then run in close to the shore and take a line to a tree. The bottom is weedy and not the best holding. Restaurant in the hotel ashore.
5. *Içmeler* It is very deep for anchoring here. Take a long line ashore if possible.

V. The Lycian coast

Marmaris to Antalya

This coast roughly encompasses the sea-girt bulge between ancient Caunos and Antalya. It is a wild and rugged region, where the mountains are split by ravines and chopped off by angular-faced scarps that plummet into the sea. In ancient times it was a coast feared by mariners, and even today this coast is not a friendly one to sailors. It presents a hostile aspect from seaward, but also some of the most majestic, almost primeval, scenery you will encounter in Turkish waters.

The coast takes its name from the Lycian cities dotted along its length. The Lycians, like the Carians, are believed to have been an indigenous Anatolian race, speaking an Indo-European language. They appeared in this region in about the second millennium BC, and quickly established a number of cities, with Xanthos as the capital. Perhaps tempered by the wild region, they became renowned for their skill in battle. Against all comers they held out against conquest for longer than other regions, the ultimate accolade coming from the Roman Senate, which declared Lycia an independent state in 167 BC. On two occasions the Xanthians fought to the last man, and burned the city, women, children, elderly, all, rather than submit. The second occasion was when Brutus besieged the city:

'It was so tragical a sight that Brutus could not bear to see it, but wept at the very mention of the scene . . . Thus the Xanthians, after a long space of years, repeated by their desperate deed the calamity of their forefathers, who after the very same manner in the Persian Wars had fired their city and destroyed themselves.'

Plutarch

We know something about Lycian architecture from the numerous surviving rock tombs, which are thought, in some cases, to be replicas of Lycian dwellings originally built in wood. These were often decorated with ornate wooden friezes, the Lycians being skilled craftsmen. They were also skilled sailors. The inhabitants of Phaselis are known to have been famed for their fast, light sailing boats, and may have been the *Lukas*, the sea peoples referred to in Egyptian records.

When the early Greek settlers arrived, the Lycians incorporated Greek cultural elements into their lifestyles, reflected in some of the rock tombs which have Ionic columns, pediments and porticoes in the manner of Greek temples. Alexander the Great conquered the region, although not without difficulty, and it was declared an independent state under Roman rule after repeated attempts by the Roman army to control it. Lycia declined under Byzantium to become the haunt of pirates, and was

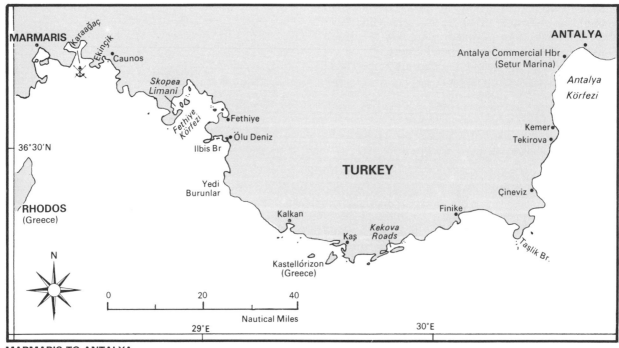

MARMARIS TO ANTALYA

known, along with the Pamphylian and Cilican shores, as the Pirate Coast.

Today the memorials to the Lycian dead, the rock tombs and massive sarcophagi mounted on pedestals, dot the coast so that it seems to be one vast necropolis. The large numbers of tombs and sarcophagi remaining intact where they were placed can partly be attributed to the inaccessibility of the region. Until the new coast road was cut the only means of communication was by sea. It remains a haunted landscape, and no doubt 3,000 years from now, when our memorials are dust, there will be a Lycian rock tomb and a sarcophagus or two somewhere along this coast.

Captain Beaufort

Admiralty chart 241, *Anchorages on the South Coast of Turkey*, bears the subtitle 'Principally from the Surveys by Captain F Beaufort, FRS, RNI, 1812'. This remarkable man surveyed the coast of Asia Minor for the Admiralty, in the 32-gun frigate *Fredericksteen*, from 1810 to 1812. These were the first accurate surveys of the coast, and the plans of the anchorages on chart 241 are still correct to this day, except for man-made additions – hotels, apartment blocks, dwellings, chimneys and the like.

Beaufort was not merely a naval surveyor, but also an amateur archaeologist and historian with an ear for a good tale. He later assembled his surveys and notes into a book, published under the title *Karamania*. The book takes its name from the Karamanids, a Turcoman tribe which held sway in this region in the 13th and 14th centuries. In the 15th century the region passed to the Ottoman dynasty, but it retained its earlier name among English travellers for some time.

Beaufort was made Hydrographer for the Navy in 1829, and served with considerable distinction until 1855. He stepped up surveys and chart production, organised surveys on a more scientific basis with specific instructions to those conducting them, organised the first *Notices to Mariners*, in 1834, and developed the scale bearing his name, for wind and sea conditions, that we still use today.

Data

PORTS OF ENTRY

Fethiye
Kaş
Finike
Kemer
Setur Antalya Marina
Antalya

PROHIBITED AREAS

1. It is prohibited to enter or land in Karaağaç Limani in the area shown (roughly N of Yilancik Adasi). Navigation is restricted in the area shown around Yilancik Adasi.
2. It is prohibited to enter Olü Deniz. However, you can anchor near the entrance and land there.

MAJOR LIGHTS

Yilancik Adasi Fl.WR.5s10/7M 086°-R-098°
Delikada Fl(2)5s8M
Baba Adasi Fl(2)5s7M (*Note* that this light is identical to that on Delikada)

FETHIYE KORFEZI

Peksimet Adasi Fl.10s12M
Göçek Adasi Fl(2)10s8M
Kizil Adasi Fl.5s15M
Fethiye Adasi Fl.R.3s3M
Ilbis Burnu Fl(2)5s7M
Kötü Burun Fl(2)10s12M
Catal Adasi Fl.5s5M

KASTELLORIZON (Greece)

Ak Ay Stéfanos Fl.WR.4·5s5/3M 095°-R-125°
Nisis Strongili Fl.5s17M

Ince Burnu (Kaş) Fl.3s5M
Kekova Adasi (W end) Fl(2)5s8M
Olü Fl.WG.3s7/4M
Kekova Adasi (E end) Fl.5s7M
Taşlik Burnu (Cape Gelidonya) Fl(3)10s15M
Kucük Cavuş Burnu Mo(A)W.15s8M
Av Burnu Fl.10s12M
Baba Burnu Fl.5s8M

Quick reference guide

	Shelter	Mooring	Fuel	Water	Provisions	Eating out	Plan	Charge band
Karaağaç Limani (prohibited anchorage)	A	C	O	O	O	O	•	
Ekinçik	B	C	O	O	C	C	•	
Delikada	O	C	O	O	O	O	•	
Baba Adasi	C	C	O	O	O	C		
Kizilkuyruk Kuyu	B	C	O	O	O	O	•	
Küçük Kuyruk	B	C	O	O	O	O		
Ragged Bay	C	C	O	O	O	O		
Kapi Creek	A	AC	O	O	O	C	•	
Twenty-two Fathom Cove	B	AC	O	O	O	C		
Ruin Bay	B	AC	O	O	O	C	•	
Wall Bay	B	AC	O	O	O	C	•	
Sarsala Iskelesi	C	C	O	O	O	O	•	
Deep Bay	B	C	O	O	O	C	•	
Tomb Bay	B	C	O	O	O	C	•	
Domuz Adasi	C	C	O	O	O	O		
Tersane	A	C	O	O	O	C	•	
Boynuz Bükü	B	C	O	O	O	C		
Göçek	B	AC	A	A	A	A	•	2
Club Marina	A	A	A	A	C	C	•	3
Fethiye Marina	B	AC	A	A	A	A	•	2
Letoonia Marina	B	A	O	A	C	C	•	2
Batikkaya Bükü	C	C	O	O	O	O		
Gemiler anchorages	B	C	O	O	O	C	•	
Olü Deniz (entrance)	C	C	O	O	C	B	•	
Yeşilköy Limani	C	C	O	O	O	O	•	

Kalkan	A	AC	A	A	B	A	• 2
Buçak Denizi	B	C	O	O	O	O	•
Longos	C	C	O	O	O	O	•
Kaş	A	A	B	A	A	A	• 2
Bayindir Limani	B	C	O	O	O	C	•
Asar	O	C	O	O	O	O	
Pölemos Bükü	A	C	O	O	O	O	
Tersane	B	C	O	O	O	O	•
Kale Köy	C	C	O	O	O	B	•
Uçagiz Limani	A	C	O	B	C	B	•
Gökkaya Limani	B	C	O	O	O	C	•
Karaloz	B	C	O	O	O	O	•
Andraki	O	C	O	O	O	C	
Finike	A	A	A	A	B	A	• 1/2
Karaöz	C	O	O	O	O	O	
Cavuş Limani	C	C	O	B	C	C	•
Cineviz Limani	B	C	O	O	O	O	•
Cirali Limani	O	C	O	O	O	C	
Tekirova	C	C	O	O	O	C	•
Kemer Marina	A	A	A	A	B	A	• 2
Setur Antalya Marina	A	A	A	A	C	C	• 2
Antalya marina	B	A	A	A	A	A	• 2

Karaağaç Limani to Olü Deniz

KARAAGAC LIMANI (Karagatch)

Note

At the time of writing Karaağaç Limani is a military zone, and a yacht should not attempt to enter, as anchoring, diving and landing are prohibited. A yacht should also endeavour to keep outside the restricted area at the entrance to Karaağaç Limani, although in practice yachts on passage between Marmaris and Ekinçik cut across it. A plan of Karaağaç Limani is included, as it is possible, though unlikely, that it may be opened up in the future.

I have had several letters advising me that it was OK to go in here, but I can only say that, when I did so, the authorities were not very polite, and I was apprehended and told in no uncertain terms to leave. No more letters, please, unless you have been in here and stayed the night and are not related to any Turkish admirals! *Gulets* sometimes anchor off the entrance to Karaağaç, but I recommend yachts to stay well clear.

TURNALI KAYASI (Edmonds Rock)

Care must be taken of Turnali Kayasi (Edmonds Rock), with a least depth over it of 0·6m/2ft, lying one mile SSW of Turnali Burnu and 1¾ miles W of Yilancik Adasi. It is now marked by a buoy.

A light is exhibited on Yilancik Adasi (Fl.WR.5s 10/7M), and there is another on the E side of the entrance to Karaağaç (Fl.3s6M).

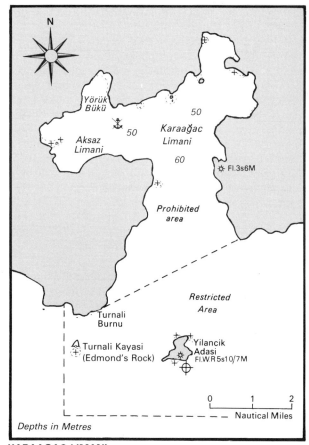

KARAAGAC LIMANI
Yilançik light 36°46'·6N 28°26'·3E

EKINCIK LIMANI

Approach

The bay lies at the N head of Köyceğiz Limani, 2½ miles NNE of Kizil Burnu.

Conspicuous Several rocky pinnacles close to the coast on the E side of Kizil Burnu are conspicuous. Delikada (Dalyan Island) and the light structure atop it are conspicuous against the flat land behind. Closer in, the light structure on the western side and

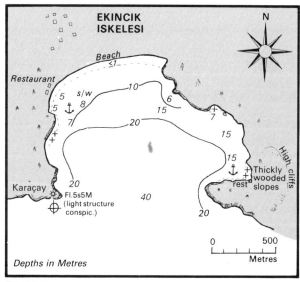

EKINCIK
Karaçay light 36°49'·4N 28°33'·0E

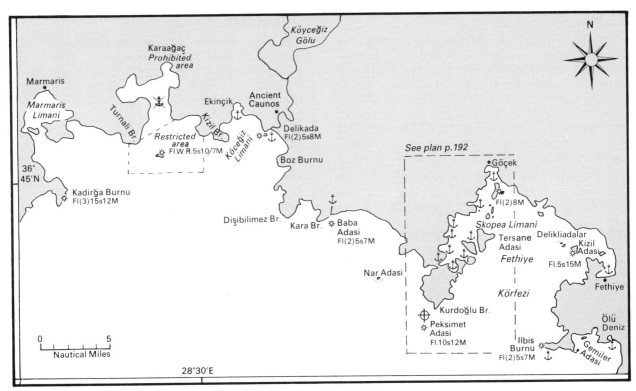

MARMARIS TO OLU DENIZ
Peksimet Adasi light 36°34'·1N 28°49'·5E

Yilancik Adasi, looking E

some of the houses of Ekinçik Iskelesi are easily identified.

By night Use the lights on Delikada (Fl(2)5s8M) and on the W side of Ekinçik Limani (Fl.5s5M).

Ekinçik: anchorage on the W side

The actual range of the latter appears to be less, probably about 1½ miles.

Mooring

Anchor off the restaurant on the W side of the bay, or in the SE corner with a long line ashore. In the SE corner there are places where a yacht can go bows-to the rough quay with care. The depths here are considerable until a short distance off, so you will usually be anchoring in 12–15 metres. On the W side there is a short quay with 1·5–2m depths off the end, but it is usually crowded with *gulets* and with local tripper boats operating between Ekinçik and ancient Caunos.

Note In the summer Ekinçik gets very crowded and some yachts prefer to anchor off in the large bay SSW of Ekinçik proper. Yachts usually anchor with a long line ashore on the S or SW sides. Good shelter from the prevailing winds in idyllic surroundings under the wooded slopes.

Shelter In settled weather the anchorage on the W side is protected from the prevailing winds, but overall the anchorage in the SE corner offers better all-round shelter.

189

Facilities

Restaurants ashore. *My Marina*, the restaurant in the SE corner, has good food and superb views across the bay at a price. Limited provisions available. Local tripper boats do a return trip to ancient Caunos from Ekinçik. They will usually come out to see whether you want to do the trip, or you can call them up on VHF Ch 6. The trip is not what could be called cheap any more – a cartel operates, keeping the price inflated over those of other boat trips – but it is not to be missed.

General

Ekinçik is the best place to leave your yacht for a visit to ancient Caunos, which is about five miles away up the Köyceğiz river. You should reckon on spending an unrushed day here, as much for the scenery en route as for the ruins of ancient Caunos itself. Neither should Ekinçik be hurried over. It is picturesque, particularly in the SE bay, where red cliffs and steep wooded slopes rise up abruptly from the anchorage. It is often very crowded with yachts in the summer, being conveniently situated almost midway between Marmaris and Skopea Limani.

DELIKADA (Dalyan)

The small islet off the entrance of Köyceğiz river. The latter leads up to Dalyan village, and to the ruins of ancient Caunos. Delikada lies 2 miles SE of Ekinçik, and stands out well against the flat land behind. In calm weather, or when the *meltemi* is not blowing strongly, a yacht can anchor off the NE tip of the islet in 4m, with a line ashore. It is never a comfortable anchorage, as any swell invariably works its way around to here. Ekinçik is much to be preferred.

Note Shoal-draught yachts have crossed the bar of the river and proceeded up-river towards Dalyan. The position and depths over the bar are constantly changing, and you should seek local knowledge and inspect the bar yourself before attempting it. There is rarely more than one metre over the bar, although there are 3–8m depths in the main channel of the river. Proceeding up the river, you must pass through the gates of a fish trap (*dalyan*, hence the name of the village), which will be opened for you. Further up the river you will come to a concrete barrier, with gates through which you can proceed further upstream. It has been reported that the high-

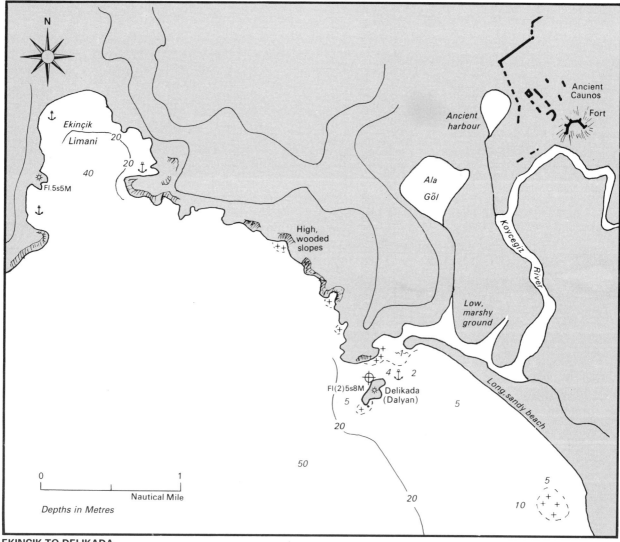

EKINCIK TO DELIKADA
Delikada light 36°47'·9N 28°35'·6E

190

tension cable with about 8–9 metres' clearance has been moved. Keep your eyes open, though. The setting in the reed-lined river, with Lycian rock tombs in the nearby cliffs, is superb.

Caunos

This ancient city was sited on the border between Caria and Lycia, and although Herodotus refers to the inhabitants as Carian, he remarks that their customs resembled those of the Lycians. This would appear to be borne out by the rock tombs (which are typically Lycian) in the cliffs nearby. The inhabitants were always considered a sickly lot, being described as much given to fevers and having a green complexion – a description probably referring to the malaria that must have been prevalent in this marshland setting.

Today it is this marshy setting, with the reed-lined river meandering under steep cliffs, that gives the boat trip to Caunos much of its charm. Turtles perch on the river bank, and herons, sandpipers, kingfishers, and hawks (the last no doubt looking for stray turtles) are prolific. Insecticides keep the dreaded malaria away.

The ruins of ancient Caunos are not spectacular like those at Ephesus or Pergamon. There are baths, a small theatre, a temple, and a market place, all of Roman origin, although on earlier sites. A medieval fort crowns a steep knoll, and the adventurous can climb up to it for a spectacular view towards Dalyan village and the sea. It is the setting that makes Caunos a special place, and one of my treasured views, a sort of archaeological satori of mine, is that looking over the shallow bathing pool and garden by the old harbour. It is quite inexpressibly and hauntingly beautiful.

BOZ BURUN

Between Boz Burun and Dişibilmez Burnu, there can be a confused sea when the *meltemi* is blowing. Close to the capes, the swell reflects off the steep-to coast to crash back into the oncoming swell. It is a good idea to keep some distance off, to avoid the reflected confused sea, although it is tempting to cut across here when on passage between Ekinçik and Fethiye Körfezi.

DISIBILMEZ BUKU

The large bay between Dişibilmez Burnu and Kara Burun. In the NW corner of the bay there is a cove that can be used in settled weather. Anchor in 10–15m taking care of above and below water rocks in the bay. Reasonable shelter although a strong *meltemi* pushes a considerable swell into here.

BABA ADASI

This island lies one mile E of Kara Burun. It is easily identified, being bold and steep-to against the flat land behind. Closer in, a large brick pyramid on the summit is conspicuous. A light is exhibited on the island (Fl(2)5s7M).

Kara Burun · Baba Adasi

Baba Adasi and Kara Burun looking E

Peksimet Adasi

You can get behind the island from the W or E. From the W there are 4 metres least depth, and from the E, 10 metres least depth. A yacht should keep well off the beach, as there are 2-metre depths 100 metres off, gradually shelving to the beach.

Anchor behind the island in 5–8 metres, with a line ashore to the island. When the *meltemi* is blowing it pushes a swell in here, making the anchorage extremely uncomfortable. The cove N of the island at the end of the beach has silted, and there are barely 2-metre depths in the entrance.

Several large hotel and apartment complexes now adorn the bay, and restaurants and bars open in the summer.

Fethiye Körfezi

APPROACHES TO FETHIYE KORFEZI

Nar Adasi, in the NW approaches, is easily identified. Peksimet Adasi and the light structure on it (characteristic: Fl.10s12M) and Kurdoğlu Burnu can be identified from some distance off. Kurdoğlu Burnu terminates in a low rocky finger, with some isolated rocks off it, which will not be seen until close in. Once into the gulf, the islands in the approaches to Fethiye harbour are easily identified, but the islands on the eastern side of Skopea Limani are more difficult to identify.

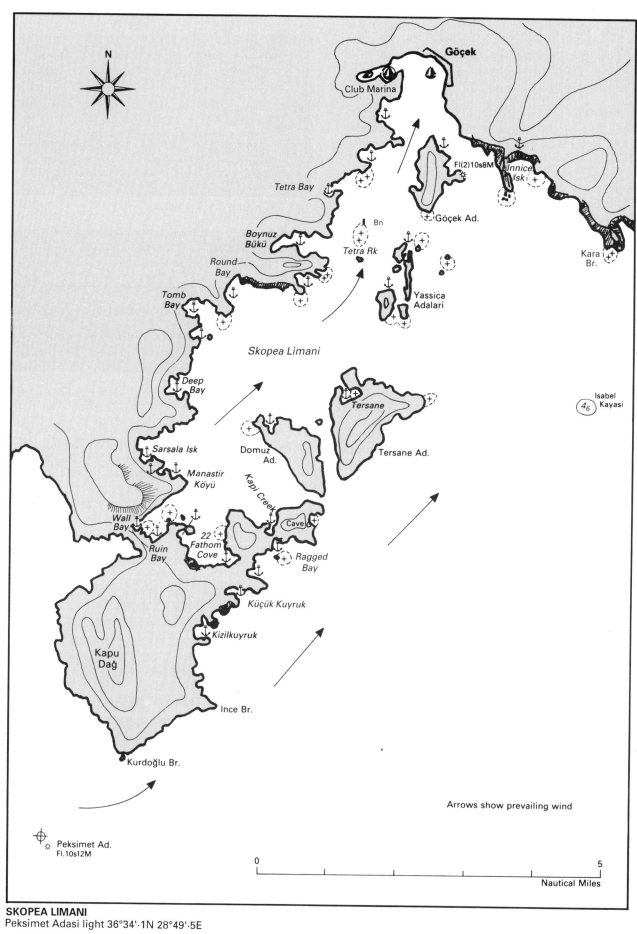

Göçek

Club Marina

Fl(2)10s8M *Innice Isk*

Tetra Bay

+ Göçek Ad.

Boynuz Bükü

Bn

Kara Br.

Tetra Rk

Round Bay

Tomb Bay

Yassica Adalari

Skopea Limani

Deep Bay

Isabel Kayasi
46

Tersane

Sarsala Isk

Domuz Ad.

Tersane Ad.

Manastir Köyü

Kapi Creek

Wall Bay

Cave

Ruin Bay

22 *Fathom Cove*

Ragged Bay

Küçük Kuyruk

Kizilkuyruk

Kapu Dağ

Ince Br.

Arrows show prevailing wind

Kurdoğlu Br.

Peksimet Ad.
Fl.10s12M

0   5

Nautical Miles

SKOPEA LIMANI
Peksimet Adasi light 36°34'·1N 28°49'·5E

Anchorages around Skopea Limani

In this small, much indented gulf, protected by a chain of islands on its eastern side, there are numerous attractive anchorages in what is almost a primeval landscape. Vast reddish cliffs, pockmarked with caves and ravines, divide steep slopes thickly wooded in pine. The water is very clear where it is shallow enough to see the bottom (most of the gulf is very deep, with the bottom dropping off quickly from the coast) and the numerous anchorages are justly popular in the summer. The prevailing wind blows up the gulf from the SW–S in the summer. It gusts over the steep slopes in places to give exhilarating sailing in flat water.

KIZILKUYRUK KOYU

Kizilkuyruk lies 1 mile NNW of Ince Burun (Kizilkuyruk Burnu), on the E side of Kapu Dağ. The entrance is difficult to see from the distance. A prominent reddish cliff lies on the N side of the entrance. The best anchorage is in the W arm, in 8–12 metres, with a line ashore to the N side. The bottom is sand and weed. In the N arm, anchor in 10–15 metres with a line ashore. Good shelter from the prevailing winds, but open to the SE–E.

From here you can visit ancient Lydae, about an hour's walk to the W. The ruins (only Roman and Byzantine buildings remain) are on a splendidly isolated site; there are two mausoleums in a fair state, sections of paved road, and columns and other ancient debris lying about. The city was never an important one, and after early Byzantine times it died out.

KUCUK KUYRUK (36°37'·85N 28°52'·9E)

A spectacular anchorage under Kuyruk Burnu. Anchor in 8–10 metres and take a line ashore to the S side. With the *meltemi* some swell works its way in

here, but it is rarely bothersome if you are tucked into the S side.

The inlet is simply superbly beautiful. It is frequented by *gulets* in the daytime, but most leave by nightfall.

RAGGED BAY

Just N of Kuyruk Burnu is a large bay, with a much indented coastline and an islet in the middle. There are several coves and bights where a yacht can anchor around the bay. Depths are mostly considerable, coming up quickly to the shore, and care is needed of some above and below-water rocks around the shore. There is also a reef extending E from the islet. Shelter with a light *meltemi* is good here, but if the breeze pushes around Kurdoğlu Burnu and up the coast a swell is pushed into parts of the bay.

The surroundings are just wonderful, with pine growing down to the water's edge.

KAPI CREEK (Karpi Bükü, Four Fathom Cove)

Approach

This small creek lies just over ½ a mile SW of the narrow channel between Domuz Adasi and the mainland coast. When approaching from the S, Domuz channel will not be seen until close to. There are good depths in the fairway, and passage

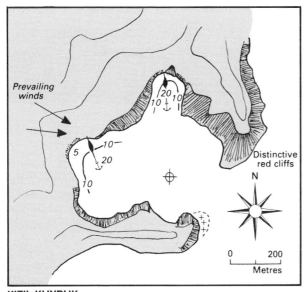

KIZIL KUYRUK
36°37'·2N 28°52'·2E

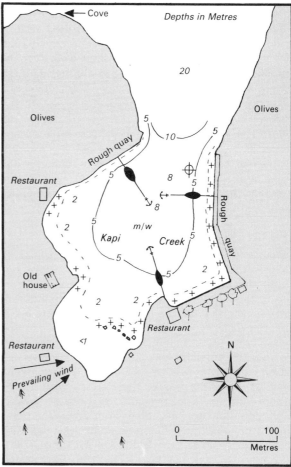

KAPI CREEK
36°38'·65N 28°53'·6E

through it presents no problems. The entrance to Kapi Creek will not be seen until close to, when the restaurant at the head is conspicuous. Proceed into the steep-sided creek, which is free of dangers in the entrance. The end of the creek is shallow (see plan).

Mooring

Go stern or bows-to the quay on the NW side or that on the E side. As soon as you get into the entrance, touts for one or other of the restaurants will be waving you onto their quay. Take your time making your choice. Care is needed off either quay, and deeper-draught craft will not be able to get right up to either quay in places. There are laid moorings off the rough quays. The bottom is covered with thick weed and is not everywhere good holding. If using your anchor, ensure that it is well in, as there can be strong gusts off the W side of the creek with the *meltemi*, and there is little room to manoeuvre if you get into difficulties. Once in here there is nearly all-round shelter.

Facilities

Ashore several restaurants open in the summer. 'Village bread' is sometimes available, and although not cheap it is delicious and lasts well on board.

General

On the W side of the creek are the ruins of two old dwellings with vaulted roofs. They look something like small chapels, but I am assured that they were dwellings. The one with a triple-vaulted roof is particularly intriguing, with no obvious explanation for its complex construction. A short walk over the saddle of the hill and you come to the sea again, on the eastern side of the peninsula. Here there is a delightful cove, shaded by pine down to the water's edge.

Note Kapi Creek is too small for very large yachts, especially in the summer, when it can be crowded. In settled weather a large yacht can anchor in the cove immediately W of Kapi Creek, with a line ashore. The cove is spectacular, with cliffs on either side split by a narrow ravine at the head.

TWENTY-TWO FATHOM COVE

This is the bay on the S side of the entrance to Manistir Köyü. The bay is difficult to make out from the distance, but closer in the rocky finger protecting the cove from the N can be distinguished, as can an islet off the headland. The entrance is clear of dangers.

Go bows-to a rough quay at the head of the cove. With care, small to medium-sized yachts can get close enough for you to step ashore. Alternatively, anchor with a line ashore. There are 10–15m depths about 50m out from the quay. Reasonable shelter, although there may be a chop from across the bay – more uncomfortable than dangerous. A restaurant ashore reported to be friendly. On the slopes about the bay the rock has been weathered into jagged columns, which poke up amongst the olive trees to create a novel landscape.

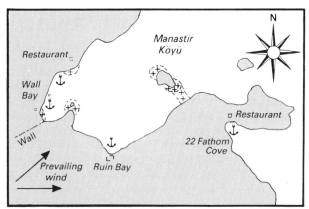

MANASTIR KOYU: 22 Fathom Cove, Ruin Bay and Wall Bay

RUIN BAY (Cleopatra's Bay)

This miniature cove lies on the S side of Manistir Köyü. Boz Burun forms the northern entrance point of the bay. The reef shown extending from the islet on the SE side of the bay in fact extends about 50–60m in a NW direction from the islet. In calm weather it is easily identified. Around Ruin Bay the conspicuous ruins of several old stone buildings, right on the water's edge, will be seen.

Anchor in 10–12m on the S or W side of the cove, with a line ashore. The jetty is used by tripper boats from Fethiye and Göcek. The setting in this tiny cove is exquisite, with thick pine covering the slopes right down to the water's edge, engulfing everything except the ruins. A restaurant opens in the summer.

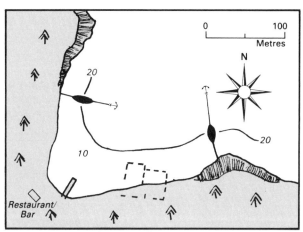

RUIN BAY 36°38'·5N 28°51'·3E

WALL BAY

This cove lies in the far western corner of Manistir Köyü. A red-roofed restaurant is conspicuous on the N side of the entrance to the cove, about due W from the 22-fathom mark on the old Admiralty chart 1886. The small bay takes its name from a high wall on its S side.

Anchor in 15m at the W end of the cove with a line ashore to a rough stone quay, or on the NW side with a line ashore to a tree. Good shelter from the prevailing wind, although there may be gusts off the high land.

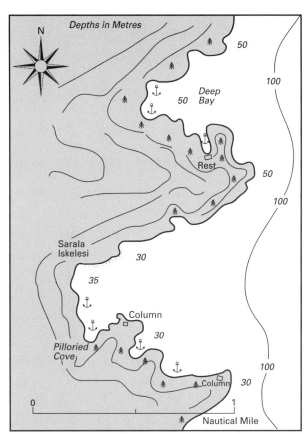

SARSALA ISKELESI AND DEEP BAY

Ruin Bay

There is a simple restaurant above the rough stone quay, as well as the more sophisticated red-roofed restaurant (Ergin Bililik) on the NW side. The setting, as in Ruin Bay, is exquisite, though I am tempted to re-name it 'Graffiti Bay', after all the graffiti with which *gulet* crews and some yachtsmen have defaced the stones around the bay.

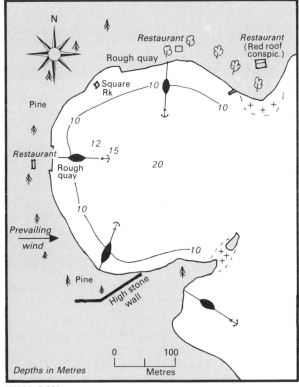

WALL BAY
36°38'.7N 28°50'.05E

SARSALA ISKELESI (Sarsila)

This is the large bay on the N side of Boz Burun. The white houses of the hamlet around the W side of the bay are conspicuous. On the S side there is an old marble column on the point and further along another fragment of column.

There are a number of coves all along the S side where a yacht can anchor with a long line ashore. Mostly it is fairly deep so you will be dropping anchor in 8–15 metres. The bottom is mostly sand, rock and stones, not everywhere the best holding so make sure your anchor is well in. Protection from the *meltemi* is good.

My favourite place is Pilloried Cove right in the SW corner. Anchor in 8–10m at the head of the cove with a line ashore. Care is needed of a rock and gravel patch off the shore. Good protection in idyllic surroundings.

DEEP BAY (Siralibük Limani)

(36°40·65N 28°51·6E)

This is the bay immediately N of Sarsala Iskelesi on the W side of Skopea Limani. There are a number of places where you can anchor around the bay, although, as its name suggests, it is fairly deep in here for anchoring (as are most of the anchorages in the gulf).

On the SE side of the bay just inside the entrance there is a narrow inlet with a catwalk along the E side. There are mostly 2–3 metre depths off the catwalk. Go stern or bow-to where convenient. Some care is needed as the holding is not the best and yachts tend to lay their anchors some way out which in the shallower water means they can be near the surface. In some cases yachts will take a line right across the bay which hinders new yachts wanting to get further in. Good shelter. At the head of the creek there is a simple restaurant.

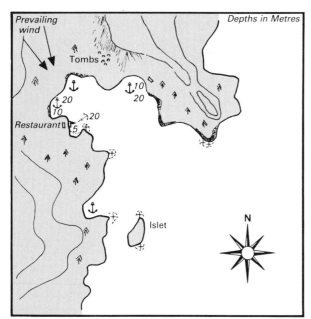

TOMB BAY
36°41'·8N 28°52'E

Tomb Bay: the anchorage just inside the S entrance (restaurant and quay opposite)

Domuz Adasi   *Tersane Adasi*

The channel between Domuz Adasi and Tersane Adasi, looking N

Alternatively, anchor where convenient off the beach in the NW corner.

TOMB BAY (Taşyaka)

This bay lies about one mile N of Deep Bay. The islet in the southern approaches is easily identified, and the channel between it and the mainland is deep and clear of dangers in the fairway.

Just inside the entrance on the S side there is a cove, with a restaurant on the W side. Go stern or bows-to the rough quay off the restaurant, where there are mostly 2–3 metre depths just off the quay. Alternatively, anchor and take a line ashore to the E side, where there is a rough quay to which you can get close in places. The bottom is mud, rock and weed, not the best holding. You can also anchor in any of the coves around the cloverleaf head of the bay. Take a line ashore if practicable. Depths are mostly 10–5 metres, coming up quickly to the shore. Good shelter here from the prevailing wind, which blows in over the high land into the bay.

The bay is an attractive spot, with the steep land, clad in pine, dropping down to the coast and beach. Oleander grows around the shore. On the steep cliffs on the N side of the bay are Lycian rock tombs, mostly of the pigeonhole variety. These house the remains of the inhabitants of Crya, an ancient provincial town sited on the summit of the cliffs. It controlled two islands in the gulf, presumably Domuz and Tersane. It is worth a walk up to the tombs, as much for the dramatic site as for the tombs themselves.

DOMUZ ADASI

This is the southernmost island of the chain of islands which protects Skopea Limani on the E. It is a private island, apparently belonging to the owners of the Turkish daily newspaper *Hurriyet* (Freedom). As might be expected, you are not allowed to land on the island. The dwellings and quay are on the N

side of the island, about due W of the islet in the channel between Domuz and Tersane Adasi. The buildings are conspicuous from the N.

At the NW end of the island there is a bay sheltered from the prevailing wind. Anchor in 15m on the W side, off a small beach.

TERSANE ADASI

The island lying close eastwards of Domuz Adasi and separated from it by a narrow channel. There are good depths in the channel, with a least depth of 11m (36ft) over a shoal patch just N of the islet in the middle.

Ruins   W entrance point

Tersane: the entrance, looking SE

There is a good anchorage in Tersane creek, with nearly all-round shelter, on the NW side of the island.

TERSANE CREEK

Approach

The entrance is difficult to pick out from the distance. The conspicuous buildings on the N side of Domuz Adasi help to locate things. Once at the narrow entrance, the numerous ruins at the head of the creek are conspicuous. The entrance and outer end of the creek are deep and free of dangers, but the two coves at the head are shallow and rock-bound (see plan).

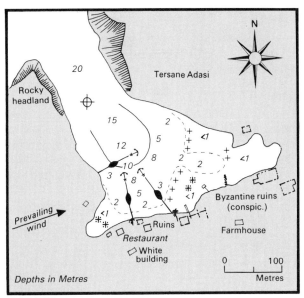

TERSANE
36°40'·65N 28°54'·9E

Mooring

Anchor where shown, with a line ashore. The bottom is mud and weed, with some loose rocks, but appears to be good holding. Nearly all-round shelter. It can get crowded in the summer, and you will have to squeeze in where possible.

Tersane anchorage, looking E

Facilities

A small restaurant opens in the summer. Limited provisions – bread, eggs, yoghurt, etc – can sometimes be obtained from the restaurant.

General

The numerous ruins around the shores of the creek date from Byzantine times and later. There are numerous substantial buildings, including a church. Many of the buildings look as if they had been lived in until comparatively recently. The only inhabitants now are the farmer and his family. *Tersane* means dockyard, so it is likely that at one time boats were built or repaired here.

YASSICA ADALARI

This group of five small islands and several islets and above-water rocks lies in a cluster N of Tersane Adasi. There is a serious error on the old Admiralty chart 1886 (on charts not corrected after 1986), which shows 43 fathoms in the channel between the two southernmost islands of the group, where in fact there is a reef just underwater between the two islands. The error is duplicated on Turkish chart 312, which shows 79m where there is less than one metre.

On the N side of the southernmost island there is a pleasant day anchorage, sheltered from the prevailing wind. At the N end of the long squiggly island and the islet off it there is also a good day anchorage protected from the prevailing winds.

TETRA ROCK AND REEF

The islet and reef shown on the old Admiralty chart 1886 (the islet is difficult to identify on the chart) are easily identified. The islet is easily seen, and the reef is now marked by a small beacon (⁑ topmark). The reef is situated approximately 400 metres N of the islet, and is orientated approximately N–S. Care is needed in the vicinity of the reef.

BOYNUZ BUKU

This is the large bay lying on the coast opposite Yassica Adalari. The entrance is difficult to detect from the distance but Tetra Rock, mentioned above, between Yassica Adalari and Boynuz Bükü, is easily identified. Care is needed off the second point in on the N side of the entrance where a reef runs out for 100 metres or so. There is mostly 5–10m over it except close to the shore where it shallows. Once into the bay, anchor at the head in 8–10 metres. The bottom is mud and good holding. Good shelter from the prevailing wind.

This fjord-like bay is covered in pine woods on its N and S slopes, but at the head there is a lush stand of deciduous trees and oleander. Reeds grow around the marshy ground at the mouths of the two creeks at each corner. The mouths of these creeks have silted, but off the stand of trees and a small jetty in the middle there are depths of 10 metres at about 60 metres off and 2-metre depths at the end. Restaurant and water ashore.

TETRA BAY

About three quarters of a mile N of Boynuz Bükü there is an unnamed bay offering good shelter from the prevailing wind. It is very deep until close to the head, but you can anchor in 15m with a line ashore, taking care of a shallow ledge near the shore. Good shelter from the prevailing winds.

Like Boynuz Bükü, this bay is fed by a small creek, and has a lush stand of green trees on the small river flat at the head.

GOCEK ADASI (Kizlan Adasi)

The northernmost of the islands in Skopea Limani. A light is exhibited on the E side (Fl(2)10s8M).

There are several coves on the NE side which afford some shelter from the prevailing wind.

GOCEK (Köçek, Paterson's Wharf)

BA 1644
Turkish chart 313
Imray-Tetra chart G36

Approach

The bay and village lie at the far northern end of Skopea Limani. The buildings of Göçek village are conspicuous.

Mooring

There are several places to berth.

1. *Göçek Town* Two dogleg piers extend off the village. Go stern or bows-to the pier where directed. The shore NW of the piers has now been quayed and yachts also berth here. Some care is needed as the depths are irregular and yachts drawing more than 1·5 metres will sometimes get stuck on the bottom. As it is all mud this is not too much of a problem except for a spot of embarrassment. Between the two piers anchors often get tangled, and *gulets* often look as if they are going to lay an anchor on top of yachts in here when they come in to berth. There is talk of laying permanent mooring lines. Good shelter, although there is a bit of popple from the prevailing wind.

2. *Iltur Pier* An L-shaped pier NW of Göçek town quay. There are 2·5–4 metre depths on the outside of the outer end, and 2–3·5 metre depths on the inside. A number of years ago the pier was partially destroyed by the town council claiming it was illegal. The status of the pier is currently unknown but in 1996 the pier was in use. It appears it will be rebuilt at some time when the legal wrangles are sorted out. Shelter on the Iltur Pier is only average as the prevailing wind sends a chop across the bay onto the pier making it uncomfortable.

3. *Iltur Club Marina* The marina tucked into the SE side of the W side of Göçek Bay. Once into the entrance, the neo-Lycian buildings of the marina stand out in startling fashion. Berth where directed. There are laid moorings tailed to the quay. Good shelter from the prevailing wind.

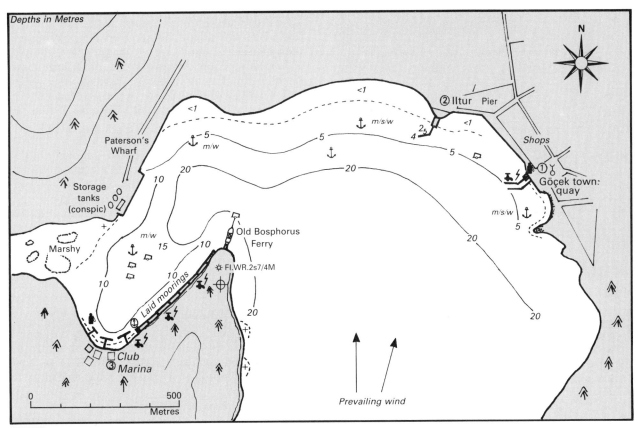

GOCEK
Göçek light 36°45'·1N 28°55'·3E

Authorities Police. Harbourmaster and marina staff at the respective marinas. Charge band 2 at Göçek town. Charge band 3 at Club Marina.

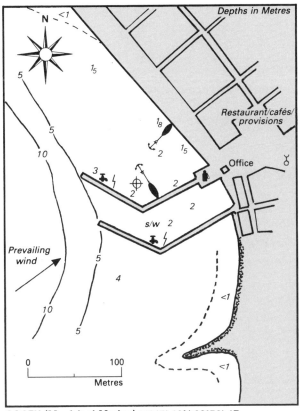

GOCEK (Municipal Marina) 36°45'·19N 28°56'·4E

Anchorages

1. The most popular anchorage is in the N of the bay, in 3–10 metres. The bottom is mud and weed, generally good holding. Good shelter from the prevailing wind, although a little swell is pushed in here.
2. In the dogleg of Göçek Bay, NW of Club Marina. There are several large mooring buoys in the bay which should be avoided. Anchor in 5–12 metres. Good all-round shelter.
3. In the bay S of Göçek town quay. This is open to the prevailing wind, and not the best anchorage.

Note

1. Care is needed of inflatables zooming around Göçek Bay with little or no awareness of the dangers they pose. In 1992 a horrific accident between two inflatables occurred when they collided, killing two and maiming several others. In more recent years there have been more accidents involving high speed inflatables, but the authorities seem incapable of acting.
2. At times the municipal authorities have tried to restrict anchoring in the bay. They have attempted to make charges for anchoring on a par with the marina charges or have stated it is forbidden to anchor here. The legality of all this is doubtful. At the time of publication there seemed to be little interference with anchoring in the bay.
3. Göçek has a reputation for heavy fines for yachts polluting the sea. Extremely heavy fines (up to £400 and up to £4,000 reported but not confirmed) have been levied for yachts pumping

Göçek: Club Marina, in the SW corner of the bay

out their holding tanks or toilets and lesser fines for diesel and detergent spills. *Gulets* however seem to be able to pump out their holding tanks, even in harbour, with impunity. Do not on any account even contemplate pumping out a toilet in the vicinity.

Facilities

1. *Göçek town* Water and electricity on the quay. Fuel quay.
2. *Iltur pier* Water and electricity on the quay. Restaurant and bar.
3. *Club Marina* Water and electricity on the quay. Fuel on the quay at the S end. Shower and toilet block. Mini-market. Restaurant and bar. Regular ferry service back and forth from Göçek.

Göçek town

Repairs Some mechanical repairs can be arranged. Sail repairs and *gardiennage*.

Göçek Yacht Service. Lutfiye Uzun who runs Göçek Yacht Service has been involved with arranging services for yachts for a good number of years. She can arrange crew, yacht spares, airport transfers, laundry, provisioning, and provides a fax service. VHF Ch 60 ☎ (252) 645 1730/645 1731 *Fax* (252) 645 1732.

Provisions Good shopping for provisions in town. Ice available.

Eating out Good restaurants, including some good fish restaurants around the waterfront and in town.

Other PO. Bank. Turkish gas and *Camping Gaz* can be ordered. Laundry. Telephone and fax facilities. Buses and *dolmuş* to Marmaris and Fethiye. International flights from Dalaman airport, about half an hour away.

General

Göçek has grown from a ramshackle little place into a bustling charter-boat base – its proximity to Dalaman airport, about half an hour away, makes it ideally placed for charter. It is a thoroughly pleasant spot – a mixture of a place, catering for the

agricultural needs of the farmers in the fertile valley behind as well as for the needs of the newcomers, the yachtsmen.

The new Club Marina in the bay has some startling but not unattractive architecture in what can only be described as a Neo-Lycian style, complete with columns and friezes. I like it, although prices are not cheap for a night or two here.

The new marina is in marked contrast to the storage tanks and buildings at Paterson's Wharf. Paterson's Wharf is in fact the old name, and its proper title is the Turkish Chrome Company Wharf, which doesn't have quite the same ring to it. Chrome ore mined inland is loaded here for export, though there are moves to have the loading point moved elsewhere, and if the owners of Club Marina have anything to do with it then it will probably be soon.

INNICE ISKELESI

On the mainland coast opposite Göçek Adasi there is a wonderful bay with steep cliffs all around it. In calm weather you can anchor here. The *meltemi* pushes a swell up into it, making it untenable.

KUCUK KARGI KOYU

The large bay on the mainland coast lying N of Katrançik Ada. Although it is deep in here local *gulets* use the bay. With a strong *meltemi* a swell is pushed into here. Restaurant ashore. Magnificent surroundings.

KARGI BUKU

The large bay E of Küçük Karği Köyü. Local *gulets* anchor in the W cove of the NE head of the bay. It is very deep in here but the surroundings are magnificent.

KIZIL ADA

On the N side there are two bights where a yacht can anchor. Good shelter from the prevailing wind although there can be gusts over the island. Open to the NW–N–NE so probably best used as a lunch stop.

FETHIYE (ancient **Telmessus**)

BA 1644
Turkish chart 313
Imray-Tetra chart G36

Approach

The town and harbour of Fethiye lie in the large bay S of Fethiye Adasi. You will not see the town and harbour until you are right around the corner into the bay, but numerous hotels around the beach N of the town are prominent.

Conspicuous The Delikliadalar group of islands and Kizil Adasi are easily identified from the distance. The small lighthouse and dwelling on the S tip of Kizil Adasi are conspicuous and, closer in, the white beacon and light on Sunk Rock (Batikkaya) are easily spotted. The villa complex on the W side of

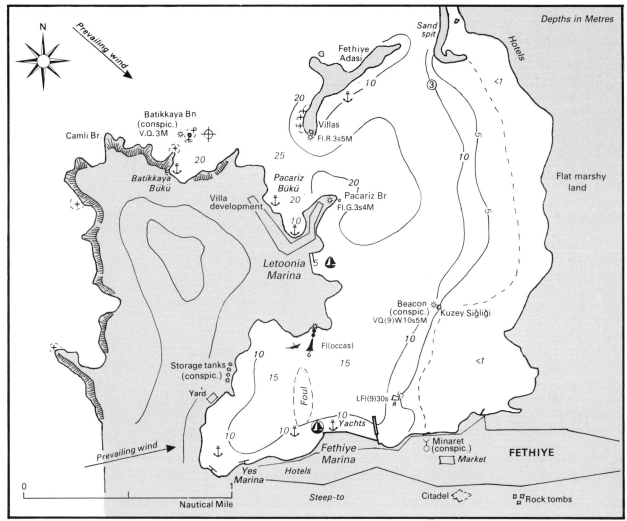

APPROACHES TO FETHIYE
Batikkaya light 36°38'·8N 29°06'·1E

the entrance, opposite Fethiye Adasi, is conspicuous. Fethiye Adasi is a low-lying island with numerous villas built around its shores. The light structure on its S tip is easily identified from the channel. Once you are into Fethiye Bay, the buildings of the town will be seen, and the yacht quay is easily identified. The white beacon marking the shoal water (Kuzey Siğligi) on the E side of Fethiye Bay is conspicuous, but the buoy further S is more difficult to see.

Fethiye: the lighthouse on Kizil Adasi, in the western approaches

By night In the approaches, use the lights on Kizil Adasi (Fl.5s15M), Batikkaya (VQ.3M), and Fethiye Adasi (Fl.R.3s3M). The beacon marking Kuzey Siğligi is lit (VQ(9)10s3M), as is the buoy (LFl(9) 30s). The yacht quay is spotlit. The light on the buoy marking the wreck on the W side of the bay (Fl) should not be relied on.

Dangers
1. Isabel Rock lies 2 miles W of Delikliadalar, with least depths of 4·6m (15ft) over it.
2. An isolated rock on which the sea breaks lies ¼ mile W of the northernmost island of the Delikliadalar group. It is now marked by a W cardinal buoy.
3. Sunk Rock, marked by the Batikkaya light structure, lies 750m E of Camli Burun.
4. Kuzey Siğligi light structure marks the western edge of the shoal water on the eastern side of Fethiye Bay. This shoal dries in places. A buoy ½ a mile further SSW also marks the edge of this shoal.
5. On the W side of the bay the wreck of the 'hotel ship' will be seen. A green buoy (⁑ topmark) marking it should be left well to starboard. The buoy is lit Fl (occas).

Fethiye: light structure on Pacariz Burnu. Fethiye town in the background

Mooring

Go stern-to the yacht quay where directed. Alternatively, there are wooden catwalks off the Hotel Likya and off the Han restaurant where a yacht can go stern or bows-to. The bottom comes up quickly to the yacht quay and the catwalks, so you will usually be dropping anchor in 10–12 metres. The bottom is mud and weed, and not everywhere good holding.

Shelter Good with the prevailing winds, but open to the N. Some swell is generated within the bay itself by the prevailing wind, but this is more bothersome than dangerous. NE gales are reported to make the yacht quay untenable, although yachts have wintered afloat here.

Authorities A port of entry. Customs are directly behind the yacht quay. Immigration are next to them. Health authorities are a block behind the immigration and the harbourmaster is near the root of the pier. Yacht marina, charge band 2. Likya and Han yacht piers, charge band 2.

Anchorage Anchor to the W of the yacht quay in 10–15 metres. The bottom is mud and weed, not everywhere good holding. Care is needed of a large foul area between the Han yacht pier and the wreck of the old hotel ship. This foul area consists of the wrecked ships anchor chain which was let go and dragged across this area when it caught fire. If your anchor snags on the chain it will require a diver to go down to free it as it is impossible to haul the chain up.

Note There are reported to be lots of mosquitoes in the vicinity of the Han and Likya berths.

Facilities

Services Water on the yacht quay, and at the Likya and the Han. Electricity (220V) can be connected on the yacht quay. Shower and toilet block on the yacht quay.

Fuel On the quay. A tanker is normally stationed permanently here.

Repairs Mechanical and some engineering work can

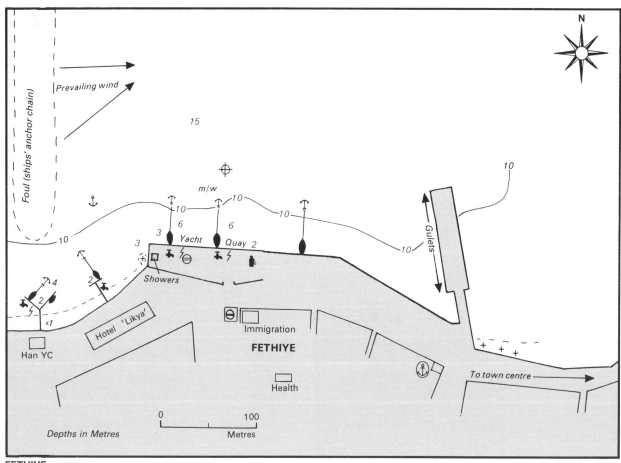

FETHIYE
36°37'·4N 29°06'·2E

202

be carried out in the town. Hardware shops and limited chandlery. A boatyard on the W of Fethiye Limani can haul yachts.

Provisions Good shopping for all provisions. Market on Monday and Wednesday. The market is situated on the eastern side of the shopping area. Ice available.

Eating out Good restaurants in the town. Look around the market area, out of the town proper, for some good *lokantas*.

Other PO. Banks. Turkish gas, and *Camping Gaz* bottles can be refilled. Buses to Muğla and Antalya. Dalaman International Airport is about an hour away.

Note Touts on the yacht quay can arrange to get everything for you – diesel, gas, provisions, etc – but this is not an economical way of doing things.

General

Fethiye was flattened in the same earthquake that destroyed Marmaris, and the modern post-quake town is mostly composed of reinforced concrete buildings of little charm. Here and there one sees older dwellings that survived the earthquake – little gems tucked into the concrete town. Nonetheless the town is a convivial place, and one that most people come to like. The market area is a fascinating warren of shops and stalls, selling things, fixing things, making things of every description, from copper plates for tourists to agricultural implements for the farmers in the hinterland.

In the cliffs behind the town are numerous Lycian rock tombs that are prominent when approaching from seaward. This necropolis is virtually all that remains of ancient Telmessus, which was the principal port of Lycia. The largest of the tombs is the Tomb of Amyntas, an imposing tomb with Ionic columns, dating from the 4th century BC. Just W of the tombs are the ruins of a medieval fort, also prominent from seaward.

AROUND FETHIYE BAY

1. ***Yes Marina*** In the SW corner of Fethiye Limani is a wooden catwalk where a yacht can go stern or bows-to. It is mostly used by a charter fleet. Water and electricity. Alternatively, it is possible to anchor off here. Restaurants not too far away. You are a bit out of it here, and in the summer it can be a hot dusty walk into town.
2. ***Letoonia Marina*** Under Paçariz Burnu there is a bay, which now has a quay around part of it, and a short pier. Berth where directed. Good shelter from the prevailing wind. Water and electricity. Restaurant and bar ashore. Charge band 2.
3. ***Paçariz Bükü*** Lies immediately W of Paçariz Burnu. Anchor in 6–10m at the head. Good shelter from the prevailing wind. The charm of the place has been somewhat eroded by the suburban villas around the slopes.
4. ***Batikkaya Bükü*** Lies under Batikkaya light structure. Anchor in 5–10m, off the beach, on a sandy bottom. The shelter from the prevailing

Ilbiz Burnu, looking S

wind is better than it looks on the chart. This is the most attractive of the anchorages, with a beach and wooded foreshore, though the threat of villa development looms over it.

CAMLI BURNU TO ILBIZ BURNU

Along this impressive bit of coast, cliffs drop precipitously into the sea, and the slopes are covered in pine for the most part. In calm weather it is possible to anchor off the holiday village S of Camli Burnu, and in a bay further W. However, if any sea is running the anchorages should not be used – it needs to be absolutely flat calm.

Around this stretch of coast there will often be flat spots with little wind when there is a light *meltemi*, though needless to say there is usually a swell, making motoring uncomfortable.

Gemiler Adasi and nearby anchorages

Gemiler Adasi and nearby anchorages lie in a large bay E of Ilbiz Burnu. The light structure on the cape is conspicuous. Care should be taken of an underwater rock, which is not shown on the chart, lying 60–70m off the cape. Rounding the cape from the N, the rock three-quarters of a mile SE of Ilbiz Burnu is above water and easily identified.

Karacaören Adalari, composed of one island and a chain of above-water rocks, connected by an underwater reef, are difficult to make out until closer in, although they stand out well when approaching from the S. Gemiler Adasi is difficult to identify from the distance, appearing as part of the high land behind. There are several anchorages in this area (see plan).

1. ***Karacaören*** Between the island with numerous ruins on it and the outermost above-water rock of the reef there is 10m least depth in the channel. The bay opposite the island, partially sheltered by the reef from the S, provides an attractive and reasonably sheltered anchorage. Anchor in 6–10m in the W of the bay, with a line ashore, or on the N side with a line ashore to a rough stone quay. There are insufficient depths to go right up to the quay. The bottom is thick weed over sand, with some rocks, and has been reported to be bad holding, although I have found it adequate. Good shelter from the *meltemi*, although some swell creeps around into the anchorage.

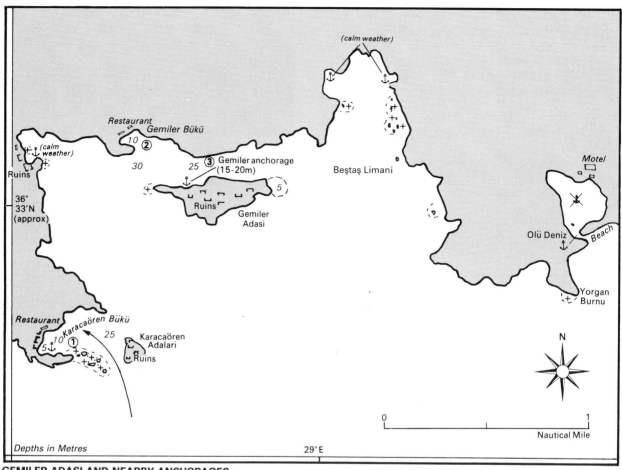

GEMILER ADASI AND NEARBY ANCHORAGES

Restaurant ashore. The bay is picturesque, with a few medieval ruins amongst the *maquis*, and the low, craggy isthmus terminating in the reef.

Note on local knowledge When I was pottering around the channel taking soundings, I noticed a 15-metre local charter boat altering course to pass through the reef. 'Aha!' I thought. 'A bit of local knowledge to enrich this pilot, along the lines of "local boats use a passage through the reef, but yachtsmen are advised to...", etc.' The *gulet* drove straight up on the reef and then turned side on, to pound slowly in what was fortunately a small and dying swell. A local fishing boat got there before I could assist in pulling off the boat. The sheepish skipper and, by now, quite frightened charterers, then entered the bay around the end of the reef.

Local knowledge and its consequences: Karacaören reef

In most of the eastern Mediterranean, items of local knowledge that should be treated with caution will often be proffered. You will often be told that there are sufficient depths off a quay when you can plainly see that there are not. Following this incident, I now regard such advice with a healthy scepticism. I was tempted to name this bay 'Wreck Bay'!

2. ***Gemiler Bükü*** This is a small, nearly oval bay on the mainland coast, opposite the western end of Gemiler Adasi. Anchor off the beach in 10m, on a sandy bottom. The best place out of the swell is in the W corner, with a line ashore, where the local fishing boats go. With the *meltemi* a swell works its way into the bay, more uncomfortable than dangerous. Two restaurants ashore amongst the olive trees. Mr Robinson's village bread from one of the restaurants is justly famous not only for its taste, but also for its keeping qualities.

3. ***Gemiler Adasi*** You can anchor off the island at the western end of the channel. There are considerable depths until close to, when the bottom comes up quickly. Anchor in 15–20m, with a line ashore. There are 8m depths until about 15–20m from the shore, where it shelves quickly to a rocky ledge just under the water. There can be an appreciable W-going current in the channel which may cause you to lie at an angle to the shore. Moderate shelter from the *meltemi*. At night there may be a katabatic wind off the

mountains from the NE, which makes it uncomfortable. Some care is needed in this anchorage.

On the slopes of Gemiler Adasi are the extensive ruins of what must have been a sizeable Byzantine community. It is interesting to wander around the remains, where there are numerous mosaics, some now sadly destroyed by visitors, in and around the buildings.

4. ***Beştaş Limani*** The bay E of Gemiler Adasi has several coves which can be used in calm weather (see plan).

OLU DENIZ (Yorgun Köyü)

This beautiful inland bay is now a prohibited area, and yachts cannot anchor in the lagoon. Being a landlocked bay, connected to the sea only by a narrow and shallow channel, it was being suffocated by the oil and sewage left by the numerous yachts that visited here, and so was closed in 1983. A detachment of *jandarma* ensures that yachts do not enter. However, if you wish to visit you can anchor just outside the entrance, with a line ashore, where there is reasonable shelter from the *meltemi*.

Approach

From the SW you will see a long sandy beach. Closer in, another beach will be seen close N of the first beach, and part of this is the sandy spit enclosing Olü Deniz. Numerous hotels, restaurants and camping grounds are conspicuous around the SE of the beach from closer in.

OLU DENIZ
36°33′N 29°06′·7E

Mooring

At present, anchor in 15–20m in the entrance, under the hook of land protecting it, and take a line to the cliff on the W side. Good shelter from the *meltemi*, although some swell may work its way around. At night there may be a katabatic wind from the NE off the mountains, which can make it very uncomfortable and possibly untenable in here.

Facilities

Several restaurants around the beach, and on the NE shore of Olü Deniz. Lots of bars and beach cafes. Most provisions can be found although at some distance from the anchorage. *Dolmuş* or taxi to Fethiye.

General

The enclosed lagoon, with its sandy beach and high mountains behind, is a place of some considerable beauty. It is to the credit of the ministry responsible that yachts have been banned from the lagoon until it recovers from the onslaught of diesel engines and human leftovers. However, there is no credit due for the rash of land-based development, which has blighted the coast with white concrete boxes. By day there are traffic jams, and a cloud of carbon monoxide over the place. At night, it throbs to the moronic beat of popular disco compilations from the numerous discos and bars. Luckily, the lagoon and the anchorage outside are away from the worst of it, so you can indulge if you wish and then retreat!

YEDI BURUNLAR

The seven capes lie 9 miles due S of Olü Deniz, and stretch for another 7 miles in a SSE direction between Kötü Burun and Zeytin Burun. These high, bold capes have a nasty reputation. When the *meltemi* is blowing there are gusts from different directions off the high land in the vicinity, and a steep, confused sea piles up for several miles off.

SE of the capes, a sandy beach and sand dunes stretch for another 7 miles. It is here that the ancient Xanthos river (present-day Esen Cayasi) empties into the sea, and for some distance off the beach there is comparatively shallow water (10–20m depths). Here, too, a confused sea piles up over the shallow water with the *meltemi*. The best policy to follow for getting past the Seven Capes and the

Kötü Burnu

Yedi Burunlar, looking SSE

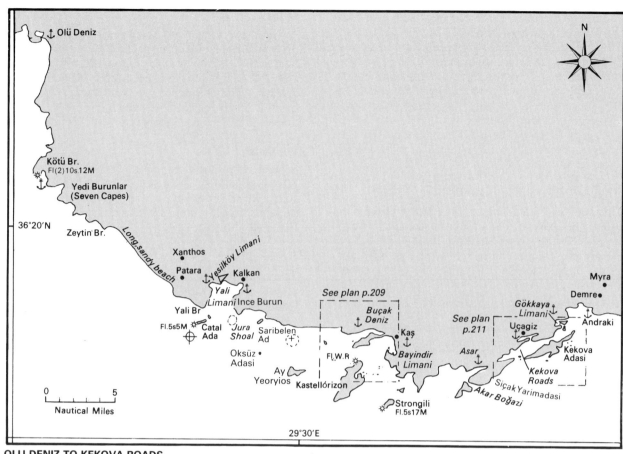

OLU DENIZ TO KEKOVA ROADS
Catal Ada light 36°12'·7N 29°20'·9E

beach is to keep about 2–3 miles off. When proceeding N from Kalkan, most boats leave at 0400 in the morning and motor as far as possible, although there may still be a lumpy sea.

At the southern end of the beach are the ruins of ancient Patara, some of which can be seen from seaward. Patara was the port for Xanthos, but its heyday was during the Roman occupation, when it served the whole Lycian coast. It was here that Bishop Nicholas of Myra, our present-day Santa Claus, was born. Like so many of the other ancient ports along the Turkish coast, Patara silted, and today sand dunes have completely clogged the entrance to the marsh that was once a great harbour. At the N end of the sand dunes a new hotel complex has been built.

KOTU BURUN

With a moderate *meltemi*, *gulets* sometimes anchor in a cove under Kotu Burun. It is quite deep, and some swell penetrates to make it a bit rolly, but the anchorage could be useful.

YESILKOY LIMANI

This is the bay on the W side of Yali Limani. The vast new holiday village on the slopes to the N is conspicuous. There is good shelter from the *meltemi* here, although there are strong gusts, and some swell penetrates into the bay. The best place to anchor is on the W side of the bay. Anchor in 10–15

metres, with a line ashore. The bottom is sand and weed, and not everywhere good holding.

The slopes about the bay are covered in *maquis* and olives, but the presence of the new holiday village and a new road cut around the bay probably means that more concrete will be poured over the rock and earth in the near future.

KALKAN

Approach

The harbour lies at the NE end of the large bay (Yali Limani) lying between Yali Burnu and Ince Burun, 3 miles further E.

Conspicuous Catal Ada, the two islands separated by a narrow channel in the western approaches to Kalkan, look like one island until close to. The new holiday village in Yesilköy, and another massive development E of the original development, are conspicuous once you are into the bay. The buildings of Kalkan will not be seen until you are right into the bay. A large hotel just behind the harbour is conspicuous. The breakwater and entrance are difficult to identify until close to.

By night A light is exhibited on the south end of Catal Ada (Fl.5s5M). The entrance to the harbour is lit F.G and F.R, though the range is limited and a flashing disco light in the development to the E has a better range.

Conspicuous hotel   Entrance

Kalkan: approach, looking NNE

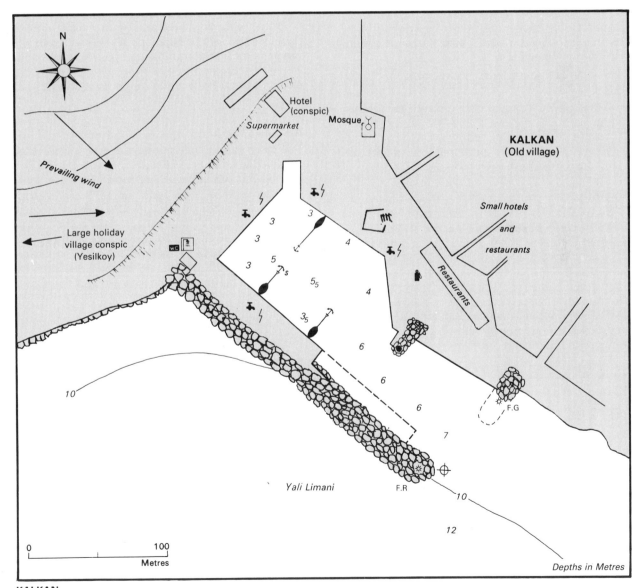

KALKAN
36°15'·7N 29°24'·9E

Dangers
1. With the *meltemi*, there are fierce gusts into Yali Limani off the high land on the W side of the bay.
2. Jura shoal, with a least depth over it of 4·6m (15ft), lies ¼ of a mile SSW of Ince Burun. It is easily seen in calm weather.
3. A rock with a least depth of 3m over it lies midway between Oksüz Adasi and the coast to its NE.

Note Part of the outer breakwater was destroyed in 1996 but it is likely it will be repaired in the near future. The partial destruction does not affect the shelter in normal settled summer conditions, but does indicate the sort of seas that hit this coast in the winter.

Mooring

Go stern or bows-to where directed. The bottom is sand, but does not appear to be everywhere good holding, for some reason. Because the harbour is comparatively narrow, anchors are often tangled between craft lying on opposite quays. There is talk of installing laid moorings.

Shelter Good shelter from the prevailing wind. Southerlies set up a surge, usually more uncomfortable than dangerous.

Authorities Harbourmaster. Charge band 2.

Note
1. A freshwater spring bubbles up into the sea near the harbour, making the water in the vicinity deliciously cool in the summer.
2. Heavy penalties for pumping out toilets and holding tanks have been levied here.

Facilities

Services Water on the quay. Electricity (220V) can be connected. Toilet and shower block.
Fuel On the quay.
Provisions Good shopping for provisions. There is a mini-market by the harbour. Ice can be ordered.
Eating out Numerous restaurants near the waterfront, many of a surprisingly sophisticated nature.
Other PO. Exchange office. Laundry. Turkish gas and *Camping Gaz*. Bus to Fethiye and Antalya. Taxi for trips to Patara and Xanthos.

General

Kalkan was a Greek village until 1922, when it was resettled with Turks. The 1958 earthquake caused considerable damage, and it was decided to relocate the villagers in the new settlement, immediately above the old village.

Some years ago most of the old village was purchased by an entrepreneur from Istanbul, and he has evidently managed to sell various buildings to others from the big city. Hence the numerous sophisticated restaurants and bars. I wonder if any of them thought that the developers would also follow them here from Istanbul, and build holiday villages the size of the original village.

The village itself still has a good feel to it. The buildings are entwined in bougainvillea and jasmine,

and there are marvellous views out over the bay. It is the nearest safe harbour from which to visit Patara and Xanthos. Both sites are well worth a visit.

Caution

An uncharted shoal patch lies about 100m S of the islet at the southern extremity of Saribelen Adasi.

Care must also be taken of the underwater rock between Oksüz Adasi and the mainland. A recent observation put its depth at around 3 metres, and suggested that its position might be slightly different from that shown on the chart. It is now marked by an isolated danger buoy (YB). A bearing of 085° or less on Gürmenli Adasi leads clear of it to seaward.

BUCAK DENIZ (Port Vathi)

This long inlet lies on the NW side of Curkurbağ Yarimadasi (Vathi Peninsula). Two above-water rocks lie on the S side of the entrance. A light structure is situated on the N side of the narrowest part of the inlet (Kaş Mevkil Fl.WRG.10s5-3M 297°-G-065°-W-071°-R-093°).

At the head of the inlet there is an anchorage in 10–15m, with a line ashore. With a light *meltemi* there is some slop in here, and if it blows strongly it can get very uncomfortable and possibly untenable. There are reported to be strong gusts from the NE off the mountains in the autumn. It is a short walk over the isthmus to Kaş village.

KAS MARINA

The town council has started construction work on a quayed area on the NE side of Buçak Deniz. This is to be Kaş Marina with berths for 350 yachts and it is hoped it will be open for 1998. All marina facilities are to be installed. Travel-hoist. Although the wind does not blow home into the end of Buçak Deniz, some swell is pushed into here with NW–W winds and it remains to be seen if the berths are comfortable with strong westerlies. It is intended that the old harbour will be for *gulets* and the marina for yachts.

KAS (ancient **Antiphellos**)
BA 1054

Approach

The numerous islands in the approaches are readily identified. From the W, Gürmenli Adasi and Gürmenli Kayalari, two above-water rocks, are easily identified. The easternmost rock looks much like a submarine from most angles. From the S, the channel between Sulu Adalari and the mainland is also easily identified.

Conspicuous The buildings of Kaş cannot be seen until you are into the bay, although the holiday village to the SE of Kas will be seen. Closer in, the light structure on the extremity of the breakwater shows up well. The entrance is not apparent until close to.

By night Use the light on the N side of Kastellórizon (Fl.WR.4·5s5/3M: the red sector covers Gürmenli

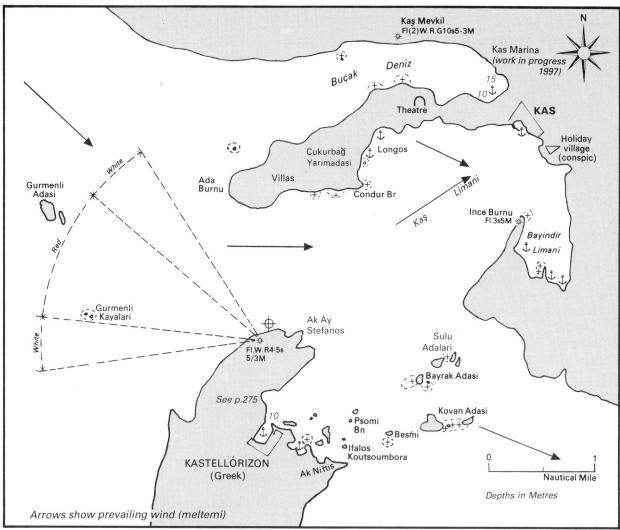

APPROACHES TO KAS AND KASTELLORIZON
Ak Ay Stefanos light 36°10'·0N 29°35'·3E

Adasi and Kayalari over 095°-125°) and on Ince Burnu (Fl.3s5M). A light is exhibited on the extremity of the breakwater: Fl.R.2·5s2M.

Dangers

1. The underwater rock between Oksüz Adasi and the mainland must be avoided in the approach from the W. It is marked by an isolated danger buoy (YB).

2. With the *meltemi*, there can be a considerable swell at the entrance to the harbour, which you must turn side on to when entering.

Mooring

Go stern or bows-to where directed or where convenient. The bottom is mud, sand and weed, but not everywhere good holding.

Shelter Good shelter from the *meltemi*.

Authorities A port of entry. Customs, police and health officials are close to the waterfront. Harbourmaster. Charge band 2.

Note As at Kalkan, a freshwater spring empties into the harbour, keeping the water cool.

Facilities

Services Water and electricity (220V) on the quay. Shower and toilet block. Laundrette.

Fuel A tanker delivers to the quay.

Repairs Limited mechanical repairs.

Provisions Good shopping for provisions. There is a small market for fresh fruit and vegetables near the bus station. Ice can be delivered.

Eating out Numerous restaurants around the waterfront and in the town.

Other PO. Bank. Turkish gas. Buses to Fethiye and Antalya.

General

Kaş lies at the foot of steep slopes, in a crescent-shaped bay, sheltered by the Greek island of Kastellórizon (Turkish: Meyisti) from the southwest and by the skinny peninsula (Curkurbağ Yarimadasi) on the north. Like many of the villages along the coast, Kaş was Greek until 1922, when it was resettled with Turks from the Anatolian plateau and the Balkans. It is a small green oasis under the scrub-covered hills, and the village, which from the distance looks nothing at all, is quite one of the most enchanting places along this coast.

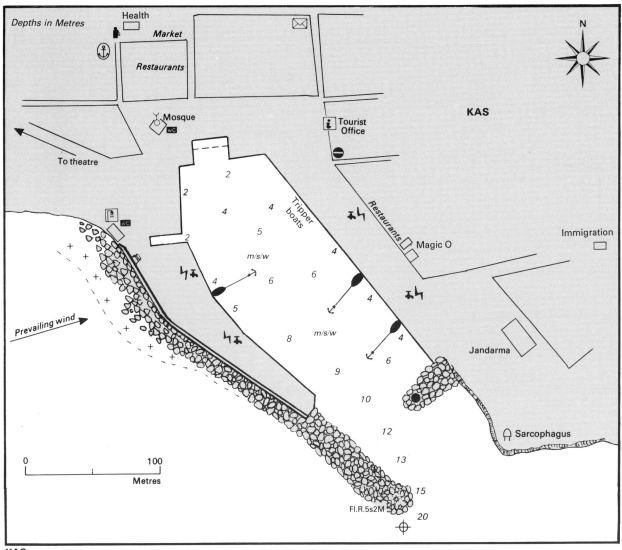

KAS
36°11'·9N 29°38'·5E

The ancients evidently thought so too. Behind the village on the steep slopes are numerous Lycian rock tombs, although they are not obvious until after dark, when spotlights pick them out like giant ancient glow-worms. A short distance W of the village is a well preserved Hellenistic theatre, with superb views over the bay.

ANCHORAGES AROUND THE BAY

1. ***Longos*** On the W side of the bay (Kaş Limani) you can find some shelter from the *meltemi*. Anchor just N of the small islet N of Condur Burnu. It is quite deep here, and you will have to anchor in 12–15m. The bottom is sand and good holding. A reasonable lee from the *meltemi*, but some swell creeps around. You can also anchor in the cove 0·4 miles NNE. Anchor in 8–10m on a sandy bottom, with a line ashore.

2. ***Bayindir Limani (Port Sevedo)*** This is the large bay in the SE of Kaş Limani. The best place is in the far SE corner, where a white house is conspicuous on the small headland. Anchor on the E side of the headland, off the beach, in 8–10m, or in the small cove in the SE corner, in 10–15m. The holding is bad in places. Good shelter from the *meltemi*, although some swell creeps around into here. You can also anchor in the bight on the W side of the bay, which some reckon is a better place than at the head of the bay. Several restaurants ashore.

ULU BURUN

On the SE side of this cape the Institute for Nautical Archaeology, under the direction of Dr. George Bass, has been involved in the excavation of a Bronze Age shipwreck since 1984. Preliminary investigation and finds indicate a large number of oxide ingots, similar to those recovered from the Cape Gelidonya wreck, as well as storage jars and tools. It is thought the wreck dates from the 14th century BC, making it the oldest Bronze Age vessel so far excavated.

Note With the *meltemi* there are fierce gusts off Ulu Burun. Some shelter can be found in a small cove on the SE side of the peninsula, about 1½ miles from the tip of the cape. Anchor in 15m with a line ashore to the W side of the cove.

Ulu Burun, looking W

ASAR BUKU

The long inlet on the NE side of Siçak Yarimadasi ('Hot' peninsula). At the head of the inlet lie the ruins of the ancient city and port of Aperlae, now partially under the water. In calm weather a yacht can use the inlet, but some caution is needed when approaching the ruins to avoid the submerged quays of the ancient city. Anchor in 5–10m on sand and weed. When the *meltemi* is blowing a swell rolls into the bay, and it becomes unsafe in here.

AKAR BOGAZI

This is the channel between Iç Ada and Siçak Yarimadasi. It is narrow, but there are good depths.

A current is said to set through it to the SE, but I have never detected any appreciable current in the channel.

Kekova Roads

Kekova Adasi is a four mile long island lying in a WSW–ENE direction, and sheltering a stretch of water across to the much indented mainland opposite. Kekova Adasi protects this roadstead from the sea set up by the prevailing winds, providing a calm area with numerous well protected anchorages. There is perfect all-round shelter in Uçagiz Limani,

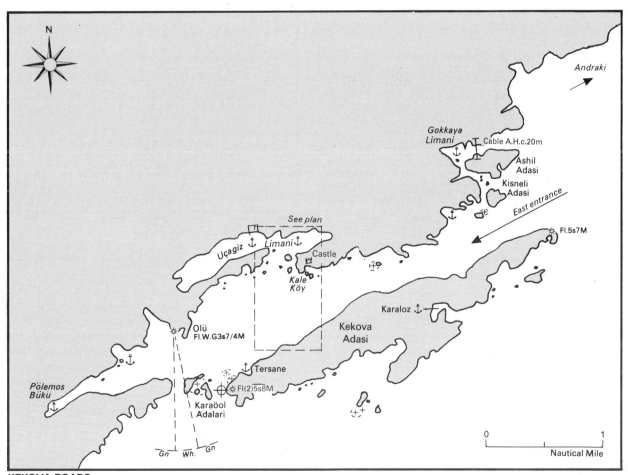

KEKOVA ROADS
Kekova Adasi W light 36°10'·3N 29°50'·6E

which is also known as Olü Deniz, because, as in its namesake further west, it is always calm in here. Kekova Roads can be entered from the western or eastern end of Kekova Adasi.

WESTERN CHANNEL

At the western end of Kekova Adasi a group of islands, Karağol Adalari (Pilanda or Karakol Adalari), lies in the middle of the channel. There are channels on the eastern and western sides of Karağol Adalari. From the distance it is difficult to distinguish the two channels, but closer in the western channel opens up, and the light structure on the mainland coast will be seen. The light structure on the western end of Kekova Adasi is partially obscured by a knoll in the approach.

Although the channel on the eastern side of the islands is considered the normal one to take, I consider the channel on the western side to be more straightforward. There is deep water in the fairway and right up close to the sides. The channel on the eastern side of Karağol Adalari has good depths in the fairway, but care must be taken of a rocky bank, just under water, lying approximately 200m due N of the light structure. The rocky patch is easily spotted in calm weather.

The light structure on the mainland (Olü) bearing 357° leads clear through the channel on the west

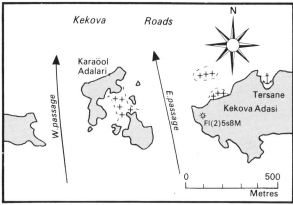

KEKOVA ROADS – WESTERN ENTRANCE

side of Karağol Adalari. (Olü light: Fl.WG.3s7/4M. The white sector covers 355°-358° and leads clear through the channel.) A light is exhibited on the western end of Kekova Adasi: Fl(2)5s8M.

EASTERN CHANNEL

The channel between the eastern end of Kekova Adasi and the coast is straightforward, and clear of dangers in the fairway. Once into Kekova Roads, the channel is deep close to Kekova Adasi. A light is exhibited on the E end of Kekova Adasi: Fl.5s7M.

POLEMOS BUKU

The long (1½ miles) inlet lying at the western end of Kekova Roads. It is free of dangers, except for several small islets on the northern side. Anchor where convenient. Most yachts proceed right up to

the end of the inlet, where there are 5–10m depths about 250m from the shore. The bottom is mud and good holding. Excellent, nearly all-round shelter. There are some gusts with the *meltemi*, but they are not bothersome.

Ashore, the slopes are covered in *maquis* and olive. It has been reported that there are some underwater ruins off one of the small islets.

TERSANE (Xera)

A miniature cove lying 450m NE of the western end of Kekova Adasi. In the approaches, care must be taken of the rocky patch already mentioned, lying 200m N of the light structure. Once the entrance is open, you will see the ruins of a church at the head of the cove, and other ruins on the eastern slopes. Anchor in 4–10m with a line ashore to the western side. The bottom is sand and good holding. Good shelter from the prevailing wind, although with a strong *meltemi* it can be a bit rolly in the anchorage.

The miniature cove is picturesque, with a small beach at the head, crystal-clear water over a sandy bottom, and the ruined church a haunting memorial to Christianity in the country of Islam.

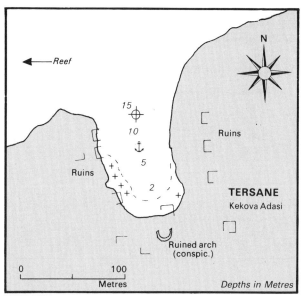

TERSANE
36°10'·4N 29°50'·9E

KALE KOY

Once into Kekova Roads, the most conspicuous object is the magnificent castle at Kale Köy. Situated on a steep ridge on the western side of the entrance to Uçagiz Limani, its battlements stand out dramatically over the hamlet below. The anchorage at Kale Köy is only suitable in calm weather, usually in the morning before the breeze picks up. Although it is partially protected from the four mile fetch across the roadstead, the bottom here is bad holding and not to be trusted.

Tersane, looking S from the entrance

Kale Köy: the rocks at the entrance with steps cut into them

Approach

The anchorage is surrounded by above and below-water rocks. The plan shows the dangers and the entrance into the anchorage. The rock on the western side of the entrance has stairs cut into it, and was perhaps a watch tower at the end of a mole that is now under the sea. The reef and above-water rocks on the eastern side are easily identified.

Mooring

Once inside, anchor in 12–15m. The bottom appears to be mud and weed, but this must be over rock, as the holding is uncertain. The bottom comes up quickly to a sunken quay that the restaurants on the waterfront have been built out upon. The NW corner of the bay is shallow. Off the easternmost restaurant there is a laid mooring usually used by the tripper boats from Kaş.

Facilities

There are numerous (for a small hamlet) restaurants on the waterfront. Limited provisions.

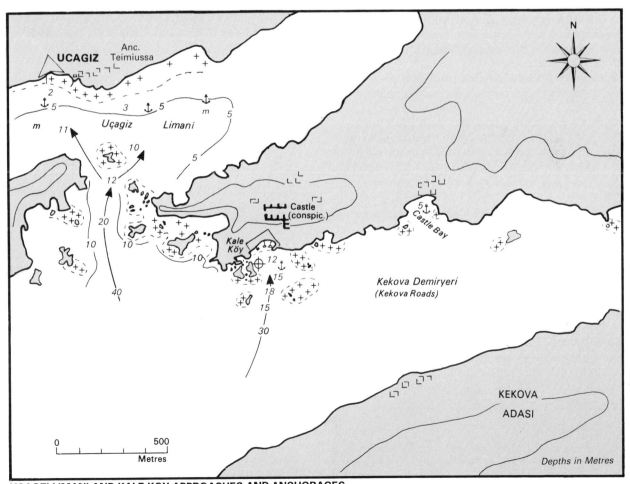

UCAGZI LIMANI AND KALE KOY APPROACHES AND ANCHORAGES
Kale Köy 36°11'·6N 29°51'·9E

Kale Köy approach and anchorage, looking NE

General

It is a short, if steep, walk up to the castle, from which you will be rewarded with a view right out over Kekova Roads. Although small, the castle is quite magnificent, partly because of the site and partly because the battlements stand out in this otherwise rocky landscape. Within the castle there is a miniature theatre, cut into the rock.

On the slopes outside the castle numerous sarcophagi can be seen. Some have toppled over, but one can only marvel that so many stand erect upon their pedestals where they were placed two or three thousand years ago. Looking down to Kale Köy, you get a proper perspective on the sunken parts of the city which was probably ancient Simena. The sunken quay that the restaurants are built upon can be clearly seen, and a lonely sarcophagus still stands half submerged on the western side of the bay.

UCAGIZ LIMANI (Olü Deniz, Tristomos)

This completely landlocked bay lies through a rocky channel immediately W of Kale Köy. Uçagiz means 'three mouths', after the three channels into the bay.

Channel   *Hamlet*

Uçagiz Limani, from the castle at Kale Köy.

Uçagiz Limani

Approach

From Kale Köy, take the main channel, which then divides into two around a low rocky islet which is surrounded by a reef just underwater. The reef is easily seen as a brown smudge. In the fairway of either of these channels there are depths of 9–10m, although there are depths of 3–5m closer to the sides. In practice, the passage through the channels into Uçagiz Limani is not as difficult as it looks in the plan.

Mooring

Once into Uçagiz Limani you can anchor in several places. The usual place is off the village, in 3–5m depths. There are piers off several of the restaurants in the village, and yachts can go bows-to with care – if you go aground it is all mud. There are 1·5m depths at the extremity, and 2m depths about 20m off. A yacht can also anchor in the eastern half of the bay. Anchor in 4–5m off the ruins ashore. The bottom is everywhere mud, and good holding. Good all-round shelter.

Note Touts in speedboats will often come out to yachts – even as far as the entrance to Kekova Roads – to entice you to one restaurant or another. I suggest you reserve your choice until you have had a look around at what is on offer. It is perfectly normal in Turkey to look politely at what is on offer in a restaurant and decide that you want to look elsewhere, though the touts will do their utmost to keep you at their restaurant.

Facilities

Numerous restaurants on the waterfront. A number of the restaurants here have their own piers, or will operate a 'courtesy boat' to get you to and from the anchorage. Water from the restaurants. Some provisions available.

General

Uçagiz is a ramshackle little hamlet that has been catapulted (not so long ago) from a former age into the 20th century and its present trade in waterborne tourists. It still has great charm, and is well worth a wander around and a quiet drink in a waterside café afterwards.

Just E of the hamlet there are numerous sarcophagi, and a rock tomb, by the water's edge. The ruins are thought to be those of ancient Teimiussa, a small provincial city that administered the surrounding area.

CASTLE BAY

About 600m E of Kale Köy there is a cove offering partial shelter from the prevailing winds. On the W side of the entrance there are some above-water rocks. Anchor in 5–8m and take a line ashore. There are numerous ruins at the head of the bay.

KARALOZ (Port Sant Stefano)

This small inlet lies on the southern side of Kekova Adasi, 1½ miles SW of the eastern tip. The entrance is difficult to pick out from the distance. From the W and E the islets off the S side of Kekova Adasi are readily identified, and from closer in a cave will be seen on the E side of the entrance. There are good depths in the entrance to the inlet and for some distance in. Anchor at the head in 6–10m, with a line ashore. The bottom is mud and weed and good

holding. Good all-round shelter.

This miniature fjord is a grand and wild place. The landscape about is rugged, with scanty *maquis* on the rocky slopes. The water is crystal clear, and the fishing in the vicinity is good.

MARTINIS REEF

Note that Martinis Reef is not in the position shown on the old Admiralty chart 241. It lies off the small island in the southern approaches to Gökkaya as a reef extending E of the islet. A search within the area where the Martinis Bank is supposed to lie failed to locate it.

Coda A friend of mine, Harry Potts, has spent some time looking for the elusive Martinis Reef and believes he has found it more or less in the position shown on the chart. Depths over the reef were around 5 metres. Care should be taken in the vicinity of the Martinis-Potts Reef and any future reports are welcomed.

GOKKAYA LIMANI

At the eastern end of Kekova Roads, a group of small islands lies close to the mainland coast, with narrow but navigable channels between them. The two largest islands are Ashil Adasi (Aşirli Adasi) and Kisneli Adasi (St Elias Island). Numerous islets and reefs are dotted about these two larger islands, but by day passage through the narrow channels is straightforward, however daunting it looks on the plan.

Approach

From the distance it is difficult to make out the islands and channels, but from closer in you will be able to identify what is what. A castellated fort on

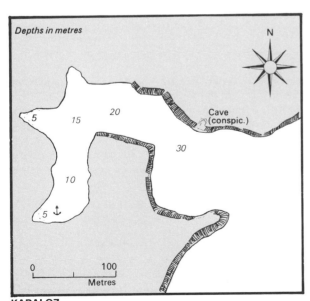

KARALOZ
36°11'·4N 29°53'·4E

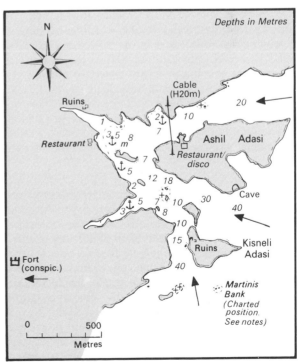

GOKKAYA LIMANI
36°13'N 29°54'E

the mainland, close to Gökkaya Limani, is conspicuous from the E. A night entry is not advised.

Mooring

Most yachts make for the anchorage in the NW creek. Anchor in 5–7m, on mud. Good holding and shelter. In settled weather you can find your own particular little niche around the channels, as there are suitable depths for anchoring everywhere (see plan).

Note The restaurant/disco on the N side of Ashil Adasi has a power cable running across the channel, supported by two pylons. It is always difficult to ascertain the least air height under the cable, but I estimate it to be around 20 metres. Yachts with taller masts should enter through one of the other channels.

Facilities

Restaurant in the NW bay. Restaurant/disco on the N side of Ashil Adasi, which some feel should be boycotted for destroying the tranquillity of the place.

General

The channels are fascinating to potter around in, being not unlike miniature fjords. A freshwater spring bubbles up into the sea, so that the water is refreshingly cool in the summer. On the S side of Ashil Adasi there is a large cave which can be visited in a yacht's tender, either from the anchorage, or while someone hovers off the entrance. It is wonderfully cool inside, and small fishing boats sometimes tie up in here to snooze away the hottest part of the day.

ANDRAKI

An open anchorage under Calpan Burnu, lying a little over 2 miles ENE of Gökkaya Limani. There is a rough stone breakwater in the NE corner used by local boats. It can be used before the afternoon breeze gets up, but it is not a secure anchorage. There is a restaurant on the shingle beach, and a taxi can be ordered from here to do the trip to Myra and Demre, about 5km away. A yacht should not be left unattended here. It is much better to go to Finike and hire a taxi from there to visit Myra and Demre.

MYRA

This Lycian city was at one time by the sea, but alluvium deposited by the Demre river (Andraki Nehri) has built up a coastal plain for several miles around, as well as covering much of the ancient city. Little is known of ancient Myra, but at the beginning of the Christian era Saint Paul was brought here, a prisoner on his way to Rome and his death. He was put on a grain ship that went south about Crete and was later wrecked on Malta.

At Myra there are numerous well preserved Lycian rock tombs that you can climb up to and examine at close quarters, and a well preserved Roman theatre. On the coastal plain laid down by

the river, and right up to the ruins of Myra, there are extensive market gardens. There are greenhouses everywhere.

DEMRE

Near the village of Demre is the church dedicated to Saint Nicholas. Nicholas, patron saint of the sailor and the pawnbroker (an odd duo, but then again, perhaps not, given the cost of sailing these days), is better known as the original Santa Claus. Many apocryphal stories are told of the good Bishop of Demre, but it does appear that he was indeed a generous man who extended charity to the poor of his town.

One story relates how he donated a bag of gold to a poor family. Wishing to remain anonymous, he climbed up on the roof and dropped the bag down the chimney. The daughters of the family were drying their stockings in front of the fire, and the gold fell neatly into one of them. A harmless enough tale to bestow legitimacy on the tradition of putting stockings out for gifts at Christmas.

Nicholas was martyred here in 655, and his grave soon became an important place of pilgrimage. His bones were stolen by merchants from Bari in Italy in 1072, and transported to a church there, where they now lie.

The small church dedicated to Nicholas has been partially restored with funds from the Greek Orthodox church. It is an atmospheric place, fairly reeking

FINIKE TO ANTALYA
Taşlik Burnu light 36°13'·1N 30°25'·3E

Above Pilloried Cove in Skopea Limani. *See page 193. Below* Olü Deniz. *See page 205. Bottom* Greek Kastellórizon looking NE from the slopes behimnd the harbour. *See page 257.*

Above Kaş looking NE. *See page 208.*

Below Uçagiz Limani and the entrance from Kekova Roads looking NW. *See page 214.*

Left Gökkaya Limani looking N across the southern entrance. *See page 215.*

Above Finike looking NW. *See page 217.*

Below Kemer Marina looking SW. *See page 221.*

Setur Antalya Marina looking WNW.
See page 222.

Above Antalya. The marina looking SW from the slopes behind. *See page* 223. *Below* Near Abana. *See page 265. Below right* Sinop. *See page 270.*

of another age, and well worth the effort to visit it. The Noel Baba festival, honouring the saint of that name, is held here in early December every year.

Finike to Antalya

GOK LIMANI

This large bay, immediately before Finike, is sometimes recommended as an anchorage. It has been reported that there is a shoal area in the entrance that comes up suddenly from 60+ metres to 4 metres. Care needed when making the approach into the bay. With the prevailing winds it is not safe, as a heavy swell rolls in.

FINIKE (ancient **Phoenicus**)

Approach

A small commercial harbour lying in the NW corner of Finike Körfezi (Gulf of Finike).

Conspicuous From the SW, the town and harbour cannot be seen until you are right into the bay, when the outer breakwater is readily identified. From the E, the houses of the town, including a number of large multi-storey buildings, can be clearly seen. Closer in, the harbour breakwaters and light structures are easily identified.

By night Use the light on Taşlik Burnu (Fl(3)10s15M), and closer in, the lights on the harbour breakwaters (Fl.R.5s6M and Fl.G.5s6M). A light is also exhibited on the radio tower one mile S of Finike: F.R.4M.

Mooring

Go stern or bows-to the quay where shown. The quay is used by a charter company but can be used if there are berths free. Alternatively, anchor off under the S breakwater. The bottom is mud and good holding.

Shelter Good all-round shelter. Although the harbour is partially open to the E, these winds are usually not bothersome.

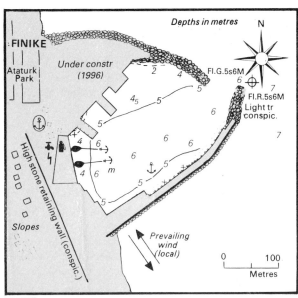

FINIKE
36°17'·6N 30°09'·2E

Authorities Port officials. Harbourmaster. Charge band 2.

Facilities

Services Water and electricity on the quay. Shower and toilet block.
Fuel On the quay.
Repairs Limited mechanical repairs in the town. Wood workshop near the yacht quay.
Provisions Good shopping for all provisions. Fresh fruit and vegetable market near the mosque. Ice can be delivered.
Eating out Numerous restaurants near the harbour.
Other PO. Banks. Turkish gas. Bus to Antalya.

General

Finike is a dusty, ramshackle town serving the surrounding market gardening area. On the alluvial plain east of the town, greenhouses occupy every square inch of fertile ground, growing early tomatoes, green peppers and aubergines for export. The

S breakwater   *N breakwater*

Finike: harbour entrance looking WNW

harbour too is like a greenhouse, for little wind penetrates here to cool it, and it can be stifling in the summer.

The site of ancient Phoenicus is nearby, though little remains. This is the nearest safe harbour to Myra and Demre. Also nearby is ancient Limyra.

KARAOZ

This is the large bay on the E side of Finike Körfezi. A large holiday village is conspicuous in the bay. Shelter can be found in a cove on the N side of the bay. The rocks shown on the Admiralty and Turkish charts are close to the coast. Anchor in 5m on mud. Reasonable shelter from the prevailing wind, although a swell rolls in.

On the S side of the bay there is a miniature cove barely 30 metres across. Here there is reasonable shelter from the prevailing winds. It is open only N. Anchor in 5–7 metres and take a line ashore. A few houses ashore.

TASLIK BURNU

This bold cape, with a number of islands lying off it, is more commonly known as Cape Gelidonya. In ancient times it was known as the Sacrian promontory, and Pliny described the rugged islands off it (Beşadalar: the five islands) as being 'fraught with disaster for passing vessels'. And so they were for at least one such vessel, the Bronze Age wreck that was discovered here by a sponge diver, Kemal Aras, and investigated by Peter Throckmorton and later Dr George Bass. Throckmorton describes what he saw when he dived over the wreck:

'Almost invisible, dozens of copper ingots lay heaped on top of a rock that pushed out of the sand. They were stuck so solidly together that they could only be moved with crowbars. When we prised one off, we found a hollow under it, full of bits of wood preserved by the sand and by copper salts released by corrosion of the ingots. There were potsherds and bronze axes, adzes and spear points.

Most startling were bits of rope twisted out of reeds or grass. It was what seamen call fox lay, two strands of fibre twisted by hand.'

Peter Throckmorton *The Lost Ships*

The artefacts from the wreck are displayed in the Bronze Age Hall in Bodrum Museum. This wreck, dating from around 1200 BC, was one of the earliest found around the Turkish coast until the discovery at Ulu Burun.

There are good depths between the cape and the first island of the group. A current is reported to set WSW at about ¾ of a knot past the cape, but there can be considerable variations in its direction and strength. From the cape to Antalya, a high and rugged mountain range runs parallel to the shore. Steep slopes, often thickly covered with pine, drop sheer into the sea, except where valleys cut across the mountains. There is often snow on the high peaks well into late spring.

SULUADA

Once around the cape, Suluada, a rocky, red-coloured island, is easily identified. The passage between the island and the coast is clear of dangers in the fairway. Opposite the island there is a cove, used by the American expedition *caïque* when the Cape Gelidonya wreck was being investigated. It provides only a limited lee from the prevailing wind, and there is invariably some swell in here.

CAVUS LIMANI

A large bay lying 7 miles NNE of Taşlik Burnu, on the SW side of Cavuş Burnu. The islet off Cavuş Burnu is easily identified, and there is a deep passage between the islet and the coast. (A perceptible current runs through the passage.) The light structure on Küçük Cavuş Burnu, the cape on the southern side of the entrance, is readily identified once the entrance is opened (light characteristic Mo(A) 15s8M).

Beşadalar   Taşlik Burnu

Taşlik Burnu and Beşadalar, looking SW

Taşlik Burnu, looking N. Note upper and lower light structures

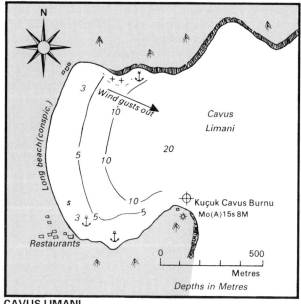

CAVUS LIMANI
Cavus light 36°17'·8N 30°29'·0E

Once into the entrance, a long beach will be seen, extending right around the western side of the bay. Anchor at the S end of the beach, or in a small cove at the S end of the bay. Alternatively, anchor in the small cove on the N side, where shelter from the prevailing winds is reported to be good. The bottom is hard sand and the holding not everywhere the best. Good shelter from the prevailing southerlies, but in the spring and autumn there can be strong gusts off the land in the evening and at night. In autumn there are reported to be strong gusts off the mountains from the NE.

Development has begun around the shores although there is still not extensive building ashore. Restaurants in the summer. A mini-market and PO The bay is most attractive with twin cultivated valleys dropping down between rocky slopes covered in pine to the long beach.

CINEVIZ LIMANI (Port Genovese)

This spectacular deserted anchorage lies 2½ miles NW of Cavuş Burnu.

Approach

The cove is difficult to spot from the distance. Cavuş Burnu is easily identified, and the long beach around Cirali Limani is also easy to identify. Between the cape and the beach there appears to be a solid wall of rock, rising sheer from the sea with no apparent openings. Musa Daği, behind the anchorage, is the highest point in the middle of the cliffs. Head for this until the group of above-water rocks at the entrance to the cove is spotted. There are good depths on either side of the rocks in the middle of the entrance.

Mooring

Anchor in 6–8m depths at the head of the cove, off the shingle beach. There are 4m depths about 50m

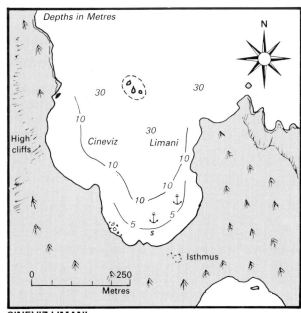

CINEVIZ LIMANI
36°22'N 30°31'E

Cineviz Limani

off the beach. The bottom is sand and shingle, and not everywhere good holding.

Shelter Good shelter from the prevailing winds. There are westerly gusts off Musa Daği, but these are not normally troublesome if your anchor is well in. In the event of a fresh northerly breeze in the morning, a sloppy swell enters the bay. It is not usually dangerous, but it is uncomfortable. Take a line ashore to keep your bow to the swell.

Facilities

None.

General

The deserted bay is magnificent, with awe-inspiring cliffs dropping sheer into the sea on the eastern side of Musa Daği. There is no other anchorage on this coast as grand as Cineviz. Pine trees grow wherever they can get a hold on the precipitous slopes. Across the isthmus, the only level ground here, there is another bay with northern and southern coves. The northern cove is rock-bound and unsuitable for a yacht, but the southern cove is suitable in settled weather.

CIRALI LIMANI

An open anchorage off the southern end of the beach about 2 miles NNW of Cineviz Limani. It is suitable in the afternoon with the S–SE breeze, although some swell works its way around. It is completely open to the N. Several restaurants and a motel around the beach.

The scenery is spectacular: steep craggy slopes are cut by ravines and scarps covered in thick growth, and near the shore sand dunes border the long beach. Water from a creek bubbles over the rocks into the sea at the southern end of the beach.

ANCIENT OLYMPUS

The ruins of ancient Olympus are not evident from seaward. They lie on the slopes N of Cirali village, much overgrown and in a ruinous state. At one time a city noted by Cicero for its riches and works of art, it declined in Byzantine times to become a haunt of pirates.

The Chimaera

On the slopes of a hill 1½ miles inland from the northern end of the beach bordering Cirali Limani is the ancient Chimaera. Today it is not the spectacular phenomenon it was hitherto regarded as, and in fact I had difficulty making it out at night, although to be fair there was a full moon.

The Chimaera was described by Homer as a fire-breathing monster, part lion, part goat, and part snake. It was slain by Bellerophon, a character very much like Heracles – a scene depicted on many early Greek vases. The fiery breath of the monster was said to be eternal, and it is that which we see today.

Or, if you prefer a more mundane explanation, it is a mixture of gases, including methane, produced underground, which on contact with the atmosphere ignites. From these beginnings, 'Chimaera' later became a name for any fantastic beast, and from that we get the modern meaning of 'chimera', a fanciful conception.

ATBUKU LIMANI

A small bay lying immediately N of Cirali beach. It is not as sheltered as it might appear from the chart.

UCADALAR (Three islands)

This group of small islets lying off the coast is easily identified. Good depths in the channel between the islands and the coast.

TEKIROVA (ancient **Phaselis**)

This anchorage lies under Ince Burnu, five miles S of the bold Av Burnu.

Approach

From the S, a plateau sloping gently down to the sea can be identified from the distance. It ends in a headland, on either side of which a yacht can anchor. Closer in, a section of ancient wall on the cliff top on the S side of the headland is conspicuous. From the N, a few ruins can be seen around the shores of the northern anchorage.

Note In both the northern and southern anchorages and around the headland there are numerous above and below-water rocks, most of them the remains of

Tekirova: the N bay and small ancient harbour (ancient Phaselis). Ancient Mt Solymnus behind

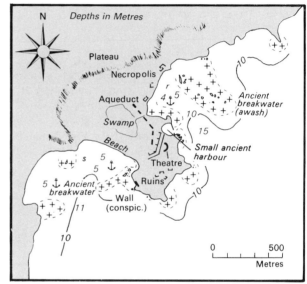

TEKIROVA
36°31′N 30°34′E

ancient breakwaters. Some care is needed when entering either of the anchorages. The sketch plan shows only the approximate position of the numerous underwater rocks.

Mooring

1. In the bay on the S side of the headland. Care must be taken of the submerged remains of the ancient breakwaters extending from the W and E sides of the bay. Anchor on the W or E side, in 5–6m. The bottom is coarse sand and reasonable holding. Adequate shelter, although if the afternoon southerly blows with any strength it can be uncomfortable.
2. In the bay on the N side of the headland. The ancient breakwater on the N side of the anchorage is mostly above water or awash. Anchor in 4–6m. The bottom is littered with large boulders and blocks, probably ancient debris. Use a trip line on your anchor. The shelter here is quite good, but the uneven rocky bottom can make anchoring tricky. It is possible that anchoring will be prohibited here in the future, because of the ancient debris on the sea bed.

Koca (Av) Burnu, looking NNW

3. The small enclosed harbour in the northern anchorage is rock-bound at the entrance, there being perhaps a 10m wide channel clear of dangers, with 2m depths in it. The bottom slopes gently to the beach within the harbour, with about 1m depths in the middle.

General

The site is one of the most picturesque along this coast. On the headland and the isthmus between the two anchorages are numerous ruins: the necropolis, with sarcophagi lying about the slopes; part of the Roman aqueduct; the harbour street with dwellings and shops; and the most pleasing little theatre I have ever sat in. Sitting near the top of the theatre, you have a view over the ancient city towards ancient Mount Solymnus (Tahtali Daği) – its peak capped in snow until late spring – and over the northern and southern harbours. The slopes about are thickly wooded in pine, and in a depression in the middle of the isthmus there is a reed-encircled swamp that was formerly a small lake.

The city was founded in 690 BC by colonists from Rhodes, and quickly grew into a prosperous trading city with three harbours, the remains of which can still be seen. It was famed for its fast light sailing boats, known as *phaseli*, but unfortunately we have no surviving illustrations of these craft. Phaselis shared the history and culture of the other Lycian cities along this coast. It surrendered to Alexander the Great in 333 BC, but thereafter remained quasi-independent under Roman jurisdiction. It declined during the Byzantine era.

KEMER MARINA

Approach

The marina lies one mile W of Koca Burnu, on the western side of a small headland.

Conspicuous From the N and S the massive Koca Burnu is easily recognised. The light structure on it is not easily seen from the distance. From the N, the numerous hotels and buildings around the shore of the bay are conspicuous, particularly the white buildings of the Club Méditerranée on the western side of Koca Burnu. Once into the bay, the small wooded headland dividing the bay into two can be identified, and the marina breakwaters will be seen. The light towers at the extremities of the break-waters are conspicuous.

By night Use the light on Koca (Av) Burnu (Fl.10s12M) and the light on the reef N of Kemer

(Fl(2)10s6M). The entrance to the marina is lit Fl.R.3s5M/Fl.G.3s5M.

VHF Ch 16, 09 for the marina (0800–2400). Call sign *Kemer Marina*.

Dangers
1. Care is needed of the reef lying 0·6M N of the marina entrance in the northern approaches at 36°36'·8N 30°34'·5E. It is now marked by a light structure and light that looks a bit like a mini-oil platform. Light characteristic Fl(2)10s6m6M. When approaching Kemer Marina from the N it is best to head for Koca (Av) Burnu and then make an approach from the NE.
2. Care is needed of the above and below water rocks around Koca Burnu and the above water rock and reef extending approximately 60m N of Kücük Burnu.
3. Care is needed of a shoal patch, least depth 3·5m, lying approximately 300m NNE of the entrance.
4. With strong northerlies there is a confused swell

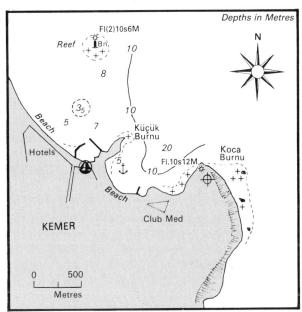

APPROACHES TO KEMER MARINA
Koça Burnu light 36°35'·8N 30°35'·3E

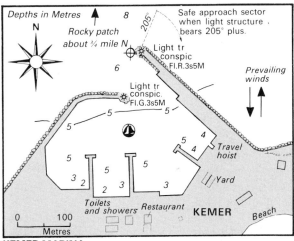

KEMER MARINA
36°36'·2N 30°34'·3E

Kemer marina

at the entrance to which you must turn side-on to enter.

Mooring

Data 200 berths. Visitors berths. Max LOA 20m. Depths 2–5m.

Berth Go stern or bows-to where directed. There are laid moorings with lines tailed to the quay.

Shelter Good all-round shelter. With strong northerlies, a reflected swell affects the eastern side of the marina – more uncomfortable than dangerous. Kemer is a popular spot for yachts to winter in.

Authorities A port of entry, with all the relevant authorities: customs, immigration, and health authorities. Harbourmaster and marina staff. Charge band 2.

Anchorage A yacht can also find fair shelter in the bay on the E side of the headland. Anchor in 3–5m under the headland, where there is some shelter from northerlies and good shelter from southerlies.

Facilities

Services Water and electricity (220V) at every berth. Shower and toilet block. Telephone connections can be made.

Fuel On the quay.

Repairs A 40-ton travel-hoist is in operation, with hard standing for about 80 boats. Most repairs can be carried out at or arranged from the marina.

Provisions Mini-market in the marina. Good shopping for provisions nearby. Ice available.

Eating out Numerous restaurants around the waterfront and in Kemer village.

Other PO. Exchange office. Turkish gas and *Camping Gaz*. Laundry. Taxi and *dolmuş* to Antalya, about 40km away.

Additional marina services Daily weather forecast. *Gardiennage*.

General

Since it opened in 1984, Kemer Marina has developed into one of the most popular marinas in Turkey. It is a popular spot for yachts to winter in, and is often booked solid from the end of summer. The holiday village and hotels around it are mostly a summer affair, and many of the associated restaurants and bars close in the winter.

From Kemer, excursions can be made to the numerous and little known Lycian sites dotted around the mountainous interior. To the W of Kemer and Phaselis, there is a cluster of sites around Karabuk on the slopes of Bey Dağ: Cormi, Idebessus, Acalissus and Arycanda.

Kemer Turban Marina, 07980 Kemer, Antalya ☎ (242) 814 1490 *Fax* (242) 814 1552.

SETUR ANTALYA MARINA
(Antalya Commercial Harbour)

BA 242

Approach

This new marina lies inside Antalya commercial harbour, 5 miles SW of Antalya city.

Conspicuous Several oil storage tanks, derricks and the breakwaters are conspicuous from some distance off. South of the harbour lie a number of unlit mooring buoys, but these are close enough to the shore not to be troublesome. NE of the harbour there are several mooring buoys for tankers unloading oil at an underwater pumping terminal to a refinery on the shore.

By night The entrance to the commercial harbour is lit Fl.G.3s6M/Fl.R.3s6M. The entrance to the marina is lit Fl.G.3s4M/Fl.R.3s4M.

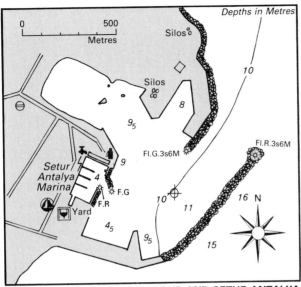

ANTALYA COMMERCIAL HARBOUR AND SETUR ANTALYA MARINA 36°50′·06N 30°37′E

VHF Ch 16, 72. Call sign *Setmar*.

Mooring

Berth where directed. There are laid moorings tailed to the quay.

Shelter Good all-round shelter.

Authorities All authorities for clearing in and out of Turkey are based here. Harbourmaster and marina staff. Charge band 2.

Facilities

Services Water and electricity (220V) at every berth. Shower and toilet block. Telephone connections can be made.
Fuel On the quay.
Repairs A 60-ton travel-hoist and hard standing area. 200-ton slipway. Yacht repair facilities can be arranged. Chandlers.
Provisions Mini-market. Better shopping in Antalya. Ice available.
Restaurants Restaurant and bar. Good restaurants in Antalya, though getting back at night could be a problem.
Other Exchange office. Laundry. A marina minibus runs between the marina and Antalya every hour from 0800–1800. Taxis.
Additional marina services 24-hour security. *Gardiennage.* Daily meteorological bulletin. Telephone and fax services.

General

Although the site of this new marina is not the most prepossessing, surrounded as it is by the storage tanks and derricks of the commercial harbour, it is likely to succeed because of the shortage of berths along the coast, and because Hasan, a name familiar to many along the coast, has been appointed director.
Setur Antalya Marina, Ticari Limani, PO Box 627, Antalya ☎ (242) 229 1340 *Fax* (242) 241 2056.

ANTALYA MARINA

BA 242

Approach

The buildings of Antalya are visible from some distance off, but the exact position of the harbour is difficult to locate until close in.

Conspicuous Numerous high-rise buildings can be seen from the distance. From the E, the Düden waterfalls, near Lara, a torrent which drops over the cliffs into the sea, are conspicuous. A lesser torrent close E of the harbour is not conspicuous until closer in. A short distance off the harbour, the Fluted Minaret and the harbour breakwaters will be seen.

By night Use the light on Baba Burnu (Fl.5s8M) and the lights at the harbour entrance (Fl.G.3s4M and Fl.R.3s4M).

VHF Ch 12, 16. Call sign *Antalya Marina*.

Dangers
1. The entrance is quite narrow and the harbour small. There can be a confused swell at the entrance with the normal southerly breeze, and it would be dangerous to enter in a southerly gale.
2. A small conical buoy off the coast W of the harbour marks a wreck. The depths over this wreck are 4–5m. The buoy is not lit.

Mooring

There are berths for 50 yachts in total, and many of these are taken up by local boats. It is recommended that yachts over 20m do not attempt to enter the harbour, and large yachts under this length should exercise caution when doing so.

Go stern or bows-to where convenient or where directed. Visiting yachts are normally directed to the pier on the S side of the harbour. There are laid moorings here with lines tailed to the quay or a small buoy. Some care should be taken over depths close to the shore.

Shelter Good shelter from the prevailing winds. Southerly gales cause a surge that could be dangerous in some berths. The best shelter is tucked in behind the fuel quay.

Authorities A port of entry. All the relevant authorities are housed close to the marina. Harbourmaster and marina staff. Charge band 2.

Facilities

Services Water and electricity (220V) near every berth. A shower and toilet block.
Fuel On the quay.
Repairs Yachts normally go to Setur Antalya Marina or Kemer Marina for hauling. In the town all manner of mechanical and engineering work can be dealt with. Electrical engineers in the town. Hardware shops.
Provisions Excellent shopping for all provisions in the town. Above the harbour there is a large and colourful bazaar, with a good fresh fruit and vegetable market. Small fish market at the harbour. Ice can be delivered.

Entrance   *Fluted minaret*

Antalya: approach, looking NE

Antalya Marina looking S

Antalya Marina: part of the restoration of the old town

Eating out Good restaurants around the harbour, and others in the town of all categories and prices. There is good food to be had in Antalya.

Other PO. Banks. Turkish gas and *Camping Gaz*. Laundries. Hospital. Buses to many destinations: Izmir, Istanbul, Ankara and Mersin. International and internal flights from the airport, about 10km out of town.

Additional marina services Telephone and fax services. *Gardiennage*. Daily weather forecast.

General

Antalya is a thoroughly pleasant city, rapidly becoming a centre for the growing tourist trade on this, the Turkish Riviera. This is reflected in the preservation and restoration of the old Ottoman village within the walls of the old citadel by the Turizm Bank. Around the harbour a number of buildings have been pleasingly renovated, and these elegant edifices, housing fashionable boutiques, restaurants, cafés and a hotel, are in dramatic contrast to some of the reinforced concrete boxes nearby. In the streets of the modern town immediately above the harbour, the bazaar is a colourful warren of alleys, crammed with stalls: the alley of shoe shops, the tinsmiths' alley, the spice alley, the tool shop alley, the new and old carpet alley, and *köfte* and *çay* shops at every turn. On the cliffs and high walls around the harbour are numerous *çay* shops that offer fine views over the water, and are cooled by the afternoon breeze denied to the harbour hemmed in below.

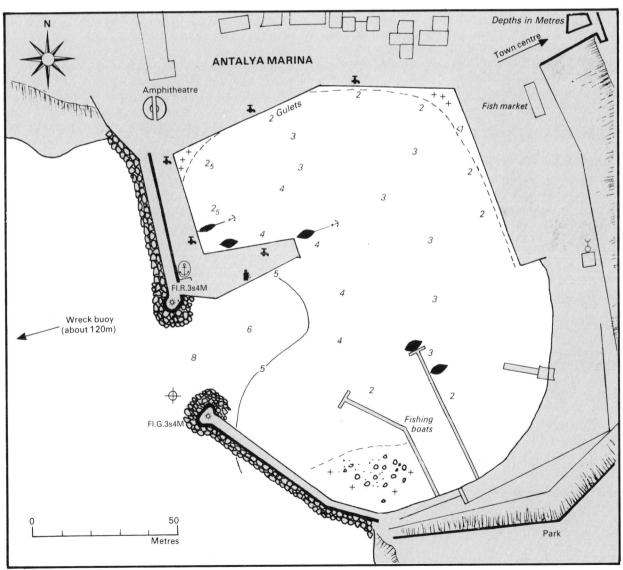

ANTALYA MARINA
36°53'N 30°42'·2E

Kaleci Turban Marina, 07980 Kaleci, Antalya ☎ (242) 242 3676 *Fax* (242) 242 3675.

ANTALYA

The city is on a magnificent site at the head of the large gulf of the same name. The rugged Lycian mountains lie to the south and west, the massive Taurus range is behind, and the fertile Pamphylian Plain spreads out to the east. The city itself sits on a hummock right in the corner of the gulf, with just enough height to survey the sea and land around.

The site was occupied in the 5th to 6th millennia BC, as finds in the Gurma Cave, east of Antalya, have shown. The original inhabitants probably spoke an Indo-European language, like the Hittites, but later adopted Phoenician, and still later Greek, as new colonists arrived. Greek settlers arrived here in about the 7th century BC. According to Homer these were survivors from Troy, but it appears now that they were the victors, the Achaeans, who spread down through the Aegean islands and into Turkey in this period. The Persians, under Darius, arrived in 557 BC, and Alexander the Great stormed through here in 334 BC.

The Pergamene King Attalus II founded the present city in 158 BC and bestowed his name on it (Greek: Attaleia; it appears to have had a similar-sounding name for most of its early period anyway). The Pergamene rule was short, and the city was soon captured by pirates. Rome eventually took the city, which then developed into an important port and remained so for the next millennium. The Crusaders used to embark here for the Levant, in order to avoid the arduous journey across the Taurus range.

The Selçuk Turks captured Antalya in 1207, and held it until the Ottomans arrived in 1387. The most prominent memorial to the Selçuk reign is the Fluted Minaret (Yivli Mianre), said to be a perfect example of Selçuk architecture, standing close behind the harbour.

For most visitors, the attraction of the place lies in its hustling and bustling warren of streets, where you can buy almost anything; failing that, someone will make it for you. Most of the old town above the harbour has been restored, and it is a joy to walk around the wonderful and quite opulent examples of Ottoman and Greek architecture – like most of the cities along the coast, the city was a melting pot of nationalities until the exchange of populations in the 1920s. The restoration work in the town, including that on the buildings around the harbour, has given the heart of Antalya a touch of 18th- and 19th-century grace, and I recommend a good day's wander, stopping in *çay* houses or cafés along the way (try one in the park above the harbour) to catch your breath and just watch the chaos of life in a living, breathing and quite sympathetic city.

Sites near Antalya

TERMESSUS A Lycian city-fortress lying in the hills to the NW of Antalya. The ruins have not been excavated, but the setting is most picturesque. The ruins are much overgrown and sarcophagi lie everywhere. It is well worth a visit.

PERGE The ruins of the ancient city lie 18km NE of Antalya. Perge was famous as the birthplace of Apollonius of Perge, a giant of early Greek mathematics who produced much of the early work on conic sections. When rediscovered during the Renaissance, this detailed work, over a thousand years ahead of its time, enabled Kepler to work out his laws of planetary motion. There are numerous ruins here, including the main street, agora, theatre, stadium and city walls and gates.

ASPENDOS Lies 46km to the east of Antalya. It was a large and prosperous city at one time, joined to the sea by the navigable Eurymedon river (Köpru çay). The most remarkable building surviving is the large theatre, which, although it has not been restored, is in an excellent state of preservation. Also remaining are part of a Roman aqueduct, and the agora.

VI. The Pamphylian and Cilician coasts

Antalya to the Syrian border

Unlike the Aegean coast, this Mediterranean coast is long and straight, with few indentations. It has comparatively few harbours and anchorages for its length, and for this reason few yachts cruise it. The region also lacks the benefit of the cooling *meltemi*, and the heat and humidity can be torrid in the summer. It used to be said that when God made Hell he was dissatisfied, so he made Mesopotamia and added flies. You are not so far away from Mesopotamia here.

Pamphylia extends roughly from Antalya to Alanya, a large fertile plain, watered by numerous rivers, that has been inhabited since Neanderthal times. According to tradition the survivors from Troy settled here, but it is more likely that the Achaeans, the victors at Troy, were the first Greek colonists. Later in the 8th and 7th centuries BC, colonists from Aeolia and Ionia settled at Aspendos, Perge and Side. There was never a Pamphylian confederacy, the various cities being subject to the diverse invaders who came through the region.

The greatest period of prosperity was under Roman rule, when the cities expanded considerably and many great monuments were built. Most of the present-day ruins of these ancient cities date from the Roman period. Pamphylia duly came under Byzantine rule, but succumbed to Arab attacks early on in the 8th century. It was taken by the Selçuks in 1207, and by the Ottomans in 1391.

Cilicia extends from Alanya to the Gulf of Iskenderun. The Romans divided the province into Cilicia Aspera, Rough Cilicia, and Cilicia Campestris, the Cilician Plain. Cilicia Aspera was the steep-to coast between Alanya and Mersin, where the lofty Taurus mountains jut dramatically into the sea. Cilicia Campestris was the fertile plain extending from Mersin to the Gulf of Iskenderun, a miniature Nile Delta where three to four crops can be grown in a year.

Cilicia figured prominently in the history of the ancient world, and like Pamphylia has been settled since the Neolithic period. Along the coast, many of the castles and fortresses still to be seen date from that remarkable period of medieval history when the Rubenid kings ruled over an area known as Lesser Armenia:

'During the first half of the twelfth century the Rubenid dynasty succeeded in creating an Armenian principality in Cilicia, and by the middle of that century they had effectively established their independence from Byzantium, as evidenced by their construction of the Corycian castles. The Rubenid kings maintained their independence largely through their close alliances with the various Crusader kingdoms in the Levant, cementing their ties by marriages between Armenian princesses and Frankish rulers. As a result, the Kingdom of Cilicia came to combine the finest elements of Armenian culture with those from Latin Europe of the early Renaissance, bringing about a curious flowering of western chivalry in south-eastern Asia Minor.'

John Freely *Companion Guide to Turkey*

In the 14th century the Armenian kingdom fell to the Mamelukes, and later to the Ottomans. For a long period Cilicia was a forgotten region, Cilicia Aspera being inaccessible and the Cilician Plain plagued by malaria. Today a new road has been cut around the coast from Alanya to Mersin, and the swamps have been drained. The traveller here should remember, though, that this region is still classified as a malarial risk area by the World Health Organisation; appropriate counter-measures should be taken.

Perhaps the overwhelming impression retained along this coast is of the lushness and incredible fertility of the land. Somehow one imagines a barren, almost desert landscape, and not the well watered market garden that borders the coast for nearly its whole length. Little wonder that the ancients fought so hard, so long, and so often over it.

Weather patterns

The prevailing winds in this region are land and sea breezes. In the summer the onshore sea breeze gets up at about midday and blows until dusk. It normally blows at Force 3–5, rarely more than Force 5–6, from a southerly direction, mostly SW. The wind tends to follow the contours of the coast. The offshore land breeze begins to blow early in the morning, and may continue until midday. At times it can blow at Force 5–6, but generally it is less.

In the spring the land and sea breezes are not well developed, and the heat is not enervating; this is the best time to cruise this coast. In the autumn, there can be exceptionally strong winds off the high mountains at night. These are most troublesome in the region of the Taurus mountains, and in the Gulf of Iskenderun.

In the summer, particularly early summer, there may be a sea mist in the morning. At times this can reduce visibility to half a mile, but rarely to less. It has usually cleared by midday.

Data

PORTS OF ENTRY

Alanya
Taşucu
Mersin
Iskenderun

PROHIBITED AREAS

It is prohibited to navigate in the vicinity of the BOTAS oil terminal in the Gulf of Iskenderun.

MAJOR LIGHTS

Baba Burnu Fl.5s8M
Side Fl(2)5s9M
Alanya LFl.20s20M (vis 249°-108°)
Selinti Burnu Fl.3s8M
Anamur Burnu Fl(2)5s15M
Aydincik Fl.3s8M
Dana Adasi Fl(2)10s10M (vis 131°-022°)
Incekum Burnu Fl.10s9M
Mersin Fl(3)10s15M
Fener Burnu Fl.10s20M
Yumurtalik Fl(2)10s10M
Iskenderun Fl.5s13M
Akinci (Resülhinzir) Fl(2)5s22M

Quick reference guide

	Shelter	Mooring	Fuel	Water	Provisions	Eating out	Plan	Charge band
Side	C	C	O	B	C	B	•	
Fidan	O	C	O	O	O	O		
Alanya	B	AC	B	A	A	A	•	1/2
Aydap	O	C	O	O	O	O		
Gazipaşa	O	C	O	O	O	O		
Yakacik	C	C	O	O	O	O		
Karataş	C	C	O	O	O	O		
Anamur Burnu	O	C	O	O	O	O	•	
Anamur Kalesi	O	C	O	O	O	C		
Bozyazi Limani	A	AB	O	A	O	O	•	1
Softa Kalesi	C	C	O	O	O	O		
Kizilliman anchorage	C	C	O	O	O	O		
Soğuksu Limani	B	C	O	B	O	C	•	
Aydincik	A	AC	B	A	C	C	•	
Sancak Burun	C	C	O	O	O	O		
Sulusalma Burun	C	C	O	O	O	O		
Ovacik Adasi	B	C	O	B	O	C	•	
Ağalimani	B	C	O	B	C	C	•	
Limani Kalesi	B	C	O	O	O	O		
Taşucu	A	A	B	A	B	B	•	1/2
Susanoğlu	O	C	O	O	O	C		
Akyar Burun	C	C	O	B	O	C	•	
Narliküyü	C	C	O	B	O	C	•	
Kizkalesi	O	C	O	O	O	C	•	
Limonlu	B	C	O	O	O	O	•	
Mersin	A	AC	B	A	A	A	•	1/2
Karataş	B	AB	O	B	C	C		
Yumurtalik Limani	C	C	O	O	O	C	•	
Ayas	B	BC	B	A	C	C	•	
Iskenderun	A	AC	B	A	A	B	•	

The coast eastwards of Antalya

Four miles SE of Antalya, Baba Burnu rises sheer from the sea to a large plateau. One mile E of Baba Burnu, the Düden river drops into the sea in a spectacular waterfall conspicuous from seaward.

LARA

About 1¾ miles E of Baba Burnu are the ruins of the harbour of ancient Lara. It is possible to anchor on the W side of the low headland, though great care is needed. A reef, probably the remains of an ancient breakwater, runs out from the headland in a westerly direction. Enter from the west and anchor under the reef in 3–4 metres, on sand. The sea breeze blows into here, and it can be very uncomfortable. Hotel to the NW. Virtually nothing remains of the ancient city.

SIDE (Selimiye)

The ancient city and harbour of Side lie 28 miles E of Lara. The coastline is low-lying, but no longer deserted, as a number of hotels and holiday villages have been built in recent years.

You can anchor on the N or the S side of the headland – the general consensus being that the N side affords the best shelter. Anchor in 3–6m, tucked as far under the headland and rocks (the

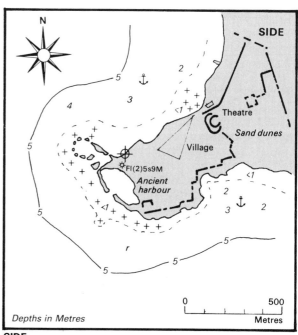

SIDE
36°46'N 31°23'.1E

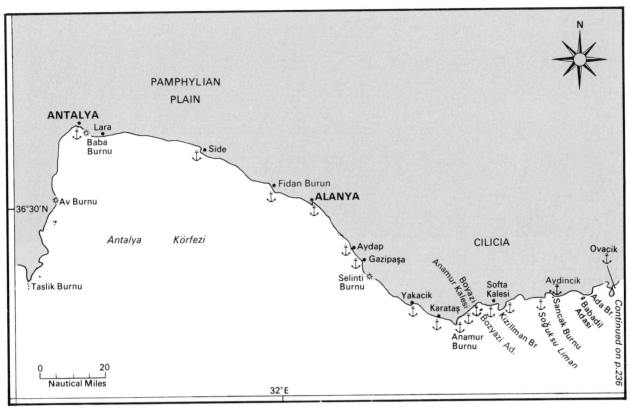

ANTALYA TO OVACIK

ancient mole) as you think prudent. The bottom is hard sand, and not everywhere good holding. Side is not a sheltered anchorage, and in the event of a southerly blow a yacht should leave and go to Antalya or Kemer. Even with the afternoon breeze you will roll around uncomfortably.

There are numerous restaurants, and provisions can be obtained. Side is now much developed as a tourist resort, with numerous hotels and *pensions* dotted about everywhere.

The ruins, particularly the theatre, are well worth seeing. Sand dunes have engulfed part of the city, reminding me of Shelley's lines:

'My name is Ozymandias, king of kings:
Look on my works, ye Mighty, and despair!
Nothing beside remains. Round the decay
Of that colossal wreck, boundless and bare
The lone and level sands stretch far away.'

Here at Side, the sands now stretch towards the burgeoning tourist resort that is growing up.

FIDAN BURUN (Fiğla)

A small bay, partially protected by a short headland (Fidan Burun), lying 21 miles ESE of Side. A white water tower is conspicuous on the headland. There are also several hotels in the vicinity. Off the cape, there are numerous above and below-water rocks. Send a dinghy in to reconnoitre, as there is only a narrow pass through the reef obstructing most of the W bay. Anchor on the W side of the headland, taking care of the rocks, or on the E side. The anchorage is very uncomfortable with the afternoon breeze, when you will roll around with the onshore swell.

ALANYA

BA 237

Approach

The high steep-to promontory jutting out from the flat hinterland is prominent from some distance off.

Conspicuous Closer in the castle walls on the summit of the promontory will be seen. Hotels line the foreshore on the flat land E and W of the promontory. Approaching the anchorage on the E side of the promontory, the long pile pier and the octagonal

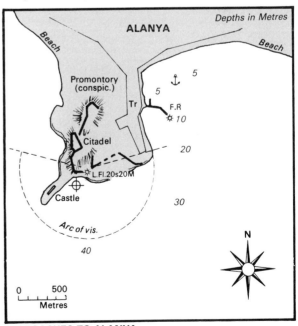

APPROACHES TO ALANYA
Light 36°31'·6N 32°00'·7E

229

Alanya: the anchorage, viewed from the top of the promontory

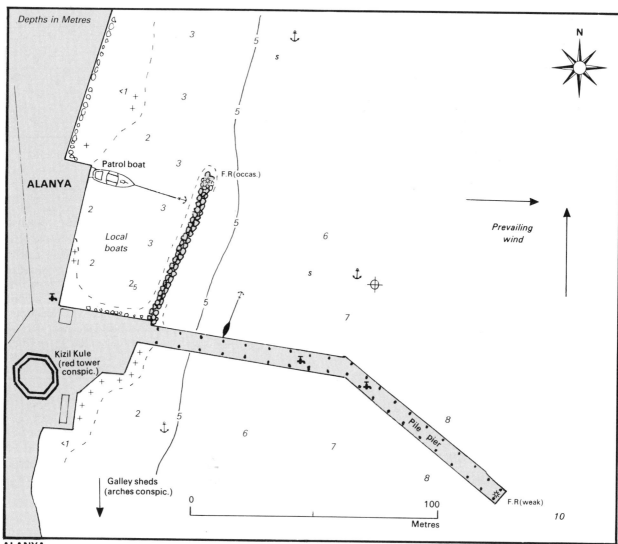

ALANYA
36°31'·8N 31°59'·5E

red tower (Kizil Kule) at the root of the pier are conspicuous.

By night Use the light on the promontory (LFl.20s20M), and closer in the F.R (weak) on the end of the pier. A weak F.R is sometimes exhibited on the extremity of the breakwater protecting the small harbour.

Mooring

Anchor where convenient off the N side of the pier. The bottom is sand and weed and reported to be not good holding. Alternatively, go stern or bows-to the pier. The small harbour is usually so crowded with fishing and tripper boats that there are no berths available, though you may be lucky.

Alanya: anchorage and small harbour, from Kizil Kule

Shelter Reasonable shelter from the prevailing summer winds, although you will roll a fair bit. Nearly all-round shelter in the small harbour.

Authorities A port of entry. Customs patrol at the harbour. Immigration police on the waterfront. Customs and harbourmaster in the town. A charge is made for going on the pier.

Facilities

Water On the pier and close by the harbour.
Fuel In the town. A tanker may be able to deliver to the pier.
Repairs Some mechanical and engineering work can be carried out in the town.
Provisions Good shopping for all provisions in the town. Ice can be delivered.
Eating out Good restaurants around the waterfront and in the town.
Other PO. Banks. Turkish gas. Buses to Antalya and Mersin.

General

The bold promontory was known in ancient times as Calonoros, the 'Good Mountain', and later, when it became a pirate stronghold, as Coracesium, the 'Crow's Nest'. The city was of little importance in classical times, being ruled by pirate overlords who preyed on the shipping travelling along the coast

from the Levant to Lycia and Caria. Pompey cleaned up the coast in his campaign against piracy, destroying a combined pirate fleet off here in 67 BC.

Alanya was of minor importance in Byzantine times, and it took little for the Selçuks, under Sultan Alćeddin Keykûbad I, to take it in 1221. Alćeddin named the town, after himself, Alaiyya, and from that the present-day name of Alanya evolved. The Karamanid Turks took the city in 1300, and the Ottomans in turn took it in 1471.

Under Selçuk rule, the octagonal reddish-coloured fort (Kizil Kule) and the naval dockyards at the water's edge were built to safeguard the town. Kizil Kule is in remarkably good condition, and is worth a visit as much for the deliciously cool interior inside the massive walls as for the interesting construction and the small museum on the ground floor. The naval dockyard (*tersane*) is the only surviving example of its type. Five vaulted galleries open directly onto the sea, and within them galleys were built, repaired and sheltered.

On the promontory, the defensive walls enclose a large area about which the old village clings to the slopes. It is a steep walk up to the top of the promontory, but well worth the effort. At the far end of the fortress, there is a platform at the edge of the cliffs called Adam Atacagi, 'Man Drop', from which, it is said, condemned criminals plunged to their death on the rocks below.

The modern resort has grown up around the sandy beaches on either side of the promontory, leaving the old village pretty much as it was fifty years ago. In common with many others, the new town is architecturally undistinguished, but it is a relaxed, pleasant place, and the locals are friendly. At night it can be fairly noisy in the anchorage from loud sound systems on the shore. A local boat can be hired to visit several caves around the promontory. One of these always has high humidity inside it, and is said to be beneficial to those suffering from rheumatoid and arthritic complaints.

AYDAP (ancient Hamaxia)

A small cove lying 17 miles SE of Alanya. It is enclosed by cliffs on all sides, with the ruins of ancient Hamaxia on top. The cove is very small, and in any case offers only limited shelter from the afternoon onshore breeze. With the latter a swell works its way into the cove. Anchor in 2·5–5 metres, with a line ashore. Local fishing boats sometimes shelter in here on their way along the coast.

GAZIPASA (Halil Limani, ancient Trajanopolis, formerly ancient Selinus)
36°15'·8N 32°16'·8E

An open anchorage off the river mouth on the N and S sides of Kale Burnu. The N side is reckoned to be the better. Anchor in 3–5 metres, on sand. With the afternoon onshore breeze, a swell rolls into the anchorage. It is not really suitable as an overnight anchorage and really is only suitable for a visit to ancient Selinus/Trajanopolis before moving on. Gazipaşa town is about 2km inland.

Selinus was founded by Antiochus IV, and was one of three fortress cities he founded along the coast, with Iotape to the NW and Antiochia further SE. It was renamed Trajanopolis when the Emperor Trajan died here on his way to Palestine in AD 117. When Beaufort surveyed the anchorage in 1812 the massive mausoleum of Trajan was largely intact. Today there are only a few ruins.

From Gazipaşa the coast becomes steep-to, with precipitous cliffs dropping vertically into the sea from the high mountains of the Taurus range behind. The slopes are mostly covered in scrub and splodges of oleander. The latter often pick out the watercourse of a ravine in a pink ribbon of flowers. Once around Anamur Burnu there are extensive pine forests clinging to the slopes. In the valleys, and on any flat land, the verdant green of banana plantations is in marked contrast to the bare rocky slopes.

YAKACIK KOYU (Kalidiran, ancient Charadus)

A bay lying 18 miles SE of Gazipaşa. A few fishing boats use the W side of the bay. Anchor in 5–6m, on sand. Care is needed of a reef and shoal water off the beach. There is some protection from the afternoon onshore breeze, but some swell invariably rolls in here. On the W side it is reported that you can anchor with a line ashore in a small cove by an old hut on a rock. Shelter here is reported to be good and out of the swell rolling into the bay. It can be useful when coasting towards Anamur Burnu, but should not be relied upon.

The slopes about the valley are a solid swathe of green. Banana plantations use every available patch of square ground, right up to the houses of the hamlet.

KARATAS (Melleç)

A small bay SE of Yakacik. Karataş Burnu, the W entrance point of the bay, ends in a low rocky finger. Care must be taken of a rocky patch just under the water in the middle of the bay. A rocky ledge runs around the edge of the shore for some 30–40m out. Anchor in 5–10m on a sand and rock bottom. It is uncomfortable in here with the afternoon breeze, when a swell enters the bay. There is only a *Jandarma* post ashore on Karataş Burnu.

ANAMUR BURNU (ancient **Anemurium**)

The cape is high and bold, with numerous Roman and medieval ruins on it. Anchorage can be obtained on the E side of the cape in 5–8m, on a sandy bottom. The anchorage is very exposed, and should be treated as a temporary stop only. A light is exhibited on the cape: Fl(2)5s15M.

ANAMUR ISKELESI

Off the hamlet of Anamur Iskelesi, there is a short pier with around 3-metre depths on the extremity. It may be useful for getting a few essentials in the

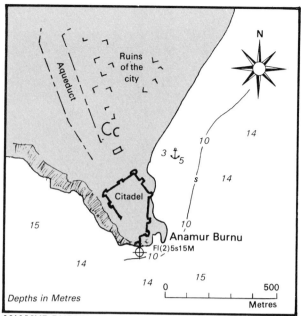

ANAMUR BURNU
36°01'.2N 32°48'.1E

hamlet. Water on the pier. Fuel in the hamlet. Limited provisions and a few restaurants.

ANAMUR KALESI

The castle, prominent from seaward, stands 6 miles NE of Anamur Burnu. In the morning, before the afternoon onshore breeze has got up, a yacht can anchor off the castle so that you can go ashore to visit it. Anchor in 3–5m to the E of the castle. A reef and above-water rock extend ESE for approximately 100m from the castle. The anchorage can only be temporary, as with the afternoon breeze a heavy surf piles up on the shore.

The castle, known to the Turks as Mamure Kalesi, is most romantic, with its towers and walls largely intact. It was built in the 12th century by the Kings of Lesser Armenia. In 1840 it was restored by the Ottomans, who used it right up until the early 20th century. It is one of the best preserved castles on Turkey's Mediterranean coast.

Anamur Kalesi

BOZYAZI LIMANI

A new harbour about three miles NE of Anamur Kalesi.

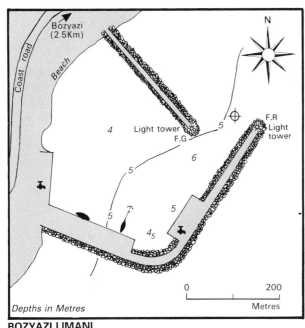

BOZYAZI LIMANI
36°05'·8N 32°57'·75E

Approach

The outer breakwater and the light towers at the entrance will be seen. The entrance is lit F.R/F.G with a limited range.

Mooring

Go stern or bow-to or alongside on the SE quay.

Shelter Good shelter.

Authorities Harbourmaster

Facilities

Water on the quay. Fuel can be arranged by the harbourmaster. Bozyazi village where some provisions can be found is about 2½km away and you will need a taxi to get there.

General

The new harbour is intended as a ferry port for a service from here to Kyrenia (Girne) in Northern Cyprus. It is also used as one of the stops in the Aegean Rally, which starts at Istanbul and finishes in Israel or Egypt. This is a convenient place from which to visit Mamure Castle and ancient Anaemurium.

SOFTA KALESI

Bozyazi Ada (Adaçik Ada), an island lying close offshore 9½ miles NE of Anamur Burnu, will be seen as you proceed along the coast. Between the island and Kizilliman Burnu (Kizil Burnu), there are several coves affording some shelter from the afternoon breeze. None of them is secure. In one of these, Cubbükonagi, a motel complex has been built. A castle on the slopes above, Softa Kalesi, is conspicuous. On the flat land along the coast there are numerous banana plantations.

KIZILLIMANI BURNU

On the E side of Kizillimani Burnu, there is a narrow inlet offering some shelter from the afternoon breeze. Squeeze into the inlet and anchor in 3–5 metres, with a line ashore. Care is needed, as the inlet is less than 100 metres wide inside. Just to the N of the inlet there is another, which could also be used with care. A few local fishing boats are sometimes moored here.

SOGUKSU LIMANI (Yenikaş)

Approach

The bay lies 11 miles ENE of Kizillimani Burnu. It is difficult to make out from the distance, but closer in numerous greenhouses and the houses of the hamlet will be seen. Care must be taken of the numerous reefs shown on the plan.

Mooring

Anchor on the E side of the headland in 5–7m, with a long line ashore. The bottom is sand and rock and good holding. Good shelter from the afternoon breeze once you are tucked under the headland. The bay is open to the S and E. In the event of NE winds a yacht can anchor on the E side of the bay. Care should be taken of the depths, as it has silted around the river mouth.

Facilities

Water from local sources. Limited provisions.

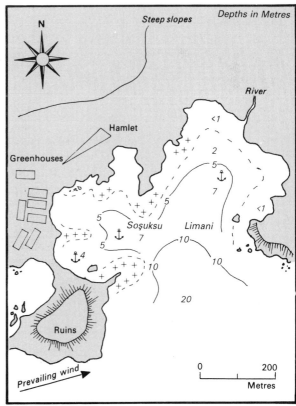

SOGUKSU LIMANI
36°08'N 33°17'·5E

Anchorage

Soğuksu Limani anchorage, on the W side of the river

General

The hamlet has recently been renamed Yenikaş, but most of the locals still refer to it as Soğuksu Limani, 'Cold Water Harbour', from the cold river water running into the E bay. It is most refreshing to swim here – a brief respite from the sweltering humidity that prevails along this coast.

AYDINCIK LIMANI (Glindere, ancient Celendris)

Approach

Aydincik lies 1¾ miles ENE of Soğuksu Limani. Büyükada, a wedge-shaped island lying one mile E of Aydincik, is easily identified. The buildings of the village and the harbour breakwater cannot be seen when approaching from the SW. Closer in, the harbour breakwater and the entrance are easily placed. A light (Fl.3s8M) is exhibited on the small headland forming part of the harbour, and a F.R (occas) is exhibited on the end of the breakwater.

Mooring

Go stern or bows-to the quay, or anchor in convenient depths on the W side of the harbour. The bottom is sand and mud, with some loose rocks in places. Good all-round shelter. The soldiers in the *Jandarma* post in the village may want to check your papers.

Note The overhead cable referred to in earlier reference works no longer exists.

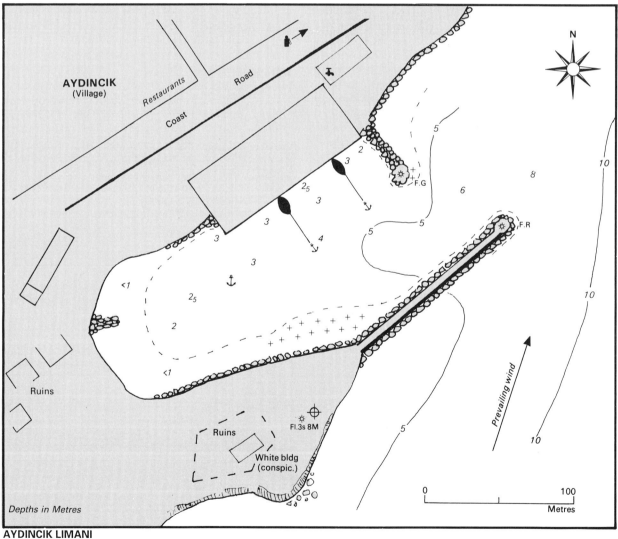

AYDINCIK LIMANI
(Fl.3s8M light) 36°08'·1N 33°20'·7E

Entrance to Aydincik harbour, looking SW

Aydincik harbour, looking NE

Facilities

Water From a tap near the harbour.
Fuel In the village.
Provisions Basic provisions can be found.
Eating out Several simple restaurants.
Other PO. Bank. Bus to Mersin.

General

Aydincik is a dusty, ramshackle little spot, but an enchanting one for all that. The locals are friendly, and most curious about visiting yachts. There are a few medieval ruins around the harbour on the W side.

SANCAK BURUN

The cape lying approximately 3 miles ESE of Aydincik. On the E side of the cape are several coves affording some shelter from the prevailing wind. The cove about 1 mile NE of the cape (Sipahili Limani) appears to afford the best shelter.

BESPARMAK ADALARI (Babadil Adalari, ancient **Grambusa**)

These two islands, separated by a narrow strait, lie close SW of Ada Burnu. On the W side of Ada Burnu there is a bay (Akkuyu), affording good shelter from easterlies, but open W. On the N side it is reported that there is a large commercial harbour under construction.

On the E side of the cape are two other coves which afford limited shelter from westerlies. The northernmost cove is reported to have a wreck (underwater – depth over it unknown) in the entrance.

OVACIK YARIMADASI (Ovacik Adasi, Kösrelik Adasi)

Ovacik Yarimadasi Burnu (Bölükada Burnu) is a bold promontory connected by an isthmus to the mainland. Ovacik Adasi (Kösrelik Adasi) and the anchorage lie on the W side of the promontory.

Approach

Ovacik Yarimadasi Burnu and Dana Adasi, to the NE of the anchorage, are easily identified.

Mooring

The best anchorage is on the S side of Ovacik island, off the beach. Anchor in 4–5m, on mud or sand. Care must be taken of the reef extending W and S from the W end of the island. Good shelter from the prevailing SW winds. Open to the E.

Facilities

A simple restaurant opens occasionally in the summer. Ovacik village lies some distance away, at the head of the bay on the W side of the cape. A mini-market and PO in the village. With the prevailing winds it is unsuitable to anchor off it.

General

In former times Ovacik Yarimadasi Burnu was known as Cape Cavalière, its bold outline being a conspicuous point for mariners to make landfall on. The cape is the last massive spur of the Taurus range jutting into the sea, and after Taşucu the coast becomes low-lying. Around the anchorage several

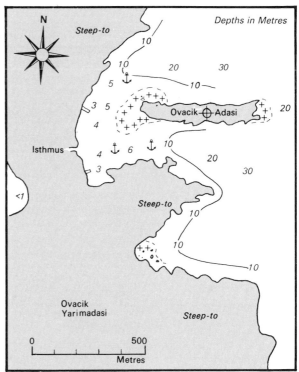

OVACIK ANCHORAGES
(Ovacik Adasi) 36°09'·7N 33°41'·7E

235

holiday villages are under construction but it remains a pleasant place to be.

DANA ADASI (ancient **Pityussa**)

A high steep-to island lying 5 miles ENE of Ovacik Yarimadasi Burnu. There are good depths in the channel between the island and the coast, but care must be taken of a rocky patch (awash) ½ a mile WSW of the SW of the island.

A light, Fl(2)10s10M, is shown from the NE end of the island, visible 131° to 022°, obscured over Ovacik Yarimadasi Burnu and Ovacik anchorage.

Taşucu Körfezi

This small gulf lies between the high land of the eastern extremity of the Taurus range and the low land of the Cilician Plain, with Incekum Burnu forming the eastern side of the gulf. Shoal water extends for some distance S of Incekum Burnu, and one mile S of the cape there is a shoal with less than 2m depth. A large shoal patch lies 2½ miles SSW of the cape, with least depths of 7·6m (25ft) reported over it. A current is reported to set across the cape to the SW, and to cause overfalls in places. The prevailing summer wind curves up into the gulf to blow from the S. In the autumn, fierce gusts have been reported to blow off the Taurus mountains from the N–W. Gusts of Force 8–9 have been recorded over several hours.

Note The shoal water off Incekum Burnu is reported to extend further to seaward than charted. A yacht should give the cape and the shoal water a good offing.

AGALIMANI (Bağsak)

BA 242

Approach

This large bay lies on the W side of Taşucu Körfezi. From the SW Dana Adasi is easily identified, and from closer in Bağsakada, the island off the southern entrance point to the bay, can be identified. On the N side of the bay the walls of the castle are prominent. A light is exhibited on the N entrance point: Fl.3s5M.

Mooring

Once into the bay, the hotel and camping ground in the SW corner will be seen. Anchor off here, or further SE, in 4–6m. The bottom is sand and weed. Good shelter from the prevailing southerlies. In the autumn it might be prudent to anchor on the NW side of the bay, on account of the gusts off the Taurus range mentioned earlier.

Facilities

Meagre provisions and several restaurants in Bağsak.

General

Bağsak is dramatically sited under the steep pine-covered slopes of the Taurus mountains, at the foot of the Cilician Plain. A small tourist resort is growing up around the hamlet, and a few boats are kept here in the summer.

Bağsakada is also known as Provençal Isle. In the 13th century the Provençal Order of the Knights of St John was given Bağsakada and up until Beaufort's time it was known as Provençal Isle. There are numerous ruins on the islet dating from the time it was occupied by the order.

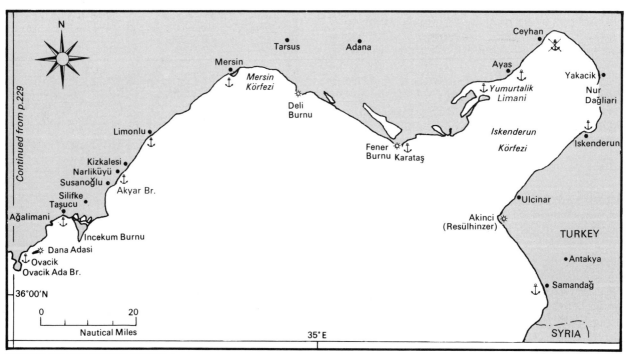

OVACIK TO THE SYRIAN BORDER

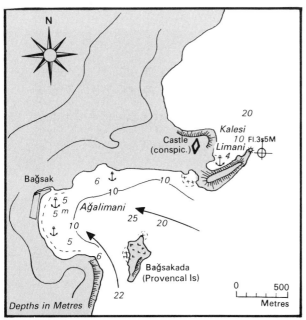

AGALIMANI
Kalesi Limani light 36°16'·5N 33°50'·5E

Ağalimani looking ENE

KALESI LIMANI (Ağalar Limani)

Good shelter from the prevailing summer southerlies can be found in this attractive cove. Anchor in 4m, on a sand and rock bottom, about halfway into the cove. A rough breakwater for local boats juts out from the W side.

The castle a short distance away was built by the Armenian kings in the 12th century, and survived as a crusader castle until the 16th century, when the Ottomans captured it. It is in fair condition, and well worth wandering around.

Anchorage   *Castle*

Approach to Kalesi Limani, looking S

TASUCU
BA 242

Approach

The new ferry harbour and the commercial harbour lie at the head of Taşucu Körfezi.

Conspicuous The large paper mill, particularly its high chimney, is conspicuous. The new high-rise buildings around the port and the harbour break-waters can be seen from some distance off. A yacht should make for the ferry harbour, not the commercial harbour to the E of the town.

By night Use the light on Incekum Burnu (Fl.10s 9M) and that at Ağalimani (Fl.3s5M). The entrance to the commercial harbour is lit: Fl.G.3s5M and Fl.R.3s5M. The entrance to the ferry harbour is lit: F.R.6M and F.G.6M.

Note The light structure on Incekum Burnu is reported to show up well on radar, and to appear as a ship, on account of the low-lying land around it.

Mooring

Go stern-to or alongside the quay on the W side of the harbour. The bottom is mud and good holding. The harbour is now reported to be very busy with ferries and local boats and it can be difficult to find a berth. Alternatives are to anchor off under the mole at the E end of the harbour or go to the commercial harbour. The trouble with the latter is that it is a fair distance from town and its facilities.

Shelter Good all-round shelter.

Authorities A port of entry. The authorities are all housed close to the harbour. The tourist office nearby is helpful.

Facilities

Water On the quay.
Fuel In the town.
Repairs Limited mechanical repairs can be carried out in Silifke. For major work you will have to go to Mersin.

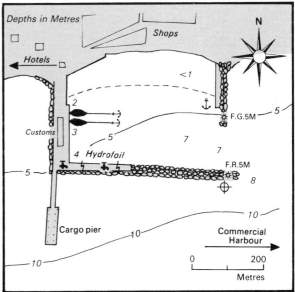

TASUCU FERRY PORT
36°18'·9N 33°52'·9E

Commercial harbour   Yachts   Cargo pier

Taşucu

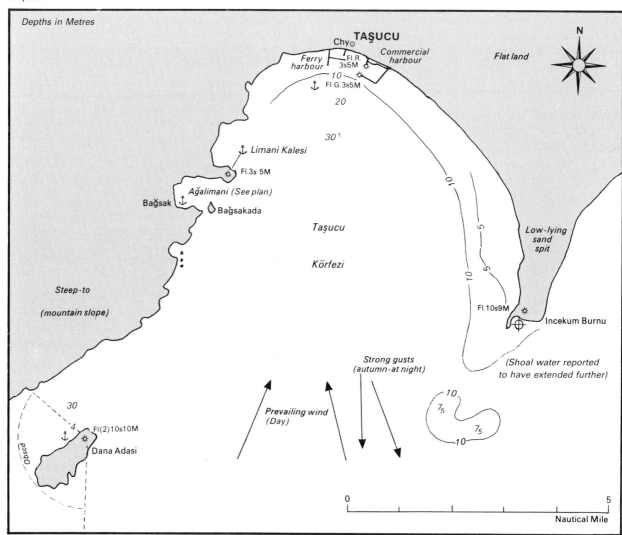

TASUCU KORFEZI
Incekum Br light 36°15'·8N 33°57'·5E

Provisions Most provisions can be found in the shops by the harbour. Good shopping in Silifke.

Eating out Numerous restaurants around the waterfront.

Other PO. Bank. Regular buses to Silifke, about 10 minutes away. Ferry and hydrofoil to Kyrenia (Girne) in Northern Cyprus.

General

Until quite recently there was only the cargo pier. The ferry harbour has been constructed to provide a link between Northern Cyprus and mainland Turkey. The new large commercial harbour nearby serves the recently constructed paper mill and the town of Silifke.

Taşucu is an undistinguished place, but the town of Silifke nearby is a bustling market town with a definite Arabic flavour to it. The castle on a rocky bluff behind Silifke, originally built in Byzantine times, is most impressive, although not in very good condition.

238

Taşucu to Mersin

Between Taşucu and Mersin there are many fine sandy beaches, to which Turkish holiday-makers are attracted in large numbers. From Susanoğlu to Mersin there is literally a solid line of camping sites, hotels and holiday villages. Behind the beaches, multicoloured tents are often five or six deep. A number of state corporations, including the Turkish post and telegraph service and several of the large banks, have gargantuan holiday villages on the coast for staff holidays.

Much of the development has occurred in recent years, and the traveller armed with a guide book written ten or so years ago may be disappointed to find a large resort where formerly there was a deserted beach.

Susanoğlu to Kizkalesi

SUSANOGLU

An open bay that the day breeze sends a swell into, making it unsuitable for anything but a temporary anchorage in the morning.

AKYAR BURUN ANCHORAGES

Akyar Burun is a fairly nondescript cape, just under 2 miles NE of Susanoğlu. There are several coves which can be used on the E side of the cape.

1. **Akyar Bükü** A bay on the tip of the cape. Anchor in the cove on the S side, with a line ashore. Good protection from the prevailing SW winds.

2. **Narlıküyü** A cove immediately N of Akyar Burnu. Anchor in 3–5m where the inlet hooks around to the W. The bottom is sand. Several restaurants ashore.

Note It is reported that the NW cove now has a breakwater at the entrance providing protection from the prevailing wind. It is possible to go on the N side with a long line ashore. The concrete steps are reserved for the holiday camp behind. Restaurants ashore.

At Narlıküyü there is a well preserved Roman mosaic representing the three graces, the daughters of Eurynome and Zeus. The spring over which the Roman bath-house was built is claimed to be the site of the legendary Fountain of Knowledge described by Strabo. Modern Turkish nomenclature is more preoccupied with the three beautiful females depicted in the mosaic, as the place is known locally as Kizlar Hamami, the Bath of the Maidens.

3. **Akisu Köyü** A narrow inlet immediately N of Narlıküyü. The prevailing wind tends to send some swell in here.

4. **Akkum Limani** A cove just E of Akisu. The least sheltered from the prevailing wind of the anchorages.

KIZKALESI

Four miles NE of Susanoğlu, the twin castles of Kizkalesi can be seen from a considerable distance off. There is no protected anchorage here but, before the afternoon breeze gets up, a yacht can anchor on the N side of the castle on the small islet. Anchor in 5–6m, on a sand and rock bottom. When the afternoon breeze picks up it sends a short swell in here, making the anchorage untenable. A resort has grown up along the beach.

The Armenian castles originally protected the town of Corycius, on the shore between them. The castle on the islet is in good repair and makes a fine

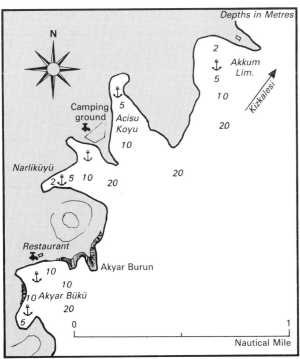

AKYAR BURUN ANCHORAGES
36°25'·1N 34°05'·6E

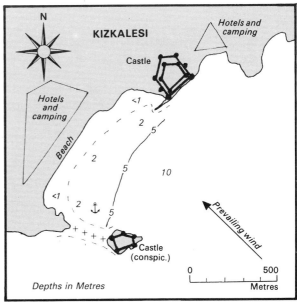

KIZKALESI
36°27'N 34°11'E

sight from seaward, appearing to hover on the water. Kizkalesi means 'the Maidens' Castle', and R P Lister makes some amusing observations on the Turkish naming of these Armenian and Byzantine castles:

'Along the coast there are many castles, which tend to be called Kiz Kalesi, the Fortress of Girls, like other castles in Turkey. The Turks, puritan Moslems, had a great idea of the wickedness of the Byzantines, and considered that their principal object in building castles was to stuff them full of girls and indulge in limitless vice. They were encouraged in this belief when, on sacking a castle, they found statues and pictures of women in it, which, of course, they usually did; though the women would be very stiff, Byzantine and saintly to any but an inflamed Moslem taste. On viewing these, they sucked in their breaths and hacked the idolatrous representations into shards and fragments, with righteous indignation and a touch of envy.'

R P Lister *Turkey Observed*

Between Kizkalesi and Mersin there are numerous ruins of the ancient cities which once dotted this coastline. Of these, Ayas (built on the site of ancient Elaeusa) and Soli (later Pompeiopulis, now Viranşehir) were the largest and most important. Some of the ruins of these ancient cities are prominent from seaward, especially the aqueduct at Ayas.

LIMONLU (Limini)

A small artificial harbour lying 11 miles NE of Susanoğlu. The breakwaters are easily identified when following the coast between Susanoğlu and Mersin. Care needs to be taken at the entrance, as it is prone to silting. Inside there are good depths. Go stern or bows-to where convenient.

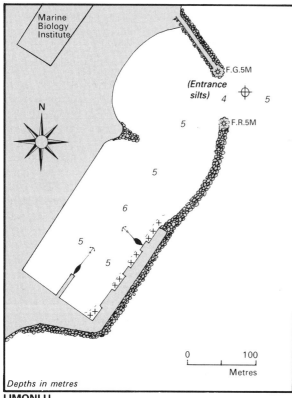

LIMONLU
36°33'·9N 34°15'·4E

The harbour is used by the Marine Biology Institute on the shore, and a *gendarmerie* post controls the harbour. Yachts are welcome to use the harbour although the authorities may want to look at your Transit Log.

MERSIN

BA 2187

Approach

The city of Mersin and the large commercial port can be seen from some distance off. High-rise apartment blocks extend some distance along the coast from Mersin.

Conspicuous There are usually a large number of ships anchored in the roadstead S of the harbour. The grain silo in the harbour and cranes and derricks within are conspicuous. The harbour breakwaters can be identified from some distance off.

By night The light on the coast immediately S of the harbour has a good range: Fl(3)10s15M. Closer in, use the lights on the buoys marking the deep-water channel (Fl(2)R, Fl(2)G) and the lights at the harbour entrance (Fl.R.3s9M and Fl.G.3s9M). The light on the crook of the S breakwater (DirFl.WR.5s 5M) is directional for the deep-water channel within the harbour.

Note There are numerous lit and unlit buoys inside the harbour. By day these present no problems, but care should be taken at night. A number of lit buoys, close to the eastern breakwater, mark the deep-water channel for large tankers.

Mooring

Caution A 1 metre shoal patch has been reported approximately 50m off the SW corner in line with the entrance to the basin. Yachts should go around

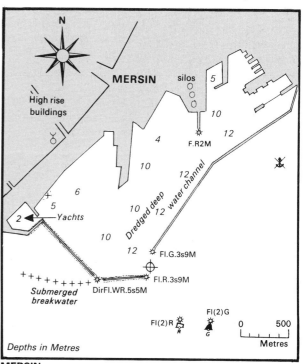

MERSIN
36°47'·1N 34°38'·5E

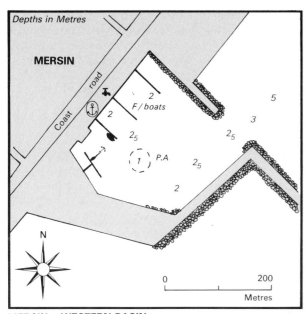

MERSIN – WESTERN BASIN

the N side where there are 2m depths reported.

Go stern or bows-to, or alongside, in the basin at the western end of the harbour. There is usually space on the pier shown in the plan.

Shelter Good all-round shelter. A few yachts have wintered afloat here.

Authorities A port of entry. The relevant authorities are within the harbour, but are unused to dealing with yachts.

Note The yacht berths are right on a sewerage outlet and it can get very smelly.

Facilities

Water On the quay.
Fuel In the town.
Repairs Engineering, mechanical and electrical repairs can be carried out in the town. Specialist yacht repair facilities are not available.
Provisions Good shopping for all provisions in the centre of town, about 15 minutes' walk away. Fresh fruit and vegetables are especially good.
Eating out Restaurants of all categories in town.
Other PO. Banks. Hospital. Turkish gas. Internal flights from Adana. Ferries to Northern Cyprus. Buses to most destinations.

Mersin bazaar

General

In recent years Mersin has expanded greatly, and this shows on the outskirts of the city, where large numbers of apartment blocks have been hurriedly thrown up. The town centre is a fascinating warren of alleys about the central bazaar; a noisy, colourful collection of stalls and barrows selling everything from watermelons to sunglasses. The surrounding area has a reputation for fine horses, and certainly in Mersin many of the horses hauling carts are not the work-weary nags one so often sees.

Mersin is a site of some antiquity, dating from Hittite times, but virtually nothing ancient remains, and the present city is a thoroughly modern one. It is a convenient place to visit Tarsus from – about ½ an hour away by bus. Tarsus has had most of the conquerors of this region trample through it, from Sennacherib, the Assyrian who 'came down like a wolf on the fold', to Sultan Selim the Grim, whose name speaks for itself. In former times Tarsus was accessible by sea along a canal, and it was up here that Cleopatra sailed for her first meeting with Mark Antony in 41 BC. It was also the birthplace of that extraordinary proselytiser for the early Christian church, St Paul the Apostle.

Note Approximately 3 miles SW of Mersin harbour it is reported work has started on a new yacht harbour. Progress is reported to be slow.

KARADUVAR

A small boat harbour for the refinery just E of Mersin. It is not for yachts, and unless you like the aroma of cracked hydrocarbons it is not even a pleasant place to be.

Iskenderun Körfezi

(ancient **Sinus Issicus**)

This gulf is entered between Fener Burnu and Akinci (Resülhinzir), 25 miles to the SE. Fener Burnu lies some 37 miles SE of Mersin, and along this stretch of low-lying coast there are no good harbours or sheltered anchorages. The two capes are lit: Fener Burnu (Fl.10s20M) and Akinci (Fl(2)5s22M).

The gulf extends almost 40 miles to the NE. It is bordered by a narrow coastal plain, behind which stands high ground. At the northeastern end, the steep-to and craggy Nur Daglari mountain range dominates the gulf. The highest peak, Migir Tepesi, reaches a height of 2,223m (7,295ft).

At the head of the gulf there are several oil-loading terminals. The BOTAS oil terminal, at Ceyhan Limani in the NW corner, is the shipment point for oil brought some 600 miles across country from Iraq. Another oil terminal for Iraqi oil is to be built in the gulf. Pleasure craft are forbidden to enter these areas.

For all intents and purposes there are two places a yacht will make for in the gulf: Yumurtalik Limani/Ayas and Iskenderun.

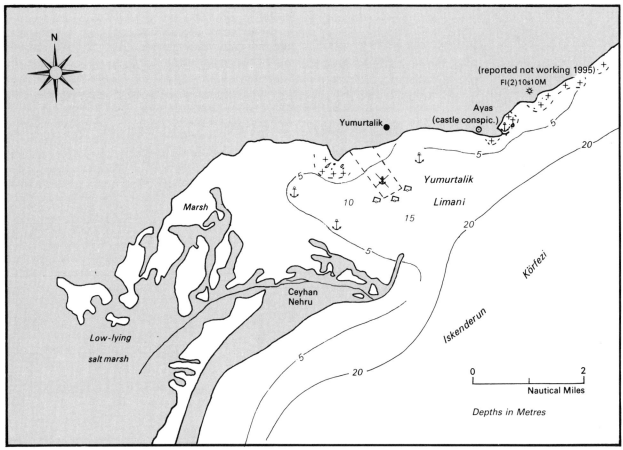

YUMURTALIK LIMANI
KARATAS (36°33'·5N 35°23'·2E)

A small harbour off the hamlet on the eastern side of Fener Burnu. Approach the harbour from an easterly direction, as above-water rocks and shoal water obstruct the approach from the S. There are mostly 2-metre depths inside. Berth alongside the quay on the eastern side. Restaurant and some provisions available in the village.

YUMURTALIK LIMANI

A large estuary formed by the Ceyhan Nehri. The upper reaches are shallow.

Approach

The castle at Ayas is conspicuous. A number of unlit mooring buoys lie at the S end of the prohibited area shown on the plan. The coastline on the SW side of the estuary at the mouth of the Ceyhan river is constantly changing. A yacht should keep well off this area of shifting shoals.

Note The light structure on the S entrance point is reported to be derelict (1995).

Mooring

Anchor on the N side of the estuary, clear of the prohibited area. Alternatively, proceed further into the estuary and anchor in convenient depths. Although an open anchorage, it is reported to be satisfactory in the summer months.

General

The estuary is home for a large number of water birds. Marine life is also said to be prolific, including large numbers of turtles.

AYAS (Kale)

Approach

The buildings of the village are easily identified. A minaret is conspicuous, and there are several large multistorey buildings in the vicinity. From closer in, the breakwater and the islet, with a small fort on it, will be seen. Make the approach from an easterly direction.

Dangers

1. Care is needed of the remains of the old mole, N of the entrance.
2. Care is needed of a sandbank that has built up on the inside of the breakwater.

Note The light N of Ayas (Fl(2)10s10M) was reported to be not working 1995.

Mooring

Anchor in 3–4 metres in the NW of the harbour. The quay is usually crowded with fishing boats, but you may find a space to go alongside.

Shelter Reasonable shelter from the prevailing S winds.

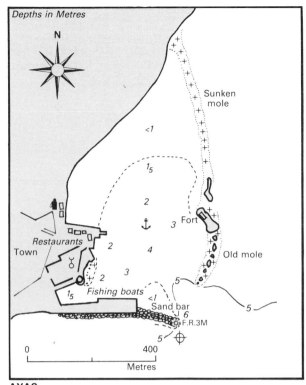

AYAS
36°46'·2N 35°47'·8E

Facilities

Water on the quay. Fuel in the village. Some provisions available. Restaurants in the village, often with fresh fish.

General

The harbour, with its castle, was built by the Genoese, and served as the principal sea outlet for goods brought across land by caravan. It was captured by the Mamelukes in the 14th century. Here at Ayas Captain Beaufort was shot and badly wounded by Turkish guards while surveying the harbour.

CEYHAN LIMANI

BA 2185
This is the oil terminal for the pipeline from Iraq. It is more commonly known as the BOTAS terminal, from the name of the operating company. It is prohibited for pleasure craft to navigate in the vicinity of the pier and shore installation.

TOROS

The Toros fertiliser pier lies 3 miles NE of the BOTAS terminal. The harbour facilities are not for pleasure craft.

YAKACIK

The old Genoese port in the NE corner of the gulf. In calm weather you can anchor off the ruined fortress and town, but it is not a sheltered anchorage.

ISKENDERUN

BA 2187
Approach

This large commercial harbour lies tucked into a bay on the eastern side of the gulf. The light structure on the SW side of the bay is conspicuous. Closer in, the harbour breakwaters will be seen.

Note Numerous oil-loading berths are located off the coast near to the harbour, extending as much as half a mile offshore. The loading point is generally indicated by a buoy or group of buoys, which should be given a good berth.

Mooring

Once into the harbour, go stern or bows-to or alongside in the inner basin. In the summer the harbour affords good protection from the prevailing winds.

Facilities

Water On the quay.
Fuel In the town.
Repairs General mechanical and engineering repairs.
Provisions Good shopping in the town.
Eating out Numerous restaurants. Iskenderun *döner* kebab is known all over Turkey.
Other PO. Turkish gas. Buses to Mersin. Internal flights from Adana.

General

Iskenderun was until quite recently known as Alexandretta, named in honour of Alexander the

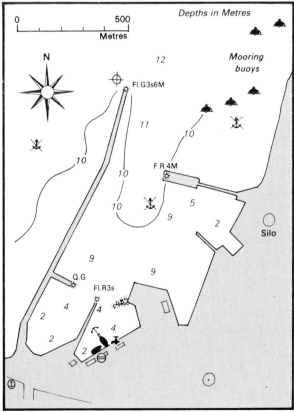

ISKENDERUN
36°36'·3N 36°11'·1E

Great after he defeated the Persians on the Plain of Issus, at the head of the gulf. Iskender is Alexander rendered into Turkish. This part of Turkey, the Hatay, was only annexed to Turkey in 1939. Formerly it was the Sançak of Alexandretta, administered by the French. In the summer Iskenderun is exceedingly hot and humid – the locals are said to migrate to the cooler mountains until the autumn.

Note The Admiralty pilot mentions the following local weather lore: Northerly gales are said to be preceded by the appearance of fleecy clouds over the Plain of Issus at the head of the gulf. The disappearance of the clouds indicates that the gale will abate.

Strong E gales, known locally as *raghieh*, occur in the winter. Ragged clouds over the nearby mountains are said to indicate the approach of these local gales. A katabatic wind, which can blow with great force (Force 10–12 has been recorded), comes from Yarik Kaya, a chasm 3 miles SE of Iskenderun. It mostly blows in the winter, and is known locally as *Yarik Kaya*, from the name of the chasm.

ULCINAR (Arsuz, ancient **Rhossus**)

A tourist resort 20 miles SW of Iskenderun. This is an open anchorage only, and not to be recommended. A short pier is used by the patrol boat, and it is prohibited to anchor in its lee.

SAMANDAG (ancient **Seleucia**)

Today this ancient port for Antioch has totally silted, and there is only an open anchorage. It is best visited by land from Iskenderun. Recent reports indicate that the harbour has been rebuilt.

HEADING SOUTH

Yachts heading for Syria, Lebanon and Israel should consult the Imray *Mediterranean Almanac* for data and harbour plans.

Hermes. *Tim Tulgar*

VII. Cyprus

Cyprus is the third-largest island in the Mediterranean, with about 400 miles of coastline. Despite its size, it has few indentations and no safe natural anchorages. All of the harbours affording all-round shelter are man-made. The island has two mountain ranges: the Kyrenia and Karpas mountains, running approximately W to E along the N coast, and the Troodos mountains in the W, with Mount Olympus rising to 1951m (6403ft).

In 1975 Cyprus was partitioned into the Turkish federated State of Cyprus in the N and the Republic of Cyprus in the S, after the occupation of the north by the Turks in 1974. The N side contains the Turkish and the S the Greek-speaking nationals (see plan). A United Nations peace-keeping force observes the border between northern and southern Cyprus. The partition of Cyprus has brought with it a set of regulations concerning navigation around the island, and landing is prohibited in certain areas. These are outlined here, but the yachtsman should keep an eye open for changes.

This chapter also covers the Greek island of Kastellórizon.

CYPRUS

Regulations

Passages

A yacht may cross from Turkey to Turkish Cyprus (or from Turkey to Greek Cyprus), and from Turkish Cyprus to Turkey, but may not cross from Turkish Cyprus to Greek Cyprus. A passage from Greek Cyprus to Turkish Cyprus is inadvisable. Please note the correspondence below from the Cyprus High Commission.

A Turkish Cypriot stamp in your passport can mean that you will not be allowed into Greece. Generally the immigration authorities in Turkish Cyprus will not stamp your passport, but will hold on to it and issue you with a landing card while you are in the country.

Note

The Cyprus High Commission has informed me of the following, and I quote verbatim from the relevant parts of their correspondence:

'The fact that part of the territory of the Republic of Cyprus is under Turkish occupation does not in any way deprive the legitimate government of the Republic of Cyprus of its legitimate rights or its rights to exercise control over the whole of its territory.

As for the ports of Famagusta, Kyrenia and Karavostasi, these are at present closed to all international shipping since October 1974 because they are situated in the areas of the Republic of Cyprus still illegally occupied by Turkey. Any ship calling at the aforementioned ports is contravening International Conventions of Safety and Laws of the Republic of Cyprus and consequently the master/ crews or owner render themselves liable to prosecution under Cyprus laws.

In view of the above mentioned facts the government of Cyprus would appreciate a correction of your above mentioned publication so that any reader and/or yachtsman may not be left in any doubt about the true situation in Cyprus and also avoid involving themselves in maritime risks which may render them liable to prosecution.'

(1990)

'One of the many tragic facets of the Turkish occupation of Cyprus and an integral part of Turkish policy to transform the character, culture and history of this area, is the changing of place names. The true names of towns and villages which date back to antiquity, have been standardised by the sole recognised competent authority in the Republic and have been submitted and approved by the Fifth United National Conference on the Standardization of Geographical Names (1987). Any arbitrary change of these names is consequently, illegal and against widely accepted principles of international law.

It is important to note again that the Government of the Republic of Cyprus, which is the only recognised authority in the country, has declared all parts in the occupied areas as inoperative and closed to passengers and trade since 1974. Entry into Cyprus from such ports is, therefore, unauthorised and, consequently, illegal. The fact that part of the territory of Cyprus is under Turkish occupation, in no way affects the application of this decision nor does it deprive the Government of its legitimate rights to exercise control over the entirety of its sovereign territory.

By presenting Cyprus in this manner, therefore, your publication appears to be condoning and supporting the illegalities which are taking place in the occupied part of the island, despite the fact that they have been widely and repeatedly condemned by the international community. By so doing, your publication seems to be introducing a political element in an otherwise non-political domain.'

(September 1992)

I would like to point out briefly in this context that I have refrained from making any political comment on Cyprus, and that plans for Northern Cyprus are included because small boats in difficulty at sea need this information. To my knowledge, no hydrographic department in any part of the world has been asked to withhold information on Northern Cyprus. I do not want to be drawn into an argument on the rights and wrongs of the tragic dilemma of Cyprus, and I emphatically do not want to introduce politics into this book. I go sailing to get away from all that. The information in this section is included solely as information essential to safety at sea.

PROHIBITED AREAS

Northern Cyprus The extent of the following prohibited areas means in effect that only Kyrenia (Girne) and Famagusta (Gazi Magusa) are available to yachts.

1. From the vicinity of Famagusta (Gazi Magusa) to the border, except for the port itself.
2. The eastern coast of the island, from Famagusta (Gazi Magusa) to Klidhes Island (Kilit Adalar).
3. From Klidhes Island to 12 miles E of Kyrenia (Girne).
4. From a point 4 miles E of Kyrenia (Girne) to a point 8 miles E of Kyrenia (Girne).
5. In the vicinity of Glykotissa or Snake Island (1·5m W of Kyrenia).
6. From Ak Kormakiti (Koruçam Burnu) to approximately Ak Kokkino (Erenköy).

Southern Cyprus Although you can anchor off in the vicinity of the British bases at Akrotiri and Dhekelia, authorisation should be obtained before you venture ashore. This can often be obtained 'on the spot'.

General information

Water

Cyprus suffers from a water shortage which can be chronic in the summer. The public water supply is turned on for only three days of the week in some ports in southern Cyprus.

Repairs

Most yachts go to Larnaca for hauling out and repair work. The yard here has recently been extended, but is nonetheless crowded in the winter. Enquire in advance for a place. Most spares can be obtained or ordered in Larnaca, and repair work can be carried out to a good standard.

Food and wine

Many large yachts go to southern Cyprus to stock up on provisions, there being a good range of English brands of packaged food. Here you can get your *Marmite*, *Branston* pickle, *Colman's* mustard, *Heinz* baked beans, Earl Grey tea, after-dinner mints, or whatever is your own particular indulgence. The locally produced wine is both palatable and reasonably priced. For whites try *Arsenoe* or *Keo* hock; for reds, try *Othello*. The local beer, *Keo* or *Carlsberg*, is quite palatable, but not cheap. The local brandy is interesting and not expensive.

Useful books

Bitter Lemons Lawrence Durrell. Faber. Written before partition, but deals sensitively with the Cypriot problem.
Journey into Cyprus Colin Thubron. Penguin. Usual penetrating and wonderfully written book.
Blue Guide to Cyprus A & C Black.
The Traveller's Guide to Cyprus Jonathan Cape.

Weather patterns

Winds

The prevailing summer wind is a westerly which gets up at about midday, blows between Force 3–6 (it is strongest in July and August), and usually dies down at sunset. In the late evening to mid-morning there will often be a NE wind around Force 2–4. Away from the coast the wind is between W–WSW, but closer in it tends to follow the contours of the coast, so that at Larnaca it blows from the SSW and even curls around into the bay from the S and SE. Yachts going W usually leave at night, when there is little or no wind, and motor as far as possible until the wind gets up in the morning. From Larnaca, a yacht will leave at night for Limassol or Paphos, departing from there for Greece or Turkey.

The winds in the winter are divided almost equally between W and E on both the N and S coasts. Gales are frequently from the S or E in the winter (see the Coptic calendar in the Introduction). Gales are rare in the summer.

Weather forecasts

A weather forecast is transmitted on Armed Forces Radio, on 1439kHz (208m) and 1421kHz (211m), after the news broadcasts at 0600, 0700, 0800, 1300, 2000 and 2200. It is not a maritime forecast, and is generally of little use. A weather forecast can be obtained at Larnaca Marina.

Fog

Sea fog often occurs along the S coast in the summer. It appears in the early morning and has usually dispersed by midday. In the early morning, visibility can be less than a quarter of a mile, but is generally more. The sea fog does not extend out to sea and generally extends no more than one mile off the coast. It is most dense around Limassol (in Akrotiri Bay), in Larnaca (in Larnaca Bay), and in Famagusta. It seldom occurs on the N coast.

Tides

The tidal range in Cyprus is small, being 0·24–0·39m (0·8–1·3ft).

Currents

In the summer, currents seldom exceed one knot. Off the N coast the prevailing westerlies induce an E-going current of 0·5–1 knot. Off the S coast there may be an E-going current of 0·5–0·8 knots.

Climate (at Kyrenia)

	Av max °C	Av min °C	Highest recorded	Relative humidity	Days 1mm rain	Sea temp °C
Jan	16	9	24	70%	13	15
Feb	17	9	31	67%	10	16
Mar	19	10	27	67%	7	16
Apr	22	12	31	68%	4	17
May	26	16	36	68%	2	19
Jun	30	20	41	65%	0	21
Jul	33	22	41	62%	0	25
Aug	33	23	42	60%	0	27
Sep	31	21	39	60%	1	26
Oct	27	17	36	62%	3	24
Nov	23	14	32	66%	7	22
Dec	18	11	24	69%	11	19

Temperatures

The mean coastal temperatures for Cyprus are around 19–20°C. In the winter, mean daily temperatures are around 13–14°C, with maximum temperatures around 16–17°, making it a popular place to winter. In the summer, temperatures sometimes reach 38–40°.

Data

PORTS OF ENTRY

Northern Cyprus
Kyrenia (Girne)
Southern Cyprus
Paphos
Limassol
Larnaca

MAJOR LIGHTS

Famagusta Harbour Fl(2)20s16M 150°-vis-290°
Famagusta (NW of town) Fl.WR.17s15/11M 178°-W-216°-R-313°
Ak Eloea Fl.10s15M
Klidhes I Q(4)20s14M
Kyrenia (Girne) Fl(3)20s15M
Ak Kormakiti Fl(2)20s15M
Karavostasi Fl.R.3s7M
Ak Paphos Fl.15s17M 277°-vis-141°
Ak Gata Fl.5s15M vis 189°-130°
Limassol Harbour Q(6)R.10s8M
Ak Kiti Fl(3)15s13M
Ak Greco Fl.15s12M

AEROBEACONS

Larnaca (34°49'·27N 33°33'·28E) *LCA* 432kHz 150M
Paphas (34°43'·10N 32°28'·77E) *PHA* 328kHz 100M

Quick reference guide

	Shelter	Mooring	Fuel	Water	Provisions	Eating out	Plan	Charge band
Northern Cyprus								
Kyrenia (Girne)	A	A	B	A	B	B	•	2
Famagusta (Gazi Magusa)	A	ABC	B	B	C	C	•	
Southern Cyprus								
Latsi	C	AC	O	B	O	C		
Loutra Afroditis	C	C	O	O	O	O		
Fontana Amorosa	C	C	O	O	O	O		
Ak Lara	C	C	O	O	O	C		
Paphos	B	AC	B	B	A	A	•	
Pissouri	C	C	O	B	O	C	•	
Limassol Commercial Harbour	B	BC	B	B	O	C	•	
Limassol Fishing Harbour	B	AB	B	A	B	B	•	
Limassol Marina	A	A	A	A	C	C	•	2/3
Larnaca Marina	A	A	A	A	A	A	•	2
Ayia Napa	C	C	O	B	C	C		
Ak Greco	C	C	O	O	O	O		
Panayia	C	C	O	O	O	C		
Figtree Bay	B	C	O	O	O	C		

Northern Cyprus

KYRENIA (Girne)

BA 849

Approach

Conspicuous The buildings of the town and particularly the Crusader castle behind the harbour are conspicuous. The long breakwater of the commercial harbour, immediately E, is conspicuous. You will not see the entrance to the old harbour until you are right upon it.

By night Use the main light Fl(3)20s15M. The entrance to Kyrenia old harbour is lit Q(6)+LFl.R.15s4M. The entrance to the commercial harbour is lit Q.G.4M/ Fl.R.3s4M.

VHF Ch 16.

Dangers Care is needed at the entrance to the old harbour, where silting appears to be taking place. Shoal water appears to be building up off the old breakwater.

Mooring

The inner harbour is very small, but a space will be found for you. Go stern or bows-to the quay on the W side of the basin. There are buoys for your lines, or use your anchor. The bottom is mud and good holding.

Shelter Good all-round shelter.

Authorities A port of entry. The authorities will come down to your yacht. Charge band 2.

Facilities

Water On the quay.
Fuel In the town.
Electricity Can be connected.
Repairs Mechanical and light engineering repairs. Specialist yacht repairs cannot be made here, and yacht equipment is not available.
Provisions Good shopping for provisions close by. Ice available.
Eating out Restaurants close by the harbour.
Other PO. Banks. Local gas. Buses to most destinations. Ferries to Taşucu and Mersin.

General

Kyrenia (in Turkish, Girne) is one of the most attractive places in Cyprus. The harbour is hemmed in by the buildings of the town and the steep walls of the castle. In the hills above Kyrenia, the Gothic ruins of the Abbey of Bellapais are intact enough for one to visualise just how beautiful it must once have been, and the views over the coast from the abbey are stunning.

In the castle you can see the Kyrenia ship, a Greek merchant ship of the 4th century BC, recovered from the sea nearby. Part of the original hull has been recovered and reconstructed by a team from the University of Pennsylvania. It was built plank upon plank, of pine upon pine frames, copper fastened, and sheathed underwater with lead sheet. A

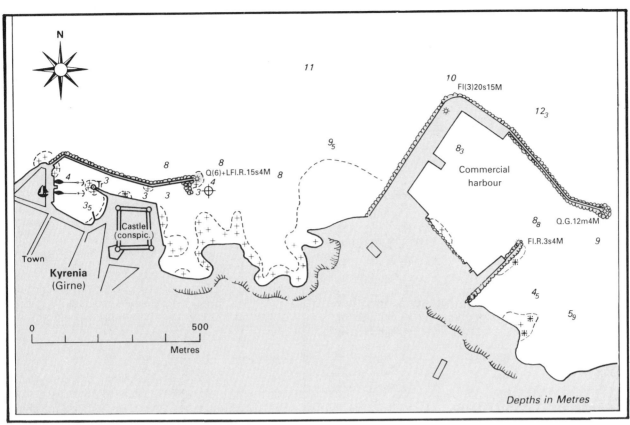

KYRENIA (Girne)
35°20'·3N 33°19'·4E

Kyrenia (Girne)

considerable quantity of cargo, including almonds, was also recovered.

    Harbourmaster ☎ (90) (392) 815 4988
    Marina ☎ (90) (392) 815 3587

FAMAGUSTA (Gazi Magusa, ancient Ammochostus)

BA 848

Approach

An area of shoal water extends some distance NW, parallel to the coast, in the approaches. A deep-water channel exists for large ships, but most yachts can cut across it as shown on the plan.

Conspicuous The high-rise buildings to the S of the harbour are conspicuous. The beacon, which when in line with the lighthouse shows the deep-water channel, is easily identified and a minaret in the old walled city is conspicuous.

By night Use the two main lights: SE Bastion Fl(2)20s16M and NW of town Fl.WR.7s15/11M (178°-W-216°-R-313°). The outer entrance is lit

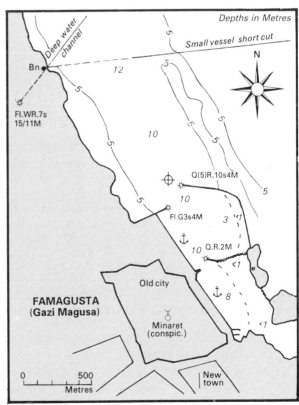

FAMAGUSTA
35°08'·1N 33°56'·6E

Q(5)R.10s4M/Fl.G.3s4M. Old mole Q.R.2M.
VHF Ch 16.

Mooring

Go alongside where convenient, or anchor off. The harbour is little visited at present.
Authorities The army is much in evidence.

Facilities

Water Near the quay.
Fuel In the town.
Repairs Limited mechanical repairs.
Provisions In the town.
Eating out Restaurants in the town.
Other PO. Banks. Local gas. Buses to most destinations in the north of the island.

General

Since 1974, this once bustling harbour and city has become a ghost town. Only about 20–30 per cent of the buildings are lived in, and only a few ships visit the harbour, where once it was difficult to find a berth.

Southern Cyprus

LATSI

A miniature harbour in Kolpos Khrisokhou. It is shallow, with depths of one metre or less for the most part. A small yacht can go stern-to, with a long line to the breakwater, just inside the entrance, where there are 2–3 metre depths. Several tavernas ashore.

LOUTRA AFRODITIS

A bight in the coast, approximately 2½ miles WNW of Latsi. The anchorage is partially sheltered by an islet on the NW side of the anchorage. There is a hotel just NW of the anchorage. Mediocre shelter.

FONTANA AMOROSA

A bay about 3 miles NW of Loutra Afroditis and about 1½ miles SE of Ak Akamas, the NW tip of Cyprus. The bay is within the limits of a firing range, but you will be advised if it is to be used. The bay has a reef and shoal water running out from the coast near the N end. The best anchorage is tucked under the headland to the N of the reef and shoal water. Alternatively, anchor S of the reef and shoal water. There is an islet connected by a reef to the coast off the S end of the anchorage. Reasonable shelter from the prevailing wind, but open entirely N and E.

AK AKAMAS (Cape Arnauti)

The NW tip of Cyprus. Off the cape is an islet, Nisis Mazaki, fringed by a reef and shoal water. There is a shallow passage between the islet and the cape, but the prudent course is to keep well to seaward.

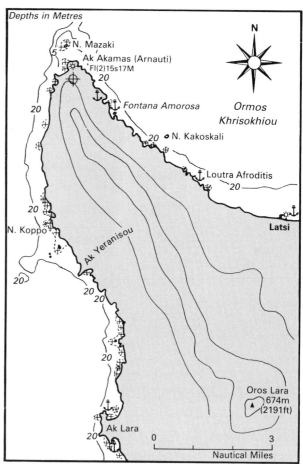

NW CYPRUS – LATSI TO AK LARA
Ak Akamas light 35°05'·3N 32°16'·9E

AK LARA

A yacht can anchor on the N or the S side of the cape, where there is some protection from westerlies. There is a taverna around the beach S of the cape.

PAPHOS

BA 849

This is the usual jumping-off spot when on passage to Greece or Turkey.

Approach

Conspicuous The white lighthouse on Ak Paphos is conspicuous. From closer in, the hotels and buildings around the shore will be seen, and the small fort and western breakwater are easily identified.

By night Use the light on Ak Paphos (Fl.15s17M) and the leading lights into the harbour F.R.2M/F.R.2M on 321°·5'. However, a night approach is not recommended, because of the reefs and shoal water in the approaches.

Dangers
1. Care must be taken of Vrakhonisos Moulia, a reef and shoal water lying 2 miles SE of the harbour in the direct approach from the S. The reef and shoal water lie between ½ a mile and one mile off the coast.
2. Care is also needed of the reef to the N if coasting down to Ak Paphos.

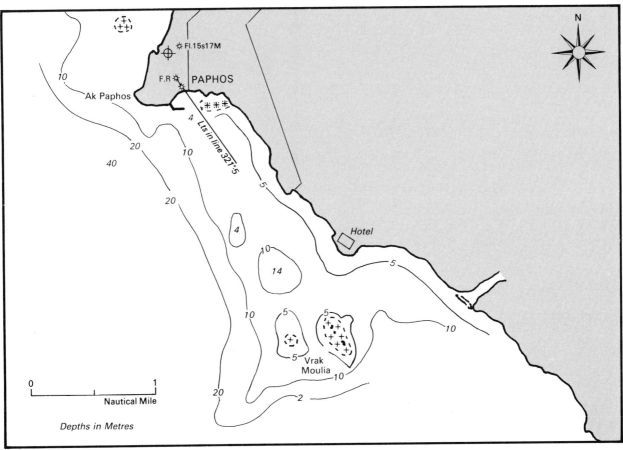

PAPHOS APPROACHES
Ak Paphos light 34°45'·4N 32°24'·3E

3. Care must be taken because the two buoys marking the entrance are not always in place.
4. The depths in the entrance may be less than charted, as it silts here.
5. Care must be taken of the eastern breakwater, which is partly submerged.

Mooring

Once into the harbour, veer to the W, as there is shoal water close E of the transit line. Anchor off, or

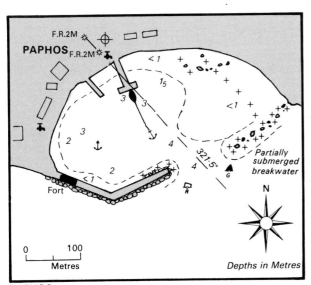

PAPHOS
34°45'·1N 32°24'·4E

go stern or bows-to the pier. The harbour is small and can be crowded in the summer.

Shelter Good shelter from the prevailing westerlies, but with strong southerlies it is very uncomfortable and may become untenable.

Dangers Care must be taken of the submerged quay and breakwater in the NE of the harbour.

Authorities A port of entry, although you may have to be stamped in at Limassol or Larnaca. You cannot clear from here, although this is likely to be changed in the near future.

Facilities

Water Near the pier.
Fuel In the town.
Repairs Minor mechanical repairs only.
Provisions Good shopping for provisions.
Eating out Good restaurants, including, it is reported, an English fish and chip shop!
Others PO. Banks. Local gas. Bus to Limassol.

General

Paphos is a comparatively unspoiled spot, although of late it has started to expand considerably. The harbour is believed to be built on the remains of the Phoenician harbour, Paphos having at one time been an important Phoenician trading post. The small fort was originally built by the Lusignan kings, and later modified by the Turks.

While in Paphos, one should visit the Roman palace, built in the 3rd century AD, and known as the Palace of Theseus after one of the mosaics found here, which depicts Theseus slaying the Minotaur. There are numerous other well preserved mosaics in the palace, and the other buildings of the same period are well worth a visit. Also nearby are some interesting underground rock tombs of the 3rd century BC, known as the Tombs of the Kings.

Note It is planned to build a small marina at Paphos, but no details of the final form are available at the time of writing.

ORMOS PISSOURI

A bay immediately E of Ak Aspro, affording some shelter from the prevailing westerlies. A large white hotel is conspicuous on the beach. Anchor in 4–5 metres. A line of buoys marks off a swimming area. Tavernas ashore.

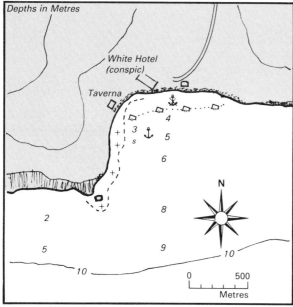

ORMOS PISSOURI
34°38'·5N 32°43'·3E

LIMASSOL

BA 849

Approach

This large commercial harbour lies in the NW corner of Akrotiri Bay, sheltered from the prevailing westerlies by Akrotiri peninsula.

Conspicuous The buildings of Limassol and the commercial harbour can be seen once around Ak Gata. There are always a large number of ships anchored in the roadstead. Two loading gantries and a silo are conspicuous in the harbour.

The entrance to the commercial harbour is lit Q(6)R.10s8M/Oc.G.7s10M. Leading lights on 248° Front F.G.2M; Rear Oc.G.5s2M.

VHF Ch 16 for port authorities.

Note Off Cape Gata close to the coast there is an area marked by three large yellow buoys (lit: Fl.5s)

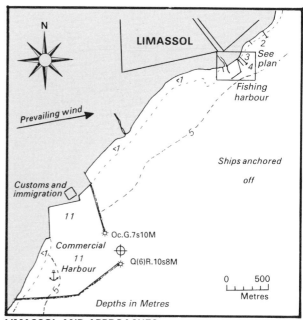

LIMASSOL AND APPROACHES
34°38'·7N 33°01'·6E

which is presumably a prohibited area. A yacht should stay outside this area.

Mooring

A yacht can anchor in the western corner of the commercial harbour, which is S of the town, but most yachts prefer to go to the fishing harbour, off the town. Go alongside in the basin, or stern or bows-to the pier immediately to the E. Good shelter from the prevailing westerlies.

Authorities A port of entry. The authorities are all housed in one building in the commercial harbour.

Facilities

Water On the quay in the basin.
Fuel Can be delivered by mini-tanker.
Repairs Mechanical and engineering repairs in the town. GRP boats are built in Limassol.
Provisions Good shopping for all provisions in the town.
Eating out Numerous restaurants on the waterfront and in the town.
Other PO. Banks. Local gas and *Camping Gaz*. Buses to most destinations in the S. Ferries to Rhodes, Piraeus, Haifa, and Alexandria.

General

The city has grown immensely in the last 10 years to become the commercial hub of southern Cyprus, and fairly hums with industry and smells of money. It cannot be described as an attractive place, and few yachts choose to stay here for more than a day, while en route to or from Larnaca.

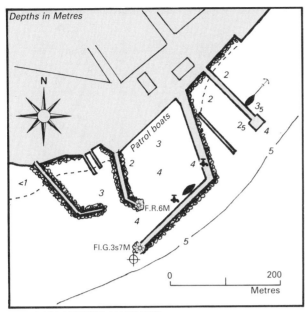

LIMASSOL FISHING HARBOUR
34°39'·8N 33°02'·5E

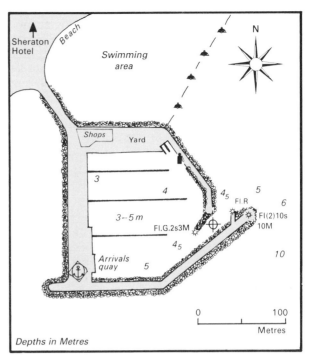

LIMASSOL MARINA
34°42'·5N 33°09'·5E

LIMASSOL MARINA

A new marina built some 6 miles around the beach from Limassol.

Approach

The position of the marina is difficult to determine until closer in. Head for the last hotel on the NE side of Limassol Bay which is the Sheraton behind the marina. The breakwater blends into the coast from the SW approach and not until you can see a few masts will you be able to determine where it is with any certainty. The entrance cannot be seen until right up to it.

By night The entrance is lit by a Fl(2)10s10M on the S mole and a Fl.G.2s3M and Fl.R at the entrance.

VHF Ch 09, 16. Call sign Limassol Pleasure Harbour.

Dangers
1. In the approach from the E care is needed of several dangers in the immediate approaches. Close W of the marina there is a fish farm with a number of fish pens. The outermost fish pen is lit Q but should not be relied on. Further E of the fish farm are a number of buoys and a pipeline terminal platform above water. When approaching from the E a yacht should keep well off the coast and make the final approach from the SE.
2. The entrance to the marina is very narrow between the low rock spur on the W side and the breakwater on the E side.

Mooring

Data 227 berths. Limited visitors berths. Max LOA 30m. Depths 3–5m. Max draught 4m.
Berth at the arrivals quay by the port office and report for a berth. There are laid moorings tailed to the quay.

Shelter Good.

Authorities Clearance into and out of Cyprus can be arranged by the marina office for a fee. Harbourmaster and marina staff. Charge band 2/3.

Facilities

Services Water and electricity (220V) at every berth. Telephone connections can be made. Shower and toilet block.
Fuel On the quay.
Repairs A 54-ton travel-hoist can haul yachts onto

Limassol Marina approach looking N. Note the square Sheraton Hotel behind the marina hard standing. Mechanical and some engineering repairs can be carried out. Some GRP and wood repairs. Chandlers.

Provisions A mini-market in the marina. A few other mini-markets on the main road to Limassol. For extensive re-stocking you will need to go to Limassol town where there are numerous large supermarkets.

Eating out Restaurant and bar in the marina and at the hotel.

Other Exchange facilities. Telephone and fax services at the marina office. Local gas and camping gaz available. Buses and taxis to Limassol.

General

This new marina has been built out to deeper water, and is connected to the coast by a short causeway. It is a fairly remote place, lacking the intimacy between harbour and town that Larnaca has. The marina is full of local yachts and visitors berths are at a premium here. The office will fit you in where it can, but it pays to book a berth in advance.

ATC-Limassol Pleasure Harbour, PO Box 1933, Limassol, Cyprus ☎ 321 100 *Fax* 329 208.

ORMOS AKROTIRI

There is a reasonable lee under Ak Gata from the prevailing westerlies, and many skippers choose to anchor under the cape rather than go into Limassol when working westwards from Larnaca.

VASSILIKOS

BA 849

About 9 miles E of Limassol Sheraton Marina there is an industrial harbour at Vassilikos. A number of tall pylons and storage tanks in the vicinity identify where it is. There are 8–9 metre depths in the entrance and mostly 6–7 metre depths inside. Although not really a place for yachts, it might be useful in an emergency.

AK KITI

This cape forms the western entrance point to Larnaca Bay. A reef and shoal water extend southwards from it for at least one mile. Shoal water extends for varying distances off the W side of Larnaca Bay and a yacht should keep well off. Tacking into the bay I was tempted to stay on a closing tack with the coast a little too long until the depths decreased abruptly from 8m to 3m. There are also reports of uncharted rocks off the airport some distance out from the coast.

LARNACA

BA 848

Approach

It is difficult to work out exactly where the marina and entrance are. There seems to be only a solid wall of rock ballasting extending along the coast. The best thing to do it to head for the commercial harbour until the masts in the marina can be identified.

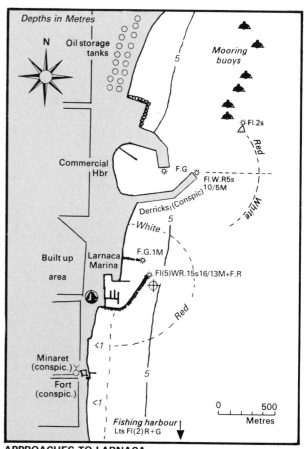

APPROACHES TO LARNACA
Marina main light 34°55'·1N 33°38'·6E

Conspicuous Two tall chimneys with red stripes are conspicuous on the NE side of Larnaca Bay. There are always numerous ships anchored in the roadstead. The storage tanks and chimneys of the oil refinery N of the commercial harbour are conspicuous. At the commercial harbour the tall crane gantries are conspicuous and a number of warehouses will be seen. The fort and minaret on the waterfront, about ½ mile S of the marina, are also conspicuous. Closer in, the breakwater sheltering the marina will be seen just S of the commercial harbour. The entrance to the marina is not obvious until close to.

By night Use the light on Ak Kiti (Fl(3)15s13M), and closer in the light on the marina breakwater (Fl(5)WR.15s16/13M+F.R). The latter is not easily seen against the lights of the town, but the light at the entrance to the commercial harbour (Fl.WR.5s 10/5M) shows up well. The flare of the oil refinery N of the commercial harbour also shows up well.

VHF Ch 08, 16. Call sign *Larnaca Marina*.

Dangers
1. To the N of the commercial harbour there are numerous unlit mooring buoys off the oil refinery.
2. Care must be taken of the shoal water fringing the coast on the W side of Larnaca Bay.

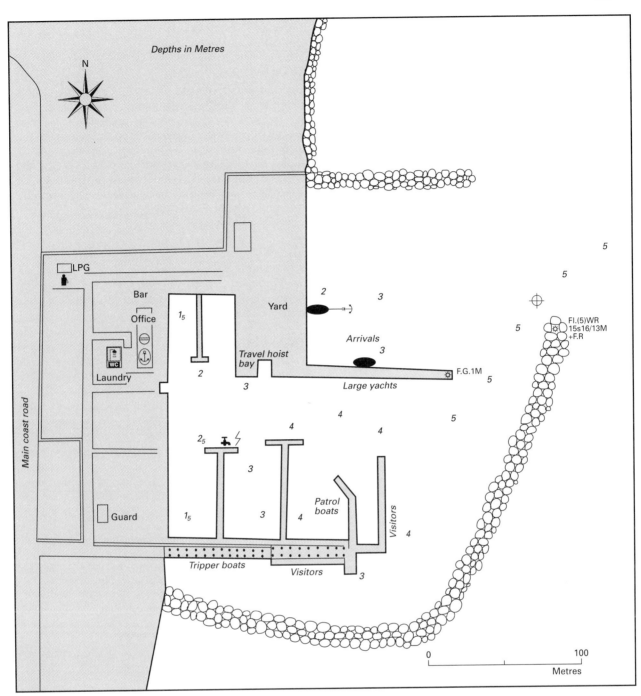

Depths in Metres

N

LPG

Bar

Office

Yard

1₅

WC

Laundry

Travel hoist bay

Arrivals

2

3

3

3

3

Large yachts

F.G.1M

Fl.(5)WR 15s16/13M +F.R

5

5

5

5

5

5

2

4

4

4

2₅

3

Guard

1₅

3

4

Patrol boats

Visitors

4

Tripper boats

Visitors

3

Main coast road

0   100
Metres

LARNACA
34°55′·1N 33°38′·6E

Mooring

Data Nominally 200 berths but more are squeezed in. Limited visitors berths. Max LOA 35m. Depths 1·5–5m.

New arrivals are asked to berth in the outside basin. Go stern-to the W quay or alongside the S quay. The bottom is mud and mostly good holding although you may have to lay a second anchor in the outside basin. With E–NE winds it gets very bumpy in here and may become untenable. Even if you have booked a berth in advance you may be kept in the outer basin for some time. Small yachts may be able to potter into the marina and find a temporary berth somewhere.

Larnaca Marina approach looking SW into the entrance. Arrivals basin on the right of the photo

Berths inside are on finger pontoons or with laid moorings tailed to the quay. Large yachts go on the N quay and use their own anchor if the laid mooring is unsuitable. Visitors are normally put on the outside E pontoon or tucked around on the S side of the marina off the pier-pontoon.

Shelter Good all-round shelter. There can be a slight surge with strong easterlies, but it is not troublesome.

Authorities A port of entry. All the relevant authorities are housed in the marina. Harbourmaster and marina staff. Charge band 2.

Note The marina has been dredged to 5m in the approaches and outer part, and to 1·5–3m in the inner part, but the bottom appears to be irregular. Yachts drawing more than 2m should proceed with care in the innermost part of the marina.

Facilities

Services Water and electricity (220V) at or near every berth. Note that water is often in short supply, and may be turned off at times or the pressure may be low. Telephone connections can be made. A shower and toilet block. Laundrette.

Fuel On the N quay.

Repairs A 40-ton travel-hoist operates, and there is hard standing for about 100 yachts. Most mechanical and engineering repairs can be carried out. Electrical and electronic repairs. Some wood and GRP repairs can be made. Several chandlers, and good hardware shops with a wide range of stainless steel and bronze hardware. Good-quality marine paint and antifouling available.

Provisions Excellent shopping for all provisions. Many otherwise hard-to-get items can be found here, and it is a good place to stock up, whether heading N or S. *Orfanides* and *Metro* supermarkets have just about everything you want. You will need a hire bike or a taxi or bus to get there. Large purchases will be delivered to the marina with a bit of negotiation. Ice available.

Eating out Numerous restaurants on the waterfront and in the town. English-style pubs, with English-style lager louts often in evidence in the summer.

Other PO. Banks. Telephone and fax service at the marina. Hospital. Local gas and *Camping Gaz*. Hire cars and motorbikes. Buses to most destinations in the S. International flights from Larnaca Airport.

General

Larnaca is a popular place for yachts wintering in the eastern Mediterranean. While the town is not architecturally inspired (like so much of southern Cyprus it has all been thrown up in the last 20 years), the marina is a safe and popular place to winter. It is something of a crossroads for yachts which have just come up the Red Sea and those that are about to go down it. The social life is rated amongst the best in the eastern Mediterranean.

Note The marina is often fully booked, so you should write in advance to see if a berth can be arranged. Write to: The Director, Larnaca Marina, Larnaca, Cyprus ☎ (4) 653110/ 653113 *Fax* (4) 624110.

AYIA NAPA

A resort area lying 4½ miles WNW of Ak Greco. There is an indifferent lee here from the westerlies, but in calm weather you can anchor off. Care is needed of a 2-metre shoal patch in the middle of the anchorage. Anchor in 2–3 metres, on sand.

The small fishing harbour here has 2m in the entrance, but barely 1·5m depths in the middle. The entrance is rock-bound, and you should reconnoitre in a dinghy before entering.

Hotels and tavernas ashore.

AK GRECO

It is possible to anchor on the N or S side of Ak Greco, depending on the wind and sea. Generally the anchorage on the N side affords better shelter from the prevailing winds.

PANAYIA

A bay about 3 miles NNW of Ak Greco. It is sheltered on the S side by a low headland and islet. Keep a reasonable distance off the islet, which is fringed by a reef, and approach the anchorage from the E. Reasonable shelter from the prevailing winds, which tend to follow the coast.

FIGTREE BAY

A bay just under a mile N of Panayia. A number of apartment blocks and hotels have been built around the nearby coast. Care is needed of the low islet, fringed by reefs, in the bay. Anchor between the low islet and the headland sheltering the bay on the S. Reasonable shelter.

Tavernas ashore. The bay has become a popular resort, and is crowded in the summer.

SE CYPRUS – AK KITI TO FAMAGUSTA
Ak Greco light 34°57'·2N 34°05'E

Kastellórizon

BA 1054
Imray-Tetra chart G36

(Castellorizon, Kastellórizou, Turkish Meis)

See plan page 209.

This small Greek island lies close off the Turkish mainland, some 70 miles E of Rhodes. For this reason, it fits comfortably into this pilot rather than the companion volume on Greek waters. It can easily be seen from Kaş, and a yacht on passage down the Turkish coast will pass between it and the mainland coast. Several of the other smaller islands in the vicinity, notably Nisis Strongili to the S and Nisis Ayios Yeóryios (Georgios) to the W, are also Greek.

In the 20th century the fortunes of the island have all been downhill. In the 19th century, Kastellórizon was an important port for the Levant trade, being strategically placed between Egypt, Lebanon and Syria in the S and the Aegean ports in the N. Photographs of the harbour from the turn of the century show it crowded with sailing ships of all types, loading and unloading cargo or waiting for a fair wind. The photographs of the crowded harbour are difficult to reconcile with the deserted quays and air of decay in present-day Kastellórizon. In the early 20th century it had a population of some 20,000. Today there are 200 inhabitants.

The period of prosperity ended with the Turco-Italian War in the early 1920s, when the Levant was effectively dismembered as a trading force. Kastellórizon was badly damaged in the Second World War, when it was bombed, and fire destroyed many of the buildings. Today it hangs on as the easternmost outpost of Greece, connected only, by ferry, with Rhodes, and nourished by a little tourism.

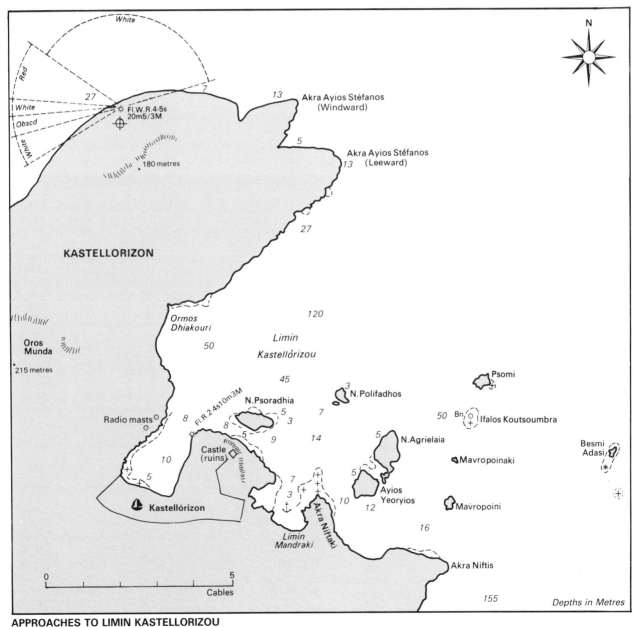

APPROACHES TO LIMIN KASTELLORIZOU

Ak Ay Stefanos light 36°10'N 29°35'·3E

The island itself is a steep-to, bare, rocky place, with barely a patch of top-soil to be seen. Here and there there is a little *maquis* or *garrigue*, but otherwise the island is just bare rock thrusting up from the sea. Only around Mandraki and in the valley behind Kastellórizon town is there a splash of green, where some underwater spring feeds the trees and vegetation and keeps the baking sun at bay.

LIMIN KASTELLORIZOU (Meyisti)

BA 1054
Imray-Tetra chart G36

Approach

From the N there are no dangers not easily identified in the approaches to the harbour. From the S, a number of islands and underwater rocks make the approach more difficult. Special attention must be paid to the underwater rock S of Besmi islet. A yacht will normally choose to stay to the N of Besmi and Psomi islets until there is a clear passage into the harbour.

Conspicuous From the N, Nisis Ayios Yeóryios and Gürmenli Adasi are easily identified. Gürmenli Kayalari, two above-water rocks, are also easily identified. On the N side of Kastellórizon, several large white rocky patches on the slopes are conspicuous from some distance off. From the S, the hump-backed Nisis Strongili and the lighthouse on it are easily identified. From the N, you will not see the buildings of the village until around Akra Ayios Stefanos. From the S, the buildings of the village can be seen once past Nisis Strongili. The ruined castle on the E side of the harbour is conspicuous.

By night From the N, the light on the northern tip of Kastellórizon (Fl.WR.4·5s5/3M) covers Gürmenli Adasi and Kayalari with the red sector. From the S, use the light on Nisis Strongili (Fl.5s17M), but there are no lights to indicate the channel between the numerous islands. The harbour entrance is lit on the E side: Fl.R.2·4s3M.

Dangers
1. Care must be taken of the numerous underwater rocks and shoal patches in the approaches.
2. When the *meltemi* is blowing there are fierce gusts off the high slopes of Kastellórizon. This makes sailing up the Turkish coast towards Kaş or Kastellórizon difficult. The gusts blow across a W-going current to set up extremely short and difficult seas.

Mooring

Go stern or bows-to the quay in the SE corner. Care must be taken of the ballasting which extends underwater in places. The bottom is mud and rocks, not everywhere good holding. The quay is also very low, making getting on and off difficult, especially when bows-to.

Shelter Good shelter from the prevailing summer winds, although there may be a surge with a strong prolonged meltemi and with strong southerlies. Open to the N and E.

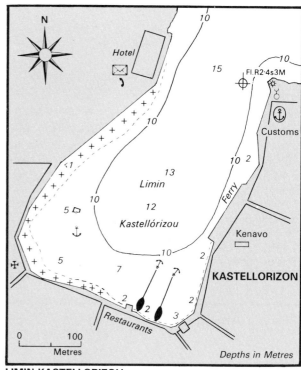

LIMIN KASTELLORIZOU
36°09'N 29°35'·6E

Authorities Customs and immigration on the waterfront. Harbourmaster. A yacht can check in here, but cannot obtain a Transit Log. A charge is made. Charge band 2.

Kastellórizon: SE corner of the harbour

Facilities

Water Scarce on the island, and limited amounts only are available. Fill up before you get here.
Fuel Limited amounts only. No fuel quay.
Repairs There is a small yard at Mandraki, capable of hauling small yachts only. Kenavo Yacht Service, located on the waterfront behind the Tourist Information Bureau, do sail repairs and can make new sails, do some engine and electrical repairs, and even have a small stock of secondhand yacht gear. They will also keep mail. They keep a listening watch on VHF Ch 67. Lisa and Shackle, Kenavo Yacht Service, Megisti, Kastellórizou, 85111 Greece ☎/*Fax* (0241) 49213.
Provisions Some shopping for provisions. Fresh produce is poor.
Eating out Restaurants on the waterfront. Avoid eating out at the bossy ones on the waterfront which help you to tie up, offer a free beer, and then overcharge for meals.
Other PO. Metered telephone. Ferry to Rhodes. Flights to Rhodes.

General

The white splash of a town under rocky slopes and bordered by the blue Mediterranean is a delightful if somewhat underpopulated place. Many former inhabitants have emigrated to Australia, and you will often meet one of these 'rich relos', making a nostalgic pilgrimage to the island.

On the east coast, the Blue Grotto is said to make that at Capri look dull. It is best visited by local boat. Underwater fishing around the coast is also reported to be good. Numerous yachts now visit Kastellórizon, and it is good to see some life returning to the place. For those looking for an out-of-the-way place, this is it, and I for one like it.

MANDRAKI

The bay immediately SE of Kastellórizon. Anchor in 3–5 metres. Good shelter from the *meltemi*. It is a short walk over the saddle to town.

VIII. The Black Sea

This is a sea of very different character to the Mediterranean. The water is less saline and, in hard winters, pack ice forms around the eastern, northern, and western shores for a distance of up to 10 miles. Pack ice has been known to reach the northern entrance to the Bosphorus, and is commonly believed to have been the floating islands that Jason and the Argonauts encountered. The rainfall over the sea and coast is much higher than in the Mediterranean (an annual average of 80in/203cm in some places), and consequently the vegetation is thicker and more lush. In places, the forests of oak and chestnut and the farming land are reminiscent of Mitteleuropa – a bit of Hungary or Austria transported to Asia.

Marine life in the sea is biologically poor, but the superficial impression from the local catches is that there is an abundance of fish: herrings, mackerel, anchovy, swordfish, tunny and flatfish. Large numbers of tunny migrate annually from the Mediterranean to the Black Sea to spawn and are easily caught in the narrow confines of the Bosphorus, as is only too evident from the large numbers in the fishmongers and restaurants of Istanbul. Anchovies (hamsi) are caught in huge numbers, and figure prominently in the cuisine of the Black Sea.

The lower layers of the Black Sea have a high hydrogen sulphide content, since the water is replaced only slowly. The surface layers are constantly renewed by the rivers flowing into the sea, but it is estimated that the bottom layers are replaced just once every 2,500 years. This water, deficient in oxygen, cannot support much in the way of marine life.

The Black Sea coast of Turkey is little visited by yachts, and indeed is little touched as yet by tourism of any sort. There are many artificial harbours along the straight coast, and a yacht can easily find shelter at short intervals when coast-hopping. There are few naturally protected bays, and no islands akin to those off the Aegean coast of Turkey. Turkish charts of the Black Sea are published, and can be obtained in Istanbul from the hydrographic office in Cübük.

About this chapter

Unlike the rest of the pilot, this chapter gives only a very brief resumé of pilotage information, and plans where applicable, for the Black Sea harbours and anchorages. It is more in the nature of an appendix than a full-blown treatment. Few boats venture along this coast, and to expand this chapter would make the book unnecessarily bulky and more expensive. Consequently, the plans and abbreviated pilotage information should be used with caution, and in this spirit I hope that those who do sail along the Black Sea coast will accept the brevity of the information supplied here. Corrections to the information are, of course, welcome.

Acknowledgement

Most of these plans were assembled by Ian and Anne Page of SY Cetos. They have been redrawn and amended with extra information from my own and others' forays along the coast. Where possible, I have checked depths close to the quay, and the overall appearance of the harbours.

Caution

Many of the harbours in the Black Sea are prone to severe silting. Depths in the entrance to a harbour should be regarded as an indication only. I have seen the entrance to a small river, used by relatively small local boats, decrease in the space of a single winter from around 1 metre to around 30 centimetres. Ian Page records that one harbour that he could not get into with a draught of 1·5 metres was clear, with good depths, three weeks later. Around some of the small harbours, gulets equipped with a small crane and grab-bucket keep the entrances dredged.

Weather

Winter in the Black Sea can be violent. Depressions often pass across Europe and dive down across the Black Sea, bringing violent winds and raising considerable seas. In spring and autumn gales are less frequent, though they occur often enough to warrant more attention than they merit in the eastern Mediterranean. Turks who sail in the Black Sea suggest that it is unwise to enter the Black Sea before June, and that it is wise to leave the Black Sea or hole up before the end of September. I have experienced gales of Force 8 in the middle of August, though on the whole gales are rare in the summer.

Having said all this, it is likely that you will only encounter regular winds of Force 3–5 in July and August. There are normally NE winds between Istanbul and Sinop, and NW winds from Sinop to Hopa. The wind fills in around midday and dies down at night. There will also be days of calm, or of little wind. In September and early October there will often be southerlies off the land.

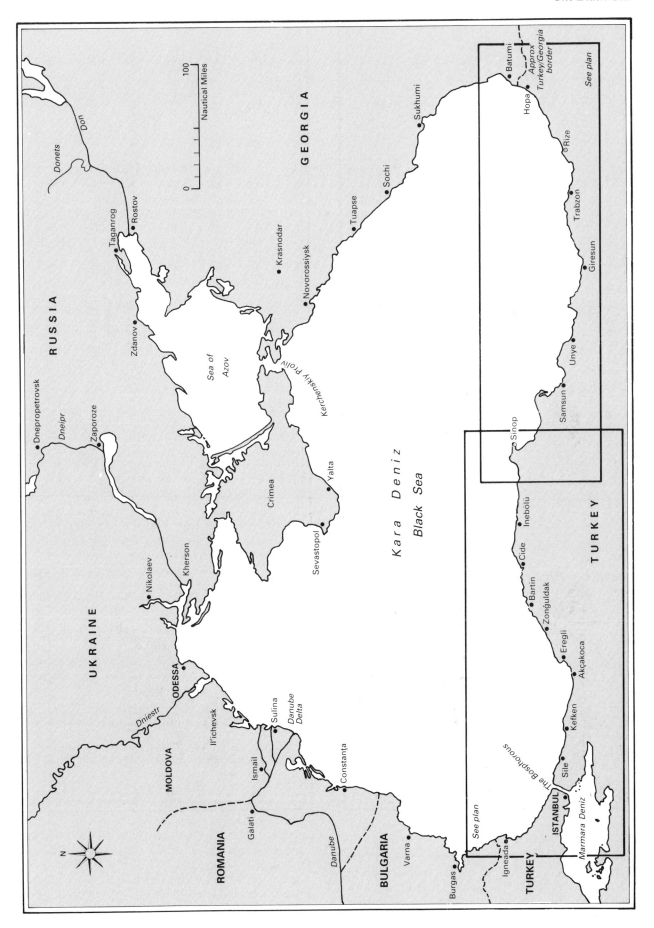

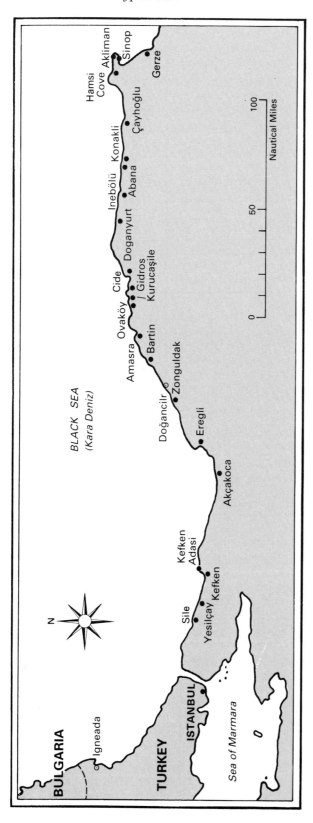

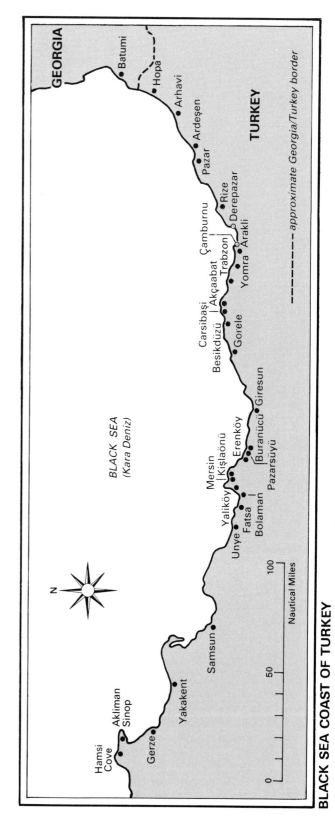

BLACK SEA COAST OF TURKEY

One of the bugbears of sailing in the Black Sea is the almost continual swell that bounces around it. With any wind, the sea builds quickly, and continues for some time after the wind has died. This can make motor-sailing in light winds or a calm uncomfortable. And you should remember that Turkey's Black Sea coast is one long lee shore. The prevailing winds are from NE–NW. Gales are often from the N–NE. And there you are on the southern shores of the sea.

Harbours

The majority of harbours along the Black Sea are man-made, with just a couple of natural harbours, or natural features partially sheltering a harbour. The longest distance between harbours is 50 nautical miles, either side of Samsun. Elsewhere there are numerous harbours, with relatively short distances between them. This means that you can stop in a number of different harbours on the return trip west along the coast, if you choose not to sail over to the north side of the Black Sea.

Authorities

There are ports of entry at Sinop, Samsun and Trabzon, but the authorities have little experience of clearing yachts in and are loath to carry out the necessary paperwork. Most of the authorities do not have the appropriate Transit Logs for a yacht, and in practice any yacht arriving from outside Turkey will be passed from harbour to harbour until it reaches Istanbul, where it should clear in at Karaköy (see Chapter I).

Useful books

Black Sea Cruising Guide Rick and Sheila Nelson. Imray. Yacht pilotage for all of the Black Sea in detail.
Guide to Eastern Turkey & the Black Sea Coast Diana Darke. Michael Haag. Covers the more major towns and resorts.
Zoom In: Black Sea Boyut Publishing Group. Available in Turkey. Mostly covers from Samsun east.
Turkey – A Travel Survival Kit Tom Brosnahan. Lonely Planet. Has a chapter on the Black Sea, covering the main towns.
The Towers of Trebizond Rose Macaulay. A classic, though a little irritating to read at times.
The Jason Voyage Tim Severin. Hutchinson. Retracing the voyage of Jason and the Argonauts along the Black Sea coast in a replica of a Homeric scouting galley.

Harbours and anchorages east of the Bosphorus

SILE

Lies about 21½ miles E of the Bosphorus. The town is built up steep slopes behind the harbour. The entrance is prone to silting, and a sand bar builds up in the winter. Entry reported to be dangerous in NW gales because of the shoals outside. Go stern or bows-to in the NE corner.

Water near the harbourmasters office. Small shop, restaurant and café near the quay. Other facilities in the town, about ¾km steep climb away.

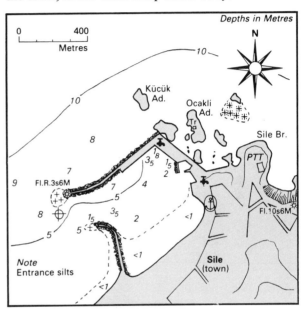

SILE
41°10'·3N 29°36'E

BOZGACA ISKELESI (41°09'·5N 29°46'·7E)

A small bay where some shelter can be gained under the headland from onshore winds. Anchor in 2·5–3m on the E side. Good holding in sand.

YESILCAY (Agva) (41°08'N 29°48'·E)

A river about 12 miles E of Sile. The pier off the river mouth is lit: Fl.3s5M. The bar over the river mouth is shallow, with less than 1–1·5 metre depths over. The entrance was recently reported to have 2m depths over the bar.

KEFKEN

A small harbour in Kefken Limani. The outer breakwater is lit F.G.5M. Go alongside the quay just inside the inner breakwater. Good shelter.

Provisions in the village by the harbour.

KEFKEN ADASI

A fishing harbour on the S side of Kefken Adasi. Care is needed of the reefs and shoal water in the vicinity. The entrance is lit Fl.R.3s5M and Fl.G.3s5M. There are fish-pens along the W side of the harbour. Anchor in the NE corner. Good

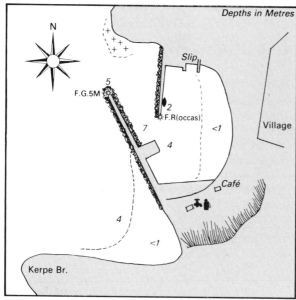

KEFKEN
41°10'N 30°13'E

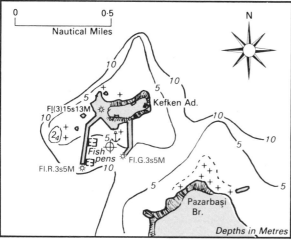

KEFKEN ADASI
41°13'N 30°15'·5E

holding. Good shelter. There are no facilities nearby.

Note A new harbour at 41°08'N 30°00'E is reported in the bay.

AKCAKOCA

A fishing harbour 38 miles E of Kefken Adasi. There are a number of holiday villages along the stretch of coast between Kefken Adasi and Akçakoca. Akçakoca Burun is lit Fl.5s5M. Go stern or bows-to the quay in the NE corner, or alongside a fishing boat if necessary. Good shelter. Reasonable shelter although some ground swell enters. Thought to be untenable in strong NW winds.

Water nearby. Fuel approximately 250m E of harbour. Some provisions. Restaurants. Market day on Tuesdays.

EREGLI

A large commercial harbour off the town of Ereğli. The S harbour is for the steelworks, and a yacht should make for the N harbour. Go alongside on the

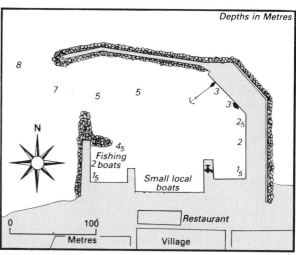

AKCAKOCA
41°05'·4N 31°07'·1E

W side of the central pier where shown or anchor off. Good shelter.

Fuel and water on the quay. Good shopping area a short distance E in the town. Restaurants and cafés.

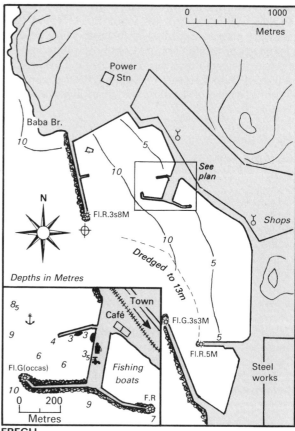

EREGLI
41°16'·9N 31°24'·1E

ZONGULDAK

A large town 19½ miles ENE of Değirmen Burnu. To the W of the town are slag heaps from the coal mining in the vicinity. A water tower is conspicuous on the headland just N of the port. Go alongside the NW quay, or alongside the coal quay or anything

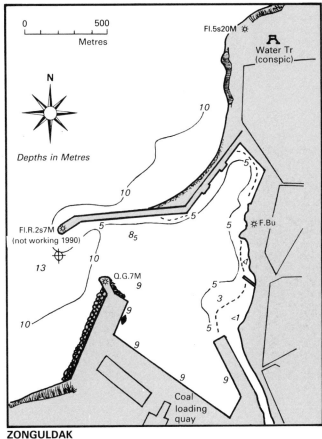

ZONGULDAK
41°27'·6N 31°46'·8E

else here. Do not anchor, as the bottom is foul and filthy (probably aeons of accumulated coal dust) and bad holding. Coal is loaded on the S quays.

Restaurants and good shopping for provisions in the town.

DOGANCILAR POWER STATION
(41°31'·5N 31°53'·7E)
A fairly large harbour for the power station, about 6 miles ENE of Zonguldak. Entry is restricted by a boom across the entrance.

BARTIN LIMANI
A commercial and naval harbour lying 25 miles ENE of Zonguldak. Go alongside the commercial quay if possible. It is prohibited to anchor in the harbour, and prohibited to enter the eastern part (Iç Limani). There are no provisions nearby.

BARTIN CAYI
Local boats use the river on the S side of Bartin Limani for shelter. Depths may alter in the mouth and inside the river itself, but generally there are sufficient depths for it to be used. Normally there are depths of 3 metres and more in the channel for 1½ miles upstream to a bridge, which opens occasionally. Anchor in the river, or nudge into the bank with a kedge out.

There is a café and a boatyard near the bridge. Bartin town, where you can get supplies, is about 5km from the bridge.

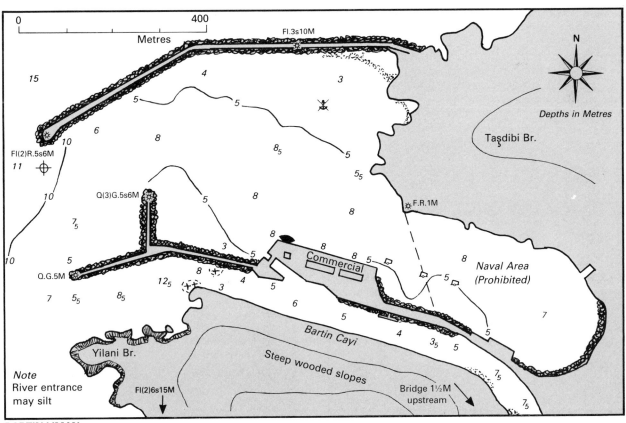

BARTIN LIMANI
41°41'·3N 32°13'·4E

Amasra, looking NW

AMASRA

A large harbour lying about 8 miles ENE of Bartin. The harbour is on the E side of the rocky headland, with the town built over the saddle. The SE corner of the harbour is a naval area, and entry is prohibited. Go stern or bows-to the quay, or alongside. There can sometimes be an uncomfortable surge in the harbour on the quay, so it may be better to anchor off in the SW corner.

Most provisions and restaurants ashore. The town is well worth a wander around, and has numerous ancient associations.

OVAKOY

A small harbour about 12 miles NE of Amasra. The entrance can be tricky with a heavy swell running. Go alongside the quay in the NW. Reasonable shelter.

Limited provisions in the village. Ovaköy is something of a boatbuilding centre, and some fine *gulets* are built here. In the village, Greek and Byzantine remains are scattered around between and in the walls of the houses.

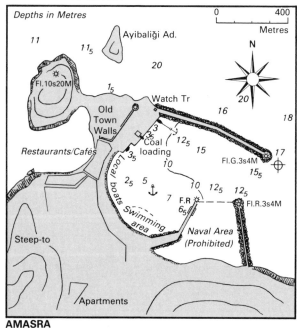

AMASRA
41°44'·9N 32°24'E

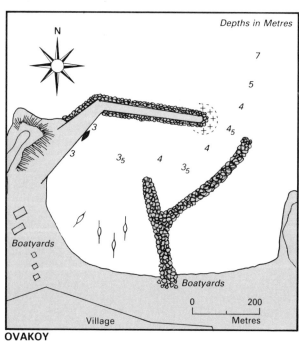

OVAKOY
41°50'N 32°40'·3E

Kurucaşile, looking WSW

KURUCASILE

A harbour about 4 miles ENE of Ovaköy, on the E side of Inebolu Burnu (lit: Fl.3s8M). Go alongside the quay on the W. Reasonable shelter. Limited provisions in the village.

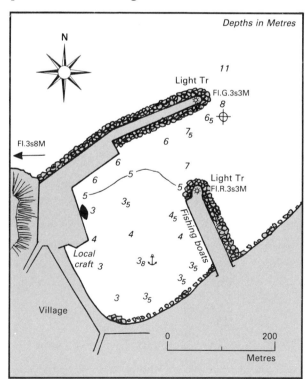

KURUCASILE
41°50'·9N 32°42'·5E

GIDROS LIMANI

An almost totally enclosed bay, lying 7½ miles E of Kurucasile. Care is needed of the reef off the W side, and of the rock and reef in the SE corner. Anchor on the W or E side where convenient. With even moderate onshore winds some swell penetrates into the bay.

Restaurant ashore on the NE. This is one of the few natural harbours along the coast, and is a spectacular spot, surrounded by steep, wooded slopes.

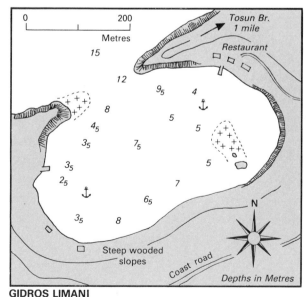

GIDROS LIMANI
41°51'·8N 32°51'·5E

Gidros, looking WSW

Cide, looking W

CIDE

A large harbour tucked under Kopekkavasi Burun, about 5 miles E of Gidros. Go stern or bows-to or alongside in the NE corner, or anchor off in the S. Good shelter.

Water from the café on the quay. Several restaurants nearby. Two shops about ½km away, and others in the town, about 2km away to the W.

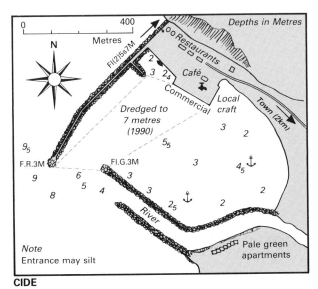

CIDE
41°54′N 32°58′·5E

DOGANYURT (42°08′N 33°28′E)

A small harbour about 5 miles E of Kerempe Burnu. Two rough rock breakwaters have been built out, with the entrance on the E side. The entrance is lit F.G/F.R. It is reported there is a 2·7m bar at the entrance with less depths to port and deeper to starboard. Once inside depths increase to 6m with 4m off the middle of the quay. Anchor in the S corner. There is a small village ashore.

INEBOLU

A large town and harbour about 19½ miles E of Kerempe Burnu. Go alongside in the NW corner.

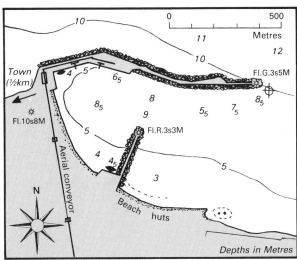

INEBOLU
41°59′·9N 33°46′·4E

Loading gantries protrude from the quay, but there is room to the W of them. Alternatively, go alongside in the SE corner. Good shelter.

Water from cafe on the S side of the harbour. Restaurants and good shopping for provisions ½km W.

ABANA

A fishing harbour 11 miles E of Inebolu. Go alongside the quay on the NW where possible. Reasonable shelter. The town is about ½km to the W.

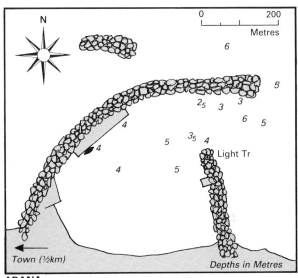

ABANA
41°59′N 34°01′·2E

KONAKLI LIMANI (Catalzeytin)

A new harbour, still under construction, about 7½ miles E of Abana. The existing breakwaters (1992) provide reasonable shelter. Anchor under the outer breakwater. No facilities nearby.

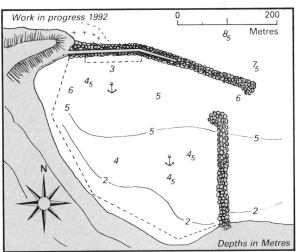

KONAKLI LIMANI (Catalzeytin)
41°58′N 34°10′E

AYANCIK

A small fishing harbour just E of a sawmill and pulp factory. A gantry off the factory is conspicuous.

269

CAYHOGLU

A fishing harbour tucked under Usta Burnu (lit: Fl.5s8M). It is important to note that the light has been moved approximately half a mile E from its original position. A quarry scar in the original position is conspicuous. The lighthouse is difficult to see from the W. A mosque in the village is conspicuous from the E. Go alongside the quay on the W side, or anchor off in the S. The bottom is mud and good holding. Good shelter.

Water at the N end of the quay. No provisions in the small village.

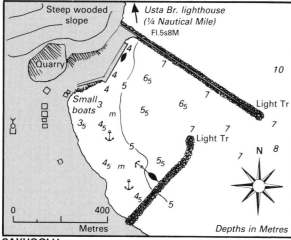

CAYHOGLU
41°57'·8N 34°30'·4E

HAMSI COVE

A tiny inlet on the E side of Ince Burun (lit Fl(4)20s9M). It affords some shelter from the prevailing wind. The sea caves just E are said to be worth a visit in calm weather. No facilities.

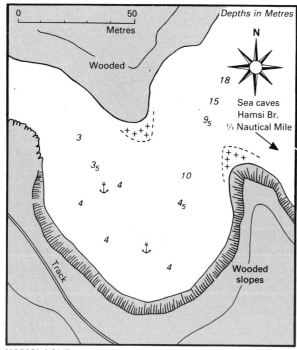

HAMSI COVE
42°04'·8N 35°02'·5E

AKLIMANI

A natural harbour at the W end of the beach running from Sinop. The end of the short breakwater is lit: Fl.R.5s6M. Anchor at the N end of the bay. Good holding on mud. Good shelter. No facilities.

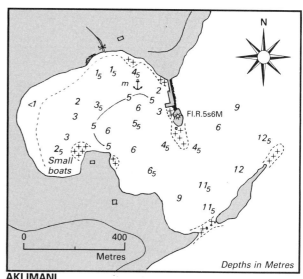

AKLIMANI
42°03'·3N 35°03'E

SINOP

The harbour lies on the S side of the headland. The town, straddling the saddle of the headland, is easily identified. Care is needed of a set-net just off the breakwater and a wreck with least depth 5·5 metres over. The inner basin is usually packed with fishing boats, but you may find a berth alongside the outer wall. Alternatively, go alongside the two small quays outside the basin, with an anchor to hold you off. It is shallow immediately off the quays themselves. Good shelter.

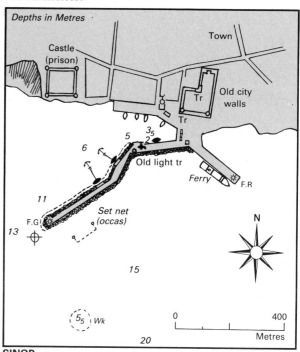

SINOP
42°01'·3N 35°08'·7E

Sinop: inner basin, looking ESE from the tower on the old city wall

Customs and harbourmaster. Water on the quay. Fuel in the town. Good shopping for provisions, and numerous restaurants. Banks. The town has numerous shops making and selling model boats; some of these are pretty awful, but some are endearing in a naive way.

GERZE

A small harbour 13 miles S of Boztepe Burun. It is really an open anchorage under Kosk Burnu (lit Fl(2)3s6M). Poor shelter. It is proposed to build a breakwater out from the headland to provide better shelter, but as yet nothing has been built.

YAKAKENT

A fishing harbour 27 miles SE of Boztepe Burun. Care is needed of the sandbank off the inner mole. Go alongside, or stern or bows-to, where possible. Good shelter.

Fuel near the harbour. Limited provisions at the harbour. Good shopping in the village 2km E. Several restaurants and cafés at the harbour.

SAMSUN

A large commercial harbour 31 miles SE of Bafra Burnu (lit Fl.5s20M). The coast around Samsun is low-lying and marshy, so that it can be difficult to estimate how far off the coast you are without any salient features to identify. Samsun is a large city, easily identified from the distance.

The authorities are unhappy if you berth in any part of the commercial area, and a yacht should make for the yacht club pier in the S of the large harbour. Go stern or bows-to, with care (see sketch plan for depths).

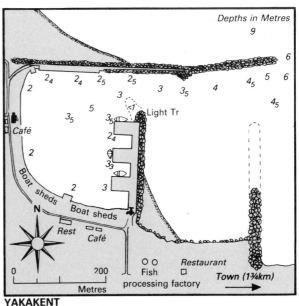

YAKAKENT
41°38'·4N 35°30'·3E

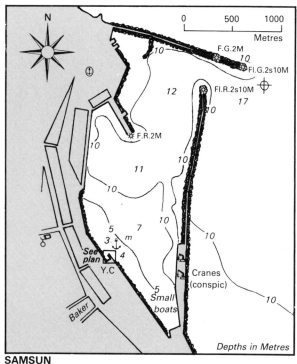

SAMSUN
41°18'·6N 36°21'·4E

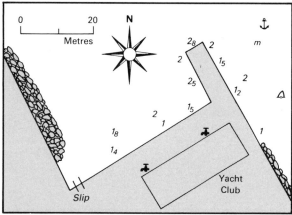

SAMSUN YACHT CLUB
41°18·6N 36°21·3E

Water and electricity on the quay. Fuel in the town. Good shopping for all provisions, and restaurants galore. Banks. The harbour is reported to be a smelly place likened to a giant cess-pool. Charge band 2 at the YC.

BELEDIYE KOYU (41°16'N 36°22'·5E)

A small and very shallow harbour immediately E of Samsun commercial harbour. There are only 1·8 metres in the entrance, and 1·5 just inside the entrance.

UNYE

A large harbour, still under construction, about 15 miles SE of Calti Burnu. A large cement works behind the harbour is conspicuous. At present (1992), the breakwaters are complete and work is proceeding on the quayed areas. The entrance is lit

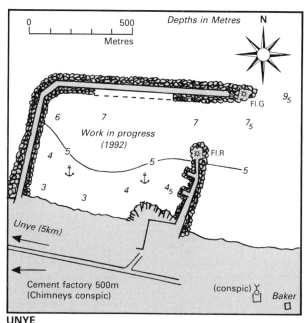

UNYE
41°06'·8N 37°19'·8E

Fl.G and Fl.R. Anchor in 3–5 metres in the SW corner. Good shelter.

Unye town is 5km to the W. The harbour is probably being built for the large cement works behind, and may become a grubby, dusty place when it is in use.

FATSA

A harbour tucked into the SW corner of Fatsa Körfezi. Care is needed of the isolated reef on the W side of the gulf. It is marked by a light structure: Fl.3s6M. The approach to the harbour is best made from the NE. Go alongside the quay where convenient. Good shelter.

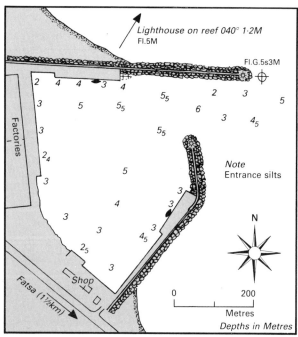

FATSA
41°02'·8N 37°29'·5E

Limited provisions at the harbour. Better shopping and restaurants in Fatsa, 1½km E.

BOLAMAN (Fatsa) (41°02'·4N 37°36'E)

A harbour on the SE side of Fatsa Körfezi. There are 5–6 metre depths in the entrance and 2–5 metre depths in the northern half of the harbour. Go alongside the quay where possible, or anchor on the S side. Reasonable shelter.

Small village nearby.

Note The harbour is reported to have silted up.

YALIKOY (Fatsa)

A small harbour just NE of Bolaman. Go stern or bows-to the quay. Reasonable shelter.

Water on the quay at the toilets. Fuel in the village. Small village nearby. Reputed to be famous for its *köfte*.

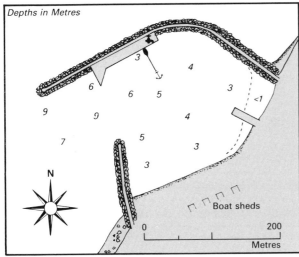

YALIKOY (FATSA)
41°03'·5N 37°36'·5E

MERSIN (Perşembe)

A small harbour close S of Cam Burnu. Go stern or bows-to or alongside the quay. There are mostly 3 metre plus depths off the quay. Good shelter.

Limited provisions and a café ashore. Better shopping in Perşembe, 6km S.

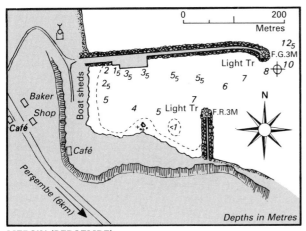

MERSIN (PERSEMBE)
41°07'N 37°46'E

KISLAONU (Perşembe)

A very small harbour just S of Mersin. Go alongside the quay on the E side. Good shelter.

Limited provisions ashore. Better shopping in Perşembe, 2km away.

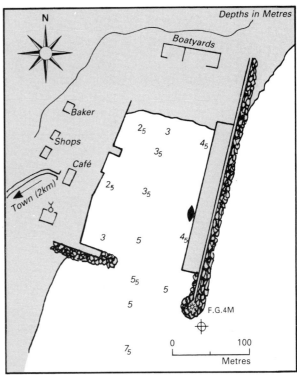

KISLAONU (PERSEMBE)
41°04'·9N 37°46'·4E

ERENKOY (41°58'·2N 38°03'·5E)

A small harbour 14½ miles SE of Cam Burnu. There are 2·5–3 metre depths in the entrance, and mostly 2–3·5 metre depths inside. Anchor, and take a line to the quay or the breakwater. Reasonable shelter.

No facilities. There is a small village 1km E.

PAZARSUYU (40°57'·5N 38°07'E)

A very small harbour 4 miles E of Erenköy. A short rough stone breakwater provides limited shelter. There are 3–4 metre depths in the outer part of the harbour. Several cafés ashore.

BURANCU (40°56'·6N 38°11'·3E)

A harbour about 4 miles E of Pazarsuyu. There are 2–2·5 metre depths in the entrance, increasing to mostly 4-metre depths inside. The entrance appears to be prone to heavy silting. Go stern or bows-to the quay in the NW, where there are 1·8–3 metre depths, or anchor off where convenient. Good shelter.

There is a village just under 1km away where limited provisions are available.

PIRAZIZ (40°55'·9N 38°18'·8E)

A short rough stone breakwater provides only limited shelter. There are 2·5-metre depths in the entrance, getting shallower behind. No facilities.

Turkish Waters & Cyprus Pilot

GIRESUN

A large commercial harbour on the W side of a rocky headland. The town and the breakwaters are easily identified. Care is needed of Palamut Kayasi, a group of rocks, just above water, approximately ½ a mile NE of the headland. Go on the quay on the S, or on the W quay with the fishing boats. Good shelter.

A considerable charge ($20) is made for using the harbour. Fuel in the town. Good shopping for provisions, and numerous restaurants. Banks.

GORELE

A fishing harbour off the town of Görele, about 30 miles E of Giresun. Care is needed of the sandbank extending some distance offshore off the mouth of the river about ½ a mile W of the harbour. The town is easily identified. There is a lattice light tower (unlit) on the extremity of the breakwater. Care is needed in the entrance of the harbour, where a sandbank and shoal water extend S across the entrance. Head for the pier off the shore and then keep outside two small red buoys marking the shoal water.

Go stern or bows-to or alongside the pier. Alternatively, anchor off and take a long line to the breakwater. Good shelter.

Provisions and restaurants in the town.

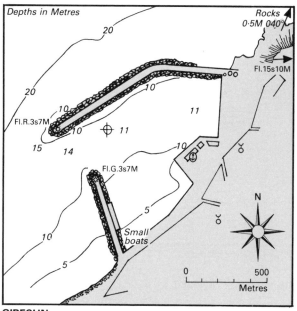

GIRESUN
40°55'·3N 38°22'·8E

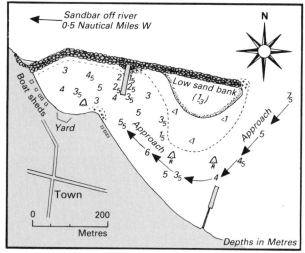

GORELE
41°02'·2N 39°00'·5E

Giresun, looking NW

BESIKDUZU

A small harbour on the E side of Bostan Burnu. Anchor in the NW corner. Good shelter. No facilities.

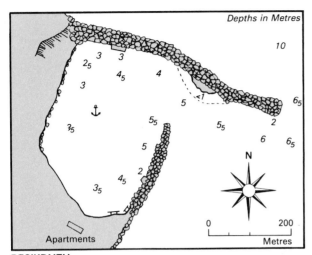

BESIKDUZU
41°04'·1N 39°13'·5E

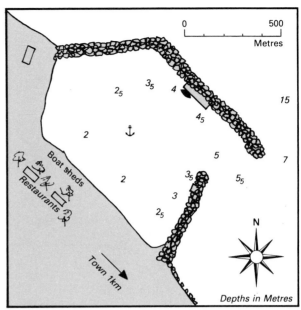

AKCAABAT
41°02'N 39°34'·3E

CARSIBASI (41°05'N 39°22'·5E)

A small harbour on the W side of Isikli Burnu (lit Fl.5s12M). The entrance is mostly obstructed by a sand bar extending out from the inner breakwater, and a yacht must keep about 3 metres off the outer breakwater, where there are 2·5-metre depths. Another sandbank obstructs the S side of the harbour, and underwater rocks and shoal water extend out from the breakwater on the N side. There are 1·5–5 metre depths inside, but the depths are uneven. Anchor and take a line ashore to the breakwater.

Good shopping for provisions in the town, just under 1km E.

AKCAABAT (Pulathane)

A small harbour about 7 miles SE of Isikli Burnu. Go alongside the quay or anchor off. Good shelter.

Restaurants by the harbour. Provisions in town, about 1km E.

YALIMAHALLE (41°00'·7N 39°42'·6E)

A very small harbour just W of Trabzon. There are 4–5 metres in the entrance and 2–3 metres just inside. It is crowded with local fishing boats and, being very small, is not really useful to a yacht.

TRABZON

A large commercial harbour under Cuzelhisar Burnu. Go alongside the quay in the SE corner where shown. Good shelter.

Customs and harbourmaster. Water nearby. Fuel in the town. Provisions and restaurants in the town. Banks.

From here you should endeavour to take a trip to the Sumela Monastery, as much for the spectacular scenery along the way as for the monastery itself.

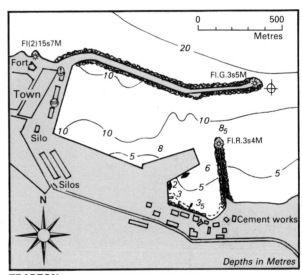

TRABZON
41°00'·5N 39°45'·1E

YOMRA

A small harbour off an anchovy factory, about 6 miles SE of Trabzon. The buildings and storage tanks are all painted light blue. Go stern or bows-to or alongside the quay. Good shelter.

Water and electricity on the quay. Limited provisions. Better shopping in the town, 1km E.

ARAKLI (40°57'N 40°03'·5E)

A small harbour under Arakli Burnu. There are 5-metre depths in the entrance and mostly 2–4·5 metre depths inside. Go stern or bows-to the quay on the N. Good shelter. Provisions in the town, about 1km SE.

275

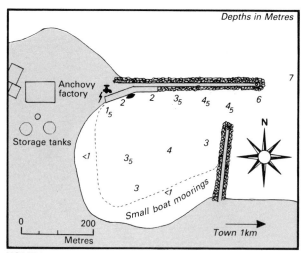

YOMRA
40°57′·8N 39°51′·6E

CAMBURNU

Lies about 5 miles SE of Arakli Burnu. Go stern or bows-to or alongside the quay on the N. Reasonable shelter. A shipyard at the W end of the harbour. No facilities. The nearest town is Surmene, about 6km away.

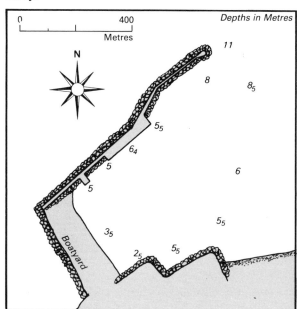

CAMBURNU
40°55′·5N 40°12′E

DEREPAZAR (41°01′·3N 40°21′·9E)

A harbour about 12 miles E of Arakli Burnu, on the NE side of Surmene Köyü. There are 3·5–4 metre depths in the entrance and mostly 2·5–4 metre depths inside. Go alongside the quay on the NW side. Reasonable shelter.

Limited provisions in the village ashore.

RIZE

A commercial harbour under Piryos Burnu. The breakwater shows up well. Care is needed in the approaches of the above and below-water rocks fringing the coast. Go alongside where convenient in the NW corner. Care is needed of the sunken wreck off the sand quay. Good shelter.

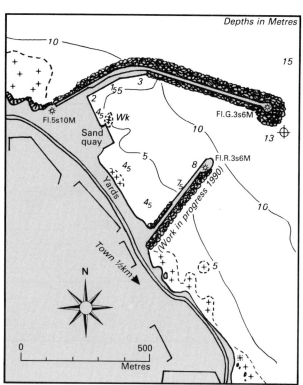

RIZE
41°02′·45N 40°30′·9E

Some provisions available near the harbour. Good shopping and restaurants in Rize, ½km to the S.

CAYELI (41°06′N 40°43′·5E)

A harbour about 10 miles E of Rize. There are 7-metre depths in the entrance and mostly 4–7 metre depths on the N side. Anchor off on the W. Reasonable shelter.

Provisions and restaurants in the town ashore.

PAZAAR

A harbour just over 2 miles E of Kiz Kalesi (lit: Fl.3s7M). Anchor where convenient, and if necessary take a long line ashore. Reasonable shelter.

A boatyard on the S. Meagre provisions ashore. Pazaar village is 1½km W.

ARDESEN (41°12′N 40°59′·5E)

A harbour about 5 miles E of Kiz Kalesi. A rough stone breakwater provides reasonable shelter. There are 6–11 metre depths in the entrance and mostly 4–11 metre depths inside. Anchor in the SW corner, on mud.

Provisions and restaurants ashore.

ARHAVI

A harbour about 21 miles NE of Kiz Kalesi. Go stern or bows-to or alongside the quay on the E, or anchor off. Good shelter.

No facilities. The village is about 1km NE.

HOPA

A large commercial harbour about 5 miles NE of Peronit Burnu. The harbour lies to the NE of the

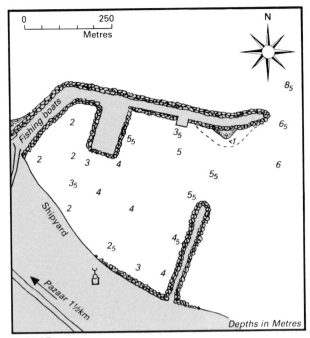

PAZAAR
41°11'N 40°55'E

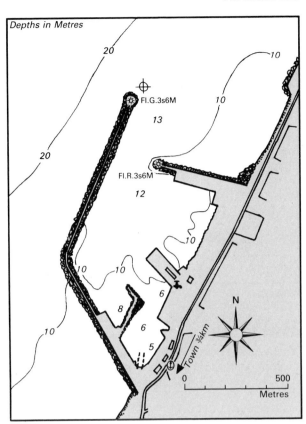

HOPA
41°25'·2N 41°25'·4E

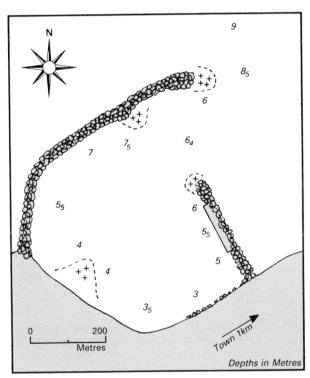

ARHAVI
41°21'·3N 41°18'·4E

town proper. Go alongside the central pier. Good shelter.

Customs and harbourmaster. Water from the toilet block on the quay. Restaurants and good shopping for provisions in the town. Banks.

From Hopa it is just 8 miles to the Turkish/Georgian border. At the time of writing, it should be remembered that northern Georgia has seen unsettled time recently.

Harbours and anchorages west of the Bosphorus

There is, in effect, only one useable harbour, at Igneada, just before the Turkish/Bulgarian border. Two other harbours have been mentioned, at Kiyiköy and at Karaburun-Terkoz, but the former is said to be shallow and the latter very small.

KARABURUN (41°21'N 28°41'E)

Rock awash N of entrance is marked by a buoy (1994). Yacht can either raft up to a fishing boat or anchor off. Water on the quay. Restaurant.

KIKIKOY (Midye) (41°38'N 28°05'·6E)

Reported possibly dangerous to enter with strong NNE winds. Only 2m depths just inside quay angle. Shoal patch at NE centre of harbour. Possible to raft to a fishing boat on NE side.

IGNEADA

A harbour under Kuri Burnu, about 68 miles NW of the Bosphorus. The rough sketch plan should be used with caution. Berth where convenient on the W quay. Care needed of underwater rocks on the W side. Good shelter.

Customs with a patrol boat based here. Fuel station with its own jetty outside the harbour. Restaurants. A village ashore.

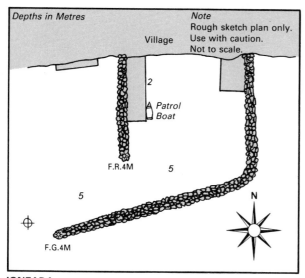

IGNEADA
41°53'·3N 28°01'·2E

Bulgaria

Yachts are recommended to go to Varna first to clear in. Burgas is also a port of entry. See *Black Sea Cruising Guide* (Nelson/Imray) for details.

Romania

Harbours at Constanta and the Danube delta. See *Black Sea Cruising Guide* (Nelson/Imray) for harbours along the coast and *The Danube: A River Guide* (Heikell/Imray) for plans of the Danube delta.

Ukraine, Russia and Georgia

See *Black Sea Cruising Guide* by Rick and Sheila Nelson, Imray.

Appendix

I. USEFUL ADDRESSES

Embassies

Ankara
American Atatürk Bul. 110 ☎ (312) 26 54 70
Australian Nenehatun Cad. 83, Gaziosmanpasa
☎ (312) 27 02 30
British Şehit Ersan Cad. 461/A, Çankaya
☎ (312) 46 86 23 0
Canadian Nenehatun Cad. 75, Gaziosmanpaşa
☎ (312) 27 58 03

Consulates

Istanbul
American Meşrutiyet Cad. 104 ☎ (212) 45 32 20
British Meşrutiyet Cad. 34 Tepabaşi, Beyoğlu, PK 33
☎ (212) 293 7540
Izmir
American Atatürk Cad. 386 ☎ 13 21 35
British 1442 Sokak No 49, Alsancak, Izmir, PK 300 ☎
(232) 4 63 51 51
Bodrum
British c/o Hamam Sok No. 4 Tepecik, 48400 Bodrum
☎ (252) 3167051

II. USEFUL BOOKS

Admiralty publications

The Black Sea Pilot NP24 Covers the Dardanelles, the
Sea of Marmara, the Bosphorus and the Black Sea
coast.
Mediterranean Pilot Vol IV NP48 Covers Turkey's Aegean
coast.
Mediterranean Pilot Vol V NP49 Covers Turkey's
southern coast (E from Marmaris, excluding Rhodes)
and Cyprus.
*List of Lights. Vol E. NP78 Mediterranean, Black and Red
Seas.*

Yachtsman's pilots

Imray Mediterranean Almanac ed. Rod Heikell. Imray.
Biennial publication.
The Aegean H M Denham. John Murray. Covers Turkey's
Aegean coast. A good general pilot (though now out of
date) with interesting historical information.
The Ionian Islands to the Anatolian Coast H M Denham.
John Murray. Covers southern Turkey. Interesting but
out of date.
Greek Waters Pilot Rod Heikell. Imray, Laurie, Norie &
Wilson Ltd. Detailed pilotage for Greece.
Black Sea Cruising Guide Rick and Sheila Nelson. Imray.
Detailed yachtsman's guide to the Black Sea.
Guide Pratique de Grèce et Turquie Jacques Angles. Editions
de Pen Duick. Covers part of the Aegean coast and the
southern coast to Keköva. Patchy. In French.
*Kreuzen Zwischen Türkischer Küste und Ostgriechischen
Insels* Andrea Horn and Wyn Hoop. Editions Maritims.

Covers part of the Aegean coast and part of the
southern coast of Turkey. In German.
Hafenhandbuch Mittelmeer Teil V DSV – Verlag. Scanty
coverage of Turkey. In German.

Other guides

Collins Companion Guide to Turkey John Freely. Readable
guide by a knowledgeable author.
Discovering Turkey Andrew Mango. Batsford. Brief guide,
but full of erudite observation, and readable.
Strolling through Istanbul Hilary Summer-Boyd and John
Freely.
The Turquoise Coast of Turkey Rod Heikell. NET.
Baedeker's Turkish Coast Good concise guide.
The Jason Voyage Tim Severin. Hutchinson.
Aegean Turkey; Turkey Beyond the Meander (covers Caria);
Lycian Turkey; Turkey's Southern Shore George E Bean.
Ernest Benn. The guidebooks par excellence to the
Graeco-Roman sites.
Ancient Civilizations and Ruins of Turkey Ekrem Akurgal.
Haşet Kitabevi. Reliable guide.
A Travel Guide to the Historic Treasures of Turkey Cemil
Toksüz. Mobil Oil Turk AS. Good guide to many of the
sites along the coast.
The Penguin Atlas of Ancient History Colin McEvedy.
Sailing to Byzantium Osbert Lancaster. John Murray.
Excellent guide to Byzantine churches in Asia Minor
and Cyprus.
The Histories (Historiaii) Herodotus. Penguin.

General

Turkey: A Short History Roderic H Davison. Eothen.
Turkey Observed R P Lister. Eyre and Spottiswode.
Amusing and erudite account of travels in Turkey.
Lost Ships Peter Throckmorton. Jonathan Cape. OOP. An
account of early attempts to locate ancient ships
underwater. Fascinating and amusing.
Memed My Hawk; Anatolian Tales Yashar Kemal. Writers
and Readers. Yashar Kemal is considered Turkey's
greatest 20th-century novelist.
Turkish Verse Penguin.
The Lycian Shore; Ionia, A Quest; Alexander's Path Freya
Stark. John Murray. Classics.
*Fire From Heaven; The Persian Boy; The Nature of
Alexander* Mary Renault. Penguin. Semi-historical
novels about Alexander the Great. Intriguing.
Creation Gore Vidal. Interesting novel covering Darius
and Xerxes.
Eothen A W Kinglake. Century. Amusing, classic account
of travels in the Levant.

Flora

Flowers of the Mediterranean Anthony Huxley and Oleg
Polunin. Chatto and Windus. Excellent guide.

Marine life

*Hamlyn Guide to the Flora and Fauna of the Mediterranean
Sea* Compact and reasonably comprehensive guide.

Mediterranean Seafood Alan Davidson. Penguin. Contains excellent line drawings and descriptions of many fish, before the pot.

The Yachtsman's Naturalist M Drummond and P Rodhouse. Angus and Robertson. About Britain and northern Europe, but this area has many species in common with the Mediterranean.

Dangerous Marine Animals Bruce Halstead. The standard reference

Food

Turkish Cooking Irfan Orga. Andre Deutsch. Mediocre.

Mediterranean Seafood Alan Davidson. Penguin. Excellent, and contains a number of Turkish recipes.

CHARTS
Imray-Tetra Charts for the Aegean Sea

Chart Title   *Scale*

G1   Mainland Greece and the Peloponnísos
Plans Approaches to Piraeus and Ormos
Falírou   729,000

G11   North Ionian Islands
Nísos Kérkira to Nísos Levkas
Plans Ormos Gouvion (N. Kérkira), Vorion
Stenou Kérkiras, Límin Kérkiras (N. Kérkira),
Limin, Alipa (N. Kérkira), Ormos Lakka
(N. Paxoi), Limin Paxon (N Paxoi)
Insets Amvrakikos Kólpos, Nísos
Othonoi   182,400

G12   South Ionian Islands
Nisos Levkas to Nísos Zákinthos
Plans Kólpos Aetou (N. Ithaki), Dhioriga
Levkadhos (Levkas Canal), Ormos Argostoliou

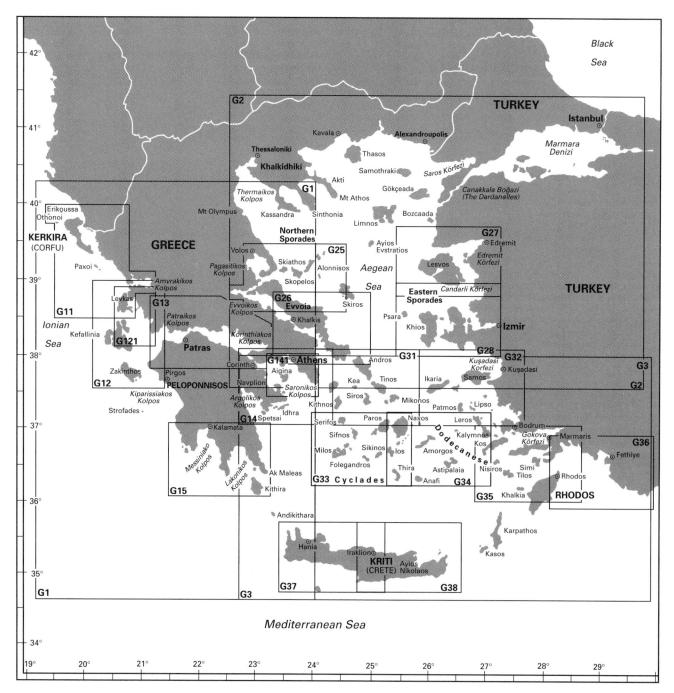

(N. Kefallinia), Ormos Zákinthou (N. Zákinthos)		188,200
G121	**Inland Sea**	
	Plans Ormos Ayias Eufimas (N. Kefallina), Ormos Frikou (N. Ithaki), Ormos Fiskardho (N. Kefallina), Ormos Vasilikas (N. Levkas), Dhioriga Levkadhos (Levkas Canal)	93,400
G13	**Gulfs of Patras and Corinth**	
	Plans Mesolongiou, Ormos Loutrákiou, Kiaton, Patrai, Ormos Andíkiron, Ormos Aiyiou, Krissaios Kólpos, Dhiorix Korinthou (Corinth Canal)	218,800
G14	**Saronic and Argolic Gulf**	
	Plans Marina Alimos, Ormos Falírou, Límin Porou (N. Póros), Steno Spétson (N. Spetsai), Límin Aiyinis (N. Aiyina)	189,000
G141	**Saronikos Kolpos** **Corinth Canal to Akra Sounio and Poros**	109,000
G15	**Southern Peloponnísos** **Ormos Navarinou to Nisos Kithíra and Akra Tourkovigla**	
	Plans Kalamata, Ormos Navarínou, Yíthion, Monemvasía (Yefira), Methóni, Koróni	189,700
G2	**Aegean Sea (North Part) Passage Chart**	
	Plans Canakkale Boğazi (The Dardanelles)	720,500
G25	**Northern Sporades and North Evvoia**	
	Plans Linaria (N. Skiros), Ormos Skiathou (N. Skiathos)	183,800
G26	**Nisos Evvoia**	
	Plans Approaches to Khalkis, Linaria (N. Skiros), Kimis (N. Evvoia), Eretria (N. Evvoia), Limenas Aliveriou (N. Evvoia), Rafina	184,600
G27	**Eastern Sporades (North Sheet)** *In preparation*	
G28	**Eastern Sporades (South Sheet)** *In preparation*	
G3	**Aegean Sea (South Part) Passage Chart**	
	Plan Límin Rodhou (N. Rodhos)	758,800
G31	**Northern Cyclades**	
	Plans Ormos Mikonou (N. Mikonos) Ormos Gávriou (N. Andros), Límin A. Nikolaou (Nísos Kea), Limin Sirou (N. Siros)	189,700
G32	**Southern Sporades and Coast of Turkey**	
	Plans Kuşadasi Liman (Turkey), Límin Karlóvasi (N. Samos), Límin A. Kirikou (N. Ikaria), Steno Samou (N. Samos), Límin Pithagóriou (N. Samos), Ormos Patmou (N. Patmos)	189,700
G33	**Southern Cyclades (Sheet 1 – West)**	
	Plans Steno Kimolou (N. Kimolos), Ormos Livadhiou (N. Serifos), Steno Andíparou (N. Paros), Ormos Naxou (N. Naxos)	190,000
G34	**Southern Cyclades (Sheet 2 – East)**	
	Plans Ormos Kalímnou (N. Kalimnos), Ormos Maltezana (N. Astipálaia)	190,000
G35	**Dodecanese and Coast of Turkey**	
	Plans Bodrum, Rodhos (N. Rodhos), Kós (N. Kos), Marmaris, Simi (N. Simi)	190,000
G36	**South Coast of Turkey** **Marmaris to Kekova Adasi**	

	Plans Marmaris, Rhodos, Megisti, Approaches to Megisti, Fethiye, Göçek 1:193,000	
G37	**Nisos Kriti (West)**	
	Plans O. Gramvousa, Hania, Rethimno, A. Galinis, Soudha, Palaiokhora, O. Sfakion	193,000
G38	**Nisos Kriti (East)**	
	Plans Iraklion, Sitia, A. Nikolaos, Ierapetra, Kaloi Limenes, Khersonisos	193,000

British Admiralty charts

Chart	Title	Scale
171	Cap Bon to Ra's At Tin	175,000
180	Aegean sea	100,000
183	Ra's At Tin to Iskenderum	1,100,000
224	Marmara Denizi	300,000
	Izmit Körfezi	300,000
236	Hisarönü Körfezi to Taslik Burnu, including Rhodos	300,000
237	Taşlik Burnu to Anamur Burnu	300,000
	Alanya	20,000
242	Antalya and Taşucu with approaches	
	Yat Limani	2,500
	Antalya Limani	10,000
	Taşucu Limani	15,000
	Approaches to Antalya	25,000
	Approaches to Taşucu	100,000
497	Izmit Körfezi	
	Yarimea to Izmit	25,000
	Tuzla to Izmit	75,000
775	Cape Limniti to Cape Aspro	100,000
	Latzi anchorage	20,000
776	Cape Limniti to Stazousa Point	100,000
796	Stazousa point to Cape Eloea	100,000
848	Ports in eastern Cyprus	
	Larnaca	10,000
	Famagusta	15,000
	Approaches to Larnaca, Gastria bay	25,000
849	Ports in Western Cyprus	
	Kyrenia: Limassol	10,000
	Vasilikos	15,000
	Moni; Paphos; Approaches to Akrotiri Harbour and Limassol; Karavostasi	25,000
850	Cape Aspro to Cape Pyla	100,000
851	Cape Kiti to Cape Eloea	100,000
852	Akrotiri Harbour and Approaches	5,000
872	Kalimno to Rhodes, including the Gulfs of Kos, Doris and Symi	220,000
1004	Canakkale Boğazi (The Dardanelles) to Marmara Adasi	100,000
1005	Marmara Adasi to Istanbul Boğazi (The Bosporus)	150,000
1006	Ports in Marmara Denizi Bandirma, Mudanya, Marmara Ereğlisi, Tukirdag	12,500
	Gemlik	15,000
	Ambarli	20,000
1030	Southwest entrance channels to the Aegean Sea	150,000
1054	Marmaris to Kaş	150,000
	Kaş Limani	15,000
	Ormos Kastellorízou	15,000
	Approaches to Nísos Meyísti	50,000
1055	Rhodes Channel and Gökova Körfezi	150,000
1057	Kuşadasi Körfezi and approaches	150,000
	Kuşadasi	15,000
	Siğacik	15,000

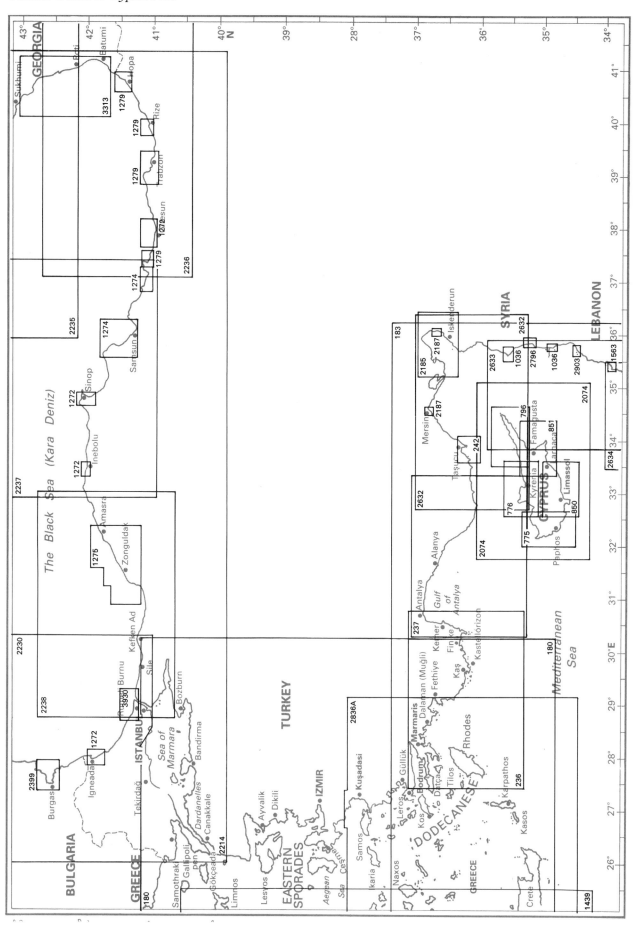

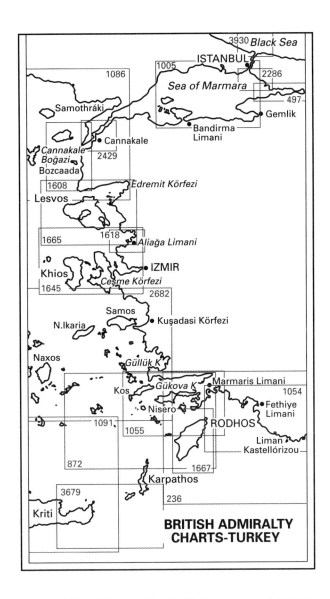

BRITISH ADMIRALTY CHARTS-TURKEY

Chart	Title	Scale
1058	Nísos Khíos and Izmir Körfezi	150,000
1061	Candarli Körfezi to Edremit Körfezi	
	with Nísos Lésvos	150,000
	Turkey – Dikili	25,000
1086	Strimonikos Kólpos to Edremit Körfezi	300,000
1087	Kölpos Petalión to Edremit Körfezi	300,000
1092	Western Approaches to the Aegean Sea	300,000
1198	Istanbul Boğazi (The Bosphorus)	30,000
	Haliç (The Golden Horn):	
	Haydarpaşa Limani	12,500
Chart	Title	Scale
1272	Giresun, Igneada, Inebolu and Sinop	
	with approaches	
	Inebolu: Giresun	12,500
	Igneada: Sinop	25,000
	Approaches to Igneada:	
	approaches to Giresun:	
	approaches to Inebolu:	
	approaches to Sinop	100,000
1274	Samsun and Fatsa with approaches	
	Samsun	12,500
	Fatsa	20,000
	Approaches to Samsun:	
	approaches to Fatsa	100,000
1275	Ereğli to Amasra	125,000
	Bartin Limani: Zonguldak	12,500
	Amasra: Ereğli	25,000

Chart	Title	Scale
1279	Ordu, Trabzon, Rize and Hopa with	
	approaches Trabzon: Rize: Hopa	12,500
	Ordu	25,000
	Approaches to Ordu: Trabzon:	
	Rise: Hopa	100,000
1522	Izmir Limani with Urla Limani	25,000
	Izmir	10,000
	Yenikale Geçidi	12,500
	Urla limani	50,000
1608	Approaches to Canakkale Boğazi	
	(The Dardanelles)	100,000
	Bozcaada	7,500
1618	Candarli Körfezi and approaches	
Chart	Title	Scale
	Aliaga	20,000
	Nemrut Limani Foça	15,000
	Aliağa	20,000
1625	Khios Strait and Ildir Körfezi	50,000
	Khios	10,000
	Cesme	15,000
1639	Nísis Ayios Yeóryios to Nísos Siros	100,000
1644	Ports and Anchorages on the southwest	
	coast of Turkey	
	Bodrum	10,000
	Göcek	15,000
	Güllük and Asin; Yediadalar; Fethiye;	
	Datça; Marmaris	25,000
1645	Nísos Khíos and Izmir Körfezi	150,000
1659	Nísos Límnos to the Dardanelles and	
	Babu Burnu	150,000
1644	Ports and anchorages on the southwest	
	coast of Turkey	
	Bodrum	10,000
	Göcek	15,000
	Güllük and Asin; Yediadalar; Fethiye;	
	Datça; Marmaris	25,000
2074	Cyprus	300,000
2185	Iskenderun Körfezi	105,000
	Ceyhan limani (Toros Gübre piers):	
	Ceyhan limani (Botas, oil terminal):	30,000
2187	Plans on the south coast of Turkey	
	Mersin and approaches	20,000
	Iskenderun and Isdenir	30,000
2200	Approaches to Kherson – sheet 1	50,000
2201	Approaches to Kherson – sheet 2	50,000
	Port Kherson	15,000
2202	Port Yuzhnyy	12,500
2214	Black sea including Marmara Denizi	
	and Sea of Azov	1,200,000
2230	Constanţa to Kefken Adasi	400,000
2236	Tirebolu to Tuapse	400,000
2237	Inceburun to Isikli Burnu	400,000
2238	Kefken Adasi to Inceburn	400,000
2285	Plans in	
2286	Southern approaches to Istanbul Boğazi	
	(The Bosporus)	50,000
2429	Canakkale Bogaz (The Dardanelles)	75,000
	Canakkale	5,000
	South entrance to Canakkale Bogazi:	
	Nara Geçidi (The Narrows)	25,000
2632	Anamur Burnu to Al Ladhiqiyah	
	including Northern Cyprus	300,000
2836a	Grecian Archipelago – southern sheet	600,000
2836b	Grecian Archipelago – northern sheet	600,000
3924	Kos island – eastern part, and entrance	
	to Gulf of Kos (Kerme Körfezi)	45,000
3930	Northern approaches to Istanbul	
	Boğazi (The Bosphorus)	50,000

III. GLOSSARY OF USEFUL WORDS
GENERAL
yes, *evet*
no, *hayir*
please, *lütfen*
thank you, *tesekkür ederim*
excuse me, *affedersiniz*
it's nothing/
that's all right, *birşey degil*
where?, *nerede (dir)?*
when?, *ne zaman?*
how?, *nasil?*
today, *bugün*
tomorrow, *yarrin*
left, *sol*
right, *sag*
big, *büyük*
small, *küçük*
open, *açik*
closed, *kapali*
goodbye, *Allahaismarladik*
(the one leaving) *Güle güle*
(the one who remains)
good morning, *günaydin*
good afternoon, *tünaydin*
good evening, *iyi akşamlar*
good night, *iyi geceler*
I don't
understand, *anlamiyorum*

one, *bir*
two, *iki*
three, *üç*
four, *dört*
five, *beş*
six, *alti*
seven, *yedi*
eight, *sekiz*
nine, *dokuz*
ten, *on*
twenty, *yirmi*
fifty, *elli*
one hundred, *yüz*
one thousand, *bin*
Sunday, *Pazar*
Monday, *Pazartesi*
Tuesday, *Sali*
Wednesday, *Carşamba*
Thursday, *Perşembe*
Friday, *Cuma*
Saturday, *Cumartesi*

IN THE RESTAURANT
appetiser, *ordövr*
baked, *firinda*
beef, *sigir*
beer, *bira*
bread, *ekmek*
breakfast, *kahvalti*
butter, *tereyagi*
chicken, *piliç*
chips, *patates (kizartmasi)*
cheese, *peynir*
coffee, *kahve*
croquettes, *köftesi*
dessert, *tatlilar*
fish, *balik*
fried, *tavada kizarmiş*
fruit, *meyve*

grilled, *izgara*
ice cream, *dondurma*
ketchup, *keçap*
lamb, *kuzu*
lemon, *limon*
lettuce, *marul*
liver, *cigeri*
meat, *et*
meatballs, *köfte*
mineral water, *maden suyu*
milk, *süt*
mussels, *midye*
mustard, *hardal*
oil, *yag*
olives, *zeytin*
omelette, *omlet*
pepper, *karabiber*
rice, *pirinç*
roast beef, *rozbif*
roasted, *kizarmiş*
salad, *salata*
salt, *tuz*
sandwich, *sandviç*
seafood, *deniz mahsulleri*
soup, *çorba*
spaghetti, *spagetti*
spicy omelette, *menemen*
steak, *biftek*
stuffed, *dolma*
tea, *çay*
vegetables, *sebzeler*
veal, *dana*
vinegar, *sirke*
(iced) water, *(buzlu) su*
wine, *şarap*
wild boar, *yaban domuzu*
    paçasi
yoghurt, *yogurt*

SHOPPING
apples, *elma*
apricots, *kayisi*
aubergine, *patlican*
bakery, *firin*
beans, *fasulye*
beef, *sigir*
biscuits, *bisküvit*
bread, *ekmek*
butcher, *kasap*
butter, *tereyagi*
carrots, *havuç*
cheese, *pyenir*
chicken, *piliç*
meat, *et*
melon, *kavum*
milk, *süt*
oil, *yag*
onions, *sogan*
oranges, *portakal*
peaches, *şeftali*
chocolate, *çikolata*
coffee, *kahve*
cucumber, *salatalik*
eggs, *yumurta*
fish, *balik*
flour, *un*
garlic, *sarmisak*
grocer, *bakkal dükkáni*
honey, *bal*
jam, *reçel, marmelĉt*

lamb, *kuzu*
lemon, *limon*
potatoes, *patates*
rice, *pirinç*
salt, *tuz*
sugar, *şeker*
tea, *çay*
tomatoes, *domates*
water, *su*
wine, *şarap*

TURKISH NAMES AND TERMS FOUND ON CHARTS
ada(si), island
adalar(i), islands
agiz, mouth
ak, white
alamet, beacon

bati, west, west wind
bo azi, strait, channel
burun, burnu, cape, point, headland
bükü, bay
büyük, big

çak, marsh

dağ, mountain
demiryeri, anchorage
deniz, sea
dere, valley
döküntü, reef

göl, lake

hisar, castle, fort

iç, inner
irmak, river
iskele (si), landing place

kale, kalesi, castle
kapi, gate, pass
kara, black
kayasi, rock, reef
kible, south
kilise, church
kirmizi, kizil, red
köprü, bridge
körfezi, gulf
köy, bight, cove, creek
köyu, village
kule, tower, peak
küçük, small

liman, harbour, port
lodos, SW (wind)

mendirek, mole
minare, minaret

nehir, nehri, river
nişan, beacon

orman, forest
ova, plain

poyraz, NE (wind)
ruzgar, wind
sançak, flag
sari, yellow
sarp, cliff, steep, rough, rocky

saray, palace
set, mole
siglik, bank, shoal, shallow
siğleri, shallows
su, water
samandira, buoy
sark, east
sehir, city, town
simal, north

tabya, battery, earthworks
tepe, hill tumulus, peak
topuk, sandspit, river bar

vilayet, province, district
yar, cliff, precipice
yarimadasi, peninsula, promontory
yol, channel, road.

PRONUNCIATION OF THE TURKISH ALPHABET
Turkish is a phonetic language, and for the most part if you say it as you see it you will get it right. The letters of the alphabet are pronounced as follows:

a as ah in father
b as b in bat
c as j in joke
ç as ch in choke
d as d in dotee
e as eh in met or ay in stay
f as f in fat
g as g in get
g a soft g, something like y or uh
h as h in hat
i as u in circus, but also as uh, i or oo, depending on
    the sounds preceding it
i as i in sit or ee in meet
j as zh in measure
k as k in key
l as l in lot
m as m in me
n as n in nip
o as o in boat or aw in saw
ö as er in sitter
p as p in pay
r as r in bray
s as s in sea
ş as sh in shall
t as t in tea
u as oo in soon
ü as ew in pew
v as v in very
y as y in yes
z as z in zest

IV. CONVERSION TABLES

1 inch = 2·54 centimetres (roughly 4in = 10cm)
1 centimetre = 0·394 inches
1 foot = 0·305 metres (roughly 3ft = 1m)
1 metre = 3·281 feet
1 pound = 0·454 kilograms (roughly 10lbs = 4·5kg)
1 kilogram = 2·205 pounds
1 mile = 1·609 kilometres (roughly 10 miles = 16km)
1 kilometre = 0·621 miles
1 nautical mile = 1·1515 miles
1 mile = 0·8684 nautical miles
1 acre = 0·405 hectares (roughly 10 acres = 4 hectares)
1 hectare = 2·471 acres
1 gallon = 4·546 litres (roughly 1 gallon = 4·5 litres)
1 litre = 0·220 gallons

Temperature scale

t°F to t°C is 5/9   (t°F -32) = t°C
t°C to t°F is 9/5   (t°C +32) = t°F

So:
70°F = 21·1°C   20°C = 68°F
80°F = 26·7°C   30°C = 86°F
90°F = 32·2°C   40°C = 104°F

Index